John Derek

Actor, Director, Photographer

MICHELANGELO CAPUA

McFarland & Company, Inc., Publishers
Jefferson, North Carolina

All photographs are from the author's collection.

Library of Congress Cataloguing-in-Publication Data

Names: Capua, Michelangelo, 1966– author.
Title: John Derek : actor, director, photographer / Michelangelo Capua.
Description: Jefferson : McFarland & Company, Inc., Publishers, 2020. |
Includes bibliographical references and index.
Identifiers: LCCN 2020009866 | ISBN 9781476675886 (paperback : acid free paper) ∞
ISBN 9781476638126 (ebook)
Subjects: LCSH: Derek, John, 1926–1998. | Motion picture producers and directors—
United States—Biography. | Motion picture actors and actresses—
United States—Biography. | Photographers—United States—Biography.
Classification: LCC PN1998.3.D4685 C37 2020 | DDC 791.4302/33092 [B]—dc23
LC record available at https://lccn.loc.gov/2020009866

British Library cataloguing data are available
ISBN (print) 978-1-4766-7588-6
ISBN (ebook) 978-1-4766-3812-6

© 2020 Michelangelo Capua. All rights reserved

*No part of this book may be reproduced or transmitted in any form
or by any means, electronic or mechanical, including photocopying
or recording, or by any information storage and retrieval system,
without permission in writing from the publisher.*

Front cover image: John Derek, 1954 (Photofest)

Printed in the United States of America

*McFarland & Company, Inc., Publishers
Box 611, Jefferson, North Carolina 28640
www.mcfarlandpub.com*

*For Marisa,
my mother*

Table of Contents

Introduction   1

1. Dare   3
2. Pretty Boy   14
3. An Attempt at Stardom   25
4. Glorious and Not-So-Glorious Days   35
5. Hard Times   45
6. The Paramount Years   54
7. High and Low   64
8. Ursula   69
9. World Traveler   79
10. New Directions   87
11. Linda   94
12. Bo   101
13. Svengali Productions   107
14. Twilight's Last Gleaming   114

Filmography and Career Record   125
Chapter Notes   187
Bibliography   191
Index   195

Introduction

"Sometimes I ask myself what there can be of interest in my life. Why are people—more or less people, according to certain periods of my life—so interested in me?"

Sixty-two-year-old John Derek asked this question in a lengthy 1988 interview in the British magazine *Hello!*

The answer is simple. Derek became an overnight sensation when his career took off after starring in the film noir classic *Knock on Any Door* (1949) opposite Humphrey Bogart. The buzz about Hollywood's hottest new male face generated such an interest in his life that suddenly movie magazines were clamoring to grace their covers with his devastatingly handsome image. Derek went on to appearances in Academy Award–nominated films such as *All the King's Men*, *The Ten Commandments*, *Exodus* and others, directed by prestigious filmmakers like Cecil B. DeMille and Otto Preminger. He was very cooperative with the press despite his reluctance to discuss his childhood. He even won the Golden Apple Award in 1951 as the most cooperative picture star of the year.

But in time, as his career began to fade, he became an intensely private man. He realized that acting was just an easy way of making a living, by engaging in an activity that he greatly despised. While his appearances became scarcer, he bloomed behind a camera, both in motion pictures and still photography. Despite his fading movie star status, his celebrity status remained intact, thanks to his marriages to three women who were celebrities in their own right. All his wives resembled each other with their high cheekbones, square shoulders and delicate features: the living proof of John Derek's obsession for perfect beauty. Due to the attractiveness and success of his wives, public interest and curiosity about John's life never waned. He gained the reputation of a Svengali, mostly nurtured by the envy of heterosexual men who often misunderstood his relationship with his wives. "I had nothing to do with their success. I did not make stars of Ursula [Andress], Linda [Evans] or Bo [Derek], they did it themselves," John stated. He admitted that he occasionally felt resentment from men for having paired with such beautiful women, thinking he had a magic formula. In reality, all he did was love them and tell them the truth all the time, even if the truth sometimes hurt.

But there is much more to Derek than his lovely wives and his unconditional love for them. Besides his great affection for all animals (horses and dogs, particularly) and nature in general, what struck me most was his integrity. He embodied a sense of honesty accompanied by a deep distaste for mendacity which, according to many, he often expressed in a blunt, direct and sometimes unpleasant way. "I've been told I'm pretty offensive on the set, and I can believe it," he once admitted. These were uncommon attributes for someone born and raised in Hollywood, where power and money were, and still are, major "values." Though some of the films Derek produced and directed are far from perfect, his creative, fascinating and often daring personality has left a mark of originality in Hollywood.

Introduction

In writing this book, I have benefited from the help of many individuals and institutions and from the assistance and support of friends without whom its completion would have been impossible. I would like to thank Yaakov Perry; the helpful staff of the British Film Institute Library in London, in particular Anastasia Kerameos and Sarah Currant for their kind help; the staff of the Performing Arts Library at Lincoln Center in New York; Christine Kruger from the Margaret Herrick Library of the Academy of Motion Picture Arts and Sciences in Beverly Hills; the staff of the Bibliothèque du Cinéma François Truffaut in Paris; the staff of the British Library Humanities Reading Room in London; Biblioteca Renzo Renzi–Cineteca di Bologna; Biblioteca Nazionale di Napoli, and Dollie R. Banner from Jerry Ohlinger's Movie Materials in New York.

Most of all my deepest gratitude goes to my editor and patient and longtime friend Stuart Williams. Without his invaluable help, completing this book would have been almost impossible. Thank you, Stu.

Chapter 1

Dare

"[He was] the most beautiful boy … like a god."—Elizabeth Taylor

John Derek was born on August 12, 1926, at Hollywood Hospital in Hollywood, California. According to his daughter Sean, his real name was Derek Dullivan Harris, while his fourth wife Bo insists it is Darec Dellivan Harris. Census sources report that Delevan was his maternal grandfather's correct name. "Dare," as his parents nicknamed him, was the only child of a couple whose marriage was already on the rocks at the time of his birth. His mother Dolores Johnson was a silent screen actress and his father, William Lawson Harris, a film director, actor, architect and (most of all) entrepreneur. Lawson, as everybody called him, was alleged to be a relatively detached husband who was seldom at home.

Dark and good-looking, Lawson was a ladies' man. He was born on June 30, 1897, in Evansville, Indiana, where, according to census records, he lived at home until he was 18. He tried to help his mother Elizabeth Hawley Harris after his father William James Harris suddenly died in 1908. He worked as an automobile salesman while completing his education as an architect. He had a sister, Artie Lee.

When world war erupted, Lawson enlisted in the army's new Motor Transport Corps and was shipped with other American automobile tradesmen to France to fight alongside the French Army. On the front, Lawson was exposed to poison gas, compromising his lungs for the rest of his life. After he returned from Europe, his interest in cinema took him to Hollywood, where he worked odd jobs in the film industry.

At the end of 1919, Lawson met Australian movie star Arthur Shirley, who had made his name in Hollywood appearing in several silent pictures, many opposite Lon Chaney. He returned to Australia, where he planned to produce, direct and star in his own films. He announced to the press that he was going to form Arthur Shirley Productions, a company worth more than $100,000, to make movies for worldwide distribution. The film studio was to operate out of a building he had bought in Rose Bay, Sydney. The studio's first production was to be *The Throwback,* written by *Saturday Evening Post* scribe Pat O'Cotter. Shirley offered Lawson a job on *The Throwback* as production manager. Seduced

John's father William Lawson Harris in the early 1920s.

by the idea of starting a new life Down Under, Lawson accepted, and asked his girlfriend Marie Pavis to join him in the new adventure.

Pavis was an English-born actress with a solid background on the American stage. She began acting in Hollywood in 1910 with the Vitagraph Company. At 30, Pavis was fully aware that her days as a Hollywood actress were limited and the opportunity to use her experience in another country seemed like a not-to be-missed opportunity. The couple agreed that Marie would join Lawson after he had settled in Sydney. Lawson traveled to Australia in the beginning of 1920.

From the very beginning of the shoot, *The Throwback* was afflicted by financial problems. The company went into liquidation just before the film was completed. Shirley attempted to finish the picture with financing from co-producer Ernest Higgins. The two business partners began to have artistic disagreements that brought filming to a halt, leaving Lawson jobless. A man of many resources, he partnered with Vera Remée to open an acting school that ultimately afforded him enough funds to create his own production company. Marie, now working under the name Yvonne Pavis, joined him at the beginning of 1922, when they partnered to establish the Yvonne Pavis Production Company. The business name was later changed to Harris Austral Super Films.

In 1922, Lawson produced and directed the low-budget features *Circumstance, A Daughter of Australia* and *Sunshine Sally*. All starred Yvonne, with Lawson appearing in the first two. In a brief interview with the Australian weekly magazine *Everyone's*, Lawson explained that although Pavis was brought out to feature in a production, she became a business associate: "She, in conjunction with myself, writes the stories and arranges the content."[1] The actress also supervised the business side of the productions.

Lawson and Yvonne managed to keep their names in the industry press where they frequently proclaimed that their company was "making films in Australia, for the world." Nevertheless, the country they fervently promoted, did not return the favor. The three pictures received a lukewarm reception from the local press and public. Their distribution across Australia suffered long delays, with some cities not showing them until long after their premieres. Lawson could not afford to wait six months or more before getting any return on the money invested in his films.

In the last week of 1922, Pavis left Sydney to return to California, where she planned to arrange North American distribution of her films. Lawson returned a few months later, after collecting the last profits from his pictures. He intended to make one more film in Australia, *Yellow*, on a Melville Island set, but the project was never realized. By the end of 1923, the couple reunited in Hollywood where they eventually married. But by 1925 they had already divorced.

While shooting the only picture he ever made in America, *Law or Loyalty* (1926), Lawson met and fell in love with actress Dolores Johnson. As John recalled years later,

> My father and my mother met in the studio environment. It was not difficult to fall in love with my mother, because she was a very beautiful woman. She had an incredible figure, and she did not look very much like other women of the time…. [She] drove all the "gentlemen" in Hollywood mad, and my father was one of those who were after her. She was very wild, crazy. It was very easy to love her, and everybody did.[2]

Like Lawson, Dolores was recently divorced (from director Percy "Scott" Pembroke, whom she had married in 1920). Born in San Francisco on April 25, 1903, Dolores was the daughter of Delevan "Del" D. Johnson (1881–1928) and Lorice C. McCallum (1885–1915). She was a stunning beauty with dark hair and mesmerizing green eyes. She would sometimes introduce herself using a combination of her parents' names spelled in different variations: "Del Oris," "Delloris" or "Dellorice," with the latter even appearing on her 1920s marriage certificate. On the set of her films, she often behaved bizarrely, refusing to shoot until her violinist put her in the right mood for the upcoming sequence.[3] By 1925, when Dolores met Lawson, she had already starred in a dozen one-reel pictures. Nearly all the films were part of a series called *The Vanity Fair Girls*, produced by Hal Roach. Those comedies had a bold innovation in that they featured "not one star but six." The shorts were usually shown to Cecil B. DeMille prior to their official release so that the director could select his future leading ladies. Dolores was one of the girls chosen.

After marrying Lawson and getting pregnant, Dolores put her career on hold, never starring in any of DeMille's productions. After her pregnancy, she briefly returned to work, appearing in a few minor roles. By 1932, her career was over.

Dare was born in the summer of 1926. "I loved that name—it suggested 'I dare you,'" John admitted years later. Dare never really knew his parents as a couple. He was only five years old, living in a small house on Laurel Canyon Boulevard, when Lawson and Dolores divorced. Being too young to have any significant feeling of loss surrounding their separation, Dare grew up knowing them separately. "Father was very cosmopolitan, not the type to go crazy over babies; when a kid gets older, that's when a father likes to take over," John commented years later.

As a baby, Dare was so strikingly pretty that he would figuratively stop traffic. Legend has it that Cecil B. DeMille was the first in the industry to spot him as a good movie bet. "He ought to be in pictures!" the director allegedly exclaimed to Dolores. At the time, Dare was only a couple of years old, speeding in his stroller under his mother's scornful eye. Dare's memories of his father were a bit confused since he lived with Dolores until he moved in with Lawson at 15. The Harrises divorced in the middle of the Great Depression and with Lawson gone, Dolores struggled to feed herself and her child. While trying to revive her acting career by appearing in minor roles, she had no other choice than to accept a part-time job as a Hollywood parking lot attendant. According to Dolores, John had an adoration for her and was tyrannically possessive. He would follow his mother from room to room, never letting her out of his sight. When she had to leave for work, he would scream at the top of his lungs in protest. "I was his slave," she recalled in an interview. "I couldn't even go shopping without his having a tantrum."[4]

On the set of the Gary Cooper film *Fighting Caravans* (1931), Dolores met 28-year-old Russell Harlan, a tall, slim and outgoing guy who was one of the several camera assistants. Starting in the mid–1920s, he had been employed by different studios as a bit player, stuntman, lighting double and camera assistant. He would later work in more than 50 westerns, including several entries in the *Hopalong Cassidy* series, before being hired by director Lewis Milestone for the World War II drama *A Walk in the Sun* (1945). The picture's success led to a long and prestigious career for Harlan, which included six Academy Award nominations for Best Cinematography.

In a *Modern Screen* magazine article written in 1951, Russ reported his very first meeting with Dare at the Lasky Ranch location on the set of *Fighting Caravans*. Dolores had brought her son along to work with her after the woman who was supposed to take care of him failed to show up that morning. Harlan wrote,

> He was a good-looking six-year-old kid. Not good-looking the way fans see him now—good-looking the way all kids are—broken-nosed, freckled, snub-nosed, or whatever.... Being a fellow who likes kids, I tried to break the ice. "Want to ride a horse?" I asked him. He managed a big smile. Borrowing

the double for Coop's horse, we had ourselves a ride. I found myself telling him about my folks' ranch down near Vista, California, where there were horses to ride any time. And somehow I found myself promising to take him down—Sunday. Well, I had me a pal then. We were Dare and Russ. He tagged after me and my movie camera until it came time to quit for the day. Then he solemnly reminded me of my promise to take him out to the ranch, so I asked his mother about it. She said she'd be grateful because he'd missed the companionship of men since she and his father divorced a year before.[5]

Russ kept his promise. The lonely Dare appealed immediately to the fatherly heart of Russ. It marked the beginning of a long-lasting friendship. He would take the little boy on hunting and camping trips every time he had time to spare. It was also a good opportunity to see Dare's mother again. Dolores and Russ eventually fell in love. More than his parents, Russ turned out to be the greatest influence in Dare's life. He became his guide, his best friend, and someone to count on for advice. Russ not only taught Dare how to ride a horse but also introduced him to photography—which eventually became John Derek's passion.

John rarely talked publicly about his childhood, but in one interview years later he recalled, "My earliest memory had something to do with horses. I began to ride them when I was five, so I scarcely remember the time when I couldn't. This time I was on a big horse that shied away from a tree on which a tire had been hung as a swing. My friend Russell Harlan made me take the horse back to the tree again, and let him see that there was nothing to fear."[6] Even though Russ was like a real father to Dare, Lawson's presence in his son's life was still very significant. He and Dolores agreed on what type of education their kid was to receive. They enrolled him in the Barton School, an alternative primary institution located in Topanga Canyon. Barton was a small co-ed country boarding school where boys and girls received a sound education at the elementary level. Teachers and pupils lived and worked together in a close family atmosphere, and each child was encouraged to develop to their full potential. The unspoiled rural setting and useful chores on the farm, which provided largely for the school's needs, balanced their studies with a natural way of life for both a healthy body and spirit.

In spite of the bucolic environment and the presence of domesticated animals, Dare despised being forced to go to school. If he could, he would have spent all his time riding a horse. Years later, when he visited the school premises for a magazine photo shoot, memories of those years suddenly surfaced:

> The school buildings are the same and the alfalfa fields; the pasture where, between lessons, we school kids raised goats and milked them, and the vineyards where the grapes were picked and later crushed are just as they were then.... Mr. Barton and his wife are no longer teaching school. They've retired, but he can still make me feel like a ten-year-old, and when he says, "Look here, Dare," I jump.[7]

Neither Dolores nor Lawson ever worried if Dare would bring home good report cards, since they believed that life experiences were far better teachers than any lesson learned inside a schoolroom. They were more concerned that young Dare learn about human values rather than literature or math.

When Dare was eight, his parents sent him to the Hollywood Military Academy where he learned to be disciplined. "I learned what the true values were," John later admitted. "Thanks to those principles, I have tried to be a good person for the rest of my life. I believe that if a boy enjoys complete freedom always, the whole time, he cannot appreciate the importance of being free. Human beings value more the things they do not have, or those they had and lost."[8] Even though those years spent at the Hollywood Military Academy corresponded to Dare's unhappiest childhood memories, they were extremely formative. After the Academy, his parents enrolled him immediately in a public high school.

Dare had not forgotten Russ after years at the Academy. Russ recalled his feelings when the two reunited. "His welcome made me a little ashamed I'd not come around sooner. He was exceptionally handsome. He looked like the idealized young military school student in an advertisement. Too perfect. When he changed into Levi's, he looked a little more natural to me." That same day, Russ discovered Dare's ability to handle a rifle, proving how well he had learned how to shoot the weapon. "Before the day was over," the cameraman admitted, "I realized my little friend was a kid who had to be tough because he was mighty handsome and because he didn't have his dad around to help him to be tough enough." According to Russ, Dare had been bullied often by his schoolmates because "he looked too perfect." He had been in a few fights already and he hadn't won every time. In the following days, Russ gave Dare some sage advice on how to handle the bullying less belligerently and more effectively.[9]

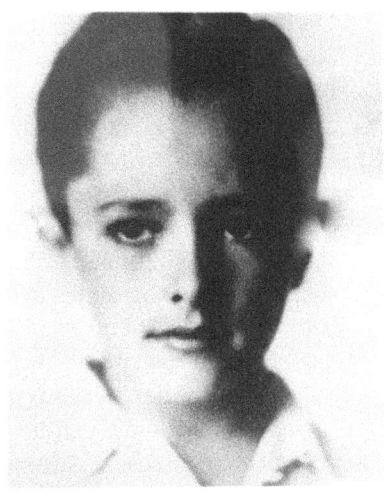

Dare Harris at age 11 in 1937.

One of his first boyhood friends was Robert "Bob" Wagner, with whom Dare would bicycle home from school. The future Hollywood star recalled in an interview with a movie fan magazine: "Dar [sic] and I grew up together. We used to keep our horses at the Bel Air Stables. Dar [sic] and I would leave our bikes at the stables and ride the horses home. You could get on a horse, and in 15 minutes you'd be up in the mountains."[10] It was Dare, who later taught Wagner to drive a car. Wagner remembered him as a kid with a warm personality, always smiling with an ingratiating way.

When not in school, Dare would spend much of his free time riding horses or painting, which had become his favorite pastime. He was a curious kid, especially interested in outdoor activities. After seeing a photograph of a skating act, he set out to be a good roller-skater. He reached the point where he would practice roller-skating over rough, vacant lots. One day with Russ, he fell and cut his knee so deeply that Russ rushed him to the hospital where he received 12 stitches. Dare held back his tears just to prove to his old friend that he had become a man.

In fact, it was Russ who later almost cried after an accident that almost killed young Dare. Since Dare had proven his skills in using a 20-gauge rifle, Russ took him along on a duck hunt to the Salton Sea. While they were on a boat in a shallow part of the saline lake, Russ brought down two ducks that fell into the swamp beside them. Russ knew that he was too heavy to walk over the crust on the surface, but thought Dare was light enough. Just as Dare got to the ducks, he suddenly sank into the swampy muck clear up to his shoulders. The boy continued to sink until Russ, horrified but resolved, managed to drag him out. Back in the boat, coated in mud from head to foot, Dare started laughing, saying that it was fun. Still shaken and feeling guilty, Russ realized that the boy was unfazed and thought of himself as a god, capable of anything.

As a teenager, Dare detested school. For him, it was too confining. Uninterested in classes, he preferred horse riding, climbing the hills, or hunting with his rifle. Since he did not show up in class often, he was forced to move from school to school. His desperate parents hired a tutor, Mr. Dean, a kind, middle-aged man who became more of a companion than a teacher. In the summer of 1939, Dare took an educational trip around California with

Dean. They traveled by car around the Golden State, stopping in various locations In Palm Springs, they camped in the canyons and rambled to all the scenic spots with their sleeping bags.

Once back home, Dare noticed his mother started to behave eccentrically. She was, in fact, drinking heavily. Her six-year relationship was over after Russ left her. He had wished to marry her and start a family with kids their own. Yet Dolores could not have another child as a result of a terrible accident she had suffered a few years earlier on a set when a stagecoach she was upturned, impaling her. That episode also marked the end of her acting career. She was now alone, living in a little Santa Monica beach house. Dare's presence was her only consolation. She had slowly developed a fear of aging, thinking that her beauty was quickly fading. She would avoid sunlight to prevent wrinkles in her face. During a drinking binge, thinking her breasts were too big, she attempted to cut one off.

"No one could touch her for her looks; she was gorgeous," John recalled years later. "People stopped seeking her out because she was unpredictable. Mother's got a tremendous temper. My father wasn't calm either but he knew how to hide it; she didn't give a hoot, she just went ahead and blew her top."[11]

When his mother's drinking got out of control, Dare, now almost 15, moved in with his father. Lawson owned a house on 14 acres in Pacific Palisades next door to Will Rogers' ranch. Dare was enrolled at the nearby Pacific Palisades Middle School, where he did not last long. Lawson was experiencing a new career as a producer of Movietone–type newsreels. He also had a small animation studio in partnership with his close friend Derek Ghent, for whom John had apparently been named. Living on a big ranch was like a dream for Dare, who had an appreciation of everything about outdoor life and all sports. He started to play polo at the nearby Riviera Polo Club where famous Australian athlete Snowy Baker taught him the game. Lawson's business was so prosperous that he bought his son a gray Arabian stallion named Spooky.

Dare's love for drawing and painting also made Lawson very happy, hoping his son one day could make a living out of his artistic talent. Soon, one of John's sketches was hung in the lobby of a popular San Fernando Valley restaurant, the Sportsmen's Lodge, making Lawson very proud. Nonetheless, Dare was happiest when he slept in the stable next to his beloved horses. He would boost his allowance by breaking in other people's horses at the Bel Air stables. "I rode a lot and hated school," he admitted years later. "One day when I was riding down a canyon, Tom Moore, the silent screen star who became a talent scout for 20th, passed." As others from time to time had done, Moore stopped and asked Dare if he ever thought of a career as an actor. John told him that his parents were actors, so Moore asked Lawson to allow his son to make a screen test. Lawson: "No. He's not going to be a commercial artist." Lawson believed that Dare had inherited his artistic flair, and wanted him to study to be an artist. But Moore did not take no for an answer, as John recalled: "We got to know Mr. Moore and his wife better, and eventually they made some voice recordings of me at their home. Then they got me my first film test at 20th. I was 16 and was supposed to be a fellow of 25 acting 18! I wore a turned-up trenchcoat to look aged and I was very bad. I underacted."[12] Despite the test result, the Moores hoped that the head of 20th Century–Fox, Darryl Zanuck, would see it. One evening, while bowling in Westwood with some friends, Dare was approached by Henry Willson, David O. Selznick's scout. Willson asked him to try out for a part with Jennifer Jones. Aware of his previous screen test disaster with Fox, Dare thought he had nothing to lose. Together with 20 other young guys who had lined up for Selznick's personal opinion, Dare was the one chosen to screen test with Jones.

He sat through a four-hour makeup job transforming him into a wounded soldier and then reclined in a hospital bed while the actress acted. He got the part eventually. Yet, when the scene was shot again for the film, the camera didn't catch his face and the entire sequence was edited out.

Still, he landed a contract with Vanguard Film, Selznick's production company, at $125 a week.

According to Russ Harlan, Dare was not as enthusiastic as most guys would have been in his situation. Selznick had nothing specific in mind for him other than keeping him with Vanguard until the right part appeared. Impatient, Dare felt it was a waste of time. Russ explained to him that Selznick had a reputation of teaching his young players something and developing them.

On December 6, 1943, *Film Daily* announced, "Dare Harris, termer, David O. Selznick" in the "Hollywood Digest column,"[13] meaning that Dare had accepted a seven-year contract with Selznick. Being still a minor, the document had to be co-signed by his parents and receive final approval by a Los Angeles court. Three weeks later, *Variety* reported, "Dare Harris' minor contract with Vanguard approved by court."[14]

"I spent every cent on having a marvelous time," commented John on his starting salary. "I was out every night. Sure, I reported to the studio's dramatic coach, but I didn't listen to her. I knew that nothing would come out of it, that I was too young to get a decent part. I wasn't ambitious."[15]

While waiting for a casting call at Vanguard, Dare accepted to appear in a short silent film written and shot between Santa Monica, Beverly Hills and Westwood by Kenneth Anglemyer, who later become known as director Kenneth Anger. Only one year younger than Dare, Kenneth was a loner and a peculiar kid. He lived not far from Dare and the two got acquainted through a common friend. Despite his age, Ken had already shown a keen interest in making experimental films using a small 16mm camera. In 1943 he shot *The Nest*, a variant on Jean Cocteau's *Les Enfants Terribles*. The young filmmaker had an interest in French Symbolist literature, especially admiring Cocteau's body of work. The 20-minute silent black-and-white short featured Bob Jones and Jo Whittaker as siblings and Dare as their friend. *The Nest* was a surreal tale of incest and narcissism with latent eroticism, as Anger summarized it years later: "A brother and sister relate to mirrors and each other until a third party breaks the balance; seducing both into violence. Ablutions and the acts of dressing and making-up observed as a magic rite. The binding spell of the sister-sorceress is banished by the brother who walks out."[16] Dare played the friend who interferes, breaking the duo's harmony. The picture was never publicly shown or released separately from the rest of Anger's prolific shorts collection.

Among the students in Dare's school was a pretty little girl named Elizabeth Taylor, who had come to the U.S. from England a few years earlier. Dare was her first crush. She wrote in her autobiography,

> There was the most beautiful boy—to me, then like a god. One day we were going down the corridor and he tripped me, then he picked me up and said, "Hi there, beautiful." Oh, you can't imagine. I was in such ecstasy, I went to the girl's room and just sat there dreaming. His name was something like Derek Hansen. Later he changed it to John Derek.[17]

One of Taylor's biographers claimed that a couple of years later, the actress lost her virginity to Dare when accomplice Roddy McDowall allowed the two youngsters to use a small dressing room beside his pool. It quickly became a sort of Sunday afternoon ritual between

Dare and Elizabeth, who would meet with other friends at McDowall's. The tryst apparently terminated when Dare began to date Shirley Temple.[18]

Dare's first part from Selznick Productions came at the end of 1943 in *Since You Went Away*. He was cast as a non-speaking extra in an invisible role of a wounded soldier in a military hospital—the scene he had auditioned for a few weeks earlier. The picture, an almost three-hour-long World War II story, showed how an American family lived coping with the restrictions of the war and the anxiety on the homefront.

Since You Went Away's cast included Claudette Colbert, Jennifer Jones, Joseph Cotten and Shirley Temple along with a bunch of future Hollywood's celebrities in bit roles. Some, like Dare, were making their screen debut, including Guy Madison, Rhonda Fleming, Dorothy Dandridge, Terry Moore and Ruth Roman. The picture was a box office and critical success, becoming Selznick's highest grossing production since *Gone with the Wind* (1939).

Only six weeks later, at the beginning of 1944, John was cast in his first speaking role as a young lieutenant and the sweetheart of Shirley Temple. The film, originally titled *Double Furlough*, starred Joseph Cotten, Ginger Rogers, Spring Byington and Tom Tully. It was filmed at the Selznick studio in Culver City with exteriors shot at Warner Bros. The story was based on a radio play about a wartime romance between a shell-shocked U.S. Army sergeant (Cotten) and a female ex-convict (Rogers). Once Selznick obtained the rights to the original song "I'll Be Seeing You," chosen as the picture's musical main theme, the producer

John Derek makes his first lobby card appearance between Joseph Cotten (left) and Tom Tully in *I'll Be Seeing You* (1944).

decided to use it also as the title. George Cukor was originally assigned to the project, but eventually William Dieterle directed. The filmmaker was not very happy about the sappy story. "I tried to keep the sentiment down, but the screenplay defeated me," he told Rogers. "The sentimental stuff kept oozing out like warm treacle. You couldn't blame the actors."[19]

Working with Shirley Temple was a pleasant experience for Dare, as he was an old friend of the actress (she and her family lived not far from Lawson's ranch). "I loved her father," John once said. "He was a great down-to earth guy. A lot of people said that her mother was a stage mama, but I never saw that. And hell, I was the black sheep in comparison to the other guys who came over. I rode a motorcycle."[20] Although Dare appeared in only two scenes, he allegedly gave Temple her first on-screen kiss. Yet the sequence wound up on the cutting room floor after Selznick decided that audiences were not ready to see that Shirley Temple had grown up. Shirley described Dare as "a self-important young man … [with] pleasing features, perhaps a little too sensitive for my taste. With a shock of dark hair cascaded artfully over his forehead and his suit shoulders padded out to disguise a rather delicate frame."[21] According to the actress, Selznick thought that, as an actor, Dare had shown promise, but had little flair. She wrote in her autobiography,

> Despite previous training, he still spoke downward and habitually missed his marks. Selznick asked me to loosen him up. Not realizing the full extent of my task, I played the role of dramatic instructor. Relax, I urged. Ignore the audience. Never mind that twitch at your mouth or the one at the corner of the eye. Nobody can see it. Instruct and cajole him as I might, Harris would not, or could not, loosen up. On-camera he still came across wooden as a post.[22]

It did not take long for people to realize what a photogenic companion Dare was for Shirley. The company arranged for him to escort her around publicly. The photographers went wild when they showed up together at the 1943 Academy Awards. On the set of *I'll Be Seeing You*, Shirley turned 15 and a small party was thrown at the studio in her honor. For the occasion, Dare invited her for lunch at La Rue, a fashionable French restaurant on Sunset Blvd. in West Hollywood. As the bill arrived, he excused himself to the men's room, forcing the actress to take care of it. Friend Robert Wagner insisted,

> Shirley was crazy about Dare, but everybody was. Without question, he was the handsomest young man I've ever seen in my life—he stopped traffic. Dare was generous to me, treating me like a young brother, and took me with him everywhere they went. In later years, he became a curmudgeon, very demanding and egotistical, but as a young man he had a charming personality.[23]

Temple admitted that there was a lot of necking but neither of the two were brave enough for sex. Dare taught her how to drive a manual transmission in his decrepit car on a deserted playing field at the Riviera Polo Club. He also impressed her by telling her extraordinary stories about his life, like claiming to be the illegitimate son of an undisclosed famous movie actress or showing off a long sharp knife he carried on him all the time just in case he had to defend them from "enemies."

Dare fell madly in love with Shirley and was very passionate in his pursuit. Once he stalked her to Palm Springs, where she was on holiday with her family, just to check if she was dating someone else. He camped out in the desert because there were no available hotel rooms. The relationship was terminated by Shirley's protective mother after Dare gave her daughter two oil paintings he had made her. Shirley recalled,

> The picture represented someone's bluish face entwined in a surrealistic background of green seaweed. In his mystical, watery depiction, Mother instantly saw a symbolic likeness between the disembodied face and mine. She forbade me to see him again, a tall order considering we were studio colleagues.

But after thinking hard about her interpretation of his painting as a foretaste of undertow and death, I comfortably distanced myself, freeing Harris to skulk after more impressionable quarry.[24]

In the meantime, alarming news from Europe continued to arrive back to the U.S. Dare, now 17, decided to enlist and volunteered for paratrooper training: "Everybody I knew was doing it and for us it was like a game." He said years later that the people who managed the propaganda business did a very good job persuading young people like him to join the army:

> We believed them, and we enlisted! … Luckily for me, I enlisted very young. I don't mean to say that I will ever forget all the horrors I saw, but I fared better than others, because being a youngster it is easier to obey orders from someone that is just a little older than you, and you also have your whole life in front of you to heal your wounds.[25]

After 17 weeks of boot camp, Dare was sent to the Philippines, where he was assigned first to the 112th Regimental Combat Team, then reassigned to a small reconnaissance infantry regiment called the Alamo Scouts. The special group was dropped by parachute over territories where enemies had infiltrated so they could spy on their maneuvers and make maps of the terrain. He was also ordered to learn how to handle a machine gun, which he used for many months against the enemy. Although he never felt comfortable in the situation, he was able to stay alive. Luck was always on his side. One day, as he and his buddies were boarding a truck for the front lines, Dare was suddenly called back. He had shared a tent with a G.I. who was up for court-martial, and Dare had to remain behind as a witness. The truck went on. Three days later, all the men on it were killed. Dare later revealed that while in the Army, he experienced his unhappiest moments. "Not being able to move on my own, and impatiently hoping for orders to take me into the thick of the fray was the acme of frustration."[26]

After almost two years and with 16 jumps as a paratrooper, he was finally granted a transfer. Once the war came to an end, Dare, eager to see the world, was not yet ready to go home. In 1946, he left the Philippines with the forces of occupation and moved to Japan. Not having a lot to do, one day with the help of two friends, he came up with the idea of opening a brothel. It was quite a profitable business which Dare, by his own admission, did more for fun than for money. "I was a child when I went to war and I was still a child in Japan. It was just one more facet of the war."[27] John's daughter Sean claims that her father told her that he was awarded the Purple Heart (apparently he was shot while in the infantry line) but did not accept it because the military would have informed his mother he had been wounded, and he didn't want to scare her. Dolores wrote to her son overseas every day. Dare would often share her letters with the other boys who found them entertaining, full of funny and glamorous details about home and Hollywood.[28]

Back home after two years abroad, Dare felt a bit like a fish out of water. Some of his friends had died in the war, others had just moved away, so he found himself alone. The aftershock of his service in the Philippines had make him grow faint at the sight of blood. He wanted to have fun and enjoy life after what he had been through. For a while he considered going to college, but quickly realized that continuing his studies was not the best choice. People kept insisting that he should be an actor, which seemed the easiest way to make a living, given his looks and previous experience. Hence, just a couple of weeks before he was out of uniform, Dare returned to Selznick's studio to renegotiate his contract. He saw that opportunities were already being given to young fellows like Guy Madison and Rory Calhoun. Wisely he requested his release, which the studio granted. He then showed up in uniform at a Christmas party at 20th Century–Fox and once again he was discovered. After a screen test, he was offered a one-year contract. This time, Dare realized that he needed to work harder. He reported devotedly to Fox's drama coach Helena Sorrell, who was amazed at his seriousness. She had been his acting instructor at Selznick two years before, when all Dare wanted was to have fun. Now she faced a motivated drama student.

Although several sources credit Dare in the cast of George Cukor's *A Double Life* (1947) in the small role of a police stenographer, he did not appear in any additional films until late summer 1948.

The first half of 1948 was very difficult for Dare. In March, his father died of emphysema at age 50. Even though Dare had been living with his mother near Malibu since his return from the war, he maintained a special admiration for his father:

Derek in a 1946 publicity shot.

> My dad was the kind of man, that if he didn't have it, he still had it, because he was a promoter, very handsome and very glib. He could talk his way in or out of anything, and everything was easy for him if he chose it to be.... I admire anybody who can get in and out of problems, who can be rich one day and poor the next, and rich again—they've got to have ability somewhere.[29]

In July 1948, Dolores, who had married a German man, attempted to kill herself with an overdose of sleeping pills. She was rushed to the hospital where her stomach was pumped.[30]

Dare's contract with 20th Century–Fox was almost over and still no offer of any role. Suddenly, things changed for the better. He was first offered a contract at Metro-Goldwyn-Mayer, which he was about to accept when a friend in the Fox reading department told his drama coach's secretary (another friend of Dare's) about *Knock on Any Door,* a novel that was about to be filmed at Columbia. The secretary thought that he would be perfect in one of the main roles. At the secretary's recommendation, Dare read the book and immediately sensed that he could play the role of Nick Romano, a wild juvenile delinquent of the slums. All Dare's tormenting self-doubts melted in his impatience to track down the producer casting that part. Nick Romano was his opportunity. He never felt surer.

Chapter 2

Pretty Boy

"You are now going to meet a new classmate with the most beautiful eyelashes of any actor in existence."—Helena Sorrell to Pati Behrs

In 1947, Humphrey Bogart formed Santana Productions, his own independent film company, and signed to appear in four pictures to be released through Columbia. The first was *Knock on Any Door*, based on African-American novelist Willard Motley's best-seller. The rights were first purchased as a vehicle for Marlon Brando by producer Mark Hellinger, who suddenly died in December 1947. Robert Lord, formerly a Warner Bros. producer, subsequently acquired the rights. When in early 1948 Bogart signed Lord to be the vice-president of Santana, the producer proposed *Knock on Any Door* as its first picture. Bogart, who loved the book, approved the idea and commissioned John Monks, Jr., to develop a script.

In March 1948, Bogart hired Nicholas Ray to direct *Knock on Any Door*. The star was a Nicholas Ray fan. He especially admired the realism and the pictorial expressiveness present in the first two films the young director had just made. At the same time, Daniel Taradash was hired to revise the screenplay started by Monks that, for censorship reasons, had to be toned down. The original novel was too provocative and full of explicit sex and police brutality, unsuitable for Hollywood's moral standards. Taradash used a flashback structure, an approach that felt right for that type of story. A combination of courtroom drama and crime film, the picture depicted the troubled life of "pretty boy" Nick Romano, a handsome young delinquent who begins his life of crime as a petty thief and brings it to a climax by murdering a policeman. The plot is told from the perspective of his lawyer, Andrew Morton, in a defense speech during Romano's murder trial. Like the defendant, the attorney was once a juvenile criminal, but he was able to redeem himself.

According to studio publicity, Bogart had discovered Dare while touring at the Salton Sea military base during the war. Apparently the star immediately liked Dare, who told him about his acting dreams. "If I can ever give you a hand, let me know," Bogart offered.[1] This discovery story, later reported by several movie magazines, fits the perfect Hollywood fairy tale on how movie stars were made. Nevertheless, the story seems very unlikely. Dare always insisted that he persistently pursued the role of Nick Romano, pleading with his agent to arrange a screen test. "My training contract was about to lapse, and I not only wanted the job but also wanted a chance to show that I could act," he told *The Saturday Evening Post* in 1953.[2]

Dare's agent was finally able to get him a screen test at Columbia, where Max Arnow, the studio's talent executive, handed Dare Nick Romano's most dramatic scene to read—dialogue taken from the book that Dare knew by heart. As part of the scene, Dare had to scream, and he did so loudly that he got a cramp that forced him to stop and lie down.

Chapter 2. Pretty Boy

Frank Sinatra, a friend of Bogart's, was after the producers to cast *him* as Romano. But Ray tested Dare more than once. According to Hollywood lore, Dare changed his name to John Derek on the advice of Lauren Bacall, Bogart's wife, who was present at the screen tests. The Bogarts believed that making his real first name into his last name, preceded by a common John, gave him a screen name that was memorable and commercially suitable. Nevertheless, many years later, John revealed that the real responsible party behind his new name was Harry Cohn. The head of Columbia thought Dare Harris sounded too sophisticated and wanted to call him Errol O'Flynn. "Even before he was going to put me in swashbucklers," John recalled, "I said, 'No way am I going to be Errol O'Flynn!' He said I could keep one of the names, so I took Derek, it's more interesting than Harris. They had the last word when they gave me the most common name on earth: John."[3]

In April 1948, John was officially cast as Nick Romano in *Knock on Any Door*. Columbia offered him a seven-year contract with a weekly salary of $250. John was ecstatic.

Everybody seemed to agree that he had the perfect look for that role with his thick dark hair and soulful eyes, evoking a Greek god. Author Motley exclaimed, "He's the exact-looking person I had in mind."[4] Only Taradash expressed a few doubts about John's ability to play Nick, questioning his capacity in showing the character's inner demons. "Can that Derek boy really play the part of Nick? It's not easy," the screenwriter wrote in a letter to producer Lord just a few days after the actor was hired.[5]

With a budget of $900,000, the shooting began on August 2, 1948. Suddenly John was overtaken by a sense of insecurity, trying to obtain from Motley all the answers about his character that Ray was not giving him. John constantly complained to the author about the production, maintaining that he was being rushed by the filming schedule and that he wasn't yet ready to do justice to his role. John wished to travel to Chicago to catch the feeling of the slums where the story was set. He expressed his disappointment when he learned that no scene was planned to be filmed on location. He was hoping for a more realistic approach. Motley agreed and wrote several letters to Ray inviting him to visit Chicago, to prowl with him on the streets of the city in old clothes during day and night, suggesting that the director shoot scenes on location with a hidden camera. Ray never replied to those letters and the film was almost entirely shot at Columbia.

Motley was also dissatisfied by how the end had been changed in the script, and considered this a sort of a betrayal of the novel, altered just to suit Bogart's character. Yet he kept giving advice to John, trying to build up his confidence. On July 25, the author wrote John from his home in Chicago, after a brief stay in Hollywood: "You are perfect for the part and know that you will make Nick live on the screen."[6] He also enclosed some newspaper clippings from a trial of a Chicago teenager on whom he had based some of the courtroom stuff in his novel. Motley thought they could help John capture the feelings of a boy on trial for his life.

In the picture, John had more scenes than any other cast member, so director Ray realized he had to pay extra attention to him. He noticed that John was giving a wooden performance, looking very tense. Ray made an effort in get John to relax. However, on several occasions John still appeared reluctant and not at ease. Seeking a certain realism, Ray coached him to slap actress Cara Williams softly during rehearsals for a scene and then hit her hard—and unexpectedly—for the actual take. John did it as told, but Williams lost her temper and punched John on his mouth so fiercely that the shooting had to be stopped while the makeup people repaired his cut lip. During a major scene in which John had to scream loudly, he was so nervous that he needed several takes; at the end he found himself

Humphrey Bogart, Derek and Lauren Bacall in 1949.

voiceless and unusable for the rest of the shooting day. Ray's biographer describes another episode of the filmmaker's frustration after John could not strike a particular pose. Suddenly the director lost his patience and tact, strode over and grabbed the young actor by the head and turned it to the left, telling him to keep looking in that direction during the scene.[7] In spite of those incidents, John remained always very grateful for Ray's direction: "Nick Ray did it. He whipped that performance out of me."[8]

Chapter 2. Pretty Boy 17

Derek and Humphrey Bogart in *Knock on Any Door* (1949).

The professional relationship between Bogart and John was of mutual admiration. "He never mentioned the fact that I was a beginner," John said gratefully in an interview. "He wasn't the big shot. There was never anything overboard about him. Even though it was his own production, he never acted out what I was to do. He let the director attend to me. Almost everybody gives a new fellow flowery advice. Bogie spared me that. What a man!"[9] The advice came later in the form of a note written by Bogart after *Knock on Any Door* was released. Bogie wrote:

> Now that you have clicked overnight, don't pull your punches! Get in there and follow up your flash. Forget your fears and don't fumble. If you do, I ought to belt you. Suddenly you've got life on the run, Johnny. If you use that brain of yours, you can wind up a long-term winner. If your Hollywood bosses give you the right breaks, in three years you can be the same sort of star Tyrone Power is.... By-pass the curse of stupid conventions. Stick to your own pattern. If you're shrewd enough, you'll be a true success.[10]

The picture wrapped on September 17, 1948. Bogart tried to rush the post-production for a possible Christmas release, but the film opened nationwide in February after a gala premiere in Chicago, where the story was set. The reviews were mixed. The film's message (a bad social environment is the breeding ground for delinquency) pointed an accusatory finger at society, and was found by some to be presented in a style a bit too melodramatic and pretentious. Not all the critics were satisfied by the film, but they generally praised John's performance. The most flattering words were printed in *The Hollywood Reporter* describing John as "a potential matinee idol, [who] performs a difficult role with finesse and professional ease."[11] The *New York Herald Tribune* added: "Derek may be a newcomer, but he knows a great deal about make-believe. His portrait of Nick Romano ... is astringent and shocking."[12] *Boxoffice* called John "an unusually promising screen newcomer who scores solidly as the young killer."[13] *Knock on Any Door* did very well at the box office and became a popular film, especially among young adults, making John Derek an overnight star. "Pretty Boy" Nick Romano's motto, "Live fast, die young and have a good-looking corpse," became a quote used by a generation of teenage fans of the so-called rebel actors Montgomery Clift, Marlon Brando and James Dean.

Derek in a publicity shot for *Knock on Any Door* (1949).

Suddenly John Derek was the face of 1949. He was famous, but no richer. "The most surprising reaction I got from this role came in Trinidad." John revealed a few years later. "I was on my way to South America with a group of better-known actors and actresses at the time. So, when we stopped at Trinidad to refuel, I tried to stay in the background and got off the plane next to last. Yet I stepped out to a shout of welcome. No one knew me—John Derek—but everyone knew Nick Romero [sic], the role that gave me my start in pictures."[14]

On the eve of *Knock on Any Door*'s premiere, the *New York Times* announced that John was currently at work in Robert Rossen's adaptation of Robert Penn Warren's Pulitzer Prize winner *All the King's Men* and that Columbia had bought the rights of Millard Lampell's novel *The Hero* as a John Derek vehicle.[15]

During that year at 20th Century–Fox, John met Pati Behrs in Sorell's drama class. A vivacious petite brunette, four years his senior, she had moved from France in January 1946. Her arrival in Hollywood was reported with fanfare by the *Los Angeles Times*. Apparently a talent scout in London heard of her beauty and flew to France to give her a screen test and signed her to a contract with Fox.[16] Pati Behrs Eristoff was a former classical dancer born in Constantinople, Turkey, on February 13, 1922. Her parents were of Russian-Georgian noble origins related on her father's side to the great writer Leo Tolstoy. Prince Andre Behrs was a colonel in the Czar's Cavalry. His refusal to lead a pogrom forced him to leave Russia. He

Pati Behrs and Derek at a masked ball in Hollywood in 1948.

traveled first to Turkey, but the unstable political and economic situation of the country forced him to France.

At age 13, Pati got her first contract to tour Europe as a prima ballerina with a French ballet company. After her father's sudden death, Pati had to leave the company to support her mother, who had joined her in Paris and was struggling with alcoholism. Pati started working in several Parisian nightclubs as a singer and dancer. Just when the war ended, she casually met Darryl Zanuck, who was in town on business. The producer had seen her dancing act at a nightclub and asked if she was interested in acting. Pati was very skeptical about that offer, and pointed out that her turned-up nose was probably not very photogenic. Zanuck convinced her otherwise and she did a screen test with French filmmaker Marc Allégret. A few weeks later she was offered a Fox contract. On December 30, 1945, she boarded on the *Edmund B. Alexander* troop ship in Le Havre, destination New York. From there she continued her journey to California by train. Once in Hollywood, she was lodged at the Bel Air Hotel.

English classes along with acting lessons became Pati's main daily routine. Her drama class was also attended by future stars Marilyn Monroe and Jean Peters (John would later deny the presence of other pretty female students, stating that it was mostly an all-male class). One day in class, the teacher warned Pati of the arrival of a student the teacher had previously coached at another studio. "You are now going to meet a new classmate with the most beautiful eyelashes of any actor in existence."[17] Pati was smitten by John's expressive eyes and his eyelashes. The two youngsters became acquainted and often studied together, occasionally rehearsing love scenes. But a few months passed before they had their first real date. John took Pati to see Ken Murray's *Blackouts*, a racy burlesque show at the El Capitan Theatre on Vine Street in Hollywood. She had expressed the wish to watch a striptease, because she had never seen one. On the way home, they stopped at a diner and over a raw steak, they talked all night, discovering a lot of things in common.

Traveling was one common interest, and in the weeks that followed, the couple visited dozens of places around California. "Then, on an afternoon some months after our first date," Pati told *Modern Screen*, "we were driving home from Santa Barbara when John suddenly pulled over to the side of the road. I was puzzled.... He wanted to say a few words—only a few—but they were enough for me. 'You are wonderful,' he said. 'Let's go to Mexico and get married.'"[18] Pati told John to wait a little longer since they had known each other for such a short time. She promised that the moment she felt ready, she would tell him. Six months later, she proposed, but this time it was John who told her to wait since he did not have enough money to support her. Pati was offended, since she knew that John's financial resources were exactly the same as when he had proposed to her six months earlier. Suddenly, the situation changed after John was offered a contract along with his "big break" role in *Knock on Any Door*. They lived together for a while. It was a great challenge for John, who had lived by himself for so long that it was hard for him to express his feelings to someone else. The relationship required Pati's understanding of John's sudden temper tantrums, his need for time alone and his constant need for physical activity. It was easier in the beginning since they were both very busy with work, seeing each other only at the end of the day.

A date for the wedding was finally set and they got married informally and very privately. According to a news article, the ceremony was briefly postponed as they waited for Pati's mother Princess Juliana Galithkaya Gouretskaya Behrs Eristoff to be well enough to cross the Atlantic. Ultimately they decided to wait no longer. On the day of the marriage, Pati was working on the film *The Beautiful Blonde from Bashful Bend* (1949) starring Betty Grable and Cesar Romero. John was supposed to wait for her to call to let him know when he had to pick her up at the studio. But the shooting finished too late for them to get married. The following day, October 9, 1948, the couple traveled to Las Vegas with their friends Candy and Bob Brand as their witnesses. On the way to the chapel, John realized he had forgotten the rings. They placed a call to the jeweler, who rushed to the airport to send the rings on the first flight to Las Vegas, just in time for the two to finally get married. According to a short Associated Press article, right after the ceremony, this marriage was to be Pati's second. She had been briefly married to Gogi Tchltchinadze, host at the Bel Air Hotel, where she resided when she was newly arrived in California. If true, for still unknown reasons, that previous marriage had been kept very quiet. The press reported that she had received the final divorce just a few hours prior her marriage to John.[19]

John's version of events is far less romantic. He confirmed that they met at Fox. Pati told him that her father, André Behrs, was a Georgian prince and a colonel in the Czar's Royal Cavalry, who had to leave the country during the 1917 revolution. André met Pati's mother, who was French, in Paris where they married and later managed little nightclubs during the Occupation.

What impressed John the most about Pati was how different she was from other American girls. She was very serious, a hard worker and, above all, she did not giggle when he spoke to her like other women would do in his presence. Even though he would see her at the drama class daily, he *really* noticed her a few weeks later at a party at the Bel Air Hotel. She was diving into the pool wearing her hair in a chignon, not worrying about her hair like most American girls would. They got engaged when *Knock on Any Door* became a success.

According to John, Pati had always been possessive but after he became popular, she turned out to be even more so. She made up her mind that they should get married. John couldn't change her mind, and one day he agreed. They had a typical quick marriage in Las Vegas and moved to a small house in Santa Monica. "The more I think about it," John confessed years later, "the less I understand why I married Pati. I don't know if we ever liked each other.... Pati interested me, but the problem was that other girls also interested me and I could not resist."[20]

The Dereks returned to their house in Santa Monica after a short honeymoon in Palm Springs. John was expected to prepare himself for his role in *All the King's Men*.

In May 1947, Robert Penn Warren, the author of the novel *All the King's Men*, sold the film rights to Columbia on a cash and percentage deal expected to yield more than $200,000. Robert Rossen, the producer-director assigned to the project, worked very closely with Warren, co-writing the script and consulting him frequently through some ten drafts. Once Columbia president Harry Cohn approved the film's budget (just under a million dollars), pre-production started. The story was loosely based on the sensational political career of notorious Louisiana governor Huey "Kingfish" Long, who became a Senator during the '30s, rising to power through dubious methods. In the picture, Willie Stark (the Long counterpart) appears as a populist politician, a twisted mixture of idealism and greed whose rise and fall is seen through the eyes of a newspaperman.

For the role of Stark, Cohn originally wanted Spencer Tracy. Humphrey Bogart was

A.C. Tillman (foreground, left), Derek (holding flyers), John Ireland (behind Derek) and Broderick Crawford (in white suit) in *All the King's Men* (1949).

also considered. Rossen, hoping to make an impact with a leading man less well-known, cast Broderick Crawford. He explained:

> [Crawford] was not, at the time of his selection for the Willie Stark role, in the category of a box office star. But he was a seasoned actor and one who we felt suited the part to perfection. While Crawford was a capable and fairly well-known actor, people just didn't turn in the street and either "ah" or "oh" or swoon in his wake.... Before the end of the first week, so deeply had the personality of the mythical Willie Stark penetrated into the consciousness of the townspeople that the vision of Gov. Earl Warren ... was temporarily dimmed.[21]

Production started on November 29, 1948. Rossen worked on location for six weeks, using exteriors and interiors of civic buildings, courthouses and hotels belonging to the towns of Stockton and Suisun City, California, which subbed for the generic state capital in the movie. Rossen's method of procuring bit players was to advertise in the papers in towns surrounding San Francisco: "If they look like people who would live in these towns," he stated in the film's press release, "they will look like the people in my picture." Realism was the filmmaker's priority in order to avoid the glossy, phony appearance of Hollywood pictures of the time. About 500 background extras were used each day for a long period. The total (tens of thousands) established a record as the highest number of extras ever used in a single picture.

John played Tom, Stark's adopted son. In an April 18, 1949, letter that Robert Warren Penn wrote to Albert Erskine regarding casting decisions, he opined, "Some of the characters are really excellent, Willie, Sadie, Lucy, Jack, Sugar, and Adam are good. Anne will do, and is good at moments. Tom Stark, whose part is much bigger in the movie than in the novel, is lousy. (Top secret: Got crammed down Rossen's throat—studio pet, Bogart's protégé, etc. But cutting may reduce him somewhat.)"[22] Penn insinuated that Bogart campaigned for John to get the part and Cohn accepted probably because Bogie was a solid box office star whom he could use in future projects.

John's role was indeed brief but highly dramatic. He played a youngster bullied and intimidated by the political demagogy of his adopted father, who forces him into a football game in which he was unfit to play. The consequences eventually make him a victim of a car accident that paralyzes him for life.

Crawford hit it off immediately with John. He wrote in an article,

> I first met Derek while I was making *All the King's Men*. My impression of him was a lot of dark, curly hair, beautiful white teeth. He was late for a shot one day and I said, "Where's 'Hair and Teeth'?" From then on, everyone called him that. I have a broken nose. My face is a little beat up. Seeing a guy as handsome as Derek for the first time was more or less of a shock—especially when I discovered that he was playing the part of my son! Don't think because Derek is so good looking, he's one of those pretty boys who tremble at the idea of having their hair mussed.... He's not afraid of anything. He plunges in whatever has to be done with a lot of spunk.[23]

John became very fond of Crawford. They worked together years later in two other pictures.

Acting with skilled players Crawford, Mercedes McCambridge and John Irelan, helped John to overcome the initial disappointment about the small size of his role. He soon realized that working alongside all these different actors gave him the remarkable chance to see their approaches to the individual problems of their parts. "I learned more in three months than I would have done in three years of drama school," he observed. Shooting was completed on January 26, 1949, but it took Rossen almost ten months to complete the editing process. Originally, Columbia expressed no intention of showing the film outside North

America. They felt that it dealt with a unique American problem and would make no sense at all to foreigners. That decision was reversed after its great success domestically. The film received enthusiastic reviews and seven Academy Award nominations; it won three Oscars (including Best Picture) and 30 other industry awards. In Singapore and in the Malaysian area, censor Jack Evans banned the picture, stating, "It gives a wrong and one-sided impression of American political life."[24]

John got flattering mentions in many reviews, the most compliments coming from *The Hollywood Reporter*: "John Derek ... shows the promise fulfilled in *Knock on Any Door* which hit release dates some time back." *Variety* wrote, "John Derek ... impresses." "Outstanding" was the comment of *New York Journal of Commerce* on John's interpretation.

On November 8, 1949, *All the King's Men* world-premiered at the Victoria Theatre in New York City, playing to packed houses for three months. A week prior to the gala event, John flew to New York for publicity appearances and interviews in connection with the premiere. Pati stayed at home because one of their dogs was having puppies. The Dereks were raising eight German Shepherds after their first dog, Annie, took three prizes at a canine show at Gilmore Stadium. They intended to donate some of the dogs to the Seeing Eye.

Arriving at La Guardia Airport, John was welcomed by three beautiful models giving him the *Photoplay Magazine* "Man of the Year Award." On the day *All the King's Men* opened in Manhattan, an estimated 5000 youngsters lined up outside the theater to see the picture. The first 500 patrons had the thrill of purchasing their tickets from John. During his publicity tour, mobs of teenagers, mostly girls, packed the theaters in three New York boroughs and in suburban parts of New Jersey just to get a glimpse of John Derek. "The sound of female shrieks and whistles was like the old times to veterans of the Sinatra campaigns of the recent past," wrote Jack Gaver of the United Press. "It's all been a little startling," John commented about that surreal situation, "and I certainly appreciate it, but actually I'd rather be a director than an actor. Too much of an actor's work in pictures isn't his own. The director tells you what to do and you do it. That's for me."[25] John also admitted feeling a little uneasy over the fact that his part in *All the King's Men* was on the small side, fearing that his fans would be disappointed. Columbia's executives cleverly had foreseen John's ability to lure younger crowds to buy a ticket for a picture whose political subject was meant for more adult and sophisticated audiences.

John wanted to see more of New York, but got very little opportunity. Columbia press agents booked him so solidly for photo shoots and interviews that he never had any time for sightseeing. "I rise at nine and make the rounds a new actor must make," he explained in a *Silver Screen* interview. "I have done a series of personal appearances, radio broadcasts, been to dozens of cocktail parties, visited magazine editors, and after 11:30 at night I sit in the hotel and twiddle my thumbs." He regretted being too much of a hurry to be as nice to fans as he wanted to be:

> Frankly, I didn't know that I loved being somebody, but I'll tell you why I have gotten such a great kick out of it. When you are a personality everybody recognizes, you are never lonely! Today when I walk into a strange town, people are friendly and I get a big smile from everyone. Yesterday, had I done the same thing, no one would have cracked his face. Sure, I could have smiled at the hotel clerk, but he has to smile back.[26]

Among his engagements, John particularly enjoyed an invitation to play host to the editors of the newspapers of the New York City high schools at a private screening of the picture at Columbia's projection room, where the student editors interviewed him. He was surprised by the quality of their questions, which he found more interesting than those professional reporters usually asked him.

A week later, *All the King's Men* had its Hollywood premiere, followed by a glittering party. John walked the red carpet with Pati in a crowd of celebrities including James Stewart, Terry Moore, Broderick Crawford and Crawford's wife Mary Alice. A couple of months later, *Boxoffice* magazine awarded him the Blue Ribbon Award after the National Screen Council voted *All the King's Men* best film of the month.

Many years later, as he reflected on his acting career, John commented,

> *All the King's Men* was the most pretentious happening I've never been involved in. They were talking Academy Awards before a foot of film was shot. It was ridiculous. I loved Brod Crawford, though. We worked together again in *Scandal Sheet*. He came in smashed half the time, read lines off the palm of his hand. There was no integrity in that film and most of the others.[27]

Chapter 3

An Attempt at Stardom

"A close-up of John Derek was a beautiful thing to look at."—Gordon Douglas

"How can you play a god?" John asked when producer Edward Small offered him the chance to play Rudolph Valentino in a biographical picture on the late silent movie star. John was not convinced, even though he admitted to the press that his look resembled Valentino a bit (although he pointed out that his nose was not as straight as Valentino's). He also feared that taking that part would brand him a dandy. Anthony Dexter was eventually given the role while John was cast in *Swords of Sherwood Forest* as Robin Hood's son. John took the part initially assigned to Cornel Wilde, who had played that same role a few years earlier in *The Bandit of Sherwood Forest* (1946). Wilde had turned it down, uninterested in reprising it. Initial casting choices originally included Gig Young to play Robin Hood's enemy King John, but the actor refused and was suspended, and replaced by George Macready. Alan Hale was borrowed from Warner Bros. to play Little John, a character he had already played in the 1922 United Artists film *Robin Hood* starring Douglas Fairbanks and in the 1938 Warner Bros. film *The Adventures of Robin Hood* starring Errol Flynn. Diana Lynn was cast as Lady Marianne, Robin Hood's love interest.

As soon the contract was signed, John, now a skilled horseman, began taking lessons in archery and fencing from Ralph Faulkner, a former member of the U.S. Olympic team. Faulkner's wife Edith Jane, an expert fencer herself, tutored him when her husband

Derek as a dashing Robin Hood in *Rogues of Sherwood Forest* (1950).

was unavailable. John played Robin Earl of Huntingdon, leading his father's veteran band of Merry Men of Sherwood Forest on yet another campaign to thwart the ambitious King John. To look the part, he had to grow a mustache which made him look like a believable son of Errol Flynn. "They wanted me to wear Errol Flynn's costumes from ten years ago," John revealed in an interview, "but Flynn's legs are too streamlined for me. My legs are much stockier and anyway the costumes looked seedy after ten years."[1] He also explained that the costume designer wanted him to make his Robin Hood sexy, but that he insisted on wearing a long jacket.

Just before filming began in August 1949, the title was changed to *Rogues of Sherwood Forest*. Shooting was done largely on location between the plateau of China Flats in the Santa Monica Mountains and the Corriganville movie ranch. Originally the exteriors were going to be filmed on a plot of giant white oaks, set in rolling hills with a stream, about 35 miles out of Hollywood where three Robin Hood pictures had been shot previously. In pre-production, art director Harold MacArthur visited the location to scout the best spot for Nottingham Forest, but the site proved to be useless. Seven very dry California summers had burned every blade of grass not under irrigation to brittle brown. There wasn't a spot of green in the place. MacArthur thought of remedying the brown terrain with 2000 pounds of green vegetable dye and 14 truckloads of burlap-backed bright green grass, which he just happened to have along with him; but there proved to be other difficulties. A stream once present had been dammed by a local farmer and many of the big trees had been badly damaged in the previous winter snowfall which had broken hundreds of limbs. With these handicaps, MacArthur had to give up. Fortunately for the picture, he discovered China Flats. With the help of the green vegetable dye and the truckloads of grass, the new location became a perfect Technicolor set lusher than anyone in the production could ever hoped.

For a spectacular fight scene in the forest between Robin Hood's archers and the crossbow- and longbow-wielding men of King John, Columbia hired 106 of Hollywood's 130 stunt men registered with the Screen Actors Guild. Their job was to leap from trees onto horsemen below, fall with horses and perform all manners of difficult and dangerous acrobatics. John did most of his own stunts and was the only actor in the cast in that particular scene. In a sequence involving a daring 40-foot leap, the producers forced him to let stuntman David Sharpe double for him. They did not want to risk injury to their new rising star, jeopardizing the entire production. "If my face gets nicked," John said in an interview, "it will heal. I don't want to be a phony Robin Hood who waves a sword at ten thousand opponents and wins. I'd really like to take on a few and see what happens."[2]

Director Gordon Douglas described the making of *Rogues of Sherwood Forest* as a fun experience. "Our leading lady [Diana Lynn] had to squint her eyes when she was in the sunlight," recalled the filmmaker. "When I saw the dailies, it looked like she had her eyes closed. I had to put her under an awning and do those scenes over. John Derek ... was prettier than the leading lady. He really was a gorgeous man. A close-up of John Derek was a beautiful thing to look at."[3]

Although the picture followed the usual lines of previous Robin Hood stories, the costumes and settings, photographed in Technicolor, were found to be very attractive by some critics who also enjoyed the film's lively pace. Generally, the press praised John's performance. He seemed very comfortable in the leading role, making a convincingly youthful, athletic Robin. At age 24, John was the youngest swashbuckler ever on screen, and his popularity was skyrocketing.

A month after *Rogues of Sherwood Forest* opened nationwide, a screenwriter named

Clifford Sanforth filed a suit in the federal court of Los Angeles against Columbia asking $45,000 in damages because the studio used a character in the picture he claimed to have created, the son of Robin Hood. His complaint alleged that he conceived the character for the 1946 Columbia picture *The Bandit of Sherwood Forest*, and that the studio had no right to re-use the character without paying him. The suit was eventually settled out of court.

When *Rogues* was about to go into production, producer Marshall Grant, who had just joined Columbia, announced his plan to make a film called *The Gainesville Circus*. In 1947, while he was still an independent producer, Grant showed an interest in producing a picture about a Texas town which had established its own community circus, but financial problems prevented further action on his project.

Derek and Diana Lynn on the set of *Rogues of Sherwood Forest* (1950).

His deal, which Columbia had taken over, provided that Gainesville would make available to the film any or all the employees of the community circus, in which virtually all of the town's 12,000 inhabitants participated. A screenwriter from Columbia was dispatched to Texas to join the annual circus tour and get background material.[4] John was cast as the male lead and ordered to visit the circus once he completed the Robin Hood film. Yet by the time *Rogues of Sherwood Forest* was completed, the Gainesville project was stalled (and later dropped) due to its exorbitant cost.

Meanwhile, Jerry Wald, a Warner Bros. producer, had tried to persuade Harry Cohn to lend John out for his remake of the 1922 First National silent film *The Patent Leather Kid*. John was very excited by the thought of playing a gangster role, which could have broken the mold of being cast because of his "pretty face" in nothing but romantic parts. But Cohn had other plans for his new leading man and refused. Wald's project was never realized.

On November 22, 1949, Louella Parsons announced in her syndicated column "Two happier young people than John Derek and Pati Behrs do not exist in our town today. They expect a baby in July and they hope it will be born on John's birthday."[5] The reality was quite different from how the gossip columnist portrayed the otherwise happy event. Reports of a shaky marriage already had appeared in the press. John was working very hard and, due to long hours away from home, felt almost as if he were single. "One night when I got home. Pati told me that she was pregnant. She had decided for herself to have our children, and when I found out I was too late."[6] According to Sean Derek, John's daughter, her father revealed during a violent verbal fight that the only reason he had married Pati was because she had threatened to kill herself if he did not marry her. That night, he was about to leave her for good, so she waited until he was outside her door. Then he heard her spinning the barrel of a gun he kept in the house. He ran back in, pleading with her to stop. John was only successful after he promised to take her to Las Vegas the next day and marry her.[7] On April 13, 1950, Pati gave birth to a son by a Caesarean section, two weeks earlier than they expected, and much too early if the November press release five months earlier was accurately timed. The Dereks named the baby Russell Andre, after John's father figure and best friend Russell Harlan, and Pati's father Andre.

Less than 24 hours after Russell Andre's birth, a nurse noticed something strange in the baby, who seemed to show symptoms of a rare condition related to a split esophagus (a separation in the baby's esophageal tube that caused food to be detoured into the lungs rather than his stomach, causing suffocation). Luck was on the Dereks' side: The only surgeon in the States capable of performing an experimental surgery for this rare condition was at the Children's Hospital. Within a few hours of his birth, little Russell underwent a long, delicate but successful surgical procedure that resulted in him being one of the first babies to survive that terrible condition. After the infant spent many weeks in observation at the hospital, the doctors discharged him, recommending maximum care at home. Russell was a very frail

Derek, his son Russell and first wife Pati Behrs in 1950.

and delicate child and had to be treated accordingly. It was a broken dream for John, who was eager to share all his hyper-masculine activities with his son.

When Russell returned home, John was already busy preparing for his next picture, *The Hero*. He played Steve Novak, a poor Polish-American boy who was halfback in his high school football team and craved a college education. The character's illusions are blasted by the commercialism and cruel brutality in the games he plays after being awarded a scholarship. Based on Millard Lampell's first novel *The Hero*, which had been purchased by Columbia in December 1948, just a few months before its publication, it was a vehicle for John. Sidney Buchman, a Columbia writer-producer, asked the author to write a script faithful to the novel. According to Lampell, Buchman's collaboration in the final script was less than 20 percent. Yet their partnership was extremely helpful in polishing the screenplay, since it was Lampell's first experience as a screenwriter. While the duo was still in the process of revising the final draft, Columbia cast the picture. Buchman had a fight with Harry Cohn over casting choices. He and Lampell wanted Jack Palance as the lead, but Cohn was determined to cast John.[8] A young and unknown actress, Karen Sharpe, was tested for the role of Melissa, John's love interest, but Cohn preferred Donna Reed, whose husband Tony Owen was a Columbia producer. Donna was eager to return to moviemaking after a brief absence from the screen. She got the part after passing a difficult screen test, a three-page scene that took two and half days to shoot. She later commented that her romantic pairing

Director David Miller (standing) with Donna Reed and Derek on the *Saturday's Hero* (1951) set.

with John, who was five years her junior, was ridiculous, since he looked even younger than his age.

Newcomer Aldo DaRe, later known as Aldo Ray, was cast in the minor but pivotal role of Gene Hausler. Ray was not interested in acting in the film; he had merely accompanied his brother Mario, a promising football player, to a casting call. But studio executives preferred him to his brother and persuaded him to take the part. It was the beginning of a promising career. Ray and John became good friends, working together on two other occasions.

At age 24, John was solidly muscled, an expert swimmer and horse rider, but had no experience as a football player. Coached by former USC football players Mickey McCardle and Paul Clearly, John went through six weeks of intensive, strenuous physical training to appear as a believable football player. His determination and the amazing natural style quickly impressed his coaches. From 8 a.m. until 6 p.m. in the days before the shooting of the football scenes began, John was mixing with hardened college and professional football players. They outweighed him by an average of 50 pounds, and they could easily outrun, out-tackle and out-rough him any time. For that role, John gave up smoking, and got a permanent so his naturally curly hair would look the same throughout the film.

The shooting lasted 83 days during the summer of 1950 and John's presence on the set was required every day. He rarely had time to spend with his family. When he was at home, he'd sit and nurse his injured legs and the bruises his body had collected. The first week he tore a muscle in his leg, followed by bumps and bruises. These included "strawberries," the marks that virtually all players acquire when their faces rub against their opponents' sandpaper-like canvas pants during tackling maneuvers. John admitted that there were days he felt he would never want to look at a football uniform again.

The football sequences were shot under difficult circumstances. The cameramen often had to use combat cameras that allowed them to be right in the middle of the action in the field without being too intrusive.

From the beginning, there were problems. First, since the story exposed the corruption of sports in college, no Ivy League university would allow the filming on their premises. The background had to be put together from different locations including Pomona College, the Pasadena Rose Bowl and the Los Angeles Coliseum with over 100 college and professional football players. Second, a strict contractual agreement forbade Columbia from giving any credit or disclosing the names of the UCLA and USC football players appearing in the film, which could have compromised their amateur status. Third, the final script ran afoul of the censors, who felt that the relationship that the Donna Reed character had with her uncle suggested incest. Director David Miller had to coach the two actors in their use of posture, movements and eye contact in a way that did not express anything remotely sexual.[9] For unknown reasons, Columbia shelved the picture for a year. While it collected dust, John made two other films, *Mask of the Avenger* and *The Family Secret*.

Prior to its official opening, the producers of *Saturday's Hero* (its new title) organized several screenings targeted exclusively to people in the sports industry. These screenings were attended by newspaper and sports writers, radio sports commentators and coaches of local football teams, all of whom were invited to fill out comment cards. Many were captivated by how the film had portrayed so accurately the commercialism in college football. John's performance earned him compliments; all agreed that never before had a non-professional player had such a natural style on screen.

Two days before the picture opened nationwide, John appeared on a popular NBC

Derek chats with some unidentified admirers on the set of *Saturday's Hero* (1951).

program called *Author Meets the Critic*. Moderated by John McCaffery, the panel included John, Columbia home office executive Paul Lazarus, Jr., *New York Herald Tribune* sports editor Bob Cooke and radio-TV personality Bill Slater, and the topic was "Is college football over-commercialized and tough business?" It was great publicity for the picture.

Reviewers generally praised the film and its honesty. *Cue* magazine wrote, "John Derek gives the best performance of his career."[10] Yet *Saturday's Hero*'s box office performance was very disappointing, even though John and Donna were sent on a promotional tour to 35 different American cities. They also participated in a Chesterfield cigarettes advertising campaign which mentioned their co-starring in the picture. One of the main reasons for the film's failure: Just a few weeks before its release, while testifying before the House Un-American Activities Committee, producer Buchman admitted to being a former member of the American Communist Party. Millard Lampell and film star Alexander Knox were also publicly accused, without any shred of proof of any Communist activities, and this was reported by the media nationwide. On the day the film opened in Los Angeles, members of the Wage Earners Committee picketed outside the theaters in protest. Columbia found the attack false and unfounded and refuted the accusations via a transcribed message which had to be played continuously in in the lobby of the two theaters stating that, at the time the film was made, none of the people involved were members of the Communist Party. Tim Cohane, sports editor of *Look* magazine, called the film "a great football story" but added,

"As a side tent of Americana, *Saturday's Hero* will please more Communist propagandists than college presidents."[11] Cohn decided not to sue the magazine to avoid extra negative publicity.

In August, right in the middle of *Saturday's Hero* shooting, John requested, in a petition filed in Superior Court, the legalization of his screen name. He explained that since he had become an actor, there was confusion when he used his real name Derek Delevan Harris. He also pointed out that his now five-month-old son had already been christened Russell Andre Derek in anticipation of their time when the Harrises would be the John Dereks. Pati also asked that she be allowed to assume the name Pati Derek. In less than a month, the Dereks appeared before Superior Judge Arnold Praeger, who formally approved their requests.

Although *Mask of the Avenger* was filmed in the fall of 1950 just after *Saturday's Hero* was completed, Columbia released it two months earlier. John was not very happy to be cast in another Technicolor swashbuckler, set this time in the mid–19th century. However, he was bound to a contract that gave him very little decision-making power, especially about casting choices. He was more disappointed and angry when he learned from his agent that Harry Cohn had refused to lend him to Alfred Hitchcock, who had asked to cast him in his upcoming Warner Brothers thriller *Strangers on a Train*. John hoped that Cohn would change his mind and replace him in *Mask of the Avenger* with Larry Parks, who was rumored to be the original choice for the lead. But the big boss of Columbia was inflexible

Derek in *Mask of the Avenger* (1951).

Derek during a promotional tour for *Mask of the Avenger* in 1951.

and determined to solidify Derek's image as a matinee idol. *Strangers on a Train* could have changed John's career completely. Farley Granger, loaned from MGM, was eventually cast by Hitchcock in the part.

The Mask of Monte Cristo was the picture's original title. Jesse Lasky's script was based on a story by George Bruce, inspired by Alexandre Dumas' novel *The Count of Monte Cristo*. Columbia hired Irving Pichel as director, and he began work on the film. A few days into the shooting, he injured his foot and was replaced by Phil Karlson. Anthony Quinn and Arnold Moss were cast as the nasty villains, while Jody Lawrance, as her first screen appearance, played as John's sweetheart. To play the role of Capt. Renato Dimorna, John resumed his fencing classes with Ralph Faulkner, who staged all the swordplay in the picture. Drama coach Benno Schneider ("Beano" to John) guided him through his lines prior to each scene. To John's delight, his part required a lot of horseback riding. He was assigned three beautiful horses for different types of scenes. One was used in the close-ups, a second for long shots, and a third for rear shots. John's favorite was Rambler, a magnificent black stallion and a veteran of the camera, who was used for close-ups. During breaks, John rode Rambler across the Columbia Ranch in the San Fernando Valley where shooting took place.

Mask of the Avenger was another adventure picture in the tradition of swashbuckling costume melodramas established on the screen by Douglas Fairbanks. Reviews were positive. Critics seemed to enjoy the story's energetic pace, its elegant costumes and the lavish settings. "Handsome Technicolor production, a splendid action-adventure fare," praised *The Hollywood Reporter*.[12] While most of the reviewers found John's performance "convincing," the *New York Herald Tribune* expressed some reservations: "[He] goes through the motions as the hero, carrying his baby-face handicap with as much dignity as possible."[13]

In July 1951, on the occasion of the nationwide release, Columbia sent John to the East Coast on a promotional tour. Baltimore was one of the main stops, since it held the largest base of his fans. John was welcomed like royalty. He was hosted at the Lord Baltimore Hotel, which was besieged by screaming fans night and day. A contest was sponsored by a local radio station and its two winners were invited to have dinner with him. John also met the members of his fan club, attending a party, etc. In public, his behavior was always very professional. He acted politely with all his fans and was very cooperative with the editors. However, he was slowly developing an animosity against the tyrannical studio rules. *Mask of the Avenger* did not do much for John's career. Columbia released it as a sort of "audience warm-up" prior to *Saturday's Hero*, a film they hoped would established John as a star.

Chapter 4

Glorious and Not-So-Glorious Days

"The ability wasn't there. The looks compensated."—John Derek

Between November 1950 and January 1951, John moved into a new home in Encino while on holiday. It was a white, Spanish-style residence with a swimming pool and two acres of land. Since he used all his savings for the down payment, he had to work non-stop in order to be current with the mortgage. Right after the New Year, he returned to Columbia to make *The Family Secret*. Originally titled *The Secret*, the picture was a Santana Production which producer Robert Lord thought would give John a change of pace. The script was based on a "scorching novel of conscience" (as the press release indicated) by Marie Baumer and James Cavanagh. Its plot was very similar to *Knock on Any Door* but lacked the pretentious social message. John played a law student who accidentally kills his best friend in an act of self-defense. He admits the crime to his father, a lawyer who refuses to tell the district attorney. His father defends a man who has been wrongly accused; the man dies before the trial is over.

John re-teamed with Jody Lawrance, who once again played his love interest, while Lee J. Cobb was cast as the prominent attorney-father. The picture, entirely shot at Columbia, took less than a month to complete. A bit of real-life drama occurred during the filming, when John proved to be a real hero. While he was taking Lawrance for a ride in an old jalopy, the motor of the doorless convertible suddenly short-circuited. As a plume of flame and smoke erupted, John quickly grabbed her in his arms and lifted her over the side to safety. Then he leaped clear just as the studio firemen ran in with chemical fire extinguishers. The incident shocked Lawrance so much that she was given the following day off.

When *The Family Secret* opened nationwide eight months later, reviewers agreed that the entire cast had given impeccable performances. *The Hollywood Reporter* gushed, "Gems of acting come from John Derek, the youth; Lee J. Cobb, as the attorney father; Erin O'Brien Moore as the mother, and beautiful Jody Lawrance as the youth's sweetheart. All turn in sterling performances, despite their being burdened with an over-abundance of dialogue."[1] But the flawless acting was not enough to save a picture that potentially could have been a great film noir, but an excessively talkative screenplay killed it. Critics also observed that the unremarkable direction of Henry Levin had failed to bring the story to life.

John tried to pitch a project to Columbia about Joaquin Murrieta, the famous Mexican civil rights leader, vaquero and gold miner during the California Gold Rush of the 1850s. After reading a book on this Robin Hood–like personage, John fell in love with the character, whom he thought would have been a perfect role for him to play. He pestered his

Derek and Jody Lawrance in *The Family Secret* (1951).

Columbia bosses for months with strong arguments supporting his idea. He even offered to do it for free, but the studio appeared uninterested. "Nobody ever listens to an actor," he complained in an interview. At his expense, John had a flier printed and distributed among his fans and around other studios hoping to catch the interest of a producer. The leaflet showed a photo of John on the set of *Mask of the Avenger* and the words:

WANTED
JOHN DEREK
FOR
JOAQUIN MURRIETA
HE IS WANTED ON THE FOLLOWING COUNTS:

  1. His fans want to see him in a western. Westerns are always good box office and the story of Joaquin Murrieta is a true story and in the public domain, waiting for someone to make it into a movie.

  2. John Derek fits the role to perfection. Also, he is an expert horseman, loves working with horses, and is at home in the saddle.

  3. John Derek would create a role that would rank with the best, for it is a story filled with excitement, emotion, drama, and suspense. The story of Joaquin Murrieta would serve as a shot of adrenalin in the arm of the box office.

YOUR HELP IS ASKED IN THIS APPREHENSION

REWARD: Thousands of satisfied fans, old and new, who will show their appreciation by box office receipts.

The ploy was unsuccessful, but John did not give up easily and cherished the idea for years. Finally, in 1955, while under contract to Paramount, he submitted the notes he had accumulated while studying Murrieta over the past years. He hoped that the studio would be intrigued enough to undertake the production. No such luck.

After *The Family Secret* was completed, John was a guest of the Uruguayan government (along with Lizabeth Scott, Joan Fontaine, Patricia Neal, Florence Marly and Ricardo Montalban) at the International Film Festival of Punta del Este, Uruguay. Six months later, the Uruguayan government awarded all the stars who took part in the festival a silver medal.

On his return from his trip to South America,

Derek relaxing at home with his son Russell in 1951.

John faced another great disappointment when he heard that Paramount had offered to buy his contract from Columbia for a handsome price; Paramount wanted Derek to replace Alan Ladd, who was planning to leave the studio after an association that lasted almost a decade. But Cohn had firmly refused. Frustrated and disgruntled, John sullenly reported to the set of his next film *Scandal Sheet*.

Faithfully adapted from director-writer Samuel Fuller's novel *The Dark Page* (a title used when the picture was released in England), *Scandal Sheet* was a small film noir. Fuller gathered the material for the book from his experiences as a writer for various tabloids, getting his main inspiration from the real story of Charles Chapin, city editor of the *New York Evening World*, who was imprisoned at Sing Sing in 1919 after murdering his wife. The plot told of the dramatic downfall of Mark Chapman, a successful and ruthless *New York Express* editor who accidentally kills his wife and tries to steer his reporter protégé away from the truth.

The film rights were originally purchased upon publication by Howard Hawks for a Humphrey Bogart–Edward G. Robinson starrer, but that project lay unproduced for years. Fuller tried to pitch it to Hitchcock, but the director dismissed it. Hawks finally sold the rights to Harry Cohn for more than six times what he paid for it. The president of Columbia

Left to right: Griff Barnett, Derek, Donna Reed and Broderick Crawford in a dramatic scene from *Scandal Sheet* **(1952).**

had Broderick Crawford in mind as the lead, and John was given the major role of reporter Steve McCleary, Chapman's pupil. (William Holden had rejected that part, perhaps knowing of the studio's intention to produce the picture as cheaply as possible.[2]) The character of reporter Julie Allison, who disapproves of sensational journalism, was played by Donna Reed, who was billed above John.

On the set, the relationship between John and Crawford was turbulent despite the fact that the two had worked together in *All the King's Men*. Crawford tried to play John's mentor, but John did not always appreciate his methods. In one scene they had together, John was having trouble remembering his lines. Since the sequence called for him to have his back to the camera, he wrote his lines on a slip of paper, intending to read them. As soon as the camera started to roll, Crawford swiped away the piece of paper, forcing John to play the part on his own. When director Phil Karlson called *cut*, an enraged John yelled at Crawford, accusing him of sabotage. The veteran actor said, "You did fine, boy. And you just learned something. You've got ankles, and you can stand on your own two feet."

John was not amused and he got his revenge in the following scene, in which Crawford had to take a punch at him. Broderick took the director to one side and told him, "I'm going to hit the kid pretty hard. You know, a real belt." Karlson agreed, thinking that it would make the scene more realistic. John, who was not alerted, got a real hard punch, but was quick enough to hit him back with all his strength, leaving Crawford breathless. When the old actor remarked to John how hard he had punched him, his reply was: "Well, you wanted to look realistic, didn't you?"[3] When *Scandal Sheet* wrapped up, Crawford told John, "You know I didn't use to like you. When you made *All the King's Men* with me, I thought you were a swell-headed, selfish kid who needed a kick in the pants. But now, I want to say I like you, I like your work and I like to work with you."[4] John appreciated those comments.

Critics disagreed on John's performance as the ambitious young reporter. Both *The Hollywood Reporter* and the U.K. movie magazine *Picturegoer* wrote, "John Derek is excellent." The *New York Times*, was on a different page: "John Derek gives a likely imitation of a high-school-paper cub." According to *Variety*, "[Derek's] youthful appearance is more in keeping with a cub's countenance than a top newshound's carriage."

In December 1951, William Holden (left), Anne Baxter and Derek received the Golden Apple pin award as the most cooperative actors.

On December 18, 1951, the Hollywood Women's Press Club awarded John, Anne Baxter and William Holden a Golden Apple for being the most cooperative film actors of 1951. The prize was presented by Bing Crosby, dressed as Santa Claus. Just before Christmas, John was asked to make an uncredited cameo appearance in the Columbia musical *Rainbow 'Round My Shoulder*. He did his duty along with Columbia stars Broderick Crawford, Gene Autry, Donna Reed and Barbara Hale, coming into view when the picture's main character (Charlotte Austin) is being shown around the studio grounds.

The year 1952 began with John's brief appearance in two shorts produced by Columbia, *Screen Snapshots: Meet Mr. Rhythm, Frankie Laine* and *Screen Snapshots: Hollywood's Mr. Movies*. Written, produced and directed by Ralph Staub, the ten-minute shorts featured behind-the-scenes footage of stars at various events or parties. *Meet Mr. Rhythm, Frankie Laine* promoted singer Frankie Laine, who starred in *Rainbow 'Round My Shoulder*. Among the other celebrities featured was actor-stuntman Jock Mahoney, one of John's good friends on the Columbia lot. John first met Mahoney at a horse ranch in the early 1940s and became like a younger brother. John's footage from these *Screen Snapshots* was reused in two future series entries, *Hollywood Stars to Remember* (1954) and *Mr. Rhythm's Holiday* (1956).

At the end of January 1952, the Foreign Press Association of Hollywood (not to be confused with the Hollywood Foreign Correspondents Association) handed out "international stardoms" awards to a list of favorite movie stars including John, Leslie Caron, Marilyn

Monroe, Tony Curtis, Mitzi Gaynor and Virginia Gibson. *Life* magazine photographer Loomis Dean captured John in an elegant tuxedo posing next to a young Marilyn as their mesmerizing beauty captivated the crowd at the award ceremony held in Santa Monica.

John's overwhelming success came at a price. Critics seemed to pick on his handsome boyish look rather than judging his real acting abilities. The "Pretty Boy" nickname that some had pinned on him made him very self-conscious about his beautiful face. In an interview with columnist Earl Wilson, John downplayed his looks, explaining that his face was not as perfect as everybody described it. His nose was actually crooked: "I busted the cartilage twice while I was in the service. I hit a rifle butt against it. I was just walking up a hill behind a guy. His rifle slipped off his shoulder and down on his arm and hit me on the nose. I just rubbed it a little and busted it. So now it goes, down here and curves at the end. I have to keep fixin' it."[5] John showed an amazed Wilson how he would straighten his nose with his fingers, an activity he repeated several times a day, especially when he was on a set. He candidly admitted that at the beginning of his career, "the ability wasn't there. The looks compensated. So, I got to pat myself on the face for that." Yet he hoped that critics now would evaluate not only his good looks but also his acting skills.

But insecurity about his looks never disappeared. Thinking of physical heft as proof of manhood, John transformed his garage into a gym, equipped with weights and bars so that he could regularly exercise and bulk-up his body to gain some muscle.

Once again Columbia tossed him into a costume adventure, *Prince of Pirates,* this time as a 16th-century pirate. The studio assumed that such a role was bound to sustain his "great romantic appeal." Unfortunately, it did nothing to advance his career. At the end of each working day, John would suffer terrible migraines that often forced him to lie in bed for hours. It was a psychosomatic reaction to a job that he began to hate; he found it humiliating to be told how good-looking he was and nothing else. Money was the only reason he accepted the mediocre swashbuckling pictures. Because of the standard seven-year contract he had signed with Columbia at the beginning of his career, his salary had never reached the size of other movie stars. There had been several raises, but the expenses with the birth of Russell and his medical bills along with the mortgage on the Encino house were enormous. Suddenly acting had transformed from pure fun and pleasure into a horrible necessity. Director Sidney Salkow's *Prince of Pirates* was a low-budget production filmed in Technicolor, with a great deal of battle footage taken from *Joan of Arc* (1948). Opposite Barbara Rush on loan from Paramount, John played the prince of a small nation aiding the French in the fight against tyranny. Upon his return home, Prince Roland discovers that his brother, the king, has allied himself with Spain. Forced to flee for his life, Roland turns to pirating and continues the battle for freedom.

Columbia shelved *Prince of Pirates* for almost a year. His agile, youthful and magnetic performance ("a role that fits him snug as a bath cap," joked the *Los Angeles Times*[6]) was cited by the critics, but the adventurous plot was not original enough to make the film a solid box office success.

At the end of February 1952, John, Pati and Russell took a brief holiday to Catalina Island, a place where he'd spent several summers during his childhood and visited after being discharged from military service. Catalina was a happy vacation spot for John. The short break was chronicled by a movie magazine in which the Dereks appear as a normal, all–American family without the glitz and the glamour of Hollywood. Once again, reality was far different from the happy façade. The marriage was still going through rough times and John was also having problems with his mother, who after her earlier suicide attempts

Left to right: Barbara Rush, Harry Lauter and Derek in *Prince of Pirates* (1953).

was now having other mental issues. Dolores often would go to a theater where one of John's pictures was playing, and in the middle of the screening she would stand up and scream: "That's Dare, my son, he's a God, isn't he beautiful?"[7] Regularly the theater manager would call John or Pati asking them to come and get her. Dolores also had a "passion" for taxis. She would hire one to drive her to San Francisco and back, just for the pleasure of conversing with the driver, and leaving John to pay the hefty fare.

In the spring of 1952, Columbia agreed to loan John to Republic to star in *Thunderbirds*, one of the studio's top productions that year. Republic was a studio that specialized in Westerns, B films and serials. It had also developed the careers of John Wayne, Gene Autry and Roy Rogers. Originally titled *Citizen Soldiers*, *Thunderbirds* was the story of the 45th division of the National Guard from Green Hill, Oklahoma, known as the "Thunderbirds." John was excited to be cast in a war picture whose story emphasized the patriotic, sentimental and fraternal sides of war. It seemed to be the perfect vehicle to boost his career and finally break the mold of being typecast as the swashbuckler hero. Most of the shooting was done in Fort Sill, Oklahoma, where the Thunderbird division began combat training after being mobilized in September 1940. John traveled to the location in April 1952 along with co-stars John Drew Barrymore, on loan from RKO, and Mona Freeman. To heighten the savagery of the battle sequences, many combat scenes set at some of the historical Italian locations in Salerno, Anzio, Cassino and Sicily were accentuated by actual wartime clips.

The shooting lasted almost a month, and the movie was rushed for a Christmas release. On November 20, 1952, Republic organized a *Thunderbirds* world premiere in Washington,

Derek (left) and John Barrymore, Jr., in *Thunderbirds* (1952).

D.C., honoring the National Guard. The stars and all the studio's major executives were among the participants along with the Secretary of the Army, Frank Pace, Jr., and National Guard Bureau Chief Major General Raymond B. Fleming.

Two weeks later, John flew to San Francisco to attend National Guard Week activities and the West Coast premiere. The event was attended by California Governor Earl Warren, the mayor of San Francisco and other dignitaries. Despite great media fanfare, critics panned *Thunderbirds* along with John's performance. Even though he had tried to use his personal military experience for the role of Gil Hackett, his acting was called "blunt and lifeless," "too theatrical," and "unconvincing." The picture was a box office disaster.

John's wish to act in a Western feature was finally granted when Columbia cast him in two medium-budget productions, *Ambush at Tomahawk Gap* and *The Last Posse*. The former, shot in only two weeks in July 1952, was directed in Technicolor by Fred F. Sears under the personal supervision of producer Robert Cohn (son and nephew of Columbia studio bosses Jack and Harry Cohn, respectively). John, as a former member of a holdup gang, seeks to recover stolen loot buried in Apache territory. John Hodiak and David Brian were cast as the other ex-convicts. Sears, knowing that John rode "as if he'd invented horseback riding," allowed him to do all his own riding without using a stuntman. During breaks, John constantly practiced quick draws for the gunfight scenes. When a friend visited the set, John thrust a cocked revolver into his hand and cajoled him to shoot. As his friend started to squeeze the trigger, John drew his own gun and snapped the hammer to beat his friend to the kill every time.

Chapter 4. Glorious and Not-So-Glorious Days 43

Left to right: Otto Hulett, John Hodiak, Derek and Maria Elena Marques in a scene from *Ambush at Tomahawk Gap* (1953).

    Almost the entire shooting of *Ambush at Tomahawk Gap* took place at Corrigan Movie Ranch in the Simi Valley with only a few interior scenes filmed at Columbia. Upon its release, reviewers and audiences seemed stunned by Sears' grim, dark direction. The unremitting violence portrayed with brutal gunfights and graphic massacres was something that was, at the time, still unthinkable for the Western genre. When *Ambush at Tomahawk Gap* opened in England in October 1953, the prestigious *Monthly Film Bulletin* wrote: "Seventy-two minutes of unrelieved cruelty, greed, and terror make up this Technicolor Western. Execution is quite competent, but the brutality appears unnecessary."[8]

    The Last Posse was an independent Harry Joe Brown production, released by Columbia. John shared top billing with Broderick Crawford, Charles Bickford and Wanda Hendrix. Although Crawford did not appear ecstatic to be reunited with John for the third time, there were no report of major clashes between the two stars. The Alabama Hills, west of Lone Pine, California, and Yuma, Arizona, were the locations where the film was shot in just 20 days in October. *The Last Posse* had a better-than-average, action-packed script that spotlighted "a group of pompous citizens who join in a round-up of thieves, but reveal frailties of their own when they think they've a safe chance to help themselves to vast ill-gotten gains."[9] Generally the picture received fairly good reviews, including praise for Alfred Werker's forceful direction and Burnett Guffey's superb photography. The *Hollywood*

Charles Bickford (holding rein), Warner Anderson (hatless), Derek (with pistol) and Tom Powers (right) in a scene from *The Last Posse* (1953).

Reporter described *The Last Posse* as "an interesting offbeat western drama holding suspense throughout its taut 71 minutes."[10]

Ambush at Tomahawk Gap and *The Last Posse* performed very modestly at the box office, once again keeping John far from getting that big chance he thought he deserved.

Chapter 5

Hard Times

"I never liked acting."—John Derek

"Is Hollywood Destroying John Derek?" *Photoplay*'s alarming headline topped an article that explored the reasons why a promising star like Derek, after a big break in *Knock on Any Door* and *All the King's Men,* was now given some distinctly mediocre roles. "His fans keep clamoring for him," wrote the magazine, "bombarding *Photoplay* with irate letters asking why they can't see him more often and in meatier roles."[1] Although not explicitly, John blamed Columbia's executives for choices they had made on his behalf; he could not object since the terms of his contract bound him to the studio for eight years. He complained that all the good parts were going to other leading men, and his whole career was being jeopardized by the silly characters he played in most of the pictures assigned to him. He detested Cohn, who remained adamantly against all requests to let him work for others. The ultimate mistake was not supporting John enough to get him a major part in *From Here to Eternity*. Author James Jones had just sold the film rights of his best-selling war novel to Columbia for $82,000. Cohn pictured John in the role of former boxer Private Prewitt, a perfect opportunity to make him a valuable star for his studio. The president of Columbia started to campaign for John with director Fred Zinnemann, but Jones fiercely opposed the idea. The author had in mind Montgomery Clift, with whom he already discussed the part informally. Convinced by Jones, Zinnemann also declared he wanted Clift. Cohn argued violently against that choice, offering Aldo Ray instead, but the director was steadfast.[2] Ultimately, Cohn gave up and John lost the part for which Clift received an Academy Award nomination.

Louella Parsons wrote, "Although the talk persists that John Derek isn't too happy about his Columbia contract, he's too smart a boy to kick up his heels and take a suspension. In the long run, Harry Cohn is usually wise in handling his stars."[3]

The rumor that a disgruntled Derek was constantly clashing with his studio was no longer a secret after Parsons spread the news through her syndicated gossip column. As a meager consolation prize, John was cast in *Mission Over Korea*. It was a war melodrama that had everything but the buzz of the star-studded *From Here to Eternity*.

Before reporting to the set of that film, John was asked by the head of a Florida Chamber of Commerce to help judge an annual beauty pageant. Previously, he had firmly refused those kinds of offers, but his current weak financial situation forced him to accept. It was a tragicomic experience, as he later revealed in an interview:

> We had about 100 girls to start off with—and at least 5000 rooting for them. We finally narrowed them down to a baker's dozen—and that's where I realized I'd made a big mistake. All those girls who were disqualified, their relatives and friends, gave me the icy stare. No fooling, even the Florida sun seemed

to chill. I realized immediately that I just lost over 5000 admission tickets. When the contest was over and the winner was chosen, I ended up with a request for an autograph from her grandma and a barrage of questions from the new beauty queen as to her chances in Hollywood. Everybody else was unhappy and sore except the Chamber of Commerce boys.... I guess that's the last time I'll ever spend a vacation in that town.[4]

Mission Over Korea, released in the United Kingdom as *Eyes of the Skies*, told the story of the U.S. Army's pilots and their daily heroic rescue work and reconnaissance during the early days of the Korean War. The genesis of the picture was detailed by Robert Cohn in an interview with the *Los Angeles Daily News*. The producer traveled to Washington to request permission to send a film company to the Korean front which, surprisingly, he obtained without difficulties. Along with director Fred Sears and cameramen Bill Whitley and Emil Oster, Jr., Cohn spent eight weeks shooting scenes on the Korea battle front as well as backgrounds in Japan. Despite not knowing the language, the crew shot several hours of film which, according to Cohn, was much better than the actual action prescribed by the script that ultimately had to be rewritten to fit the action shot.[5] On a studio lot, a Korean village that looked bombed-out had to be rebuilt, since all the villages on location, made mostly of thatch, had been rebuilt already.

Principal photography began on January 13, 1953, at a ranch in Soledad Canyon in Los Angeles County. John was re-teamed with John Hodiak after *Ambush at Tomahawk Gap*. They played pilots with clashing personalities. Hodiak was the captain of an army

Maureen O'Sullivan, John Hodiak and Derek (right) in *Mission Over Korea* (1953).

observation plane, John was the headstrong rookie he commands. They had a very different approach to military discipline that showed the contrast between two generations of Americans fighting for the same cause. A respected actor, the 39-year-old Hodiak was married to Anne Baxter and would die prematurely two years later of cardiac arrest. Maureen O'Sullivan, known for playing Jane in the Tarzan film series, and Audrey Totter played supporting roles.

A few days into shooting, while rehearsing a scene on location, John was miraculously saved by a set worker from falling rocks. He was acting out a scene calling for him to dodge several rocks which had come loose from a cliff overhead. Sears called a halt to the rehearsal. After the large stones came dangerously close, a plaster rock builder was called. A few hours later, the scene was resumed, but this time with realistic plaster stones.

Although it had a very authentic feeling, especially in the aerial scenes, *Mission Over Korea* was a trite war melodrama, a propaganda tool that did not rise above other average movies in the same genre. Upon its release in August 1953, just after the Armistice, the picture stayed in the theaters for only a couple of weeks, practically ignored by filmgoers who did not wish to be reminded of the terrible war that had just ended.

On the set of *Mission Over Korea*, John discussed his lack of free time with the press:

> It is true that actors have more time between chores than the average person. This does not mean that it's idle time. Actors can be as busy as anyone who has an 8–5 daily job. As for myself, leisure is impossible. I handle all my correspondence, which includes fan mail. This takes about two hours of each day. Sometimes more. Actors, like everyone else, can gain weight. I must exercise to keep those excess pounds from gaining headway. Actors realize that appearance is one of their most important assets. Therefore, it is a prime requisite that they keep themselves in tip-top physical condition at all times. Instead of gymnastics, I take my exercise horseback riding. I have a couple of fine animals on my Encino ranch. I take a workout each day for at least an hour or so depending upon other chores. Then of course there is time taken up reading and analyzing books and scripts sent by the studio. This is absolute required reading for any actor. A good story is half the battle. And if I come across one which the studio doesn't own, but which I think would give me a great opportunity, I try to persuade the studio to buy it. As you can very well imagine, this is a real time-consuming job. It can take four or five hours a day. So you see, I have already gone over the eight hours of the average man's work day.[6]

A few days later, in another interesting interview with United Press Staff correspondent Ben Cook, John sarcastically stated:

> Most actors suffer from inferiority complexes.... An ordinary guy can very well do without press notices, fan mail, and the extra-low bow from the doorman at Ciro's. But to some actors, those things are as important as a mink coat to a Broadway cutie. Some of the biggest hams I know are only trying to give an impression that they are superior human beings. Actually, they are frightened little people who sneak up on their mirrors at home when they have to look at themselves.[7]

John had become the antithesis of the Hollywood star. He detested the big egos that some of his colleagues would show on and off the set. Out of the spotlight, his life was so "ordinary" that several fan magazines complained about his "normalcy" and his failure to live like "a proper Hollywood star." No glamour, no haunting the trendy Hollywood spots, and above all no fancy clothes. His love for casual wear made his name a regular on the list of the "worst dressed actors" along with Montgomery Clift, another reluctant star, and Louis Jourdan. Gardening, carpentry, horseback riding and do-it-yourself activities were his favorite off-screen occupations. These were all interests deemed right for the middle class, but considered inappropriate for a celebrity.

Just when *Mission Over Korea* was completed, the press announced that John was to star in *Renegade Canyon*, a new Columbia Western based on Peter Dawson's suspenseful

Derek (left) and Richard Jaeckel in *Sea of Lost Ships* (1953).

Saturday Evening Post serial. He was to play a young cavalry officer of the 1880s, the survivor of an Indian massacre, who sacrifices his career to prevent his commanding officer from learning that his (the commander's) son was a coward. For unknown reasons, the project was aborted.

John was borrowed by Republic to star in *Sea of Lost Ships* (pre-production title: *American Eagle*). The screenplay, based on actual events taken from Coast Guard files, paid tribute to the International Ice Patrol activities and the U.S. Coast Guard's battles with huge icebergs. John and Richard Jaeckel portrayed Coast Guard ensigns raised like brothers by Jaeckel's father Walter Brennan. (John's late dad heroically gave up his life to save the Coast Guard base at Argentia, Newfoundland.) When the two young men, both cadets at the Coast Guard Academy, fall for the same woman, Brennan has to mediate.

Cameras rolled on March 30, 1953. Candid photographs taken behind the scenes revealed a relaxed environment on the set with John and Jaeckel having a good time, laughing and cutting up for the camera.[8] Jaeckel was an old friend of John and *Sea of Lost Ships* marked their first professional association. They worked together three more times over the next decade.

The picture was made with the full support of the U.S. Coast Guard, which provided some of its stock footage. One of the most exciting sequences was taken from their archive. It showed a huge polar bear lunging across a glacier and diving into the sea. The shot had been captured a few months earlier by a Coast Guard helicopter that hovered very close to the bear and recorded the chase as he fled from the noisy machine.

Chapter 5. Hard Times

Sea of Lost Ships was completed in one month. The world premiere was held on October 21, 1953, at the RKO Keith's Theatre in Washington, D.C., before civic and military dignitaries as well as a contingent of Republic executives. The stars were present except for John, who was busy on the set of *The Outcast*. The picture went into general release a few days after the event. There were lukewarm critics from a few industry publications; major newspapers did not bother to review it.

While shooting *Sea of Lost Ships*, John learned that Pati was pregnant again. He did not take the news well. By his own admission, he was not in love with his wife and felt he was being tricked by her. Pati allegedly revealed her pregnancy at a very late stage. John candidly confessed many years later,

> I was too young, too concerned with living my own life, to understand the responsibilities of a family. My father had not stayed for long with my mother and me, so it was hard for me to imagine what a family was all about.... I don't remember my marriage to Pati being a happy time. Actually, I hardly ever think of those years. Sometimes I talk about my three wives and forget about Pati.[9]

In spite of the reality of the Dereks' marriage, the fan magazines persistently showed them smiling, enjoying each other's company in their domestic routines, presenting John as a loving husband and a caring father. "I Live and I Love My Man John," "Father's Day," "The Triumphant Years," "Kiss Tomorrow Hello" and "You Need Love in Your Life" were some of the many cheesy headlines, that advertised the fake façade of what was already a shattered marriage.

On July 7, 1953, John and Columbia amicably severed relations after he announced plans to enter independent production and do television work. The contract would not have expired until April 1954, but with his agent's help, John was released from the balance of his contracted term. "I feel as though I were freed from prison," the actor commented after he heard the good news. He told *Silver Screen*,

> It was the future I was thinking of. I stood to make $44,000 this year on my contract. That's a lot of money, although movie-wise it's not a fortune. Yet I was willing to risk the security of that regular salary in order to do what I felt was best for my career in the long run. Sure, I could go along on my contract for the next few years, collecting my paycheck and being able to pay my bills. But what would I have in the end? I was afraid I'd have a career that would deteriorate and that by the time my contract was over, John Derek would mean nothing as an actor.... I knew that if I were to survive as an actor and keep my own self-respect, I had to get out of my contract and go out on my own.... I never had a chance to play a gutty character.[10]

That chance came with Republic's *The Outcast*, made two months after leaving Columbia. John played a determined young cowboy who hires nine gunmen and returns to his native town in Colorado to reclaim his ranch, stolen by an unscrupulous uncle. Based on "Red Horizon" (the film's working title), an *Esquire* story by Todhunter Ballard, and his novel *Two-Edged Vengeance*, *The Outcast* was an action-packed Western directed by William Witney. Most of the outdoor filming took place in the Wet Mountains, near Cañon City, Colorado. The high altitude of the location proved a problem for the 143 cast and crew members. Accustomed to the near-sea-level altitude of Hollywood, they found themselves tiring quickly from the slightest exertion, slowing down he production until they adapted to the change.

"Making a picture in Colorado is hard on the breathing but awfully easy on the eyes," John commented. He had the time of his life working in the picture, as he revealed years. "I never liked acting. Or my films. Maybe one, cheap little western called *The Outcast*. I liked that because I love horses."¹¹ One hundred horses were used in the picture, supplied along with the cattle by a local ranch. John picked the stallion that he rode for the entire three-week, on-location shoot. The production was completed at Republic Studios. One day while shooting a sequence outside a saloon, John Ford's unexpected visit created a bit of commotion among the cast and crew members. The director's charismatic presence suddenly brought silence on the set when the cameras were about to roll. After politely greeting William Witney and Derek (Ford was one of his favorite directors), the 59-year-old filmmaker asked for actor Harry Carey, Jr., with whom he had worked in the past. The reason for the visit was to offer Carey the part of Dwight Eisenhower in his upcoming project *The Long Gray Line* (1955).

The Outcast (renamed *The Fortune Hunter* for British audiences) was a better-than-average Western.

Derek and one of his many horses.

When it opened nationwide a year later, *The Hollywood Reporter* compared John to Montgomery Clift: "Derek, the hero, has that brooding Montgomery Clift quality that makes you wonder if the hero will turn good or bad. And a flashing smile that rewards female audiences that wait for it."¹² Yet despite the cost of making the film on location and with the new expensive Trucolor process, the picture fell short of success. Once again, John was greatly disappointed.

Since the big roles continued to elude him, John decided to accept his first TV part: "Tomorrow's Men," a 30-minute episode of NBC-TV's *The Ford Television Theatre*. Opposite Pat O'Brien (who reprised the football coach role he played in *Knute Rockne—All American* [1940]), John played Allan Malone, a promising football athlete; he resents his coach father, who is keeping him from the team to avoid being accused of nepotism.

On October 16, a few days before "Tomorrow's Men" aired, John became a father to a baby girl, Sean Catherine. "We'd decided if the baby was a boy, we'd name him Sean," John explained, "and I've got a little bit of Irish in me, enough to make it legitimate.... Somebody suggested it was cute for a girl too."¹³ The happy event did not smooth away the serious troubles afflicting his marriage. The arguing escalated, especially now that John was more regularly at home and out of work. His quick temper often made him burst into rage. "Sometime I'd like to hit something ... someone ... and get anger out of the system," he once confessed in an interview. "But you don't go around hitting people, so I go off all alone with my horses and soon I forget about what made me so furious in the first place. Then I relax."¹⁴

Before long, John realized that the expectations he had for his career were not coming to fruition. Although he was now freelancing, his agent was not receiving any interesting offers. Unlike other stars, John was *not* a gifted charmer, by his own admission. "I can't say glowing complimentary things to people when I don't mean them. I don't go to many parties. I'd much prefer to ride my horse with no one but me, the horse and the mountain trail for company."[15]

In a town like Hollywood where public relations, networking and schmoozing industry people potentially helpful to your career was a second profession, John's reputation for being candidly outspoken, not having patience for duplicity or double talk, was seen by many as career suicide.

But John's popularity with fans did not diminish during this period of comparative inactivity. Fan letters continued to pour in at a rate of several hundred a week and articles about his life appeared regularly in the movie magazines. Yet his financial situation was bleak, especially with Pati and the two children to support, a large mortgaged house, and the expensive hobby of breeding horses. He spent most days trying to figure out how pay his bills. Then, John recalled:

> One night my agent called. He asked if I would be interested in doing a [live] *Lux Video* show. They were producing "A Place in the Sun" and I was wanted for the Montgomery Clift role. I thought about it. The scenes in movies are short. You know that they can always be re-shot if you flub a line. A television show would mean learning an hour's worth of dialogue at a time, sustaining a characterization. And what happened if I couldn't remember the lines? I gave my agent a reply. "No," I said. "Think it over," he suggested.[16]

The remake of a top film like *A Place in the Sun* into a TV production was an experiment in joining forces between Paramount, the producer of the picture, and the CBS network. Based on Theodore Dreiser's best-selling novel *An American Tragedy*, "A Place in the Sun" told the triangle love story of George Eastman, who falls in love with a factory co-worker. After getting her pregnant, the young man switches his affections to a wealthy, beautiful girl, giving him no other choice than to get rid of his girlfriend.

Montgomery Clift and Elizabeth Taylor, stars of the original film, snubbed the telecast. Farley Granger, Jeanne Crain, and Gloria Grahame were announced as the possible three leads. George Stevens, producer and director of the Paramount film, was hired as an adviser on the project and Buzz Kulik as the director. But a few days before rehearsals were about to begin, negotiations with Granger, Crain and Grahame failed for different reasons. With a talent budget of $50,000, the producers offered the parts to Ann Blyth and John Derek. Sixty-seven cast members were hired in total, including Marilyn Erskine, in the role originated by Shelley Winters, and Raymond Burr reprising his movie role as the district attorney.

"A Place in the Sun" was one of the most lavish and expensive productions in the history of live television. Seventeen sets (three times as many as most TV dramas) were spread across two giant Hollywood stages. The set for the lake scene where a rowboat tips over took up an entire stage alone. It included a large boat on real water and had to be shot live with a sort of camera trickery.

At the first meeting with the director, John, despite a strong underlying belief in some of his acting abilities, appeared to be so nervous that Kulik had to reassure him more than once. John explained that his fear was based on the fact that the character of George Eastman showed a full range of emotional acting that frightened him since his acting experience so far had mostly dealt with horses, swords or military weapons. Acting live in front of millions of viewers required him to play it right through, from start to finish, and no faking. A skilled TV director, Kulik had worked with many stars, often dealing with different forms of egotism and arrogance; he was impressed by John's honesty and humility. The director found it refreshing. Now more than ever, he knew he wanted John for this role. After considerable persuasion, John accepted the part. "I was afraid I might flub it," he recalled in an interview. "When I finally said that I'd do it. I insisted that if I pulled a fluke, I'd quit right in the middle of the performance and go on home and the producers would have to make any apologies they could to the viewers."[17]

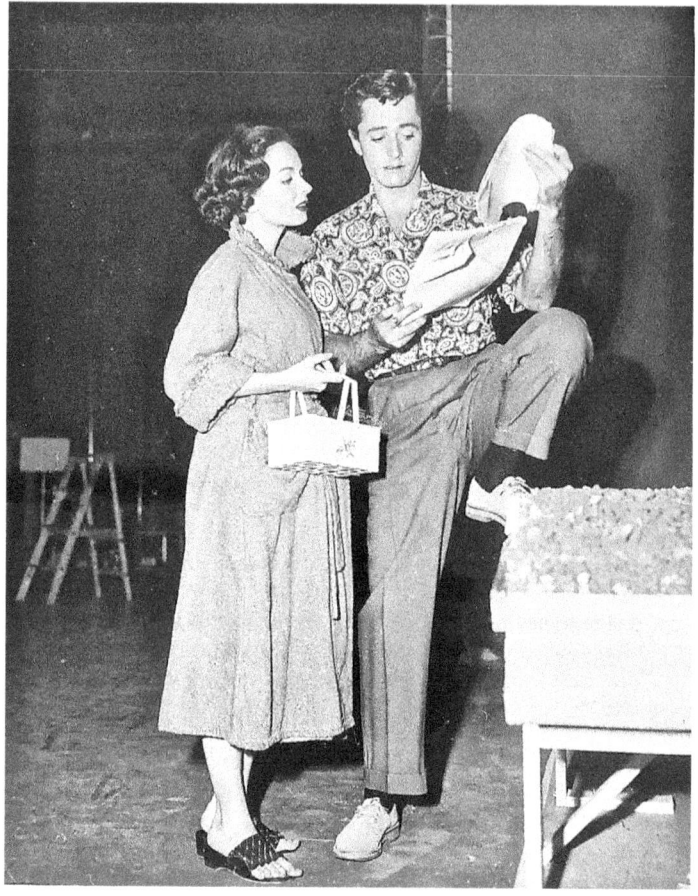

Ann Blyth and Derek on the set of CBS-TV's "A Place in the Sun" (1954).

The cast had ten days of rehearsal before the live broadcast. John learned a lot of new things, and above all, timing. In a live telecast, time had to be perfect to give it a smooth flow of continuity. Each scene was worked out in careful detail and each bit of action was meticulously rehearsed. Every speech had to be delivered at exactly the right place so that the cameras and microphones would catch both the pictures and the sound. John had to learn the art of blocking, understanding where to stand and move correctly across the stage floor, covered by a maze of chalk marks and tape lines to guide the cameras and the actors.

January 28, 1954: the night of the performance. John felt awful, on the verge of throwing up. His hands were shaky, and his mind was completely blank, incapable of remembering any word of the dialogue. Kulik reassured him that once he (John) was in front of the cameras, all the lines would resurface miraculously.

For a while, the broadcast went on without trouble. Then unexpectedly there was a moment of panic. For a telephone scene, John and Marilyn Erskine had to talk from widely separate parts of the set, and the phones had to be connected so that they could hear each other. This had worked well during rehearsals. But the phones had gone dead. John was afraid that the whole scene would go to pieces. Suddenly he remembered what he had learned about tempo. He started to speak his lines just as they had rehearsed them with the same pauses, the same timing, and the scene worked out fine. No one in the audience suspected that they couldn't hear each other. The broadcast lasted 60 minutes, twice as long as the ordinary *Lux* shows. The teleplay lasted 50 minutes and 10 minutes were devoted to the sponsor and other announcements made by Ronald Reagan, host of the show. There were some technical glitches: a man's shadow visible on a mansion exterior, the sound of voices behind intimate scenes, an insignificant shot of a stage curtain or a flash of Reagan caught off guard before a commercial. But otherwise, everything went relatively smoothly. The *Lux Video Theatre* production was a hit. That evening, NBC got one of the highest audience ratings of the season. John walked away feeling lighthearted and content that he had given a convincing performance as George Eastman and the favorable reviews the next day proved it.

At home later that night, the telephone began ringing and telegrams of congratulations began to arrive. In the following weeks, three studios contacted his agent and offers poured in.

While evaluating the incoming proposals, John agreed to play in *The Big Moment*, a 25-minute TV film featuring a cast of 16 stars including Donna Reed, Robert Young, Thomas Mitchell and Forrest Tucker. The picture, produced by Mel Epstein in cooperation with Paramount, was made up of three separate segments telling the story of ordinary people located in different parts of the world whose lives were changed thanks to the United Jewish Appeal, sponsor of the production. John and Donna Reed played Avram and Deborah, a settler and a Holocaust survivor living in an Israel border settlement. Their difficult love story was the longest segment in the film. *The Big Moment* aired on NBC on May 2, 1954, and the ratings were so high that it was rerun the following September to mark the opening of the Jewish New Year. John and other cast and crew members received silver plaques from the United Jewish Appeal as an award for the outstanding support they gave to the UJA.

In February 1954, John's four-year-old son Russ suffered a terrible attack of rheumatic fever. Doctors had to perform a delicate abdominal surgery. The child spent the next several weeks in a wheelchair. Debts related to the new medical bills hung over John along with all the other household expenses.

Suddenly, like a miracle, the tide changed.

Chapter 6

The Paramount Years

"A player must have a certain amount of ego, of course, but in John's case it's well under control."—James Cagney

One early morning in February 1954, John's telephone rang. "I was sitting at home chewing the end of a pencil, trying to figure out how to keep my budget balanced when the call came," John recalled. "Cecil B. DeMille wanted to see me. Could I come over to the studio that same afternoon?"[1] Going up the stairs to DeMille's office at Paramount, John felt butterflies in his stomach, wondering about the reasons behind the meeting. All his nervousness disappeared once the kindly-faced elderly man shook his hand with genuine friendliness. Once John sat down across a large oak desk from DeMille, the director came directly to the point. He was considering John for the role of Joshua in his upcoming production *The Ten Commandments*.

"As we talked," John remembered, "he seemed to be measuring me physically, and I thought I detected a shadow of disappointment. A few minutes later he told me very frankly that I wasn't tall enough for the part of Joshua … the one whom Moses appointed to command the conquest of Canaan, and he had to be pretty impressive in stature."[2] In a meeting that lasted more than an hour, John became increasingly astonished when he discovered that DeMille had been observing him for a considerable period. DeMille had seen all his pictures and was able to discuss John's entire body of work. With utmost professionalism, the director listened thoroughly to each word when John spoke; there was none of the dismissive attitude John had experienced when dealing with other producer-directors. Before long, a burning desire to play Joshua along with a new enthusiasm for acting filled John. He promised DeMille that by the time the director was ready to shoot, he would build up his body to the proportions DeMille wanted by weight lifting. He would be the best Joshua the filmmaker could find. The director promised to see him again before pre-production.

That pleasant meeting was one of the determining factors in John's decision to accept the contract offer which was soon made to him by Paramount.

William Meiklejohn, head of Paramount's talent procurement department, said, "It seemed pretty clear to me what should be done with John Derek. He had grown out of 'the pretty boy' parts that he had done for too long and was ready for almost any type of role—the hard, gutty, things."[3]

"I was so hungry, when I signed it," John joked, "that I wanted to eat the paper." His future was suddenly brighter. He felt less tense, and realized that being a freelance actor, especially one not too well established, had been very risky not only for his career but also for his financial situation. "While you're still a kind of toy with producers, they can promote you wonderfully. Then if the public likes you, you've got a chance at a solid career."[4]

Chapter 6. The Paramount Years

John's association with Paramount was reported by the media along with the news that director Michael Curtiz and producer Pat Duggan had lost no time in snagging him for the romantic lead in *Angel's Cooking*, a comedy about three convicts escaping from a penal colony. However, when the film was about to go into production under the new title *We're No Angels*, John had already committed to star in *Run for Cover* and was replaced by his friend Aldo Ray. However, Paramount allowed John to star in 20th Century–Fox's exotic production *The Adventure of Hajji Baba* before filming *Run for Cover*.

In November 1953, Allied Artists struck a 50-50 deal with 20th Century–Fox in which they would make three films together in CinemaScope and DeLuxe Color. In return, Fox was to receive all the foreign grosses and Allied the domestic ones. *Hajji Baba* was the first picture to be made under the agreement.

The unexpected box office success of Allied Artists' *Riot in Cell Block 11* (1954) had made Walter Wanger Allied's hottest producer. Richard Collins provided

A Paramount publicity shot from 1954.

Wanger a screenplay "suggested by" (as the film credit indicates) rather than based on the novel *The Adventures of Hajji Baba* by the 18th-century British author and diplomat James Justinian Morier.

Wanger immediately liked it. *Hajji Baba* was a desert fantasy about a young, handsome Persian barber who falls in love with a caliph's daughter after rescuing her from an evil prince whom she had planned to marry. The producer believed that such an adventurous story with sexy lavish costumes in exotic locations was the perfect choice to be filmed in CinemaScope. Yet when he pitched the project to Allied and Fox, not everybody was as convinced, as a Fox executive noted:

> This is a formula story that has been done before and sometimes very successfully. A great deal depends upon who the princess is and how voluptuous she may look to the morons who like the sort of thing; and, also who the brave Hajji Baba would be. However, for its type I guess it is no worse than its predecessors. This is the kind of picture that is known to the vulgar trade as t[its] and s[and].[5]

Director Don Siegel, who had successfully teamed with Wanger on *Riot in Cell Block 11*, shared that same negative opinion about the script and refused to make the film. "It bored me," Siegel affirmed in an interview. "I thought it was dull as dishwater and [Wanger] was a little upset that I turned it down. Don Weis directed the picture.... I thought it was a mistake for Wanger because it started to take him in a different direction."[6]

Once the production received the green light, the cast was quickly assembled. John was chosen for the title role along with Paul Picerni as the evil Prince Nur-El-Din and Elaine Stewart as Princess Fawzia (a part originally assigned to Linda Christian). Stewart was a hot name after her impressive appearance in Vincente Minnelli's *The Bad and the Beautiful* (1952). MGM agreed to lend her only if Wanger would have hired one of their younger contract directors along with her. The producer did not want that, but was forced to accept and the director hired was Don Weis.

Cameras rolled on April 12, 1954, at Lone Pine, California. A week later, while filming in the Mojave Desert, John and two supporting actresses sustained minor injuries in an almost too-realistic battle scene. Then a strong wind blew away a dozen tents wherein the cast and crew were quartered. The gusts also shifted some necessary sand dunes an eighth of a mile away, forcing the company to relocate to a different location near Panamint Mountains.

In his autobiography *Steps to Stardom*, Paul Picerni remembered John as

> probably only about five-nine, but he was a well-built, handsome guy along the lines of Tyrone Power. He was *so* handsome, almost *beautiful*, that it was as though he had the face of a woman. But he was a masculine, very athletic guy who was good at *every*thing. He was good with the sword, he was a marksman with the bow and arrow, and he was *very* good with horses. In fact, he had his own, beautiful horses up there at the Lone Pine location. John also loved the girls…. I don't remember if he was married at the time we did *Hajji Baba*, but that was when I found out how much he liked girls—no matter what age! … In the final sequence of *Hajji Baba*, I have a big swordfight on horseback with John…. John and I did a lot of the swordfight ourselves.[7]

Left to right: Rosemarie Bowe, Elaine Stewart, Amanda Blake and Derek in *The Adventures of Hajji Baba* (1954).

John was busy on the *Hajji Baba* set about three weeks, working on location and then doing a few scenes at the Monogram-Allied Artists studio.

Despite a tight budget, a new color technique was employed. The new process consisted of using different color themes to symbolize the traits of the principal characters as well as help identify them in the crowd scenes: orange, red and brown for the caravans; green for the Turcoman women's camp; blue for the bazaar sequences; white for Princess Fawzia; and black-against-white for the desert encampment of Nur-El-Din.

When *Hajji Baba* was released in North America, critics roasted it, while audiences perceived the production as unintentionally funny, a tongue-in-cheek Oriental fantasy extravaganza rather than a serious adventure feature. In France, the picture created a rift between film buffs and critics. Some found it the setting design archetype of pure *mise-en-scéne*, while others dismissed it as just childish nonsense. It became a sort of a cult movie and was showed for months in Parisian cinemas.[8]

In spite of the negative reviews, the box office total gross was $2,019,100, at a cost of $816,813. The picture was considered quite the success for such a small-budget production.

John's first assignments under his new long-term contract at Paramount was for producers William Pine and William Thomas. He was cast opposite James Cagney in *Run for Cover*. The western was intended to be filmed in VistaVision, Paramount's new screen process, a competitor to Fox's CinemaScope. Once Winston Miller finished the script, a $1,600,000 budget was assigned to the film and it was scheduled for a late spring start. Cagney's presence gave the project an A-star status. Although the actor had approval over the studio's choice of director, he endorsed Paramount's choice of Nicholas Ray, who had just completed his first Western, *Johnny Guitar* (1954), for Republic.

Run for Cover told the story of Matt Dow (Cagney), an ex-convict who had been jailed for a crime he did not commit. While heading West, he meets Davey Bishop (Derek), a boy the age of his dead son, and he becomes a kindly father figure to Davey. Riding along, the pair are innocently involved in a train robbery that triggers a series of dramatic events.

From the very beginning, Ray thought of John for the part of Davey, a crippled young man who tries to prove his manhood, a role that much resembled Nick Romano's tortured personality. The director believed that this was the perfect opportunity to improve on John's inhibited performance in *Knock on Any Door*, a failure that still annoyed him after so many years.

"If Nick [Ray] asked me to crawl across a room crying like a baby, and then turn over and kick my heels, I'll do it. I trust him,"[9] John revealed. He was thrilled to be once again under the direction of one of the few people for whom he had a deep respect. He liked the script, a generational conflict echoing the themes of many of Ray's previous successful films. "The roles are reversed; I'm playing a Cagney part," he joked in an interview. John was referring to his unsympathetic character as the bad guy, in opposition to his co-star's role as a compassionate human being, far from the evil gangster parts he was famous for.[10]

Filming began in the small town of Silverton, 50 miles north of Durango, Colorado, in the last week of May 1954. Working with Cagney was a special treat for John. Cagney told an interviewer, "This boy is a pretty dedicated youngster. And he has just the right mixture of brashness and unaffected humility that a young actor needs. A player must have a certain amount of ego, of course, but in John's case it's well under control."

It did not take long for John to discover how generously Cagney would behave with his colleagues, being attentive to the director and the other players' needs, especially in front of the camera. Once, during a dramatic scene, Cagney gently touched his arm and motioned

Derek in a *Run for Cover* (1955) publicity shot with James Cagney (left) and Viveca Lindfors.

for him to turn toward the camera a little more. When Ray called cut, the star grinned and winked, reassuring John that everything went fine.

Supporting actor Ernest Borgnine recalled in his autobiography Cagney's generosity:

> Cagney was so easy to work with. He did his work, knew his lines… [I]n the evening, when we'd finish, people would congregate around his dressing room. After he'd change, he'd bring out a little square piece of wood and tap-dance on it. Everybody would hum a tune and he'd dance like crazy.[11]

The harmony on the set was spoiled slightly when a special effects explosion hurled a tiny piece of glass into Ray's eye, forcing him to wear dark glasses for the rest of the shooting.

Chapter 6. The Paramount Years

Twenty days later, the cast and crew returned to Paramount where they filmed all the interiors shots.

According to Ray's biographer, the director got frustrated since he still could not find the key to unlocking John's potential. He wasn't as stiff as in *Knock on Any Door*, but neither film seemed to have caught completely both the repression of his character and the violence necessary to break through himself. John seemed unable to deliver his big emotional scenes and make Davey Bishop as well-rounded or as sympathetic as Nick Romano. Some believed that the reason was the script, which was not always clear and logical about John's character. Others thought that John was simply nervous because he felt that Ray nursed a platonic crush on him.[12]

The picture's subtext was clearly inspired by McCarthyism paranoia and the Cold War. All the characters had a dark past and a marked distrust of strangers. Paramount's editors seemed uninterested in making the picture different from anything they had seen before. Cagney and Ray were appalled when watching the final cut when the film opened almost a year later, in April 1955. "We tried to make as offbeat a Western as possible, but whoever cut the film was evidently revolted by anything but clichés," Cagney commented in his autobiography. "As a consequence, little things that the director, Nick Ray (a good man), and the actors put in to give the story extra dimension were excised very proficiently. The result was just another programmer."[13]

Most of the critics found *Run for Cover* an above-average Western, memorable primarily for its impressively vivid color photography. *The Hollywood Reporter* described John's performance as "excellent" and *Variety* "very good." Other reviewers were not as generous. The *New York Times*' Bosley Crowther panned the picture and opined, "John Derek's portrayal of a weakling [is] random and watery."[14] *Run for Cover* ultimately did not recoup its cost, grossing a disappointing $1,500,000.

Following completion of filming, John had only a few weeks before starting work on two films shot almost simultaneously in the summer of 1954: *An Annapolis Story* and *Prince of Players*.

While at home, he did anything but rest. Not satisfied with already being an expert at bull-whipping, knife-throwing, archery, judo, swimming, boxing, wrestling, shooting and of course riding, John decided to learn bullfighting. He had become deeply involved in the art after meeting a young matador. John worked out his calves. He went to the bullfights with his friends and stood on the walkway watching and absorbing the technique of matadors. He learned the passes, movements and the best possible way to avoid being gored. "Once again, I want to know how much guts it takes to get there. Oh, I don't have to prove anything to myself any more, but this thing scares me. It scares everybody else, too. I don't feel bad about admitting it, especially when the matadors admit."[15] Even though he denied it, for some reason, John had to constantly prove his physical superiority, getting into hyper-masculine, often dangerous, activities that offered him an adrenaline rush.

Adrenaline was exactly what was missing in *An Annapolis Story*, the first picture John shot that summer while on loan to Allied Artists. The film's genesis began in August 1952 when executive producer Walter Mirisch approached the Pentagon with the idea of making a film about life at the U.S. Naval Academy in Annapolis that featured many of the traditional and social events that were part of the educational and training program. Mirisch's tentative storyline did not fully convince Col. Clair Towne, head of the motion picture section of the Department of Defense. Yet the producer obtained full collaboration. The approval was provided on the condition that the Navy could monitor the project, providing constructive

Diana Lynn and Derek in *An Annapolis Story* (1955).

criticism and suggestions to ensure that it respected the traditions and discipline at the Naval Academy. It took almost two years for Mirisch to produce a suitable script and start production. To save costs, any kind of color footage dealing with Annapolis, including combat and carrier operations material from earlier Navy pictures, was "borrowed." The cut-and-paste style was very ineffective due to an awkward mix of World War II and Korean War aerial combat footage. Not one scene was shot at Annapolis. The entire production was made on the small Allied Artists backlot. "In the history of motion pictures, no color film could compare to the mishmash of pieces of color film we ended up using—all sizes and shapes, including 16mm and 8mm," director Don Siegel revealed in his autobiography. "We used an old Technicolor camera in a huge casing. The oddity was that, despite the clumsily, hot, uncomfortable casing, it was manned by a most brilliant cameraman, Sam Leavitt."[16]

John reported to the set on July 21, 1954, after getting the crew cut that his military role required. The plot was simple: Brothers Tony and Jim Scott, while on active duty as jet fighter pilots based on an aircraft carrier off Korea, resolve a bitter quarrel which originated in their competition over Peggy Lord, a naval captain's daughter they met during their Annapolis training. John was originally cast as Jim Scott, the brother who eventually gets the girl (Diana Lynn, in a part originally assigned to Debra Paget, whose previous commitments did not allow her to be in the picture). He did not like his part and insisted to the director that he play Tony, the other brother, a role originally intended for Kevin McCarthy. Siegel pointed out to John that his was the better role, but John disagreed so resolutely that the roles *were* switched. This change, according to Siegel, made not the slightest difference in the film outcome. Future filmmaker Sam Peckinpah was Siegel's dialogue director and personal assistant, and also played a pilot. Despite being rushed by Mirisch to complete the film as quickly as possible, Siegel admitted, "The picture *was* fun to do. I liked my cast; I liked my crew. Unfortunately, the one thing I didn't understand was the picture. I should have understood it. I had seen other versions many, many times. I'm afraid the supposed audience agreed with me."[17]

In February 1955, Mirisch screened the final cut at the Pentagon; he had not yet come up with a satisfactory title. He was worried over the tentative name *The Annapolis Story*, where the definite article implied a historical and documentary film, something Siegel's film was not. Eventually the Pentagon approved the picture, Mirisch changed the *The* into *An* and the title got endorsed by the Navy.[18] For marketing reasons, *An Annapolis Story* was released in the United Kingdom as *The Blue and the Gold* and in other English-speaking countries as *Navy Air Patrol*. The film performed moderately well at the box office, despite the lackluster reviews. Critics found John very convincing; *The Hollywood Reporter* even forecasted, "This picture should do a lot for young John Derek."[19]

As soon as his presence was no longer required on the set, John moved to 20th Century–Fox to work on the major production *Prince of Players*. His dynamic *Hajji Baba* performance had rewarded him the role of John Wilkes Booth, President Lincoln's slayer. Originally intended for Jay Robinson, the part was given to John after Fox studio chief Darryl Zanuck glimpsed John's work in *Hajji* at an industry preview.

Playwright Moss Hart had completed a script based on Eleanor Ruggles' bestselling biography that traced the tragic story of Edwin Booth, the 19th-century Shakespearean actor, and his actor brother John Wilkes. Fox acquired the rights to the story in January 1953. Zanuck passed Hart's script to Philip Dunne, a skilled screenwriter-producer who found it too long and verbose and felt that it required a major revision. When he told Hart of all the necessary changes, the playwright said: "Fine, I agree with you completely. Write it just like that,"[20] leaving the stunned producer in complete charge of all the script changes. In a few weeks, Dunne finished the alterations under Hart's supervision and with Zanuck's approval. Since it was a period film dealing with historical facts, several months of research were necessary before shooting could begin. For the Shakespearean scenes, special costumes, duplicating those worn by the actors of that time, had to be sketched and made. The interiors of different American theaters had to be reproduced with the aid of vintage photographs.

Welsh-born Richard Burton (age 29) was cast as Edwin Booth. Dunne remembered seeing him in 1949 at the Globe Theatre in London in *The Lady's Not for Burning* and being struck by his talent. In 1953, Burton starred in *The Robe* (co-written by Dunne), the first-released CinemaScope production. Zanuck agreed with the screenwriter that Burton's background as a leading Shakespearean actor was a great asset. In his diary, Burton recalled, "I remember the high hopes I had of that film and my disappointment at its indifferent reception. The original script by Moss Hart was very good when I agreed to do it but a year later when I actually did, it had been murdered by Zanuck and his hacks. Some of it was savable, however, which accounts for what little success we had."[21]

Maggie McNamara was cast as Edwin's young wife and Raymond Massey as his extravagant father, Junius Brutus Booth. John was pleased to be part of such a prestigious production. Finally he had a role that gave him the opportunity to showcase his full acting ability. He diligently studied his character, trying to understand the psychology behind the jealousy John Wilkes Booth felt toward his brother, and behind his crazy act of shooting President Lincoln.

Several scenes called for John to do some hard riding which he performed without the use of a body double as usual. The dramatic scene in which John shoots the president with a derringer, then jumps to the stage of Ford's Theatre and breaks his left ankle, was one of the hardest to do. The director was afraid that John would break a leg in the 15-foot jump from the box to the stage, and a stuntman was summoned. The stuntman made the leap, landing in a nest of rubber cushions below the level of the stage. Then John jumped, but only to another platform a few feet below the presidential box. Asked if he felt uncom-

Sarah Padden, Derek and Stanley Hall (right) in a dramatic scene from *Prince of Players* (1955).

fortable in playing one of the most despicable villains in American history, John replied: "Not at all. They gotta hate me before they love me."[22]

Some of the horses used in the production belonged to John, who had recently leased some stables at the John Carroll Ranch in Granada Hills in partnership with an expert handler named Bob Smith. Together they bred and trained cutting horses.

Right from the beginning, *Prince of Players* seemed to be destined for disaster. Dunne, who also directed the film, was too inexperienced to lead the complicated production, which required that several powerful theatrical moments be translated into a cinematic experience. Although the director was aided in the staging of the Shakespearean scenes by noted stage actress Eva Le Gallienne, who made her screen debut in the picture, the Shakespearean extracts were pitched like songs in a musical, making the magnetic stage acting style of some performers unsuitable for the screen. Yet everybody in the production seemed happy with the result when the picture wrapped in September 1954. "The best thing I've had so far," was John's comment about the experience.[23]

The film premiered in New York on the rainy afternoon of January 10, 1955. The unusual time choice was made to enable Broadway stage personalities to attend. The unique screening marked the first daytime bow of a CinemaScope production on Broadway. The only star of the film to attend the event was Maggie McNamara. The picture opened nationwide the next day, playing in a few theaters in stereophonic sound. There were mixed reviews for the picture itself, but John's acting was very well received. *Variety* called it "a fine performance," and the *New York Times* said it was "aptly flashy and grandiloquent." Unfortunately, on both sides of the Atlantic, the movie played to many empty seats. *Prince of Players* was the first flop in CinemaScope.

Chapter 7

High and Low

"I don't respect men that aren't physical. I don't care how mental they are. If you develop a mind, you can develop a body."—John Derek

At the end of October 1954, John was assigned to co-star with Kathryn Grayson and Oreste Kirkop in *The Vagabond King*. The offer came on the same day he received confirmation that he was cast as Joshua in *The Ten Commandments*.

In director Michael Curtiz's *The Vagabond King*, John was set to play a young officer in the court of Louis XI. When shooting was postponed until December 27, John was forced to bow out due to a scheduling conflict with DeMille's *Commandments*.

Derek was not DeMille's first choice for the Biblical character of Joshua the stone cutter. Hugh O'Brian, Jeff Chandler, Eric Fleming, Dale Robertson, Michael Pate, George Nader, Vince Edwards and Tony Curtis were all previously considered. The final serious contenders were Brian Keith, Cornel Wilde, Clint Walker and John. After their first meeting, DeMille was not entirely convinced by John, noting sourly, "He knows nothing about the Bible."[1] But the director liked John and intended to assign him a different part.

"I was extremely honest in my reply," said John, recalling being asked what he knew about the Biblical character. "I told Mr. DeMille that beyond the name and what he stood for in the Bible history, my knowledge of Joshua was slight to the point of scantiness. Then Mr. DeMille went into detail on Joshua and I was fascinated by his storytelling. When I left his office, I vowed to myself that when Mr. DeMille saw me again, I would be up on my Joshua lore."[2]

DeMille decided to cast Cornel Wilde, who had worked with him in *The Greatest Show on Earth* (1952), and offered him the part. But the actor was unconvinced about the quality of the character and pulled out. In the meantime, John was still determined to get the part, knowing that it was still uncast. He loved the idea of playing Joshua, a sort of military leader, a hyper-masculine character that would have helped him move away from his pretty-boy image.

Three months after his first meeting with DeMille, a smiling John, with a trimmed beard, strode into the Paramount commissary in tennis shoes, riding pants and a blue T-shirt ready to show the director his physical achievements. He had devoted every extra hour in the last months to researching Joshua. His greatest pre-production feat was getting into extremely fine physical condition for the role as the rebellious slave, who sweated as a stone cutter while craving freedom from his Egyptian masters. John had worked out every day in the studio gym and through outdoor activities at his ranch, becoming leaner, agile and stronger, and cutting his weight down to 165 pounds. To guard against fatigue, he took vitamins and mineral supplements, and lunched on a combination of whipped eggs, milk, orange juice and honey. For John, the challenging training was not as hard as it sounded. It

Chapter 7. High and Low

was in line with his philosophy of life "*mens sana in corpore sano*": a sound mind in a sound body. Said John, "I don't respect men that aren't physical. I don't care how mental they are. If you develop a mind, you can develop a body. They're both equally important. A great mind with no physical power is dissipating half the stuff that's given you."[3]

DeMille was impressed by John's physical shape. That, along with the beard, made him appear manlier and more resembling the director's idea of how Joshua should look. Two screen tests were immediately arranged—a silent, color one to see how John would photograph, and a black-and-white sound one directed by DeMille's associate producer Henry Wilcoxon (who was campaigning for beefcake Clint Walker to play Joshua).

Wilcoxon in his autobiography stated that the true reason behind John's casting was Debra Paget. DeMille wanted her as Lilia, but 20th Century–Fox said that they would loan the actress only if Paramount was willing to cast John, in a role equally as important as Paget's: "They're grooming both kids for stardom and they don't want Derek in anything but a co-starring role,"[4] Wilcoxon told DeMille, who (according to Wilcoxon) was ready to give the part to Walker.

Fox's demand that DeMille cast John in order to get Paget was shrewd studio strategy. After leaving Columbia, John was not contractually bound to any studio except Paramount. He had, in fact, done *The Adventures of Hajji Baba* and *Prince of Players* for 20th Century–Fox on a loan from Paramount. His casting in *The Ten Commandments* would have meant enormous visibility and indirect publicity for Fox's soon-to-be-released two films. No matter the real reason behind John's casting, DeMille was satisfied with his screen tests and assigned him the part.

It did not take long for the director to recognize John's insecurities. The filmmaker treated him as if he was valuable and worthy of giving the best. "Mr. DeMille made me ashamed of doing some of the pictures I've done just to exist," John admitted. "He's made me want to give my best—really learn to express myself and work."[5] Thanks to DeMille's advice, John slowly emerged from the deep water of self-doubt. Since he had rushed his lines at an informal 15-minute reading of the script, the director suggested that he work with a diction teacher. Aware of his own fast talking, John acquiesced.

Before leaving for Egypt to film on location, DeMille asked John to report to the studio on the last week of March for his first scene. The sequence called for Joshua to climb up and then down a 30-foot rope and then fight his way through a group of taskmasters to help an old slave woman. "That's rough…. That's going to put callouses on my hands," John commented.[6]

Once on the set, Donald McLean, a dialogue supervisor, was assigned to

Derek in a publicity shot for *Photoplay* magazine in 1955.

rehearse all John's scenes with him before they were filmed. DeMille explicitly requested that the dialogue had to be spoken exactly as scripted, without the slightest deviation. The director realized that many of the speeches spoken by the principal characters, including Joshua, came from the Bible in direct quotes.

All of John's *Ten Commandments* scenes were shot in Hollywood, on 12 of Paramount's 18 sound stages used for the occasion. He did not travel to Egypt where DeMille photographed some of the exteriors with Charlton Heston (who played Moses) and swarms of extras.

On the set, John got acquainted with Yul Brynner, who played the pharaoh Rameses II. The baldheaded star spent much of his spare time photographing the director and his fellow actors, using a camera hidden behind his throne or his chariot. John had a passion for photography, which later would develop into a real profession, and was fascinated by Brynner's technique after seeing some of the beautiful shots he had covertly taken of him. While waiting for their scenes to begin, the two would often occupy their time talking about cameras, lenses and exposures.

John and Heston developed a solid friendship. Sharing a passion for horses and sports, they'd often spend their free time together exercising at the studio gym or horseback riding around John's hilltop house in Encino. They agreed to pose together for a fan magazine while plunging into John's 60-foot-long pool with scuba equipment.[7]

On a warm Saturday of April, not having any scheduled scenes, John, along with his friend Roy Camp, took the opportunity to participate in a boat race between the mainland and Santa Catalina Island sponsored by the Sportsmen's Club of Van Nuys. About 45 minutes after the competition started, his motorboat ran out of gas and he quickly started to drift toward the treacherous currents of the San Pedro Channel. His little wave-tossed boat was soon lost in a sudden shroud-like fog. The next day he was spotted by a civilian pilot who dropped flares to mark the location. A Coast Guard cutter sped to the scene and towed John to Avalon Harbor at Santa Catalina. When rescued, John learned that a total of 12 boats had been reported lost during the race because of the thick fog. Coast Guard vessels along with private yachts equipped with radar were cautiously probing through heavy waves in search of survivors. John realized how very lucky he had been. When Paramount executives heard the news, he was summoned immediately to the office of one of the executive producers who scolded him for his reckless act. John had, in fact, signed a contract in which he had agreed not to engage in any behavior that could put him at risk of injury. The discussion escalated quickly into a heated argument, with John storming off the lot and returning the following morning after he had cooled down.

Years later, John opened up on how it really was working under DeMille's direction. "DeMille was a caricature of himself ... a god in his own cloud. He built his cloud and got on and he lived there." He also recalled a moment when the filmmaker started to direct John's horse instead of him:

> We are getting ready to cross the Red Sea. It had just opened and I had to lead the goddamned people down into the thing. We had about 3000 extras on stage—they'd opened these two stages—and he's up there with his megaphone hooked up and *he's talking to my horse*! That was his way of knocking the pins from under you. I just slipped off the horse, went to the commissary and said, "If he ever talks to me again, he's going to apologize." And he was gracious enough to do so—in person. That wasn't enough for me. I said, "You chewed my ass out on a megaphone, give the apology on the megaphone." So, after lunch, he gave me the apology on the megaphone, on the set and in front of all the extras ... and we crossed the Red Sea![8]

The Ten Commandments reached a final cost of over $13.5 million, becoming the most expensive production in film history until 1963 when *Cleopatra* hit $20 million. After undergoing a long editing process, supervised by DeMille, the final cut ran 221 minutes. It was previewed in Salt Lake City on October 5, 1956, followed by a gala evening in Los Angeles and another in New York a month later. *The Ten Commandments* was nominated for seven Academy Awards, but it only won one (for Best Special Effects). It received generally positive reviews, although some critics noted its divergence from the Biblical text. Still, it was unanimously praised for the extraordinary cinematography. Only a few reviews mentioned John by his name, but they were universally positive. "John Derek makes a good Joshua," wrote *The Hollywood Reporter*; "Competent work is done … by John Derek as Joshua," *Variety* chimed in. Ultimately the story of Moses grossed an astounding $122 million worldwide, becoming the highest-grossing film of 1956 and the second most successful film of the decade.

In June, the press announced that after finishing his co-starring role in DeMille's picture, John planned to scout Arizona for a ranch property to cater to tourists and vacationers. He and his family would operate the venture and keep part of the land for themselves. But the ambitious project was abandoned when at the end of August, just a few days after the completion of *Ten Commandments*, John announced the end of his stormy seven-year marriage. He told Louella Parsons, the first to print the news on September 10, 1955, "I left home once before and then we straightened everything out. This could be a temporary thing, or it could be permanent. Basically, my wife and I have nothing in common and I think it's better to make a clean break." The columnist explained that when John had left home last time, he asked for her advice and she urged him to try again because of the children. John came back to his family with good intentions, but after three months, the situation was so hopeless that he decided to see an attorney to put an end to it. Pati blamed John's decision on the fact that he was romantically involved with someone else: "I don't want to say anything, but I'm afraid somebody is trying to break up my home. It's a terrible thing because of our children."[9]

Firm in his desire for marital freedom, John filed for divorce on September 16. He made a general charge of cruelty, stating that his wife's actions caused him mental anguish that interfered with the performance of his professional duties. He did admit that Pati was a fit person to have the custody of Russell, now five, and Sean, two. He asked only for reasonable rights of visitation and offered to make provisions for the support of his family.

While Pati was still hoping John would return, he declared to the press, "Pati and I have been discussing divorce for a long time. I think we both will be happier when it is accomplished."[10] On October 19, Pati was awarded temporary support payments of $1750 per month from John, pending their divorce hearing.

The following day, a false report that Pati had committed suicide hit Hollywood. When the news reached her at home, she appeared to be baffled:

> I just don't understand who could have done something like this.… I have no reason to do such a thing. I have two wonderful children and they're here in the house with me and the nurse. I still hope that my husband will come back to me, but I wouldn't do such a thing to bring him back. He knows that. No, I don't think this false report is likely to bring about a reconciliation. But we do have so much in common—our wonderful children. I still love him very much. It's humiliating to say. But it's the truth.[11]

According to John's daughter Sean, John gave the story to the press, making her mother look distraught and suicidal.

In the *Photoplay* article "The Truth Behind John Derek's Bust Up" (December 1955), John and Pati, interviewed separately, revealed details of their marriage and separation. Convinced that his marriage was over, John had rented a small Sunset Boulevard apartment. He had visited the Encino house only to pick up a few clothes and to see Russell and Sean when Pati was away. He was aware that the kids being exposed to their constant arguments wasn't healthy. Since he and Pati argued about everything, even how to raise them, tension and bickering were having an impact on them. "Pati and I don't belong under the same roof. It isn't a healthy situation for anybody," he remarked with conviction. With brutal honesty he also revealed that he had seen a marriage counselor without telling his wife: "But when you come right down to it—your problems are your problems and the answers have to come from you. Distrust and too much discord—constant discord—can be difficult to overcome. And let's face it, I'm not too great to live around. I'm selfish and I have a very bad temper. I'm impulsive and when I want to do something—when I want something—I want it now."[12]

He described Pati as "a wonderful mother," but her practical and conservative behavior did not match with his impulsive way of living and artistry. Also, her lack of enthusiasm about everything he would do had put a dent in their relationship. Another cause of friction was Pati's prudent style of living that clashed with John's extravagance. John would forget his family necessities and the unpaid bills, and Pati was infuriated by his lack of common sense. Pati had often turned a blind eye to the many "girlfriends" John brought home, but now the situation seemed unbearable. The Dereks had been living in a doomed marriage for many years and their separation was inevitable. Despite John's denial, a rumor had spread that a third party had finally pushed the situation over the edge and broke the couple apart.

The third party: Ursula Andress.

Chapter 8

Ursula

"Until I met Ursula, I didn't know what love was."—John Derek

John met Ursula Andress during a lunch break in the studio canteen while he was making *The Ten Commandments*. With most of the tables taken, he spotted an empty chair at a table where a group of young contract players were discussing their careers. John was not in the mood for conversation but took the seat and ordered his lunch anyway. Most of the players recognized him and quickly overwhelmed him with questions about his picture. While he was trying to answer patiently, one of the guys motioned to a girl and asked, "What do you think about that, Ursula?" The question was directed to a short-haired honey blond with light brown eyes and thick eyebrows, sitting silently at the other end of the table. She half-smiled like someone who did not understand a word of what had been said and politely replied: "It iss vereee niess." Everyone at the table burst into laughter. Another guy from the group said that no matter what you ask her, she would always give the same answer. John recalled in an interview,

> The whole table was laughing at her.... She realized it, of course, but she was regular enough not to get angry. I looked down the table. Our eyes met only for an instant, and that was just how long it took to happen. Then Ursula and I started to laugh. Here was a girl I didn't even know, had never spoken to. Yet the two of us were now laughing at the rest of the group and they didn't know why. She understood that I understood. Suddenly, she began to talk in very bent and broken English. After each sentence, the group would break up at her inability to express herself. Then I found myself laughing harder than anyone. Not *at* Ursula, but *with* her, at the others. For she was putting them in their places so adroitly they didn't know it.[1]

John revealed many years later that he did not particularly like the blond on that first meeting. "She was a little fat. Her hair was very short and her eyebrows—she had incredible eyebrows—were very big and very black. They were so big you could hang your washing on them. And she had very red lipstick. No, I didn't like her looks at all."[2] In addition, Ursula was often in the company of her secretary Barbara Bachelor, who helped her with everything because of her limited English, and two Alsatian hounds.

One afternoon days later, John entered the Paramount canteen and saw her there, alone at a table for two, staring at the menu. He sat with her and helped her order. He attempted to have a conversation with Ursula, communicating in broken English often accompanied by colorful gesturing or pronouncing funny foreign words. "In the beginning, I regarded her as everybody else did. I thought she was a character, laughable, and even a little weird. But after I got to know her better, I realized that she wasn't weird at all. She was ready to accept, rather bravely, I thought, every challenge that life had to offer."[3]

Andress arrived in Hollywood when she was only 17. She was born on March 19, 1936, in Ostermundigen, a little village located a few kilometers outside Bern, Switzerland. The third of six children, she was the daughter of Ross and Anna Andress. After she completed high school (and became fluent in German, French and Italian), she went to Paris to study art for a year. During a trip to Rome, a producer signed her for a tiny role in an Italian production called *The Many Loves of Casanova*. This was followed by three others. Then a Paramount talent scout spotted her and offered her a screen test. Ursula accepted even though she did not know a word of English. In London to do the screen test, she stayed with Audrey Hepburn's mother, refusing to be in a hotel after having a bad experience in Rome hotels where men tried taking advantage of her. After a successful screen test, she was flown to Hollywood and put under contract for Paramount.

> There I was in Hollywood with a contract that said I was a star, so I behaved the way I thought a star acts. The studio wanted me to learn acting, and take speech lessons and dancing and singing, but I just laughed and said, "No, I want to play." So, I played…. The whole Hollywood bit … tennis, swimming, lying by the pool, men, nightclubs, men, parties, men, everything.[4]

Although she received a weekly salary of $250, Ursula did not work at all. She refused to learn English with her assigned coach, rebelling against the strict studio discipline that demanded that she give no interviews until Paramount decided that their "creature" was ready to face the public. Tired of coping with her wild behavior, the studio fired her just a few weeks after she met John.

"Ursula was crazy, completely crazy," John said in an interview. "She was like a wild person, she lived her own way—fast, very fast. She had come to the United States on a contract with Paramount Studios to become a star. But she couldn't care less about being an actress and the cinema world didn't interest her in the least."[5] The first official date John and Ursula had happened when she surprisingly asked to go diving with him. That day, John had arranged to meet some real diving champions. Initially, he did not like the idea of bringing along a beginner, especially a girl, but eventually invited her. John marveled as Ursula, who had never been diving, proved to be much braver than some of the expert divers. After observing the others doing everything she was supposed to do, she jumped into the pool without hesitation and displayed her diving skills amazingly. John was so impressed that he kissed her.

Ursula was smitten by John's eyes:

> His eyes were the most beautiful eyes I ever saw in a man. I think he had gorgeous eyes. Green-blue with this sparkling inside. Plus, he had the eye to see beauty and to appreciate beauty…. Lana Turner didn't want to work with him, because she said he's too beautiful, because he had longer eyelashes than hers and he had such a perfect face. It's hard for a woman to be next to John… [T]hough John had a beautiful face, he was not a narcissist.[6]

Their subsequent dates turned out a bit differently. He had to compete with a flock of guys eagerly waiting their turn to take her out. Her tiny bungalow was always crowded with people—mostly ardent admirers—including Marlon Brando and James Dean. Intrigued by the fact that this Swiss beauty had so many men in love with her, John wanted to discover what this strange foreign girl had that was so desirable to almost every man.

Thanks to his charm, he was able to beat the competition and go out with her again. Rumors of the two being a couple ultimately reached Pati, to whom John was still legally married. John claimed that Pati engaged a private detective to follow him to find out who John was seeing, but apparently she discovered the affair after finding Andress's dog's collar in the back seat of their family truck. Pati dialed the telephone number engraved on the metal dog-tag and reached an office at Paramount. She was transferred to Ursula's drama coach, who told her the name of the dog's owner. Pati didn't say anything and waited for John to make the first move. She realized that this time something different was happening to her husband. In the past, she had often turned a blind eye to John's brief escapades, but now she sensed that Andress was a real danger for her family, and that John would eventually leave her. As she feared, a few weeks later John asked her for a divorce. (According to Sean Derek, her mother kept Ursula's dog collar for 17 years in a deposit box just in case she needed to use it as proof of John's infidelity.)

Pati threatened to bring legal action against Andress, who was still underage. Since the Swiss girl had arrived in America on a work visa, a lawyer informed Pati that litigation could have led to Ursula's deportation on moral charges. This move had been a trick that Dolores, John's mother, had attempted on Pati when she disapproved of her son relationship's with her. To protect Ursula, John decided to stop seeing her, even dating another girl for a while. Ursula went back to her wild Hollywood life and got closer to James Dean, who was madly in love with her and was trying to win her back. On several occasions, the temperamental young actor proved his jealousy by racing his car against John's when John was out on a date with the actress. On September 30, 1955, when Dean crushed his Porsche 550 Spyder and died, Ursula was devastated. Only a few days earlier, John had been taken on a fast ride in that car. Like a proud father, Dean was eager to show off his new "fireball" with Ursula at his side. However, when she refused to get in the car, John, who was in her company, accepted the invitation instead. During the entire high-speed ride, he mocked Dean's new "toy," making him furious.

In the days following Dean's tragic death, reporters chased Ursula everywhere, hoping to get a statement. John took her away from the Hollywood commotion, whisking her off to a secluded countryside location. They spent a lot of time together, and John finally captured Ursula's heart. As a sign of love, he gave her a beautiful watch and a silver keychain with a boat he handmade for her.

The couple realized that something serious was happening to them. For the first time in his life, John fell in love. "Until I met Ursula, I didn't know what love was," he later confessed. He admitted that he had heard thousands of stories about love but he had never experienced those feelings. Finding Ursula, he realized he did not need any other woman, not even as a friend. So he got rid of all the others. The two became extremely close, pledging to each other eternal and faithful love, planning to get married as soon John got a divorce.

* * *

Emotionally indebted to DeMille for the tremendous opportunity to co-star in *The Ten Commandments*, John made another picture with Paramount. Unfortunately, it was not of the same caliber. *The Leather Saint* was the story of a young Episcopalian minister who secretly becomes a professional boxer in order to finance new hospital equipment for his polio-ravaged parish. Alvin Ganzer and Norman Retchin wrote the role of boxing priest Father Gil Allen for Montgomery Clift, who was a close friend. In early 1954, producer Leonard Goldstein purchased the rights intending to make the film for Universal. Clift was considered as Father Gil Allen, but the actor, who had already worn the priest's frock in Hitchcock's *I Confess* (1953), turned down the offer. The second choice was Ricardo Montalban, who also declined. In the fall of 1955, a revised script was sold to Paramount after the character of the Roman Catholic priest was changed to an Episcopalian. The writers had in fact learned that a Mexican priest, who had boxed professionally to raise money for

Derek gets ready to film a boxing scene for *The Leather Saint* (1956), with the help of an unidentified crew member.

charity, was severely punished by his bishop. In November 1955, just a few days before the beginning of pre-production, the screenplay got the green light from the National Council of Churches' Broadcasting and Film Commission and John was cast as Father Gil.

Paramount reported that one of the reasons John had been chosen was for his experience as an amateur boxer five years earlier when he had allegedly trained for two months with Mushy Callahan to star in Columbia's never-realized remake of *Golden Boy*. Richard Thorpe was considered for the job of director, but Paramount decided to give screenwriter Ganzer, who had also been an assistant director for several years and a TV director, a

Derek and Jody Lawrance in *The Leather Saint* (1956).

chance to make his first picture on the assumption that the writer himself knew the material best. Paul Douglas and Jody Lawrance were cast in the other main roles along with Cesar Romero, who was returning to work at Paramount after a 20-year absence.

As soon as John was confirmed in the part, he got a butch haircut and began to train with Joe Gray, a former actor and professional boxer, who supervised all the boxing sequences. Shooting began on January 9, 1956. Much of *The Leather Saint* was filmed on location in the San Fernando Valley, Malibu Beach and downtown Los Angeles. The production was permitted to film inside the Episcopalian All Saints Church in the heart of Beverly Hills in return of a generous contribution. This meant that Paramount didn't need to build a church from scratch on a sound stage. On the set, John and Jody Lawrance started a feud that tabloids called "the buzz of the Paramount lot."[7] The two had worked together in *Mask of the Avenger* and *The Family Secret*, yet on this occasion John had become the most fervid critic of Lawrance's diva-ish behavior, initiating continuous quarrels that disrupted the harmony on the set.

While post-production was in progress, the industry press revealed the high hopes Paramount had for this picture. Some spoke of the possibility that John would be in line for an Academy Award nomination, stating ludicrously that every actor who had portrayed a man of the cloth in pictures had wound up with an Oscar nomination (Bing Crosby in *Going My Way* and *The Bells of St. Mary*, Spencer Tracy *in San Francisco, Boys Town* and *Men of Boys Town*, Gregory Peck in *The Keys of the Kingdom*, Karl Malden in *On the*

Waterfront). In an interview, John candidly admitted to not being interested in being a "serious actor," fully aware of his own artistic limitations. His objective was to be a movie star "for the masses," and to just make money. "I want money and the motion picture industry is a good place to make it. The big stars aren't products of any of those dramatic schools. They're personalities. I want money to spend on my hobbies. Why knock yourself out to win Oscars? I want to have fun without a struggle." John also insisted that he had never complained about his handsome face preventing him from getting more dramatic parts, and wished he *hadn't* been born with a pretty face so he could win more serious film roles instead of beefcake parts. "I'm glad I look this way. I wouldn't have gotten in movies if I didn't." Morosely he admitted that he hadn't liked any of the movies he had made to that date except *The Ten Commandments*. Commenting on *The Leather Saint*, he *said*, "The role is pretty similar to all the others I've done. It just doesn't go far enough. I'd like a part that doesn't flatter you, so you are not a living doll. I'd rather lose the girl. Then you get better notices from the critics."[8]

The Leather Saint opened at the end of the following May, receiving fairly good reviews that generally praised his likable characterization as a priest. "Derek is very good as the handsome and manly priest, making believable both his churchly vocation and his boxing interest," noted *The Hollywood Reporter*.[9] The film performed disappointingly at the box office.

On February 24, 1956, two weeks after *The Leather Saint* was completed, John boarded a plane destined for London. Unhappy that his Hollywood career seemed to be going nowhere, he eagerly accepted the invitation to star in his first British production, *The Flesh Is Weak*.

Originally titled *Women of the Night*, the picture was the idea of Raymond Stross, a British producer interested in making a film on the delicate theme of postwar street prostitution in England. The idea came to Stross after reading an article in the *Sunday People* campaigning for a cleanup of London's prostitution areas, exposing a notorious racketeer family, "The Emperors of Vice," as primarily responsible.

Stross assigned the job to screenwriter Leigh Vance, who spent days and nights researching the subject visiting the streets, alleys, bars and clubs of London's West End: picking up information, learning methods and habits as to how the racket operated. He wrote it down in the form of a screenplay telling the tragic story of a pretty and naïve small-town girl Marissa Cooper (Italian starlet Milly Vitale), coming to London and falling in love with Tony Giani (John), who blackmails her emotionally into working as a prostitute for him and his two brothers.

"*The Flesh Is Weak* puts a spotlight not only on the girls who ply their tawdry trade, but on the men behind them—the men who live on their immoral earnings," Stross explained in an interview.[10] To sell the film overseas, the producer cast John in the lead believing that a well-known Hollywood name would add to its marketability. Don Chaffey, a young documentary TV and film director, shot all the needed background shots around London's Soho, Shepherd's Market and Curzon Street areas before principal photography began. Once John arrived in England, most of the production was filmed in five weeks at Walton Studios, about an hour from London.

Landing at London Airport, John was met by Stross, who had alerted the press as to the star's arrival and called him "the world's most handsome man." *Confidential* magazine later published a story about John's alleged encounter with "Tania," a local prostitute who picked him up in the street one night. Oddly, the article seemed in line with the film's subject, appearing almost as a set-up to create more buzz around the film that was about to open in America.¹¹

In England, *The Flesh Is Weak* was a financial triumph. In spite of mixed reviews (many newspapers condemned its explicitness and tasteless subject matter) and the unsurprising X certificate from the British Board of Film Censors (who demanded a series of cuts), the film drew more attention than expected. Audiences crowded the theaters for more than four months due to the publicity about the shocking subject.

Milly Vitale and Derek in *The Flesh Is Weak* (1957).

John turned in a fine, convincing performance as the devilish, dashing pimp, pleasing the British reviewers. *The Flesh Is Weak* is considered by many to be Britain's first exploitation film. Its success started a trend of productions deliberately attempting to test the nerve of the British censors by dealing in scandalous subjects. U.S. censors were more lenient than those in England, leaving streetwalker scenes that were cut for London audiences. But censors in Memphis, Tennessee, banned the movie, rating it as "immoral."¹²

On his return to the States, John realized that his film career was proving to be a source of frustration once again. While Ursula had signed a new contract with Universal, he accepted a role of the medieval Persian poet-mathematician-astronomer in Paramount's lavish production *Omar Khayyam*.

Producer Frank Freeman, Jr., first become interested when he studied Khayyam and his work *The Rubaiyat* in college. He proposed that Barré Lyndon write a script; after more than a year, Lyndon completed a manuscript of 1.5 million words, from which he condensed a 118-page shooting script. Paramount assigned the Technicolor-VistaVision production to director William Dieterle, with whom John had debuted as a credited actor in *I'll Be Seeing You*.

Cornel Wilde played the title role (beating out the competition of John Forsythe, Robert Wagner, Rossano Brazzi and John Neville), Raymond Massey played the wise Shah, Debra Paget was the shah's fiancée Sharain, Michael Rennie played Hassan the villain, and John was Prince Malik the shah's heir. Peruvian-born singer Yma Sumac appeared as Karina, a confidante of Sharain; her phenomenal vocal range was displayed in three songs during the course of action.

Except for a few sequences shot on desert locations in the Indio and Palm Springs regions of Southern California, *Omar Khayyam* was entirely filmed on the Paramount lot, where the shah's court was reconstructed. According to a press release, the production assembled 25,000 props that were true to the 11th-century Oriental tradition, along with an impressive number of costumes faithfully reproduced from original art of the time. John was its only leading player to handle some swordplay in some of the battle scenes.

Derek and Cornel Wilde in *Omar Khayyam* (1957).

Omar Khayyam was completed in six weeks at a cost of approximately $2,272,000. Originally the picture was scheduled to premiere in Teheran, Iran, but the studio abandoned that extravagant idea. During the editing process, for unknown reasons, a few retakes appeared to be needed. Yet it took an entire year before they were completed since many cast members were unavailable. (John's presence was not necessary.) The picture was finally released in August 1957. In the New York metropolitan area, *Khayyam* was shown simultaneously in 66 neighborhood theaters. Reviewers praised the opulent sets and costumes along with the cinematography but dismissed the confusing and wordy script. *Harrison's Report* pegged the film as "a routine costume adventure melodrama that it is only spottily entertaining."[13]

Chapter 8. Ursula

On April 4, 1956, while John was shooting *Omar Khayyam*, the Superior Court in San Fernando California, granted the interlocutory decree to Pati on her cross-complaint charging John with mental cruelty. She received custody of Russell and Sean. Finally, the Dereks were officially divorced. Tabloids disclosed some of the financial details that included John keeping the family home and giving Pati the money to buy a smaller place in Van Nuys, where she and the children moved the following month. John revealed his intent to sell his house and look for a place big enough to keep horses.

Desperate for money to pay Pati's alimony, John became discouraged when he learned from his agent that no work was on the horizon. After he failed to sell Paramount on the concept of his old project on Murrieta, he reluctantly accepted the lead in *Fury at Showdown*, a B western, followed by two TV appearances.

Produced on a limited budget by Bob Goldstein and released through United Artists, *Fury at Showdown* was shot at RKO in only one week in July 1956. The script, originally titled *Showdown*, was based on the novel *Showdown Creek* by Lucas Todd and had plenty of typical Western action, gun battles, and fistfights. John played Brock Mitchell, a gunfighter trying to reform himself and live a life of peace, only to run into opposition from town bullies. Brock's young brother (Nick Adams) desperately tries to divert him from the quick road to death that awaits most gunslingers. Carolyn Craig starred opposite John as his love

Natalie Wood visits Derek (left) and John Smith on the set of *Fury at Showdown* (1957).

interest. The actress had recently been discovered in a community playhouse by a talent scout who got her cast as Elizabeth Taylor's sister in *Giant* (1956). Natalie Wood was an unexpected set visitor and the tabloids speculated about an affair between the 18-year-old star and John. Both dismissed the notion.

Duty-bound to lie to the press, John expressed fake enthusiasm about starring in the picture, which was not much different from the other Westerns he had done in the past. "It's the type of role I want," he commented. "Lots of action and lots of character. I'm sullen, bitter, brutal kind. I'm a young guy with an old heart, redeemed by his kid brother and the girl he loves."[14]

The pictured featured a lengthy fight sequence between Derek and John Smith, both of whom refused a stuntman. The scene was referred to by the *New York Times* as "a humdinger of a fistfight."[15] Despite its limited budget, the picture turned out to be a sleeper, receiving positive reviews.

On the eve of turning 30, John was now showing a touch of silver hair at the temples, a startling contrast to his handsome profile. This was a sign of aging that John happily welcomed, as he believed that the gray could help him convince producers that he was ready to abandon the "pretty boy" characterizations that were still haunting him. John told the press, "When I found the tinge of gray in the temples and displayed it to producers to prove that I was grown up, the good roles started coming my way."

John next appeared on the small screen in two prime-time western dramas. The first was "Black Jim Hawk," a 30-minute episode of the ABC series *The Ford Television Theatre*. Directed by Arthur Hiller (later the director of such successful films as *Love Story* [1970]), John played notorious gang leader Hawk, who swore vengeance on the president of the Republic of Texas (the man had refused to pardon Hawk's father, who had been sentenced and hung for murder). *Variety* called Derek's performance "forceful."[16]

Two months later, John starred in "Massacre at Sand Creek," an episode of CBS-TV's 90-minute drama series *Playhouse 90*. He played Norman Tucker, a good-hearted lieutenant who tries in vain to stop a vengeful colonel from provoking an Indian war. The shooting was an enjoyable experience for John since the cast was joined by 75 horses. Just being on a saddle made him a happy man. He joked with the press that the horses were getting better treatment than *he* was. His horse was actually three identical animals: a trick horse for the jumping and the falling scenes, a running horse for the chases, and a dialogue horse which had to stand perfectly still while he spoke.

Chapter 9

World Traveler

"You tell me you are one of the greatest actors in the world. In which case you need to find the greatest director in the world, which isn't me."—Sergio Leone to John Derek

In the first week of 1957, there was a dramatic accident when John's speedboat suddenly overturned in the ocean off Alamitos Bay Peninsula near Long Beach, California. He and his friend Buddy Railsback were rescued by a lifeguard launch, and John was taken to the Community Hospital in Long Beach for treatment of a possible rib injury. John had been steering the 16-foot outboard motorboat when it struck the wave that flipped it. He and Railsback, who was unharmed, were preparing the vessel to a race the following day between Ocean Park and Paradise Cove.[1]

The accident did not delay John and Ursula's plans to get married. She was 20 years old and, through the help of her powerful friend Harry Kissinger, had been able to apply for a green card as an alien of extraordinary ability. On February 2, 1957, John and Ursula had a very unconventional marriage ceremony in a Las Vegas wedding chapel. The minister arrived in a pink Cadillac and a taxi driver was asked to be the witness. Ursula was very emotional and cried during the entire ceremony. With John free from any work engagements, the newlyweds made plans to travel across Europe. Fluent in three languages, Ursula was John's translator during the trip.

Paris was their first stop, followed by a short visit to the Andress family in Switzerland. Then the couple crossed the Alps, driving through Italy to Rome, where they were guests of Italian producer Dino De Laurentiis and his actress-wife Silvana Mangano. A rumor circulated about the possibility of John and Ursula making a film together in Italy, tentatively called *Love Is My Shame*, but the project never materialized.

In Italy, John had the opportunity to watch *Knock on Any Door*. It was a curious experience that he enjoyed as he had been dubbed by an Italian who, according to him, had a lot of fire in his voice. John usually detested watching himself on the screen since he detested his own voice, which he thought was too monotone.

During his Roman holiday, John was approached by the FBI: The minions of the law were looking for information about John's old friend and colleague Mickey Knox, who had appeared in *Knock on Any Door* and *Saturday's Hero*. Knox had been accused of being a member of the American Communist Party. John, who was never involved in any political activity, did not divulge anything, but alerted his friend about the investigation.

While in Europe, John's agent informed him that there was interest in him playing the lead in *High Hell*, an American production scheduled to be shot in Europe. In urgent need of money, John accepted the offer without reading the script. *High Hell* was a gold rush story

Left to right: Al Mulock, Patrick Allen, Derek and Elaine Stewart during the shooting of *High Hell* in Switzerland in September 1957.

of the late 19th century, based on the novel *High Cage* by Steve Frazee. In the movie, five miners and a woman (Elaine Stewart) are trapped for the winter in a cabin atop a high peak in the Canadian Rockies.

At the end of August, John and Ursula traveled to London, where Burt Balaban, son of Paramount president Barney Balaban, and co-producer Arthur Meyer had assembled the rest of *High Hell*'s cast. On September 16, a Swissair plane carrying the stars and a crew of 30 members left London Airport heading for Basel in Switzerland. From there, the group went by train to Interlaken in the Bernese area, a location scouted a month earlier by the director, and made the steep 11,333-foot climb up the side of the Jungfrau mountain by mountain railway. From the very beginning, Balaban knew that the picture would be unsatisfactorily if made only in a studio. Location work would be necessary. Many places were suggested that resembled the original Canadian Rockies setting, but they were ruled out primarily because there was no nearby hotel that could accommodate the entire crew. The Cheddar Gorge in the Somerset area in England was also dismissed due to the unpredictability of the British weather; rain could have spoiled the tons of salt they intended to use as "snow." Switzerland turned out to be the best bet.

The weather was good at first, and despite the fact that several people got severe altitude sickness (including Balaban and Elaine Stewart), the shooting went along well. After a few days, once everyone was accustomed to the altitude, the sickness and headaches were almost gone. But a week later, a number of people, including Stewart, had to be rescued by local guides after being caught in a sudden blizzard while heading back to their lodge.

Another accident, one that could have jeopardized the entire production, occurred a few days later. While experimenting with a camera angle, Balaban slipped from the face of a glacier. Luckily, a guide present on the set grabbed a rope around his waist and held him dangling until a heroic John volunteered to help pull the filmmaker to safety.

After two weeks of hard work on location, the shooting continued for another four weeks at the Elstree Studios outside London. Over six tons of salt were needed to dress Stage 5 to make it look like a perfect replica of the snow-covered top of the mountain. Instead of the usual "quiet everyone please" when silence was required for shooting, Balaban blew a very effective blast on his Swiss Alpine Horn. Filming was going according to schedule and luckily the production was not held up by the wave of influenza which had swept England at the time, halting several other productions.

High Hell was released in the U.S. through Paramount in February 1958. Despite tepid reviews, the picture's total gross at the box office was more than satisfactory, doubling the $400,000 film cost.

The Dereks returned to Rome, where they spent a few months enjoying *la dolce vita*, along with the large colony of American stars in town working at Cinecittà Studios, the Italian Hollywood. John and Ursula loved strolling around the Eternal City; the Roman paparazzi often captured them while having a drink or dining in one of the many fancy establishments around the glamourous Via Veneto. Later that winter, the Dereks flew to the Middle East, stopping in Israel and later in Iran. In Teheran, they met the shah. John tried to pitch to him an idea of a movie that involved Arabian horses. Knowing that the Iranian ruler was a fan of blondes, he brought Ursula to the meeting.

South America was the Dereks' next destination. John had visited Argentina and Uruguay at the beginning of his career and had nice memories of that trip. In a letter he wrote to a friend in Tel Aviv, John and Ursula expressed their intention of putting together a "gaucho picture"—probably a variation of the original Arabian project. John was toying with the idea of becoming a director starring in his own films.

They returned to Italy where John found himself dead broke, a circumstance that forced him to star in two unmemorable Italian-French co-productions just to meet his financial needs. The first was a low-budget swashbuckler adventure, *Il Corsaro della Mezza Luna* (*The Pirate of the Half Moon*). It was filmed on the Tyrrhenian Sea not far from Rome. As in *Prince of Pirates*, John played a nobleman who turns to piracy after a traitor gains control of his homeland. Despite the questionable quality of the picture, shooting a film in Italy proved to be an extraordinary experience for John. Everything was done at a slow pace, in a very relaxing environment, and included a lot of improvisation. Working on this film was less rigorous than the Hollywood routine John was accustomed to.

Quickly forgotten in Europe, *Il Corsaro della Mezza Luna* did not receive any theatrical distribution in the U.S. The picture was released directly to American television seven years later.

John had only a few weeks between completion of *Il Corsaro della Mezza Luna* and the start of filming *Prisoner of the Volga*. The international cast was headed by John along with Italian actress Elsa Martinelli and English star Dawn Addams. They traveled by train from Rome to Belgrade where they were joined by thousands of extras playing the rugged boatmen of the Volga. John was a cavalry officer in Tsarist Russia, seeking revenge on an evil general who had seduced his new bride. Although this period adventure was set in

Russia, it was shot around Belgrade (then the capital of the former Yugoslavia), allegedly by two co-directors: Victor Tourjansky (born Vyacheslav Kostantinovich Turzhanskiy) and Arnaldo Genoino. The first was a Russian-born filmmaker who had fled his country during the Revolution, working as an actor, screenwriter and director in several European countries and in America. The second was an Italian journalist and painter who had some experience in directing a few shorts. A little mystery surrounds Genoino's persona: Some film scholars believe that the real Genoino was not involved in the production but it was just an alias of Victor Tourjansky. Why the filmmaker used both names (especially one of a real director) and had them both credited for the same film is unclear. That same year, both names were used once again in *Herod the Great* (1959). Several sources erroneously indicate that *Prisoner of the Volga* was adapted from *The Volga Boatman* (1926), a silent picture directed by Cecil B. DeMille. However, there was no correlation between the two films, John's being an adaptation of an original screenplay by Salka Viertel.

Elsa Martinelli in her autobiography remembered Tourjansky as a very old man, but still full of life and strength that made him appear like he was the youngest crew member. Every night, once the shooting was over, the cast would gather around the filmmaker, who would share his stories and tales about Russia, whence he was once forced to flee.[2]

Prisoner of the Volga opened first in Italy in January 1959, achieving very modest box-office success. When Paramount distributed it in the States in the summer of 1960, it failed to impress reviewers and its audiences. Many complained about the ineffective dubbing (due to a diverse international cast), resulting in a few unintentionally funny moments.

In September 1959, Austrian-born director-producer Otto Preminger requested that John be part of the stellar cast of *Exodus*, a $4 million production scheduled to be shot in Israel the following spring. Preminger was so impressed after reading the three-volume manuscript of an unpublished novel commissioned by MGM to Leon Uris about the founding of the state of Israel, that he convinced the studio to sell him back the rights for $75,000. Supported by financial backer Arthur Krim at United Artists, Preminger began to work on a script with Uris, but the author turned out to be a disappointing screenwriter. The filmmaker replaced him with Albert Maltz, but Dalton Trumbo, one of the

Derek and Elsa Martinelli in *Prisoner of the Volga* (1960).

Chapter 9. World Traveler

Eva Marie Saint and Derek in *Exodus* (1960).

Hollywood Ten, who was working under pseudonyms to get around the Blacklist, was the one who did the job.

With the first draft delivered, Preminger started the casting process. Paul Newman was his first and only choice for the lead Ari Ben Canaan, a young Haganah officer who sails the *Exodus*, a shipload of Jewish refugees, to Israel. Once he secured Newman for $200,000, he signed Academy Award winner Eva Marie Saint in the leading role of an American nurse. Gregory Ratoff, Sal Mineo, Ralph Richardson, Lee J. Cobb and Peter Lawford were cast in supporting roles. John was asked to play Taha, the leader of a small Arab village and the son of a prominent landowner who gave some land to Ari Canaan's father to set up a school for Jewish children. Taha and Ari grew up together and learned that it is possible for Jews and Arabs to co-exist in peace.

After six months of pre-production work, *Exodus* began filming in Israel on March 27, 1960, the first major picture ever to be made in the country. John and Ursula had landed at Lod International Airport outside Tel Aviv for the start of the production a few days earlier.

It was their second trip to the Holy Land in less than a year. The cast stayed at the Hotel Zion in Haifa, while the international crew of 160 members was scattered all around town. Preminger, whose brilliant directorial skills had earned him an Academy Award nomination in 1944 for *Laura* and the Cannes Film Festival's Palm d'Or in 1955 for *Carmen Jones,* was also temperamental and not particularly pleasant to work with. He notoriously bullied his actors, who often hated his methods. After learning how vehemently Preminger had dismissed Newman's suggestions about a few possible script revisions, John wisely decided not to interfere with the director's work to avoid any argument. He was assigned to a technical advisor, who taught him how to look like a genuine Arab *mukhtar* and properly wear an Arab headdress. He also had to grow a beard like he had for *The Ten Commandments*'s Joshua.

John and Newman got along perfectly on the set, and had great chemistry on screen. Their relationship was so famous that a Newman "biographer" years later absurdly implied that a sexual relationship existed between the two.[3]

The atmosphere on the set was often tense, especially at some of the locations where John had to play his scenes. To give a feeling of reality to the story, Preminger tried to shoot in the places where the historical events had occurred, and some sequences were filmed in areas where the Arabs predominated. While not materially affecting work on the picture, several threats were made, and an already difficult location became *more* difficult. Several incidents halted production. Preminger and some of the stars received anonymous letters urging them to quit and get out of Israel before it was too late. Cars from the production passing through Nazareth were stoned, including one with John. Rocks were hurled from rooftops at the cast and crew. In addition, Communists had published leaflets attacking the production. The only comment Preminger made to the press regarding those incidents: "I didn't come to Israel to have a picnic. I came to make a film."[4]

Every day El Al, the Israeli airline, flew the exposed film to the States to be printed so that rushes could be viewed by the moviemakers four and half days later.

John and the rest of the cast were lodged at the King David Hotel in Jerusalem for the last 12 days of filming, and then traveled to Cyprus for the entire month of June. Preminger completed *Exodus* ahead of schedule, finishing post-production in London, on time for a pre-holiday world premiere held in New York on December 15, 1960.

In spite of the great financial investment, *Exodus* was a major critical flop. Bosley Crowther of the *New York Times* offered one of the most brutal reviews, calling the picture "a massive, overlong, episodic, involved, and generically inconclusive 'cinerama' of historical and fictional events." The critic devoted a few ambiguous words to John's performance: "As for a well-bred friendly Arab whom John Derek plays stoically, it is hard to make out what he is thinking, except that he's in a nasty jam."[5] *Variety*'s point of view was positive: "The picture has the ingredients for mass audience pull: fresh, exciting, pictorial (Technicolor), atmosphere. Pulse-quickening action and agreeable romantic interest.... John Derek stands out too as an Arab."[6] The mixed reviews had an impact on audiences that flocked to the theaters and made the three-and-a-half-hour picture a major hit. *Exodus* grossed $8.7 million in North America and more than $22 million worldwide, becoming one of the top five American moneymakers of 1961.

On February 8, 1960, John received more public recognition when his name was engraved on a star on the Walk of Fame at 6531 Hollywood Blvd. in Hollywood, making John proud of his work, despite the highs and lows of his profession.

A few weeks after *Exodus* was completed, John learned that MGM was showing an interest in casting him as Dario, the leading character of *The Colossus of Rhodes*. "Sword-and-sandal" movies had become extremely lucrative in several European countries. Even though his name was number seven in the list of the prospective stars, after long discussions, the producers considered John's swashbuckling ability as an asset for this Spanish-Italian-French co-production and offered him the lead. The picture was scheduled to be filmed first on a soundstage at the C.E.A. Studios in Madrid, where John arrived in July 1960. There were problems on the very first day of work, when he refused to rehearse his scene with Alfio Caltabiano, the sword master hired for the occasion. John told director Sergio Leone that he was in perfect physical shape and that he had always done his own stunts. John felt it was unnecessary for him to rehearse the sequence, preferring to improvise in front of the cameras when they were ready to film it. Leone, who was making his directorial debut (he would become one of the most acclaimed Italian directors and credited as the creator of the Spaghetti Western genre), insisted on the importance of a rehearsal, explaining that he was incapable of shooting a battle scene without planning certain details that would have helped him position his camera. The director's insistence eventually convinced John. A few hours later, another argument arose when the filmmaker found his star in the shade of the soundstage framing the set with his fingers. John was apparently calculating the distance from the camera to the position where he was expected to stand in his first scene.

"You're supposed to be in front of the camera, not behind it." Leone exclaimed. John explained that he was only testing to see if the camera could pass between two columns, thinking that there wasn't enough space. Annoyed but without saying a word, Leone moved the fake pillar, showing the actor that they were on a set and therefore such things were possible, and gently reminding him that those were his (Leone's) problems since he was the director. John smiled, affirming that he had complete confidence in him and left.

But that wasn't the end of problems.[7] The next crisis came during the rehearsal of the first battle scene that John had agreed to do. Apparently, he waved his sword around all over the place, making fun of the master of arms, Caltabiano, who complained to Leone. The director summoned the star and with a thick Italian accent gave him a piece of his mind:

> You have just made the man whose job it is to help you rehearse look ridiculous. But in fact you are making *me* ridiculous. If you don't like the one who is rehearsing you, you come and tell *me* and demonstrate to me that he is incompetent. Right? But you have no grounds to complain that he is incompetent. It is about time you understood a few things around here. *I* am the director. If I say I want you with a beard, you put on one. If I change my mind five minutes later, and say you should be clean-shaven, you take off the beard. If I think you look better with half a beard, you put on half a beard. If I think about it for an hour and decided after all that you should have a full beard, you put it back on. You *do it*. And I am in the position to make you put on and take off that beard all day if I feel like it. I make the decisions. Savvy? Right now, you tell me you are one of the greatest actors in the world. In which case you need to find the greatest director in the world, which isn't me, I can assure you. I'm going to send a message to MGM and Procusa—the message being that, in my opinion, you have screwed things up. If you are still here tomorrow, then I'm off.[8]

Despite Andress's attempt to try to reconcile the situation between Leone and John, the young director was firm about having John sacked immediately; otherwise he was determined to quit. Two days later, the production officially fired John and secured the services of Rory Calhoun, who happened to be in Rome and available. John's reaction was to sue producer Procusa and its Italian co-producer Cine Produzione Associata before a Spanish labor tribunal. He claimed that his contract entitled him to final say in the staging of all scenes in which he appeared. A few months later, a court verdict granted him the sum of 1.6M pesetas (at the time $27,500). But in May 1961, after the production company appealed, Spain's Supreme Court judges reversed the lower court verdict. The decision was based on the incompatibility of introducing lawsuits brought by actors before labor tribunals, since actors were not ordinary workers and could only plead in ordinary law courts. John's ten-month effort to collect his money suddenly collapsed and he received no compensation. In October 1962, Italian newspapers reported that a court in Rome had ordered John to pay the production 27 million Italian lire in damages as compensation in addition to nine million Italian lire he received as an advance sum to star in *The Colossus of Rhodes*. The court confirmed the confiscation of some properties John had in Italy, which had been frozen a year earlier, until a final decision was reached.

Chapter 10

New Directions

"I'm not a charming guy: I don't have a Ferrari and fancy clothes. Just some good old American honesty."—John Derek

After almost four years of living and traveling around the globe, John and Ursula returned to California and bought a home at 15656 Vandorf Place, in the Encino Hills, not far from where Russell and Sean were living with Pati. The house was originally Bermuda-style architecture, but the couple transformed the pool area to Grecian style with an Arab tent as the pool house. The new home was furnished with items they had collected during their trips overseas, and later enriched by several props that producer Sam Spiegel gifted Ursula from the set of *Lawrence of Arabia*. John turned the hill behind the house into a big waterfall with a fishpond at the end. John spent much of his time supervising these renovations.

What prompted the Dereks to return to Los Angeles had mostly to do with a picture deal John expected to make in South America. After the project fell through, it became imperative that he accept an offer for a major recurrent role in a new CBS-TV series called *Frontier Circus*. (Prior to starting on *Frontier Circus*, John appeared in "Storm Over Eden," a May 1961 episode of the CBS series *Zane Grey Theatre*.)

"It's better than most of the [other shows] on television," John told John Hyams in a very candid interview, explaining why he agreed to star on *Frontier Circus*:

> I couldn't do what I wanted to do in this country, so I went to Europe to try and set up productions there which I could direct as well as act in. I was in Italy, Spain, France and Greece and I found every deal I became involved with was phony. It was based on lying and cunning. I started three pictures that never finished. I even went to Yugoslavia on one deal, was on location ready to shoot and found the producer didn't have a nickel in the bank. He floated everything on speculation. Europeans think that picture-making is a big chess game in which everyone else is a pawn.... The only nice thing I can say about being in Rome is that it's nice to be broke in—the easiest place in the world. All you need in Rome is a nice suit, a Ferrari, a friend with an apartment and some charm and you're in business. But I'm not a charming guy. I don't have a Ferrari and fancy clothes—just some good old American honesty. I believe in a clean deal—and I got taken to the cleaners....
>
> I don't want to be an actor. It's not my preference because when the workday is over, it's not a job you can leave behind. You're stuck with your face and prejudged constantly. People either love you to death or hate you. You're a piece of putty to producers and you're not asked to do anything, just look like something. I still want to produce and direct, but to do it you need your own money. I've come back here to get well-heeled, to make enough money to produce and direct and then I'll go back to Europe and try again.... In Europe, people are a little closer to the basics, they feed their faces, here they feed their ego.[1]

Frontier Circus was a weekly 60-minute series created by future *Star Trek* writer Samuel A. Peeples, about a one-ring circus traveling through the American West in the 1880s. The show was inspired by NBC's hit *Wagon Train*. After taking a ratings whipping from the

Clockwise from top left: Richard Jaeckel, Chill Wills and Derek in a publicity shot for the television series *Frontier Circus* (1961).

NBC show for several years, CBS approached the makers of that series about creating a series along the same lines, but different enough that it wouldn't be labeled an imitation. The result was *Frontier Circus* in which three leading characters (played by Chill Wills, Richard Jaeckel, and John) were the operators of T n' T Circus, America's first traveling circus. The actors were hired after a screen test. Jaeckel and John had been friends since they starred together in *Sea of Lost Ships*.

Chapter 10. New Directions

Although all the interiors were filmed on Revue Studios' back lot, the cast and the crew had to travel to various locations across California and Nevada to shoot each episode in a different setting with a famous guest star. These included Aldo Ray, Irene Dunne, Mickey Rooney, Sammy Davis, Jr., Vera Miles, Elizabeth Montgomery, Barbara Rush, Stella Stevens, Red Buttons and Thelma Ritter.

Although John had lost interest in being in front of a camera, he enjoyed playing Ben Travis the circus junior co-owner and Civil War veteran, a role that gave him the opportunity to work with wild animals. A believer in authenticity, he also convinced the producers to let him use his own horse on the show. John told the press,

> He's got such a great face. He's a six-year-old stallion named Mark Owen, a Quarter Horse whose head is being used for Quarter Horse standards. Heads, like he has, are hard to find. And I think he'll photograph very well. I always figured they cast interesting looking people on TV shows and in movies. So why not cast an interesting looking horse?[2]

Among the wild animals on the set, including an elephant, zebras, giraffes, tigers and bears, there was a big lion. Often sedated, the lion was still so threatening-looking that John refused to pose with his arm around the feline until Wally Worsley, Jr., the assistant director, first put his arm around its neck and had his picture taken. Only at that point did John agree to pose.

An Academy Award nominee for his supporting role in The *Alamo* (1960), Chill Wills was the only cast member who created some trouble with the production, due to his heavy drinking.

Don Weis, who had directed John in *The Adventures of Hajji Baba*, and William Witney, who helmed *The Outcast*, were the directors of some of the 26 episodes of the series. Another was future Academy Award winner Sydney Pollack. *The Hollywood Reporter* called *Frontier Circus* "a novelty, which in itself makes it a standout show of the current TV season… If it can sustain the pace of the opener, [it] could be a real winner." *Frontier Circus* ran every Thursday from October 1961 until May 1962 and they were also seen in England on the BBC. After a very good start, the ratings dropped consistently, forcing CBS to cancel the series at the end of the first season.

Ursula Andress was still relatively unknown in Hollywood. Even though she had been under contract to two major studios, she had not yet appeared in any film. One day a Columbia executive placed a call to the Dereks explaining that he had seen a photograph of Ursula on the desk of John's agent in London: a stunning black-and-white close-up of Andress, just out of a swimming pool, wearing a wet black shirt with the hair pulled back on one side. It was a shot John had taken when they were in Greece.

The man thought that she was very beautiful and offered her a small part in an upcoming action film. A script titled *Dr. No*, based on a book by English journalist-author Ian Fleming, arrived at the Dereks' doorstep a few days later. That same day, Kirk Douglas visited John and together the three read bits and pieces of the script, laughing out loud at the ludicrous plot.

Ursula asked John to read it in its entirely and give her his opinion. John did, and found it awful. Since she seemed uninterested in making films ("Acting is so much work, and I'm lazy," she would often tell the press), Ursula trusted her husband's judgment and was ready to pass. But then on second thought, John, who was seldom at home due to his seven a.m. to eight p.m. six-day-a-week *Frontier Circus* engagement, advised her to accept it. Knowing that Ursula was bored at home all day, he thought that taking that small job would provide his wife with a nice paid holiday in the Caribbean. Hence in January 1962, Ursula traveled to Jamaica where the picture was scheduled to be partially shot, and the rest … is history. Her character Honey Rider, coming out of the sea in a tight-fitting white bikini with a pearl diver knife strapped to her waist, became an iconic scene in film history. *Dr. No* turned her into an overnight international star: the first, and ultimately the most popular Bond Girl in the 007 franchise.

In February, while Ursula was in Jamaica, their new home was inundated by a mudslide during some heavy rains. John was buried in mud for 20 minutes and only saved by their huge Afghan hound, Dimitri Mazuri Shem of Scheherazade. A few months later, John filed a suit in Superior Court seeking $190,000 in damages from his four neighbors and three companies, claiming they had divided and graded a hill near his property, causing a change in the natural flow of water, and this resulted in the mudslide.[3]

In March 1962, the American press announced that John, after completing *Frontier Circus*, would direct his wife in *May the Sea Take This Island,* a movie he had written, set to be filmed in Yugoslavia. The project was aborted for lack of funds. While Ursula's career was taking off, with offers pouring in from all over the world, John was struggling to try to direct his first film. Then in the summer of 1963 it was confirmed that Afilmco, a production company formed by Ricky DuPont, Leo Samuels and Sanford Fishbein, had given the green light to *Nightmare in the Sun,* a crime tale scripted by Fanya Foss and Ted Thomas. John would co-produce and co-star with Ursula. "Officially," former actor Marc Lawrence (*Cloak and Dagger*, *Key Largo*, *The Asphalt Jungle*) was the director, but John later became

Derek and Ursula Andress in *Nightmare in the Sun* (1964).

an uncredited co-director. For the first time in his career, John co-produced and co-directed a film in which he also starred. He played a cross-country hitchhiker falsely accused of the murder of a boredhouse wife (Ursula) with whom he had a brief affair.

In an interview, Lawrence revealed that *Nightmare in the Sun* was made possible by the bizarre millionaire Ricky DuPont, who was willing to put up a quarter of a million dollars on the condition that her name appear in the credits and that the moviemakers respected astrology on the days of the shooting. Lawrence told DuPont that her request was impossible to satisfy because if the other people involved in the project knew the provenance of the money,

> they'd cut my throat. If I sell the picture and your name is on the screen, I won't get a penny for it.... Then I cut John Derek in as my partner because he gave me Ursula Andress, who was a hot girl then. He said, "Let's do a nude scene." I thought, Jesus, if she does a nude scene at the beginning when Aldo Ray rapes her, it'll sell the picture. The day before we started to shoot, he changed his mind.[4]

The Daily Cinema labeled *Nightmare in the Sun* "a steamy tale of sex and violence in a torrid Western setting." During the shoot (it was filmed on location in Calabasas, California), the script was constantly revised, since the co-screenwriter, Fanya Foss, was Lawrence's wife and part of the on-site crew. The director was able to involve several big names he personally knew: Aldo Ray, Sammy Davis, Jr., Keenan Wynn, Richard Jaeckel and Robert Duvall all agreed to play bits for a minimal fee. The filming was completed within budget after just two weeks of work. Once Lawrence assembled a rough cut, DuPont bought it from him for a $50,000 guarantee against 23 percent of net grosses. Yet only a $9,000 payment was made by the millionaire, who was sued by the director. A few months later, DuPont sued Afilmco demanding $500,000 she allegedly invested in the picture with the understanding that Fishbein, the second producer, would invest the same sum. After the film was completed, according to DuPont, Fishbein transferred assets from Afilmco to a company named Zodiac Film, assets she was now claiming. Both lawsuits, whose outcomes were undisclosed, dragged on and on, delaying the film's release for almost two years. Finally, *Nightmare in the Sun* had its American limited release in the fall of 1964, followed by an opening in England in February 1965. *Variety*, one of the few publications to review it, called it a "trite script with generally poor performances."[5] The U.K. *Monthly Film Bulletin* opined, "Photographed in effectively stark colors, intriguingly cast and containing a number of out-of-the-way touches, this is nonetheless a thriller which fails to thrill."[6]

John's dream to become a full producer-director ultimately came true in the spring of 1964, when he struck a two-film deal for Ursula with F8 Production and Hammer Films producer Anthony Hinds, who wanted her as the lead in *She*, a film to be distributed by Seven Arts. Acting as Ursula's agent, John agreed to have his wife to star in the picture on the condition that F8 Production would financially back it and Seven Arts distributed *No Toys for Christmas*, a movie Ursula was about to make under John's direction.

John had secured the rights to Anthony March's 1945 war novel *Quit for the Next*, loosely based on the U.S. cavalry troops' actions during the retreat to Bataan in the Philippines in 1942. John asked screenwriter Vance Skarstedt, whom he knew from *Frontier Circus*, to include in the script some of the adventures that he and some of his friends had during their time in the army. Skarstedt had to also insert into the original all-male story a female character that would allow Ursula "to let her personality come out." John told a *Newsweek* interviewer, "Without being beautiful, this will be the best thing that ever happened to her. You'll have to fall in love with her—not as a sexpot but as a human being."[7]

After casting his friends Richard Jaeckel and the athletic Ron Ely (who would soon portray Tarzan on the 1966 NBC series *Tarzan*), John and Ursula flew to Manila to begin filming. Actor Jock Mohoney, an old friend of John's who was in the area shooting another movie, made an uncredited cameo as a major. Since the film's budget was low, Mahoney agreed to be symbolically paid with a free hamburger lunch.

From the very beginning, *No Toys for Christmas* proved to be a frustrating experience for John and his small crew. The equipment, rented locally, turned up to be obsolete and unreliable. The local technicians were, according to John, "good eager hearts, but without the ghost of an idea of how a professional picture is made."[8] Many of the camera trucks were so wobbly that the best camera angles had to be abandoned. While filming in the little village of Cavinti, a powerful typhoon hit the area, leaving three inches of mud all around the set. The houseboat where John and Ursula were sleeping was lifted out of the river by the typhoon and deposited in a swimming pool when the water level of the nearby Pagsanjan River rose over 35 feet.

In the local press, John openly criticized the lack of communication between his American crew and the Filipino actors. As a result of some remarks which he allegedly made, one of his Filipino actors, Ronald Remy, quit the picture. Meanwhile, the locals complained about John's lack of direction, the fact that they never got call slips and that he seemed to shoot according to his whims. A few days later, when the film was retitled *The*

Ursula Andress and Derek in *Once Before I Die* (1966).

26th Cavalry, John added fuel to the fire, declaring to the media that he *had* planned to produce another three or four films in the Philippines—but not now. "I'm 37 and I don't want to be 62 in a year," he joked. At the same time, he harshly criticized the "lack of respect by the [Philippines] government to the film industry." He complained that import duties and taxes on movie equipment were so high that no updated equipment seemed to have been acquired for years by local moviemakers. "There is a great potential in the Philippines for making pictures, but the government is missing the boat by not encouraging quality movie production, not only by domestic companies but by foreign film groups." He also stressed that if the right kind of movies filmed in the Philippines were circulated around the world, they would be the most effective propaganda for the country.[9]

Some of Ursula's scenes had to be postponed after she suffered a bad fall while riding a carabao, a local black water buffalo. That same night, she broke out in a rash and realized that she was allergic to the animal's hair. Despite the lengthy stay on location, the completion of the picture had to be rushed since Ursula was expected in England on the set of *She*.

In an interview, Richard Jaeckel called the film "very beautiful. But the released version was completely re-cut, and in fact cut to pieces."[10] Seven Arts not only butchered it, changing the title to *Once Before I Die,* but shelved it for two years. That explained the lack of reviews at the time of its release in December 1966. According to John, *Once Before I Die* had been a way for the producers to secure Andress' presence in a more prestigious production at a bargain price.

Once Before I Die marked the end of John's career as an actor. Without any regrets, he left a profession that he had come to detest. He was finally beginning to enjoy the ability to go anywhere without anybody recognizing him.

From now on, all his efforts were concentrated on his professional photography and into directing and producing his own films.

Chapter 11

Linda

"I spent many hours staring into his beautiful eyes."—Linda Evans

In June 1965, a year prior to *Once Before I Die*'s release, *Playboy* magazine published a 12-photo nude centerfold of Ursula Andress. Hugh Hefner and photography editor Vince Tajiri suggested to John that they should use the backdrop of a Los Angeles mansion. But not all the pictures taken captured her extraordinary beauty. John knew exactly what made her gorgeous, enhancing her cheekbones and, the shape of her eyes, after having studied her intensely. Being a true aesthete, John preferred using shots he took during the filming of *Once Before I Die* with the exotic backdrop of the Philippines jungle. The issue was a hit.

In prior years, John had developed a passion for photography, born from an appreciation for other photographers. (He admired Leni Riefenstahl's work, and the beauty of some of Richard Avedon's photography.) John progressed into a real profession during his travels around the world. One of his first published works appeared in 1963 when *Look* magazine featured Ursula on a cover and in an article illustrated with John's photographs. As Andress pointed out years later, he became a perfectionist:

> One thing that made John different [from other photographers] whenever he took a photograph, he would not allow a lousy photograph of you to be seen. You could offer him anything. If you have the wrong position and didn't look beautiful, he would never let anything to be published. He protected people he shot in every way to show them in the best way they can be seen. He did everything.[1]

When the *Playboy* issue hit news stands, the Dereks' marriage was on the rocks. Ursula was alone in Hong Kong filming *Up to His Ears* (1965) opposite French heartthrob Jean-Paul Belmondo, who had become an international star after the success of 1960's *Breathless* and *Two Women*. Some whispered that John and Ursula had several fights over suspicions that she'd been cheating on John with Ron Ely before her departure. Russell, John's son, now 14 years old, moved in after being in trouble with Santa Barbara police for stealing a car. All his life, John had been an absent father. Now the authorities insisted Russ needed a father figure, and John agreed to have his son live with him. Russ did not stay out of trouble and spent time in a juvenile jail on more than one occasion. Meanwhile, Pati sued John for $27,000 in unpaid alimony. The court awarded her $14,000, which John still refused to pay.

During the daily long-distance telephone conversations John was having with Ursula in Hong Kong, he realized that she was acting funny. When gossip from her Far East set leaked about an alleged torrid affair between Andress and Belmondo, John became impatient. He knew that Ursula, "the wild bird," as he often defined her, was a free spirit. In the past seven years of their marriage, they had made just one promise to each other: to be honest no matter what. But this time, John sensed there was some truth in the circulating rumor, despite Ursula's insistent denial. John flew to Hong Kong to confront his wife, who kept denying a relationship with Belmondo (who was married for 14 years with three children). Eventually the truth came out. John was hurt, especially by the fact that Ursula had deceived him. Before flying back to California, he broke up with her, commanding that she not return home.

Their separation proved to be extremely difficult, especially at the beginning, since John was still very much in love with her. Even though they were no longer together, he loved her. But with time, they became best friends. Theirs was a true friendship that lasted a lifetime. (After John's death, she was quoted as saying, "I see John as the most important man in my life.") Ursula told interviewer Roderick Mann: "John still has all my things at his house in California. There's no point in him in sending them here until I have a place of my own. Yes, John will always be in my life even if I marry again 20 times. I had a fantastic time with John, but things happen and now we are better apart. But he is my best friend: the only human being I really trust."[2]

Linda Evans in a publicity shot for TV's *The Big Valley* (1965).

John was not a rich man and quitting the acting profession made it harder for him to earn a living. But his reputation as a good photographer was slowly growing and he amassed a small list of clients that used his professional photographer services. He was always on the lookout for new subjects, and his next great find came after watching a few episodes of *The Big Valley*, a popular western television series. Set on a ranch, the series starred Barbara Stanwyck and a beautiful 23-year-old blonde named Linda Evans. John called the producers to ask if he could photograph the young Evans. Informed of John's exceptional skills behind the camera, Evans accepted. John did not know that the teenager had a big crush on him. The actress wrote in her memoir,

> When I was 12, I saw the movie *The Adventures of Hajji Baba*, which I thought was incredibly romantic. With a turbaned John riding across the sand dunes on an Arabian horse.... I had a picture of John over my bed (next to Tab Hunter) and I spent many hours staring into his beautiful eyes. I remember being heartsick when I read in a movie magazine that he was married with two children.[3]

Linda Evanstad was born in Hartford, Connecticut, on November 18, 1942. At six years old, she moved with her parents, both professional ballroom dancers, and her sister Charlie to Hollywood where her grandparents were living. Although painfully shy, she dreamed of being part of the entertainment industry and studied drama at Hollywood High School. An actress friend insisted she screen-test for a commercial, which she eventually got. A few commercials later, John Forsythe (her future "husband" on the '80s series *Dynasty*) cast her in an episode of his TV series *Bachelor Father*, which was followed by her appearance in five episodes of *The Adventures of Ozzie and Harriet*. Three years later, after she changed her last name to Evans, she got her breakout role as Audra Barkley on *The Big Valley*.

John and Linda met for the first time in the fall of 1965. Linda agreed to be photographed at John's house, a location she found extremely romantic. To her, his house was like one of the *Hajji Baba* sets with handmade Oriental-looking furniture covered by silks and furs and candles everywhere. John shot pictures of Linda the entire day. They met again several times in the following weeks. Despite swearing that he would never really love anyone else after Ursula broke his heart, John was quickly smitten by Linda's beauty and personality. He told an interviewer, "We realized that we wanted to spend more time by ourselves and to cut a long story short, she came to live with me. It was really easy to live with Linda because she is very good and very affectionate. Linda has a very tender way of dealing with people. She is very different from Ursula."[4] Often in the evening, Linda would return home after filming *The Big Valley* to find the house filled with twinkling candles and a romantic dinner set by John in front of the fireplace.

In January 1966, newspapers announced John's intent to divorce Ursula, but the couple did not legalize their separation until April when Ursula flew to Los Angeles from the London set of *Casino Royale*.

That spring, John's old friend and colleague, actor Don Murray (whose debut in 1956 in *Bus Stop* opposite Marilyn Monroe made him one of Hollywood's most promising new stars) decided to cast Linda in a movie he had written while intending to produce and star in it. *Night on the Street, Cock a Doodle Doo* and *Tale of the Cock* were titles used at one point or another to advertise the film, which opened in North America three years later as *Childish Things*. Murray asked John to be the cinematographer, knowing of his experience in still photography. On the set, John cooperated so closely with director David Nelson that they eventually shared a co-director credit. Limited in budget, Murray employed only the minimum crew required by union regulations, which meant: a camera loader, two men on sound, and a couple of electricians. John would have preferred to bootleg the picture, avoiding the union altogether and employing young men interested in filmmaking. He explained in an interview,

> I wanted to work with people who would be excited about what we were trying to do. It is very frustrating when no one in the crew is enthusiastic and excited about trying to do something new, taking the time to do something different with the camera to get something unusual on the film. I have been in pictures longer than any of them, and yet they all look bored with it. I would much rather have gone down to UCLA and picked up some kids who wanted to go into directing and photography, kids who are really interested in film, and worked with them.[5]

Telling the story of the spiritual conversion of an immoral man, *Childish Thing* was loosely based on the life of Tom Harris, a man who, thrown out of the army, divided his life between amateur boxing and collecting money for the mob. After marrying a girl he had raped years earlier, he radically changed his life, redeemed by love and spirituality. The picture was all shot on location in Southern California with additional scenes in Las Vegas.

It briefly played in Beverly Hills in July 1969 without a distributor in hopes of attracting one, but the mixed reviews, condemning the dull and melodramatic story, did not attract someone interested in releasing it nationwide. The film was shelved until a new production

Linda Evans in a lobby card for *Tale of the Cock* aka *Childish Things* aka *Confessions of Tom Harris* (1969).

company, Getaway Films, a branch of the American Baptist Convention, decided to purchase it. Watered down (several scenes were considered too violent or sexy), the picture was released nationwide at the end of 1972 as *Confessions of Tom Harris*. It was generally ignored by the public and critics.

In a revealing September 1966 interview with British editor Donald Zec, John opened up for the first time publicly about his ongoing relationship with Linda:

> After Ursula and I were divorced, people started calling me a Svengali. It's true, I guess. I suppose all men are like that. I guess I'm the same. Give me a horse, a dog or a woman and I have to be the Svengali. But something went wrong with Ursula. She lost her identity completely. She became an anatomical animal. All body. But with Linda it's going to be different. Love is the most important thing in her life. Her love for me, the success, she'll take as it comes.... She has a very sensuous quality. On the face of it, she's a tomboy. Underneath there is a great woman eager to break out. Phenomenal figure too, for a girl of 23. She was not the sort of girl I'd normally be attracted to. I'd seen her on television and as far as her looks go ... pow! But she wasn't my type. Then we met ... what bugged me.... She was the first girl who came into my life that didn't try to flirt with me.... I've known her for a year and the change in her is remarkable. She's more sophisticated, less naïve, even her body has taken a new dimension.... She is a very good listener.... We talk a lot and I made her visually aware of the world around her.... I love beautiful things, beautiful women in particular.... Funny thing about women whose beauty is the best thing they can offer. They take on the characteristics of the last person they met.... Supposing you'd met Ursula and you liked her. Well, you'd like me too because so much of her was me too. If the last person Linda met today was the man at the gas station, then you can be sure she'd be talking like him.[6]

John was an incredibly romantic companion. He'd organize intimate dinners, horseback rides into the sunset, long walks and picnics on a beach with their dog Hajji. He loved to make gifts for Linda: soft leather clothes, a pair of boots, western-style jewelry. Every night he'd write her a love letter that made her feel like the most important woman on Earth. "Men rarely focus that much attention on someone they love," Linda said in an interview. "John isolated the world, and you became his world." He'd often organize camping trips in an Excalibur styled after a 1928 Mercedes convertible, and set the white tents in an Arabic style where they would spend their magical nights. John and Linda were inseparable, and even though they did not have a lot of money, he convinced her to stop working. On John's advice, after 112 episodes, she dropped out of *The Big Valley*. He represented for her a sort of a father figure (John was 16 years her senior) since she had lost her own father when she was 15. She put her career in his hands, encouraging him to do everything for her. He would help her choose her clothes, her look, and what to eat. She slowly gained more confidence thanks to his advice. Since no job offers came that John thought suitable, she began to assist John in his work as photographer.

John's ability behind the camera reached Evel Knievel, the popular motorcycle stunt performer. Knievel planned to do his most challenging jump ever at Caesars Palace in Las Vegas on New Year's 1967 and wanted John to shoot it. John agreed to film using two cameras in different locations. For this reason, one of them had to be operated by Linda. She had learned from John how to use a still camera, but needed a crash course in motion picture photography. Once they got to Vegas, Knievel told them that he was feeling unsure about the stunt (planned to be done outside on two ramps set on either side of the casino's fountains), but since too much was at stake, he would do it no matter what. John's immediate reaction was to quit, not interested in working with someone who thought they would likely fail. But since it was too late to find replacements, ultimately he agreed to shoot.

The following day the couple positioned John's camera on the side view, and Linda's at the far end of the jump. Linda's challenge was to keep the camera focused throughout the entire stunt since the motorcycle was riding toward her. After shooting off the first ramp, Evel dropped toward the second ramp, and crashed down with the bike slipping out from under him. Security and emergency responders immediately surrounded him. His injuries were not serious. The stuntman kept his word, paying John for his camerawork—footage that Knievel later used in a movie about his reckless life.

In a lengthy *Los Angeles Times Sunday* interview, John talked about how he was striving for a wardrobe that was practical, comfortable and dignified. He explained that to solve the problem, he had started designing his own clothes, inspired by his stay in the Philippines when filming *Once Before I Die*. He had returned to the U.S. with a safari jacket and wardrobe of 50 pieces. "Seven–dollar pants are what I want because I'm always on my knees. I want to be able to stuff camera equipment in my pockets, noy pay homage to them." He talked about the possibility of producing a line of men's fashions "where you don't have to break in your shirt at the expense of your neck."[7] John was now in partnership with Jack Hanson, the owner of the popular sportswear chain-store Jax, who agreed to produce John's new film *A Boy ... a Girl*. John did not dismiss the idea of extending their collaboration into a joint venture deal with men's fashion.

Hanson gave John a budget of $200,000 and complete artistic freedom. John wrote, directed, photographed, designed the costumes and wrote the lyrics of its five songs.

A Boy ... a Girl starred 15-year-old Dino Paul Martin, son of actor-singer Dean Martin. Dino previously had a couple of uncredited roles in two of his father's films. Opposite

Martin, John cast an unknown teenager named Airion Fromer, whom he had spotted on a beach. Although cast in a minor role, Kerwin Mathews (best known for playing the titular heroes in *The 7th Voyage of Sinbad* [1958], *The 3 Worlds of Gulliver* [1960] and *Jack the Giant Killer* [1962]) was the only solid name in the production.

The story was about a young teenage couple who get involved in a triangle love affair with an older, more experienced man, something very much in line with the hippie style of the time, with dialogue about love, peace and LSD. According to Sean Derek, many of his father's friends constantly teased him, saying that the picture was John's own sexual fantasy.

Since both of the movie's stars were minors, a nude scene in the desert had to be performed with body doubles behind a white screen. A welfare worker supervised the set at all times. "It was silly," Martin commented in an interview two years later, when the film was released, "because you don't really see anything: I could have done the scene with tight trunks." He added, "I hardly remember the picture. I made it more than two years ago, when I was 15. It was fun to do. We shot it all over California, and I got a chance to ride my motorbike a great deal. I was riding it before I could drive a car. Steve McQueen taught me."[8]

According to Hanson, the picture, shot in 16mm (later blown up into 35mm), "took two years to make because the directors and the actors had to have time out for other commitments. The two stars were in school."[9] In reality, the producer had struggled to find a distributor and only in the spring of 1969 was *A Boy ... a Girl* finally released through United Artists. The opening night was scheduled on April 24, followed by a big party at The Daisy, a nightclub owned by Hanson and his wife.

The premiere was a disaster. First, to get into the United Artists Westwood Theatre in Westwood, the spectators had to cross a picket line thrown by some employees of a local union. Twenty minutes into the film, someone broke a stink bomb into the air conditioning system set into a wall of the theater. About 600 people were forced to abandon the auditorium and the screening was cancelled. The film was re-screened the following afternoon, mostly for reviewing. Critics panned it. "[A] stinker ... a bomb of purest ray serene ... lush mush.... It's instant camp," wrote the *Los Angeles Times*. "Amateurish and overly contrived," was *Variety*'s verdict. John's photography was found to be imaginative but mostly overdone. In 1970, the picture was re-edited and released under the title *The Sun's Up*, again to no great acclaim.

An advertisement for the worldwide premiere of *A Boy ... a Girl* (1969).

In 1969, after three years living together, John finally proposed to Linda. She accepted with great enthusiasm and the two drove with John's daughter in their Cadillac to Tijuana, Mexico, to tie the knot. Like in his previous marriage with Ursula, a taxi driver was John's witness, while Linda's bridesmaid was Sean. It was a quick, simple ceremony, with both lovers wearing off-white jeans. John wanted to keep the wedding a secret from the public mostly because he wanted to tell Ursula at the right time, but gossip columnist Rona Barrett found out and spread the news.

Although John and Linda's marriage seemed to be idyllic, Ursula continued to be a strong presence in John's life. Friends kept telling Linda that John was still in love with his second wife and sooner or later he would return to Ursula. Ursula often wrote affectionate letters to John, even sending "Happy Anniversary" cards on the date of their own marriage and visited him when in town.

The truth was that John was still very fond of Ursula but, as he candidly admitted in more than one interview, he was not in love with her any more and had no intention to rekindle their relationship.

Since no interesting job offers had come in for Linda, John decided to make her the star of *Wildflowers,* a film based on a script he had written that he intended to direct and produce in Ursula's homeland. When the Dereks landed in Zurich, they bought a silver-gray Jaguar and drove to Ursula's family in Berne. There they were reached by Andress' attorney, who told them that under the Swiss law, John was still married to Ursula, and hence a bigamist. (The couple had been divorced for years, but apparently not under the Swiss law. Ursula in fact had not bothered to register the divorce with local authorities, most likely because of tax issues.) "Tell her to get it sorted out," John yelled at his ex-wife's attorney. "I think she must have sorted it out, because Linda and I made the picture (real rubbish) and went back to our house in California."[10]

Wildflowers was about a woman's incestuous fantasy with her brother. It was mostly shot in the Swiss Alps, but also in France and Norway, since the couple drove all over Europe. John was dissatisfied with the outcome and decided not to release it. Linda insisted that it was "something more than a puppet part" and was relieved that it did not get released.[11]

A few photographs taken on the set portraying a stunning nude Linda appeared in *Playboy* in July 1971. According to John,

> Before a camera, Linda is absolutely natural and uninhibited—with or without clothing. So often a woman tries to act seductive during a nude shooting, usually because she must overcome a fear of being photographed unclad. But then the finished picture strikes you as fake. That's never the result when I photograph Linda. She's completely at ease and doesn't have to fear the camera, because she's in extraordinary shape—as you can tell from my pictures.[12]

John and Linda's ten-year marriage was a happy one. She became a close friend of John's daughter Sean ("A wonderful stepmother," Sean recalled in her memoir), who lived with them for a while, and of Ursula, accepting her larger-than-life personality. "Our life was still as good as the first day," John admitted years later. "Everything was perfect between us, and suddenly I spoilt everything. I don't know why she didn't cut my throat. We needed a young girl to star in a film. I had written the script and intended to direct it. We hunted all over and finally we found Bo."[13]

Chapter 12

Bo

"I'm not a magician. I make women look beautiful, because I shoot beautiful women! I can't make a silk purse out of a sow's ear."—John Derek

After the disappointing result of *Wildflowers*, John and Linda agreed that the next film would be healthier for their relationship if she didn't have to act in it, since John often displayed very impatient and bossy behavior on the set. Having just completed a new script entitled *And Once Upon a Time*, John planned to shoot it on a Greek island. He organized a casting call to find the right female protagonist. Among many girls auditioning, a striking 16-year-old, Cathy, stood out from the crowd.

Christened Mary Cathleen Collins, known as Cathleen or Cathy, she was born on November 20, 1956, in Long Beach, California. Her father Paul was of Irish descent and her mother Norma Bass of German-Dutch descent. Cathy was the oldest of four children (the others were Colin, Kelly and Kerry). Paul Collins had a motorcycle shop in Inglewood, California, and supplied the motorbikes for the film *Bye Bye Birdie* (1963) starring Ann-Margret. Soon Ann-Margret and her husband Roger Smith became close family friends. When things got financially difficult for the Collins, Norma learned hairdressing and makeup and went to work for Ann-Margret as her personal assistant. Cathy, who never took school seriously, preferred to spend her days hanging out with friends at the beach, mostly surfing or tanning. When their parents separated, the Collins' children stayed with Norma. Ann-Margret's agent friend Kevin Casselman suggested Cathy take modeling and acting lessons, and audition for commercials or a small movie role. When Norma heard that John Derek, one of her favorite actors from the '50s, was casting a role in his next film, she accompanied her daughter to the audition.

Impressed by Cathy's beauty, John arranged a photo test in the Collins' backyard, followed by a second the next day at his house, where he profited from proper lightning equipment and Linda's help. Although the results of the printed photographs were stunning (many were shots of Cathy by the pool wearing a bikini borrowed from Linda), John was still unsure if she really was the right girl for the film. "At the time, Bo was rather lazy, she lived at the beach, ate hamburgers and her life was reduced to surfing with friends ... she didn't seem right to me," John confessed years later.[1] At Linda's insistence, he reluctantly agreed to cast her. Since Cathy did not yet have any acting experience (she had only been a model for a corn flakes company), John asked his wife to coach his new discovery. The two women spent a lot of time together, getting along very well.

However, as soon as Cathy started rehearsing with Peter Hooten, the male lead, she had a series of serious arguments with John. More than once she thought of quitting while *he* thought of replacing her. "They argued about everything," Evans wrote in her memoir.

"From his wanting to dye her hair brown to his thinking she needed to lose weight."[2] Eventually Cathy agreed to change her hair color. Finally, in November 1973, after the production had been delayed two months because of financial problems, the crew, including Cathy's mother Norma, flew to the island of Mykonos.

In Greece, the quarrels between Cathy and John escalated with Linda in the middle trying to patch things up. When Evans was offered a guest star role in an episode of the TV series *Banacek* with George Peppard, she accepted mostly for financial reasons. The money John had was tied up into the film production and very little was left to pay everyday bills. Leaving Greece, but worrying about the relationship between her husband and his young film star, Linda returned from California three weeks later, astounded to find that John and his barely–16 leading lady had fallen in love. Linda: "Some part of me couldn't believe that their relationship would last. It made no sense; he was 30 years older than Bo—surely he'd come back."[3] She was wrong. That was just the beginning of an extraordinary 25-year love story that led to a marriage lasting until John's death.

John often stated that there was something different in Cathy, something in her beauty, that made him believe that in time she would blossom into a very special person. His hunch was right and slowly she became the love of his life. After her husband admitted the affair, Linda left the set and flew back home.

At the beginning, the relationship between John and Cathy was not a bed of roses. He was full of guilt for the way he had treated Linda, resembling the way Ursula had left him for Belmondo. Meanwhile, Cathy had to face her mother, who was outraged after discovering the affair while reading her daughter's diary. Despite all the tensions, the picture was finished in eight weeks as scheduled. After shooting the final sequences on the small island of Delos, Cathy and the rest of the crew was ready to go back home. But John invited Cathy to Germany for the film's post-production. After Cathy convinced Norma that hers was not a mere infatuation, Cathy traveled with John to Munich and later to Venice. She left him in Italy and returned to her mother's home. When John was finally ready to go back to the States, he learned that since Cathy was still a minor, he could be charged on his return home with statutory rape, contributing to a delinquency of a minor and a slave act. In fact, a complaint had already been anonymously filed. A few weeks later, Cathy left for Germany and took a long car trip around Europe with John, as he had done years earlier with Ursula and with Linda. This time he feared every time they cross a border that he would be arrested by Interpol. In the meantime, the American press had become aware of the relationship between John Derek and an unknown underage girl. A Svengali, "a person who exercises a controlling or mesmeric influence on another, especially for a sinister purpose"—this was the term the media recurrently used from that moment on to define John's relationship with ex-wives and for the latest girlwho had "fallen under his spell."

In a letter dated November 9, 1974, John expressed his concern over the dubbing in the film. It was "on the minus side of mediocre," especially for the male character, which he felt handicapped the part, along with other minor problems that he wished could have been fixed for the final print. "I think the film is exactly what the script said it would be … A SWEET LITTLE FAIRY TALE," John writes full of hope.

A few weeks later, John learned that Studio Bavaria had confiscated the negative of the film, locking him out of the final stages of the editing process. One of the two producers, Canadian Edmund McMullen (the other was Kevin Casselman, Cathy's agent), had failed to pay long-overdue film processing bills to the studio lab; therefore the studio had decided to seize the picture until the payment was made in full. The film remained in a German vault until 1980.

Meanwhile, John and Cathy traveled to Mexico. After a few days in Merida, the couple reached Tijuana, where John decided to settle down in a small hotel while Cathy returned to her mother's house. During that long trip, Cathy had often expressed the desire to change her name. After playing the name game with John and some friends, someone said they knew a girl named Boo, which Cathy found cute. Somebody else mentioned Bo and she liked it instantly, so "Bo" became the final choice.

While in Tijuana, John was told by Linda's attorney, who represented her in their divorce, that he (John) could return home—but advised him to avoid being seen alone in public with Bo until she became of age. In the following three months, Bo lived at her mother's house. She'd visit John in Encino during the day, often chaperoned by one of her younger sisters, and be back to her family's house by bedtime. On November 20, 1974, Bo's 18th birthday, she moved in with John. They happily lived together until they were out of money. A second mortgage was arranged but the money did not last long. John, who had no intention of resuming his acting carrier, refused a million-dollar salary to appear in a TV series based on a Harold Robbins bestseller, preferring instead to sell the house and travel again by van.

On June 10, 1976, the couple drove to Las Vegas and at two a.m. got married in a tiny chapel named Wee Kirk o' the Heather. A female minister performed the rite wearing pajamas, while the bride and the groom were in jeans and a sweater. This time the witness was not a taxi driver, as with John's previous marriage, but someone from the chapel. The newlyweds spent their first night sleeping in their van in a Caesars Palace parking lot. The following day, Bo flew to Canada where she was expected to film *Orca—The Killer Whale* (1977) opposite Richard Harris and Charlotte Rampling. John reached her ten days later in the van. On the set, he got into a row with one of Bo's co-stars, a young actor who falsely claimed to have started a romance with her. Like a *deus ex machina*, Richard Harris solved the situation by exposing the liar. *Orca* was produced by the Italian producer Dino De Laurentiis, who had signed Bo up exclusively. After having a few disagreements with John, the producer released her from her contractual obligations.

For a year and a half, John and Bo lived in the van, traveling all over America. They finally parked the vehicle, first in a Solvang parking lot and later at the ranch of a friend, where they stayed for a few months. However, living in such a limited space was beginning to hurt their relationship, especially when the money ran out again. Things slowly improved after they spent an evening at Hugh Hefner's mansion (the *Playboy* magazine owner was an old friend of John). Years later, Hef described John as "an exquisite man, strikingly handsome, a woman's man, a man who is sufficiently sensitive so that he is able to relate to women."

An X-rated film was showed in the entrepreneur's private screening room, but many guests, especially women, refused to watch it, claiming that pornographic films were boring and tasteless. Consequently, John and Bo got involved in an animated conversation about pornography. It was the general opinion that X-rated films were all badly made and often degrading to women. Unexpectedly, a lady among the guests asked John, who was well known for his love for beauty and women, if one day he would be interested in directing a tasteful X-rated film: something sexy, erotic, but at the same time appealing to a female audience. John was intrigued by the idea. When a couple of people that same night offered to sponsor such a film, offering altogether $30,000 with the understanding that John would find another $30,000 to finance it, a joint venture was formed. Two weeks later, John completed the script of *Love You!* which, according to him, would be the first classy and well-produced porno ever made. For this story of two young couples who decide to swap partners on a secluded island, John appointed Bo as producer. Her task consisted of raising the $30,000 needed to meet the agreed-upon $60,000 total budget. It was not an easy assignment, but it was accomplished. Linda agreed to invest in it and with the help of an old friend of John's, they at last found a man with a shady background in Chicago interested in backing the film. John's children Sean and Russ were also involved on the film as production assistant and script girl, respectively, and both were paid a minimum wage. While professional porn stars had to be cast (Bo even visited the Porno Awards in Las Vegas), to save money, three qualified film students were hired as technicians as part of a very "reduced crew" that followed John and Bo to Hawaii, where they had spent a couple of weeks scouting the perfect location. Honopu Beach, on the island of Kauai, was only accessible by helicopter, an ideal spot for the privacy the production needed. But it was difficult to transport all the equipment needed for the shooting to the spot.

Bo recalled in her autobiography that her husband kept postponing the filming of the most graphic scenes: "He was so uncomfortable with it from the beginning…. John played with some light effects to make it pretty, and we settled down to get the film shot."[4] According to Sean, her father had quite a few fights with Wade Nichols and Rob Everett, the two male stars, especially on the extreme living conditions on the primitive island. Annette Haven, the "star" of the film, intervened and put an end to some of the arguing.[5] Tensions arose again while making the sex scenes, which they were all performed in the last days. John was dissatisfied with the performances and kept yelling at the stars; a four-day shooting turned into 11 long days of work. Since it was difficult to record the sound on the island, the dubbing track had to be synchronized and Bo's voice had to be used for an actress who was unwilling to do it.

Once the movie was completed, John offered it to various distributors, but the porno houses refused to play it after classifying it as not "raunchy" enough and too classy for the genre. Meanwhile, the regular cinema circuits found it too daring for a public release. According to Bo, *Love You!* was shown to 600 members of the National Organization for Women and got a positive reaction from the audience: They did not find it offensive or pornographic. It took almost two years before *Love You!* was shown at a cinema. Finally, in April 1979, the film's world premiere was held at a hardcore theater in Blaine, Washington, followed by an exclusive eight-week engagement. "The cleanest hard house I know of," John called that odd location choice. "The audience comes in couples and that's what I want."[6] The picture drew its audiences from Canada, where at the time hardcore porn was prohibited. To promote the film, John traveled to Vancouver and gave a lecture at the University of British Columbia about sex, Hollywood executives, and his desire to see screen pornography move into an art form. "It was a kind of challenge, and I'm arrogant and I wanted to do it," he explained. "I made [*Love You!*] for women, I enjoy women and they've been kind to me…. Pornography is not yet a legitimate screen form, eventually you will see better people getting into the porno business and it, too, will graduate into an art form."[7] The theatrical release of *Love You!* was very limited and the film was not commercially successful. However, in the early '80s, the sale for the home video release was extremely profitable.

Just when the filming of *Love You!* was completed, the casting of Bo in Blake Edwards' comedy *10* came as a blessing for the Dereks' still dire financial situation. According to *Variety*, Bo's salary was $35,000. Edwards had launched an international casting search for a young, unknown, beautiful girl to star as the incarnation of beauty perfection in his upcoming production. On the suggestion of a friend, Bo tested for the part and got it. John read the script and disliked it. (Years earlier, he had disliked the *Dr. No* screenplay and discouraged Ursula from accepting it.) He claimed that the story was so bad that no one would watch it. Once again he was proven wrong.

Despite her husband's hasty judgment, Bo loved the irony in the script and accepted the part that later made her and her distinctive braided corn-row hairstyle into an overnight sensation, but also marked the end of the Dereks' privacy.

Bo Derek in Blake Edwards' *10* (1979).

John's name appeared once again in the news in February 1980, when Bo was making a film called *A Change of Seasons* (1980) with Anthony Hopkins and Shirley McLaine. The press reported that director Noel Black had "creative differences" with John, who allegedly was on the set to shoot stills. The fight led to the director's being replaced by Richard Lang. At a press conference a few days later, the producer Martin Ransohoff stated that John had not caused any upheaval during filming and that purely "artistic differences" between himself and the director led to Black's dismissal. According to Bo, John never once set foot on the set, but someone from the press found a picture of a makeup artist fixing her mascara between takes and published it, writing in the caption that the man was John. That was followed by all sorts of faked reports. The truth was that Black did not get along with any member of the cast, bringing out the worst in everybody, and Ransohoff had to act accordingly.

The enormous popularity Bo gained from her short appearance in *10* convinced Kevin Casselman, Bo's former agent and co-producer of *And Once Upon a Time*, that it was the right time to pay their debts and bail out their film from the German vault, to cash in on Bo's current star status. Despite legal efforts by John to stop its showing, the film was set for distribution in North America, Europe and most of the Far East. First, the Dereks sought a temporary restraining order in Los Angeles Superior Court against the film that had been re-edited and re-titled *Once Upon a Love,* but withdrew the application when distribution details couldn't be obtained according to their attorney. John objected to any reference to Bo Derek in the picture's title and advertising, reasoning that her present name and following came after the film, which she made under her real name Cathleen Collins. Casselman told the press that in the picture there was some frontal nudity, something that constituted another of John's objections, claiming the implication of his wife being in a film at such an early stage could seriously offset her potential employment in the future.[8] The lawsuits also stated that the agreement entered into in October 1973 between the producers and John was for him to receive $30,000 and 50 percent of the net profits

Then the Dereks no-showed in court, putting an end to all their efforts to ban the film. *Once Upon a Love*, now re-titled *Fantasies,* opened in the States in November 1981.

"The Movie Bo Tried to Ban" was the slogan used to promote the film. Critics unanimously panned it, mostly because of its boring script, containing nothing spicy as promised by its advertising campaign. *Fantasies* quickly went straight to VHS, wrongly marketed as Bo Derek's pornographic debut.

Bo's phenomenal success was enhanced by her appearance on the cover of the March 1980 *Playboy*, photographed by her husband on the beautiful location of Lake Powell, Arizona. John was very skeptical about the photographs since he thought they were very artistic and less typical of a *Playboy* centerfold. The issue sold a record number of copies and five months later Bo reappeared on the August cover. Thanks to John's talent as a photographer, Bo became a sex symbol, appearing on the cover of hundreds of magazines all over the word. When she was invited on several popular TV talk shows, John went along but never appeared before a camera. One of the few times he decided to appear with his wife was on *The Barbara Walters Summer Special* in April 1980. According to Bo, John had refused to be on TV because of the way they had been labeled by most of the media "a dumb blonde under a Svengali's spell." But Walters' charm won him over and he agreed to be interviewed with his wife. "I'd never seen anyone have this kind of effect on him before," Bo wrote about Walters' effect on John. "He was smiling and laughing, something he rarely did anyway."[9] Interviewed in their tiny one-bedroom rental apartment in Marina del Rey, decorated with large pillows and John's photographs of Bo hanging on the walls, the Dereks appeared like a happy couple very much in love with each other. "To me, Bo is my everything," John told Walters, explaining that when he loves someone, he enjoys being with her all the time. Walters asked what the biggest misconception was that people had about them since they appeared almost like one entity. "That I am her Svengali. I am not her Svengali…. I don't lead Bo's life for Bo."[10]

Being 30 years her senior, he clarified, it was normal to guide her and occasionally help her avoid mistakes. At the end of the interview, Walters asked the Dereks if they'd continue to love one another when they get old, or if something happens to mar their beauty. Bo affirmed unhesitatingly, while John replied:

> That's a tough question. I've thought about that. I would assume that I would because I'm a nice person and that I love what's inside of her now. But that's not what I met. I didn't meet her insides. I met her outsides. I don't know what I would do. I can't tell you what I would do if this place catches on fire, I assume I'd jump out of the window, but I don't know that.[11]

In the spring of 1980, John and Bo were sued for $400,000 by a former friend, Karen Callan, who claimed that the couple reneged on a 1977 oral agreement in which she was to act as Bo's personal manager in return for ten percent of her gross earnings. Callan claimed that she was the one who recommended Bo to director Blake Edwards, who cast her in *10*. Callan claimed she was entitled to Bo's *10* salary ($35,000), the other films she had made after that, and all the promotional products, posters, T-shirts, etc., connected to the pictures. In a July 9, 1980, statement, the Dereks denied ever entering into an agreement with Callan, and that she wasn't a licensed agent. In January 1982, the Labor Commission ruled that Callan was not entitled to any commission or compensation whatsoever, dismissing her claim.

Chapter 13

Svengali Productions

"We have a 24-hour-a-day relationship. John is not my manager. He is my lover. I am not his wife. I am his life."—Bo Derek

The incredible success of *10* in America catapulted Bo into superstardom. In a vain attempt to escape the frantic media attention, Bo accepted the opportunity to promote the film abroad. Australia, New Zealand, Japan and Singapore were some of the destinations the Dereks visited in the first three months of 1981. Even though *10* had not yet opened in those countries, Bo was already a celebrity. Crowds of excited reporters and idolizing fans often chased the Dereks during their promotional tour. While job offers started to pour in for Bo, the husband-and-wife team seemed more interested in making their own movies. There was talk of a film produced by Harry Saltzman (*Dr. No*), tentatively titled *Monte Carlo*, in which John would direct Bo and Ursula in a story centered on the reconciliation of a mother and a daughter (even though they looked more like sisters) after a separation of 20 years. The project never came to fruition. While in Singapore for the *10* press junket, John and Bo discussed the film proposals she had received through her agent. Many were romantic romps like *10*, while others were based on popular comic heroines to be adapted into feature films: Brenda Starr; Sheena, Queen of the Jungle, and Dazzler. Those offers inspired the Dereks to make a film based on the legendary story of Tarzan but with a new, different, more feminist angle, enhancing the role of Jane. They called it *Me Jane: You, Tarzan*.

"All I had," John recalled about that early stage of the project, "was the title ... and the final scene where Jane asks Tarzan if it isn't the time they start thinking about Boy."[1] During the final stretch of the promotional world tour of *10*, the Dereks' new agent, Marty Baum, pitched the idea to several studios. MGM welcomed the project, offering to produce and distribute a new film on Tarzan directed by John with Bo starring and producing. The couple signed a three-picture deal with MGM, under which John would make his major studio directorial debut. Svengali Productions was the name of the company the Dereks formed. Its logo, designed by artist Frank Frazetta, showed Bo dangling John on a puppet string. It was a way of mocking all those who had accused John of being Bo's Svengali.

"I wish he were a Svengali," Bo said. "I wish he did make all the decisions for me. It would be a lot easier. But he won't. He says: It's up to you, it's your decision."

The pair settled in an office at MGM in Culver City and started to plan the production. Reluctantly, John had to join the Directors Guild ("He's not much for unions," Bo revealed).[2] While having the difficult task of being the producer, Bo had to exercise and diet to keep her body toned in preparation to play the role of Jane. "She can be very lazy and undisciplined," John said to *Newsweek*. "It's a matter of developing that minute discipline that makes the difference between a very beautiful girl and a stunningly beautiful girl."[3]

When the Dereks completed the first draft of the screenplay, the studio told them that, legally, they had to follow the original storyline. Bewildered and disappointed, the couple had been working on the project for too long to let it go, so they had no other choice than to accept the script revision. Yet the final version of *Tarzan* was not the film they had planned to make. MGM held remake rights to the previous Tarzans films, while Warner Brothers was also in pre-production with *Greystoke* (1984), holding a Tarzan option with Edgar Rice Burroughs' estate. In July 1980, Burroughs' heirs sued MGM, claiming that the studio did not have the right to remake the movie *Tarzan, the Ape Man*: They said that the 1978 copyright law permitted them to terminate Metro's "remake rights." To avoid further complications, MGM asked the Dereks to conform their script to the storyline of the classic starring Johnny Weissmuller and Maureen O'Sullivan, and to reinstate the original title: *Tarzan, the Ape Man*. John and Bo had no choice except to comply. But when MGM's production chief Lew Rachmil asked them to shoot at the Los Angeles Arboretum, John wanted to film in the jungle. The Dereks traveled to Brazil, visiting suitable sites, including the Amazon jungle and the Iguacu Falls, which seemed perfect. But then they came to the realization of the high cost of shipping elephants and other African animals to Brazil. Kenya was the second choice but the country's president made it clear that a native Kenyan had to play Tarzan or no authorization would be given to film in their territory. On a stop in Europe, John was captivated by the beauty of some photographs Ursula had shown him taken on the set of two films she had made in Sri Lanka. A few days later, he boarded a plane destined for Sri Lanka with Bo and six crew members. There he found the perfect stand-in for Tarzan's unspoiled jungle and, 1,868 miles away, in the Seychelles, the sea, the beach and the high cliffs.

While in Sri Lanka, John was involved in a fistfight in a bar with a pair of burly sailors, punching one of them after they made a pass at Bo. The intervention of some of John's crew members stopped the fight from escalating further.[4]

On January 13, 1981, John, Bo and a crew of 23 (including five animal trainers) landed in Sri Lanka with an old lion named Rocky (later replaced by a younger, inexperienced feline, Dandy), an orangutan who answered to the initials C.J. (Clyde Junior), two chimps called Eve and Louie, two Irish wolfhounds and a 17-foot python, 12 inches in diameter and weighing 120 pounds. The immigration officials made it clear that all the animals had to be shipped out again at the end of the film, particularly the python.

The crew settled in the small port city of Trincomalee on the country's northeast coast. What was normally a 20-week shooting was condensed into six-and-a-half weeks, working hard 15 to 18 hours a day. John said in an interview,

> Sleeping was the only other thing we did. We'd wake up and be on the set in minutes. That's part of the fun of filmmaking.... [B]ut the time we spent there was the toughest six weeks of our lives. I can't compare them to the war—or maybe even the freeway. Your life is in jeopardy out there—though now that I think about it, there were a few moments in Tarzan that Bo came close to the edge.[5]

John's input on Gary Goddard's script was heavy, although the original basic plot and characters remained for legal reasons. Some revisions and updated material for contemporary audiences were made, especially for the character of Jane, who became the focus of the picture. "We're not creating a definitive masterpiece," John explained. "The story is a remake and we weren't allowed to change it. There's no heavy message, just fundamental entertainment, every girl's wet dream. I hope with Bo in it, though, it will be more entertaining and beautiful."[6]

Oliver Reed was signed to play Jane's father, but delays prevented the British actor from participating and Richard Harris replaced him. Casting the character of Tarzan was also a challenge. The media reported that the actor selected for the part, 6'4" Lee Canalito, a former heavyweight boxer, injured his arm badly (others reported a knee injury) during his first days of filming. This affected his ability to swing from trees, and therefore he was laid off. Some members of the press speculated that one of the scenes between Canalito and Bo got too steamy for John, who sacked him. The reality was different: Canalito was fired on the third day of the shoot because he was unsuitable for his role. Apparently John found him too fat. The actor was called into the production office and handled a letter written by Bo breaking the bad news. "Lee had a beautiful quality with a Michelangelo face but he wasn't the proud Lord of the Jungle. We wanted him to look like a sculpture, but John knew it wasn't right first. Then I did and finally Lee did as well."[7] With Canalito leaving (he was paid in full), a new Tarzan had to be cast.

C.J. the orangutan, Miles O'Keeffe and Bo Derek in *Tarzan, the Ape Man* (1981).

Jock Mahoney, who had starred in two Tarzan pictures in the early 1960s, was appointed as stunt coordinator of the production. He also had joined the Dereks in the auditioning process as a consultant. For the Tarzan role, Mahoney recommended a 26-year-old, 6'3" former football player-turned-model named Miles O'Keeffe. In John's script, Tarzan had no lines, just a few grunts and his signature yell, so O'Keeffe's only screen test consisted of having him swing from a tree on a rope in a local Hollywood park.

The first week of production was the most difficult. Inclement weather halted the filming, and dysentery afflicted many crew members. The climate, the hard conditions, the mosquitos and John's complex temperamental character quickly reduced the 35 laborers to 17. The group included a disappointed Mahoney, whose friendship with John went back three decades. The stuntman was relieved of his stunt coordination duties by a letter he found under his pillow.

In a *New York Times* interview the week *Tarzan, the Ape Man* was released, Bo recalled how the production fell into pure chaos:

> On the first day's shooting, the problems were horrendous, and they weren't the fault of the Sri Lankans, but of our group. Nothing was right—or even there. Sri Lanka is overflowing with elephants and we had ordered 150 of them. On the first morning we only needed two, and they weren't there. Nobody

had ordered elephants and you can't just truck them in. They need a week to walk anywhere and our two were still on their way—20 miles out of town. John was screaming and yelling. I was screaming and yelling and I looked around at our group from Hollywood and I saw some of them were rolling their eyes and saying, "What do you expect with this couple in charge—here we go again." I knew some of them weren't going to last very long—and they didn't. So every day, as people goofed or didn't do their jobs, I said: "Walk!" And they did.[8]

When MGM cabled asking what replacements should be sent out for the crew, the Dereks declined the offer, explaining that they would manage. Bo's mother Norma, who had come out as a hairdresser, took on wardrobe and makeup duties. Bo's sister Kerry helped as assistant director. When the production manager was asked to leave, Bo's assistant Eva Chun took over. Every one of the remaining members of the original Hollywood crew did about ten jobs each. John, who loved to be a one-man band as a director, got involved as a lighting man and camera operator. *Tarzan, the Ape Man* was the first Hollywood picture filmed in Sri Lanka since *The Bridge on the River Kwai* in 1957. The crew had left behind all its lightning and grip equipment, which were still in perfect condition. Although heavy and unpractical, John decided to use it to contain the costs, while all the other materials and supplies had to be shipped from Europe.

On the set, there was a doctor with a cooler filled with snake antivenin since the region was full of dangerous reptiles. An actor from Hollywood, who specialized in playing parts in an ape suit, finally decided to opt out of the film because he objected to scenes in which Bo bared her breasts. He claimed it was against his religious beliefs: John Derek remembered him saying, "I wouldn't mind a see-through blouse—but for my ape suit to appear with nudity wouldn't be right. I'll help you as a man, but not in my ape suit and I'll pray for you." John said, "You know who Bo is and how she appeared in *10*. Don't pray for us—just leave us alone."[9]

Despite all the difficulties, John refused the use of stock footage, preferring to shoot his own animal scenes. He also filmed with a long camera lens, believing it to be less intrusive to the actors. Such a technique gave his actors a greater feeling of independence, a sense of not being under the scrutiny of the camera lens, resulting in natural performances that blended well with the wild flora and fauna around them. Being an instinctual filmmaker, John also never looked at dailies because as the film's photographer, he knew exactly what was shot. If the lab did not report any scratches or imperfections, he did not see the film again until editing began. On March 11, 1981, the Dereks wrapped the filming in the Seychelles and flew back to Hollywood. To the surviving members of the original Hollywood crew, John gave special armbands with these words printed in gold: "I finished Tarzan."

There were a few complaints about John and Bo's "slave-driving," especially by members of the crew who were dismissed earlier, but Richard Harris gave high marks to both Dereks. "John knows exactly what he wants to see on film, and Bo made sure that when John was ready to shoot a scene, everything he needed was there. She's incredible."[10]

Even though MGM had approved a $5.3 million budget, the final cost was reported as $3 million, with $1 million in advertising. Despite the loss of a good portion of money on strikes and cancellations, John claimed that if a studio wasn't involved, they could have made the film for a third of the amount. He said years later,

> When Tarzan appeared with Bo Derek's name as producer, people laugh. But she is the one who did the work. She knows where every dollar was spent…. Before beginning a film, she has everything prepared. She has her computers, about which I know nothing, and controls every dollar, every bill…. Bo and I have never ripped anybody off. Most of the time we have even saved the producers money and finished shooting before schedule. And it's all basically thanks to Bo.[11]

Tarzan's post-production was rushed because MGM wanted to release the picture by July. During the final editing process, the heirs of the Burroughs estate tried to stop the release of the picture. Their claim was that it was "too sexy" and the story was not faithful to its original. Although nobody except John, Bo and their editors had seen one frame yet, the estate accused the production of undermining the family-friendly Tarzan franchise. After watching two versions and a final print of the picture in one week, New York District Court Judge Henry Werker denied the Burroughs heirs' contention that the new picture departed from the original licensed source in virtue that it was no longer suitable for children, stating that even though he had noted occasional differences, the core plotlines were consistent. Still, he suggested that 20 frames of nudity had to be cut.

To avoid further delays, MGM agreed to cut four minutes of nudity from the final version. John was outraged by that decision and fought it fiercely, claiming that the integrity of his film had been attacked by censorship. In a last-minute meeting with MGM top executives, he quoted the First Amendment and used his sharp dialectic. John urged MGM to postpone the picture's release and fight censorship. But *Tarzan* was the only film the studio had ready for release that summer, and nobody wanted to miss that opportunity. John's last resort was to alert the media, presenting the case as an example of reactionary censorship. He, with Bo and C.J. the orangutan, organized a protest against Judge Werker's verdict at Foley Square in New York. Yet the press twisted the story, interested more in the content of the edited scenes rather than focusing on the actual censorship issue. John was so outraged that, in an interview, he screamed, "Blood will flow on the streets of Culver City if the film is cut."[12] It was a lost cause. He was banned by the editing room and, on July 24, 1981, *Tarzan, the Ape Man* opened nationwide as scheduled, the first Tarzan film rated R.

O'Keeffe did not take part in any publicity campaign. Only John and Bo appeared on national TV and on the press junket tour. O'Keeffe had a confidentiality clause in his contract, which meant he was unable to talk about the film or promote it until weeks after the official release. That gave the impression to the press and to the public that O'Keeffe was all muscle with no brain. It was John's idea that the focus of the film's promotion had to parallel the film's thematic focus on Jane's character and therefore on Bo, rather than on Tarzan, to create an allure of mystery around the character.

Critics were very harsh on what MGM advertised as "the most erotic adventure of all time." *The Wall Street Journal* described the acting as "insufferable," the direction "hopeless" and the script "idiotic."[13] Vincent Canby of the *New York Times* was less harsh: "[T]o call the film inept would be to miss the point.... Viewed stone-sober, it's a movie of more squirms than screams." He spared some good words for John, however: "Mr. Derek is a great still photographer."[14]

John was mostly disappointed by the reviews: "*Tarzan* is just a lightweight bit of fluff, with half-dressed pretentious photography so people think we're being serious. It's not supposed to be erotic and it's certainly not a masterpiece. But that's how I make films. I just go out and make itsy-bitsy little movies and have fun doing it."[15] Movie critic Gene Shalit of the NBC *Today Show* seemed to be one of the few who truly understood the film's spirit:

> [It's] a spoof, a laugh, a lot of fun.... The film is never teasing. It is never salacious.... What matters is the light-hearted point of view, the lively story ... the muscular, masculine, timid Tarzan, and best of all, Bo Derek, so sweetly appealing in her Jane Parker role.... The enjoyable *Tarzan, the Ape Man* will be one of the summer's hottest box-office hits.[16]

Shalit was right. In its opening weekend, the picture opened at #1, grossing $6,700,809 in 930 theaters nationwide—the biggest MGM opening ever. After one week, it set another record for the studio, earning $10.1 million, reaching $17 million after two weeks, setting a studio record for the biggest three-day opening in New York City and the most profitable first three weeks ever. *Tarzan's* final gross reached more than $36 million worldwide.[17]

After the smashing success of *Tarzan,* MGM made a bid for Bo's services for a two-picture deal for $5 million. The proposal was rejected, countered by the Dereks' bid to make their own movies.

John was very sore about how his original idea of Tarzan had been manipulated from the very beginning by MGM along with the final editing of the film. He bluntly revealed his frustrations in an interview with *People* magazine: "I am just sick of all this crap. Hollywood is now and always has been a hellhole. I learned a long time ago that there is no one you can trust in this business…." John continued with a checklist of complaints: "MGM failed me, the Burroughs family is arrogant and sue-happy, Judge Werker had made the Constitution a joke, the press is out to get us."[18]

Eventually the Dereks made a deal with the CBS film division that gave them total creative control and guaranteed completion on a not-yet-written $8 million feature tentatively titled *Sea Mistress*. Principal photography for the project, later renamed *Pirate Annie*, was scheduled to begin under John's direction in the fall of 1981 in the Caribbean. John outlined two stories inspired by the life of pirate Anne Bonny that Gary Goddard was supposed to adapt into a script. A casting call was placed to search for a new Errol Flynn–like actor to play the English pirate Calico Jack. Richard Harris was asked to play the role of Blackbeard the Pirate opposite Bo in the leading role; John described her character as a sort of "female Douglas Fairbanks." Bo took fencing lessons with 90-year-old Ralph Faulkner, who had taught John for *Rogues of Sherwood Forest.* Even C.J. the orangutan, after touring with Bo for *Tarzan,* was set to appear in the film. In November 1981, right in the middle of pre-production, after location research in Yugoslavia, Greece and the Caribbean, the project sank unexpectedly on account of budget problems and creative differences between John and CBS.

At once, John and Bo put all their energy in a new project called *Adam and Eve,* ultimately entitled *Eve and That Damned Apple.* Based on Mark Twain's *The Diaries of Adam and Eve,* it was a comedy the Dereks planned to make in New Zealand after spending some time seeking the right location for the Garden of Eden. George Hamilton, an old friend of John, was rumored to play the Devil while Richard Harris was to play God. The industry press reported that producers Zev Braun and Carlo Ponti both showed an interest in the project. But John accepted an offer from Universal, as the company was willing to spend $7.5 million to produce the film. A big unexpected argument between Bo and a senior studio executive, who wrongly accused the Dereks of secretly planning to shoot a different version of the approved screenplay, made the couple abandon the *Eve* project.

With the first money they earned from *Tarzan's* unexpected success (the Dereks' contract included ten percent of the gross), John and Bo bought a 5000–square foot Spanish style house built on an amazing 45-acre horse ranch in the Santa Ynez Valley, north of Santa Barbara. It was a beautiful oasis of tranquility two hours from Hollywood. John welcomed all sorts of domestic animals including his beloved horses, dogs and cats. In an old barn, John set up a leather shop, filled with old sewing machines, and he enjoyed spending some of his free time creating unique pieces. He made leather boots, chaps, vests, shirts and all sorts of accessories, mostly for Bo but also for his ex-wives and very close friends. Each piece bore a personalized inscription. A leather bikini worn by Bo on the cover of *Playboy* was one of John's original creations. It was so popular that several leather designers created knock-offs.

In spite of a pretty healthy lifestyle, 55-year-old John, who was never a drinker or a smoker, was suddenly struck by a scary case of high blood pressure which "shocked the hell" out of him, as he exclaimed in an interview:

> I used to work out with weights, because it looked cute walking by a mirror, but I've been procrastinating the past few years. I've got a pot belly and a half, but I cover it with clothes, so I can still strut around like a peacock. Lately, I have been finding the stairs are longer than my ability to climb them, not just because of my age, but my laziness, I have to work out.[19]

Disappointed by the outcome of their two latest unborn projects, John and Bo tried to pitch their ideas in the offices of producers. One day a friend suggested they talk to Cannon Films, a new production company run by Israeli cousins Menahem Golan and Yoram Globus. In just one meeting, the two parties reached an agreement on a five million dollar production with the Dereks in total artistic control. The agreement included a combined salary of $1.5 million, half of the film's profit, and half of its copyright. In addition, the lucrative contract gave John the rights to the film's final cut. It was also agreed in the five-page contract that the film's subject would be tastefully erotic, giving *carte blanche* to the Dereks on the story. As John candidly told Bo, "They just want to see you fuck to 'Bolero' [Ravel's piece for orchestra, used on the soundtrack in a scene with Bo in *10*] again. Let's go make a film called *Bolero*."[20]

Inspired by a coffee table photo book about girls riding their horses around the world, John and Bo got the inspiration about a romantic film set in Spain. They outlined a story set in the 1920s about an outgoing American heiress and a shy Spanish girlfriend. The two young women head for Morocco in hopes of losing their virginity to a sheik. But when the dream doesn't come true, they travel to Spain in search of a bullfighter.

Chapter 14

Twilight's Last Gleaming

"John was a talented, totally self-oriented bully boy who could find fault with anything and anyone but himself."—George Kennedy

In October 1982, John traveled to Spain with Bo looking for the perfect locations for *Bolero*, even though he had not yet written one word of the script. They toured the city of Seville and visited several ranches in the area with the help of a local paparazzi-turned-guide. They returned to Spain in April 1983, this time traveling to the north of the country, near the city of Santander, to finalize their choices before shooting began in the fall.

Upon his return home while outlining a script ("an erotic, sensual, silly, fun picture to show how sexy Bo can be," as he would define it[1]), John started the casting process. Ana Obregon, a popular Spanish socialite-starlet, was picked for the role of Catalina, Bo's cohort in sexual adventures. George Kennedy was chosen as Bo's chauffeur, guardian, confidant and pseudo-father figure.

Years later, Kennedy dedicated an entire chapter of his autobiography to the experience of working with the Dereks. In Kennedy's memoir, he portrayed Bo as a sweet girl who was often a victim of her husband's narcissism and sadistic behavior:

> John Derek—writer, director, photographer whiz, and conservative—was born in the wrong era. He would have carried President Theodore Roosevelt up San Juan Hill just to beat Teddy by a neck when they got there. He was a pettifogger, requiring unquestioned obedience from Bo and everybody. He loved knives, and would challenge you to spread your hand wide open on the dinner table, close your eyes, and—as he would to himself—stab down between open fingers. It was a sure attention getter, but it didn't catch on.[2]

Kennedy recalled a few times that John jeopardized Bo's safety for the sake of getting a great shot. Once he forced her to swim at night in an icy English pond, and yet another time he had her dance around a Spanish bullring while a raging bull almost attacked her. Kennedy described John as bossy and rude, remembering him giving instructions to his interpreter with an acidic tongue, often making abusive remarks to the people around him. Victoria Hughes, who worked briefly as a translator, said, "I was shocked by Mr. Derek's vocabulary."[3] When a group of Moroccan warriors, used as extras in a sequence shot in the Sahara Desert, did not follow John's instructions properly, his expressions were so insulting and verbally abusing that once the scene was completed, the men were ready to retaliate against him. Only the intervention of the local police prevented the situation from becoming violent. Early the next day, the entire crew had to be escorted to the airport until all members safely boarded a flight to Madrid. On the air-ramp stairs, John dramatically gave Morocco the finger.

Despite John's rough manners, Kennedy wrote that they never exchanged a cross word:

I liked John Derek because there was nothing wishy-washy in his makeup. He was strong, bright, self-centered, spoiled, thoughtless and overbearing—brilliant. His road was the only road.... It bothers me that everything I remember about John and *Bolero* gives little evidence that when his heart stopped, it was the only heart he really cared about. He was a talented, totally self-oriented bully boy who could find fault with anything and anyone but himself.... He was like Popeye in many ways: "I yam what I yam and that's all I yam." That, in itself, is a worthwhile summation of an artistic icon. It takes a strong will to make your presence felt in the Hollywood area. John was that, and like it or not he was right there in your face. I just wish it hadn't been Bo's face.[4]

Bo Derek in a publicity shot for *Bolero* (1984).

Italian hunk Fabio Testi was cast as Bo's bullfighter lover based on a recommendation from his former girlfriend Ursula Andress. Together they were supposed to perform some of the steamiest love scenes. John was happy because he got the actor at a very good price. But three days into the shooting, Testi showed up on the set with a virulent herpes sore on his lower lip. John was upset but was determined to keep filming Testi, disguising the sore with makeup. Kennedy felt right to intervene. He told John that the Italian actor was very contagious and kissing Bo in those scenes would endanger her. He advised John to play the role himself. The director's reaction was vehemently negative, affirming that he hated acting, he always did, and he had promised himself never again to appear in front of a camera. After it was confirmed by more than one doctor that it was herpes, the insurance company insisted Testi be replaced. Testi was dismissed, but the producers claimed that they later had to pay him $60,000 to keep him from suing them for millions. Golan also revealed that even with Testi gone, tensions mounted, claiming that three entire crews had to be replaced. John argued that there were never three crews, that not even *one* full crew was assigned to *Bolero*. The "friends and family" team included Bo's mother as the makeup artist and Bo's sister Kerry as her personal assistant. Mickey Knox, John's old friend who had appeared with John in *Knock on Any Door* and *Saturday's Hero*, was the dialogue coach and played a tiny role as a Moroccan guide. John did admit that some local crew members were fired, because they did not speak good enough English. The reality was that the producers were very slow at dispatching funds, something that delayed the production. The Dereks were forced to use their credit cards to pay the expenses and the transportation of their equipment from Germany. In addition, they had to personally guarantee everything on the shoot to get official permits. Even Elmer Bernstein, the Academy Award–winning composer, who scored a part of the film along with his son Peter, had to pay some of the musicians against a draft on his credit card.

Despite great disorganization, the shooting went on. To find Testi's replacement, the Dereks went to Rome and cast the new "toreador" with unknown 26-year-old Andrea Occhipinti (now an established film producer). According to *Bolero*'s press release, the handsome Italian was too thin for the part. Before appearing in front of the camera, he was urged to eat more and exercise under brief but intense supervision with a personal trainer. Three weeks after the shooting resumed, Occhipinti had to be flown to London for an operation to have a cyst removed from his eye. Only upon his return to Spain was John able to shoot all the key love scenes. Prior to shooting the sexy sequences, John was very clear with the Italian actor that it was unnecessary to be close to Bo in order to perform the scenes realistically, should Occhipinti have "strange ideas." "Our lifestyle is very moral," he told a British newspaper, "We are faithful—completely. That is the way we are and if others want to be different, that is fine too. But not for me."[5]

Once the editing was completed, the Dereks went to Rome to score the film and dub some scenes. Four weeks later, a couple of sneak previews were held to see if changes were necessary. Some viewers found the film on the verge of pornography. In January 1984 *Bolero* was screened at MGM/UA, the studio originally contracted by Cannon Films to distribute it. After the event, Golan dispatched a telegram to the Dereks defining *Bolero* as "completely insufferable and a total embarrassment," adding that the film, as it then stood, would have received an X rating that would jeopardize its distribution deal with MGM/UA. As Golan had foreseen, a few days later the motion picture rating board members gave *Bolero* an X rating, forcing the distributors to back out of the deal. On the eve of its scheduled release date, the film had to be distributed under the banner of Cannon Releasing Corp., without the help of any major studio. Golan explained in an interview with the *Chicago Tribune*,

> When we decided to do the movie, we decided to do the most erotic film ever to get into the legitimate theaters … we wanted to do an erotic film, but not a pornographic film. The fact is that with few changes, we could eliminate the problem of the X or the R—because they were willing to give us an R with just a few changes—but John didn't want to consider them, and that was part of our feud.[6]

Apparently 90 percent of the changes Golan proposed to John were refused:

> I was enraged. [John] wouldn't listen to me. I thought a few cuts would have made the movie much better and without problems, and in order to shake him, I used some strong words in my cable that enraged him even more. Maybe he's really, truly, honestly fighting for art. Maybe he's a crazy guy who says, "This is my art." But then the question is, who can work with such an ego?[7]

At one point, Golan even considered the possibility of shelving the completed movie, but the production company couldn't afford *not* to release it. According to Golan, John eventually made some changes, but without telling anyone. John and Bo vehemently denied any changes were made, stating that the picture was only shortened but never censored. The quarrel escalated. Golan took the Dereks to court over a $50,000 payment they allegedly received for photographs from the film that were published in the July issue of *Playboy* without his authorization. Cannon Films also filed a complaint against the couple on another five counts, including refusal to hand over still photographs for the promotion of the film and for interfering with its distribution.

The erotic subject and the turmoil surrounding the several lawsuits generated a lot of buzz around *Bolero*, which opened in 1022 North American theaters on August 31, 1984. It was released with no MPAA rating, with a disclaimer on ads that no children under 17 would be admitted. What remained unclear was who was responsible for the film's final cut. In her memoir, Bo stated that Cannon reedited the love scenes, making them longer, while Golan in more than one interview said that John made very few changes to the original cut, leaving in almost all the "pseudo-erotic scenes."

Critics found *Bolero* extremely tedious; one reviewer sarcastically wrote, "Boring with a capital BO." Roger Ebert predicted, "The real future of *Bolero* is in rentals, where fast forward and instant replay will supply the editing job the movie so desperately needs."[8] Yet a morbid curiosity brought the public to the theaters: opening weekend, *Bolero* grossed $4.5 million. But the excitement died off quickly. It was reported that the much-anticipated sex scenes frequently provoked fits of audience laughter. The final ticket sales in America reached $8.9 million, not bad for an independent production but still a disappointing profit of just $1.9 million compared to *Tarzan*'s revenues. "The only positive thing that came out of *Bolero*," John commented, "was that we showed people we can do things properly. And we showed the public that we can make a love film with some very strong scenes which are not vulgar. Everyone who saw the movie was able to appreciate how beautiful Bo looked and how genuinely pure those love scenes were."[9]

In 1980, the press talked about a project Sean Derek had in the works: a tell-all memoir about her father and his four wives. A TV serial called *My Four Wives* was also said to be in talks. That same year, John closed a deal with Simon & Schuster which published *Bo*, a 100-photo book-essay celebrating his wife through his amazing photographs. An instant best-seller, it went quickly into several reprints. When Sean's book was announced, gossip columnist Liz Smith reported that John and Bo were about to sign an agreement with their close friend, actress-turned-photographer Claude Albuquerque, to do a book showing them the way they really were—a highly disciplined couple who led a non-glamorous, down-to-earth life. John planned to illustrate it with his own photographs, but the project was never realized.[10]

Sean's candid memoir *Cast of Characters* was published in October 1982. John and his estranged daughter hadn't spoken to each other for almost three years after the two had a violent argument during Bo's first *Playboy* magazine shoot. According to Sean, John was so abusive, yelling and name-calling, that she decided not to see him again. "Avoiding him is probably healthier than anything else." Sean told the media. "If I don't do things his way, he thinks I'm an idiot. Well, there's only one person who can live that way—and it's him. He's very unusual, believing he's God, living from hand to mouth.... He doesn't like people. He judges them, physically and emotionally. My father is obsessed with beauty."[11]

Cast of Characters appeared in bookstores just a week before John's location-scouting trip to Seville for *Bolero*. When John and his crew arrived in Spain, he was surprised to find a crowd of journalists waiting for him to answer their questions. Usually Bo had been the target of the media, but on this occasion, he was the center of their interest. The mystery was quickly solved. *Hola!*, a popular Spanish gossip magazine, was serializing Sean's book.

Defending himself, John dispatched a package to Hollywood columnist Marilyn Beck: letters in which Sean assured him of her love and her approval of the manner in which he has led his life, and promised that John and Bo would have a chance to read her book before it went into print and that she would re-write or delete anything he and Bo didn't like. John recalled that a few years earlier, Sean had asked him to tell her some stories about his life. He told her that he did not *have* any amusing anecdotes to tell. She explained that she wanted to write a book. John thought that, for Sean, that project was just another way to make easy money, but Sean dismissed the accusation. John suggested that she instead write a novel, avoiding real names, explaining that readers would still believe the characters were based on her family and they still would buy the book. In this way, she would have avoided hurting the feelings of anyone she knew. Sean did not follow her father's advice, and in 1979 John received the first few chapters of the first draft of her memoir. According to John, the final version had been entirely changed since then and had no idea what was in it until he read it.

Reading *Cast of Characters* enraged him. He told *The National Enquirer*, "If you cut my daughter open, you won't find a heart inside." He also felt that being abroad prevented him from responding to the accusations in Sean's book. He dismissed the idea of suing his daughter because "I'm sure that's exactly what she wants us to do—to draw attention to her piece of trash." He was determined to let people know "that there wasn't a word of truth in the book—just lies and hideously distorted stories. It is so vicious that I'm surprised she didn't title it *Daddy Dearest* [a reference to Christina Crawford's vitriolic memoir *Mommy Dearest*, about her mother Joan Crawford]."

John told Beck, "I do not mind so much about the lies she tells about me, but to attack Bo in such a vicious manner, and to taint the memories of innocent people who are no longer here to defend themselves, well, it makes me sick."[12] Speaking to a *New York Daily News* columnist, Sean said, "My father knew I was writing this book and tried to stifle it. But I still love him. It may seem strange, but he's still my father and I care about him." She claimed that writing the memoir served as an emotional catharsis. "His movies make me cry when I watch them ... because he's the same man who told me a million times, 'You're fat and ugly. I'm not your daddy.'"[13]

Sean's memoir was generally reviewed as a sad tale of rejection and estrangement—the story of a difficult relationship between a selfish, absent father and a child in desperate need of love and approval. Linda Evans came over as a supporting, loving stepmother with whom Sean had a solid and long-lasting friendship. But Sean's relationship with Bo was never a bed of roses, since the blond actress, according to her stepdaughter, would always side with John, even when he proved to be clearly mistaken. Once the buzz around the book cooled off, the father-daughter relationship did not heal. They would not speak to each other for 17 years.

Difficult, but not as stormy was John's connection with his now adult son Russ, who in 1969, at age 19, had been involved in a motorcycle accident that had left him a quadriplegic. From complications of his paralysis, Russ was often hospitalized, but he was always able to recover. In 1984, he made John proud, working as the head of the Los Angeles Olympic Handicapped Services Department, overseeing the organization of people with disabilities, campaigning to assure their participation in the Games as spectators, workers and possibly as athletes. Russ drew high praise throughout the disabled community for his successful efforts to bring handicapped issues to the attention of the Olympic planners.[14]

At the end of 1985, John and Bo's names appeared in the news as Ronald Rewald, a man convicted of 94 counts of fraud, perjury and tax evasion, tried to defraud them. Apparently Rewald was interested in financing their next three movies by investing $21 million, along with young producer Ron Kauffman. Rewald also claimed that thanks to his ties, he would have been able to stifle any negative press. However, when he strongly implied that he had connections with the CIA and that he laundered their money (and hinted that "unseen people" were watching the Dereks), John and Bo's suspicions were triggered and they alerted the FBI. Rewald spent almost ten years in prison before he was released on parole in 1995.

On the night of June 1, 1986, John suffered from strong abdominal pain. Thinking it was indigestion, he took several antacids. Herb Tanney, the Dereks' family physician, was staying at their ranch, but when Bo suggested they get him, John refused to have him disturbed. At five in the morning, she noticed that her husband's face had turned gray and he was still in a lot of pain. She called Tanney, who immediately realized John was having a heart attack. The doctor administered some medication and called for an ambulance, despite John's protests. He was rushed to the Santa Barbara Cottage Hospital where the doctors confirmed a mild heart attack that did not require heart surgery. He was kept under observation and discharged after a week.

Within days, John was back to work on *Ondine* (later renamed *The Last Knight*), a script he had been preparing for months. It was a romantic story based on the mythological legend of Ondine, a water nymph tired of being immortal after 3,000 years underwater. She longed to become human, going ashore in search of her knight on a white horse. John would write and direct, while Bo was appointed to star in and produce it. In November, they spent a couple of weeks in Denmark and Germany scouting locations, studio facilities and acting talents, having seven speaking parts of water-nymphs to fill. Hundreds of young women flocked to the Nordisk Film Studios at the invitation of John and Bo to be screen-tested. The press reported that during a visit of some Danish breweries, the Dereks spotted a young tour guide named Caspar Hedegaard. After convincing him to do a screen test, they offered him the male lead in the movie. According to *Variety*, shooting of *The Last Knight* was scheduled to begin in May 1987 on a $5 million budget. As before, the inability to find financial backers made the project impractical.

Bo and John Derek at the Beverly Hilton Hotel for the American Film Market (1987).

After several attempts to find funds for a new film that would mark his return behind the camera, John was able to finally direct what would be his final movie. In May 1988, the media announced that Trans World Entertainment would produce *Ghosts Can't Do It*, a romantic comedy written and directed by John and starring his wife.

"What's it about? ... Our relationship," John told the press. "It's to show people that we have a sense of humor about the difference in our age. If I were watching what was going on, I'd be ticked off, too, that this old man has been married to three beautiful women."[15] John presented the story as a light comedy that casts Bo as Katie, the wife of Scott, a wealthy businessman 35 years her senior. After experiencing a heart attack, Scott commits suicide, but returns at his funeral as a ghost that only Katie can see and hear. The ghost's plan is to get her to help him take possession of a young man's body so that their relationship could continue. *Ghosts Can't Do It* was really a story about John's own fear about what would happen to Bo after he died. The heart attack had suddenly given John, now 62, a sense of mortality and a new awareness of the 30 years' difference with the love of his life.

George Grizzard was cast as Bo's husband while John's old pal Don Murray and Julie Newmar landed supporting roles. Production began in Hong Kong in the fall of 1988, but almost immediately turned into disaster when budget problems halted it, concurrent with the sudden resignation of the production manager, Tony Ray—and then Grizzard. The official reason for the lead actor's departure was given as the illness of his mother, which caused him to fly back to the U.S. Anthony Quinn replaced Grizzard and some scenes were re-shot. The last-minute intervention of a new group of producers rescued the project.

After Hong Kong, the crew filmed in Sri Lanka, the Maldives and Jackson, Wyoming, where *Ghosts Can't Do It* wrapped in February 1989. In May, the Dereks traveled to the Cannes Film Festival to promote the film and to look for European distribution. The supernatural comedy was shelved for several months before premiering first in Europe in the spring of 1990. It opened in 16 cities across America in June of the same year and grossed only $25,000 in two weeks. The Dereks told the media that *Ghosts* was "nice, intimate entertainment which means it is difficult for it to compete theatrically," professing that the $3 million movie could have gone straight to video.[16] The picture drew extremely negative reviews, winning in several categories Worst Picture of the Year awards. In 2017, *Ghosts Can't Do It* gained new popularity after the election of Donald Trump as president of the United States. The Donald cameo-ed in the film, playing himself in two short scenes shot in his New York office boardroom. Apparently, Trump was given a script which he did not really follow, ad libbing most of it. John was pleased with the results. Trump said that he did the film because he and the Dereks were friends and "it was fun looking at Bo."

According to filmmaker and close friend Frank Harris, John was frustrated by the harsh critiques of his final films, and also buckling under the weight of the mortgage of the ranch and other loans. "When I think, he even closed himself up a little more. I would say, 'John, let's do another movie.' And then he would back off. And he hated it when Bo finally had to go out and work without him."[17]

In the early '90s, John never stopped traveling around the world despite suffering from minor ailments. In January 1990, he accompanied Bo to the Fantastic Film Festival in Avoriaz, France, where she was a member of the jury. Their presence made the news all over France. That August, while in Washington, D.C., for the International Horse show, the Dereks had a private tour of the White House and met President George H.W. Bush, just when America was on the brink of the Gulf War. Even though John was never involved in politics, his personal ideas seemed to be liberal but not to be part of any particular group. There was a second meeting with President Bush a couple of years later, at a formal dinner in Doha, Qatar; the Dereks were attending an endurance horse race and the president was on a state visit.

In September 1994, after the Dereks took a trip to Hong Kong, the press announced that they were closing a deal for a leather clothing line designed by John and sold by Bo on a home shopping network.[18] It was wrongly reported that they were launching a themed international restaurant chain, similar to the Hard Rock Café, managed by John in partnership with Ursula, Linda and Bo.

In the fall of 1994, John was approached by Mary Bailey, manager of Canadian country singer Shania Twain, and asked to take photographs for Twain's new album cover. John wasn't interested, but Bo eventually convinced him to do it. On the day of the shoot, John made clear to Twain that he was making an exception since he had stopped taking photographs of any women other than Bo. He explained that he had stopped because no other woman could tolerate his severe honesty, and he mentioned that the last time he photographed Raquel Welch, she ran off crying. As Twain recalled in her autobiography, "He would express this honesty by telling me that I was overweight at 115 pounds and, yes, my nose is crooked, so he was right."[19] John's remarks did not bother the singer, who was comfortable with her own look. She assured him that she was not there to be photographed as a movie star or a model, but just as an artist in need of album cover artwork. (Some of the photographs were also used for a calendar promoting the album release.) John appreciated her honesty. Before the photo session began, he prompted her to take off her makeup and loosen her hair, making everything very natural.

After a few shots, John started to show his temperamental character, getting frustrated because Twain's nose was posing all kind of issues for him. "He started cursing and swearing about as if it were a person itself, like me, the person, didn't actually belong to it.... He finally piped up to say something to the effect of, 'Someone give me a goddamn knife so I can cut off that nose.' Although not OK with him cutting off my nose, I was fine with the fact that he wished he could, and we just carried on shooting."[20]

Finally, with Twain wearing Bo's cowboy hat, after she was kept soaking in the Dereks' cold swimming pool for almost an hour, John took the right shot that ended up being the album cover for *The Woman in Me*. The collaboration was so mutually successful that John directed videos for Twain's songs "Any Man of Mine" and "Whose Bed Have Your Boots Been Under?," both shot at the Dereks' ranch. Twain noticed the amazing teamwork and harmony of John and Bo. "The one thing that made me settle into working with him without feeling intimidated is that everyone around him loved him so much.... And I thought, how can this be a mean man? How can these people around him love him so much? It must be something I'm missing. It didn't take me very long to realize there was something very, very special because everybody around him would have done anything for him."[21]

Bo's sister Kerry was John's assistant photographer while Bo's mother did hair and makeup, while Ramon, their personal horse trainer, helped out. It was a formative experience for Twain:

> I loved working with John and greatly respected and admired him very much. Both he and Bo were incredibly professional in their commitment to work and took it all very seriously. I appreciated this, and it made me want to keep up and do as good a job as I could possibly do. They made me want to work for the best results. I matured a lot working with them, and I believe being in their company so early in my career, I learned a great deal about my face, lightning, shooting, filming and, maybe most of all, about tolerance and teamwork.[22]

Only once, in the middle of the "Any Man of Mine" shoot, was there a bit of friction between the bossy director and the singer. John insisted they do something his way while Twain wanted to do it differently. That ignited a short confrontation, but the country singer was able to speak her mind and finally John let it go. He carried on with the shoot, respecting her stance without any further comments. The video won several international music awards including the Canadian Country Music Award for Video of the Year (1995).

In the last years of John's life, some of his close friends noticed how he had mellowed, most likely because of his weakening health. After suffering a light stroke in 1991, he had become more careful about his lifestyle. The way he had softened was not much in terms of his business, but in dealing with Bo and with other people.

The 30-year age difference in his marriage now seemed to matter to him more than ever. He thought often of 15 years down the line, as he stated in several occasions, "It will be awful for Bo because I will be slowly falling apart and no matter what she says, the person she fell in love with won't be there anymore."[23] Bo, now 37, always dismissed John's contentions, stating that as she was maturing, the age gap and the personality gap and all the other things started to get smaller. She explained how they have managed a May–December marriage which the critical press predicted would fail. "Neither of us smoke or drink; I've never been one for parties, neither has John. He has lived his life much longer than I have, and very fully, and I enjoy learning from him.... John and I have a good supporting system. He worries about me; I help him. When I fuss or talk back too much, he says he's going down to the local high school and find another."[24] She added on another occasion, "Rarely does he ever get me confused with his other blonde wives now.... He used to say, 'Remember when we went here or there and did this?' I'd say, 'No, that wasn't me.' We'd argue and he'd say: 'Oh, that was the other blonde.'"[25] John was not happy about Bo working without him, but he came to terms with it. There was often talk about his return behind the camera as a filmmaker but for one reason or another, it never happened. He spent his last years at his ranch, surrounded by his 26 beloved horses, one donkey, nine dogs, three cats and a parrot.

On May 20, 1998, while saying goodbye to a visitor at the ranch, he felt a sharp pain in his chest and collapsed. The visitor called an ambulance. By the time it reached the house, John was unconscious and not breathing. On the way to the hospital, he regained consciousness, becoming so belligerent that in the altercation with the paramedics, he broke some of his front teeth. Bo, who was in Los Angeles promoting a TV series, was told by a girlfriend that her husband was recovering at the Marian Medical Center in Santa Maria, California, 150 miles north of Los Angeles. Bo reached the hospital while John was in surgery. She learned that he couldn't speak but he had blinked his eyes when the surgeon asked him if he accepted the operation, which she had also co-authorized on the mobile phone. After an apparently successful two-hour surgery, John returned to his hospital room. But a few hours later, his coronary artery ruptured, and he was rushed once again into the operating room. He came out of it on life support.

While waiting, Bo called Sean. The father and daughter had just reunited after many years of estrangement. Linda Evans and a few very close friends were also alerted. Luke Faber, John's surgeon, informed Bo that her husband was suffering from an irreversible aortic dissection, but for legal reasons, he had to be kept on life support for at least 24 hours to see if he might regain consciousness. On May 22, two days after John was admitted, Bo, after consulting with Sean, ordered the life support turned off. At 12:45 p.m., John was pronounced dead. His beloved Bo, his daughter Sean, Bo's sister Kerry and a close family friend named Lyla were all around him.

One of Bo's first thoughts after John's death was making sure that John's son Russell not hear the news on radio or television. She dispatched a family friend to the Santa Barbara Hospital that was home to Russell, who was still suffering from his motorcycle accident. He learned the sad news just 15 minutes before the media announced it.

Some of John's obituaries portrayed him mostly as the Svengali husband who controlled the careers of his beautiful ingénue wives. They omitted the number of notable film roles he had played and his ability as a skilled photographer, preferring to stress more his flops as a director.

As per his wish, John's remains were cremated. A few days later, Bo organized at the ranch a private memorial, inviting all of John's wives. Pati, Ursula, Linda and Bo celebrated John's life, sharing tears and laughs, telling stories and anecdotes about their husband.

"There wasn't a big Hollywood turnout," Liz Smith wrote in her column, "mostly friends and neighbors," but the event was "a big love-in."[26]

All his life, John had always spent all the money he earned. According to his wives, he did not know the concept of saving. He invested most of his earnings in his own productions or on home improvement and horses. At the time of his death, he did not own any major asset except for the Santa Ynez Valley ranch he had purchased with Bo, who inherited his part. When she sold it in 1999 to actor Noah Wyle, Bo did not end up with much, after paying off the mortgage and some money owed to the government in back taxes.

In 2002, the *New York Times Magazine*'s style editor Steve Kurutz published "Ranch Dressing," a long article with several photographs, in which he explained how John's particular but impeccable sense of style had influenced the fall men's wear collections that season. He wrote:

> The rugged, macho glamour that John Derek embodied, burly coats as leathery and weather-worn as his skin; enough shearling to start a farm; and denim distressed by actual labor—is being embraced by designers like Dolce and Gabbana and Dsquared. Even Louis Vuitton's fall collection features the multipocketed photo vest that was the bedrock of Derek's wardrobe during the days when he was trotting around the globe, snapping soft-focus shots of semi-nude women (his wives, mostly) in exotic locales.[27]

All his life, John had a distaste for glamour, dressing always very casually. Still, his outfits had a sophisticated rusticity, something that he once called, tongue in cheek, "primitive chic." Once he quit his career as an actor, John stopped dressing up even for public occasions. Photographs of him in a suit or tuxedo are almost non-existent, with the exception of when he participated in a Trans World Entertainment annual gala dinner in December 1988 at the Beverly Hilton Hotel, where he was photographed wearing a smart, dark double-breasted suit and a tie, holding hands with the elegant Bo.

In 2002, Bo published *Riding Lessons—Everything That Matters in Life I Learned from Horses*, an eye-opening memoir about her life, particularly the 25 years spent with John. In the book, she rectified all the misconceptions about their relationship, giving an honest portrait of her marriage with John, who was her ultimate man as she was, for him, physically and emotionally his ultimate woman. They appeared to be an intensely devoted, happy couple, rarely out of each other's sight, but still with their own independence, far from the Svengali relationship the media always tried to portray them in.

Bo was once invited to rate John as a husband. Without any hesitation, she answered: "For me, he's great." Then when she was asked if he had any faults, her reply once again was immediate: "No." But after a short pause she added, "Well ... he is very opinionated. And ... sometimes he's hard to live with. He wants things done now ... he has no patience. Most of all he can't understand carelessness ... but I love him."[28]

Nowadays John Derek is unknown to the younger generations and almost forgotten by the old ones. Those who do remember him, mostly think of that lucky, ruggedly handsome man who married three beautiful blondes, all uncannily resembling each other. John Derek was also a true maverick who happened to be, for a while, a reluctant Hollywood star.

Filmography and Career Record

As Actor

Author's note: Plot synopses are from studio publicity and promotional materials, distributed to the press and to theaters.

Since You Went Away

Selznick International Pictures, Vanguard Films
B&W, 172 minutes
Premiered in Los Angeles on July 17, 1944

CREDITS: *Producer-Screenplay:* David O. Selznick; *Director:* John Cromwell; Based on the book *Since You Went Away ... Letters to a Soldier from His Wife* by Margaret Buell Wilder; *Production Designer*: William L. Pereira; *Photography*: Stanley Cortez, Lee Garmes; *Settings*: Mark-Lee Kirk; *Special Effects*: Jack Cosgrove; *Supervising Editor*: Hal C. Kern; *Production Assistant:* Barbara Keon; *Music*: Max Steiner: *Associate Editor*: James E. Newcom; *Interior Decorator*: Victor A. Gangelin; *Assistant Director*: Lowell J. Farrell; *Associate Music Director:* Louis Forbes; *Sound Recordist*: Percy Townsend; *Technical Advisor*: Lt. Col. J.G. Taylor

CAST: Claudette Colbert (Anne Hilton), Jennifer Jones (Jane Hilton), Joseph Cotten (Lt. Tony Willett), Shirley Temple (Bridget "Brig" Hilton), Monty Woolley (Col. William G. Smollett), Lionel Barrymore (Clergyman), Robert Walker (William G. "Bill" Smollett II), Hattie McDaniel (Fidelia), Agnes Moorehead (Emily Hawkins), Alla Nazimova (Zofia Koslowska), Albert Basserman (Dr. Sigmund Gottlieb Golden), Gordon Oliver (Marine officer), Keenan Wynn (Lt. Solomon), Guy Madison (Harold Smith), Craig Stevens (Danny Williams), Lloyd Corrigan (Mr. Mahoney), Jackie Moran (Johnny Mahoney), Jane Devlin (Gladys Brown), Robert Anderson (Patron at bar), Charles Williams (Man in cocktail lounge), Irving Bacon (Bartender), Leo Mostovoy (Headwaiter), Cindy Garner (Sugar), James Carlisle (Sugar's officer friend), George Chandler (Taxi driver), John A. James (Friendly sergeant at dance), Mary Anne Durkin (Frightened girl at dance), Joyce Horne (Swenson's girl friend), Anne Gillis (Becky Anderson), Grady Sutton (Southerner), Ruth Valmy (Tony's friend), Buddy Gorman (Short soldier), Patricia Peters (Tall WAC), Andrew McLaglen (Former plowboy), Addison Richards (Major Sam Atkins), George Lloyd (Motorcycle policeman), Barbara Pepper (Pin girl), Jill Warren (Waitress), Byron Foulger (Principal), Harry Hayden (Conductor), Edwin Maxwell (Businessman), Russell Hoyt (One-armed sailor), Loudie Claar (Young mother), Don Najarian, Jon Najarian (Babies), Helen Koford [Terry Moore] (Refugee child), Florence Bates (Hungry woman), Conrad Binyon (Page boy), Theodore Von Eltz (Desk clerk), Adeline deWalt Reynolds (Elderly woman), Christopher Adams, Jimmy Dodd, Martha Outlaw, Verna Knopf, Robert Cherry, Kirk Barron (Train passengers), Earl Jacobs (One-armed boy), Cecil Ballerino (Patient at Potters Wheel), Jack Gardner (Patient in wheelchair), Doodles Weaver, Paul Esburg, Richard C. Wood, Ralph Reed, James Westerfield, Warren Hymer (Convalescents), Dorothy Adams (Nurse), Willard Jillson (Marine lover), Dorothy Mann (His girl friend), Peggy Maley (Another girl friend), Robert Johnson (Black officer), Dorothy Dandridge (Black officer's wife), Shelby Bacon (Black officer's child), Eddie Hall (Eager sailor), Warren Burr (Serious soldier), Lela Bliss (Gabby woman), Eilene Janssen (Sergeant's child), Harlan Miller (M.P.), Mrs. Ray Feldman (Soldier's grandmother), Neyle Marx (Grandson), Johnny Bond (AWOL), Ruth Roman (Envious girl), Betsy Howard (Friend of envious girl), Stephen Wayne (Bearded sailor), William B. Davidson (Taxpayer), Tom Dawson (Tough Bronx soldier), Marilyn Hare (Merchant Marine's wife), Jonathan Hale (Conductor), Walter Baldwin (Gateman), Eric Sinclair (Voice in convalescent ward), Jerry Revell (Foreman), James Clemons, Jr. (Caroler), Dick Whittington, a dog (Soda), Neil Hamilton (Photo of Tim Hilton), Rhonda Fleming (Girl at Dance), Aileen Pringle (Woman at Cocktail Lounge), Wallis Clark (Man at Cocktail Lounge), Neila Hart, Florence Allen, Lulu Mae Bohrman, Dulcie Day (Extras), Dare Harris [John Derek] (Soldier)

PLOT: Tim Hilton goes to war, leaving his wife Anne and his two children Jane and Bridget. Suddenly their income is reduced to the usual allotment from the government, which does not permit of keeping their maid Fidelia. At the instigation of her daughters, Anne boosts the household income by taking in a boarder, the grumpy Col. William G. Smollett. The old man is upset because his grandson Bill has flunked out at West Point; the colonel feels that this has brought disgrace upon his ancestors. On a visit to his grandpa from a nearby Army camp, Bill wins the heart of Jane, the older of Anne's two daughters. Ordered to an embarkation port, the young soldier becomes engaged; and subsequently dies in battle. Although she is devastated by the tragic news, Jane continues her work as a nurses' aid in a rehabilitation hospital. Anne's husband is reported missing in action in the Pacific. Welcome as a sustaining influence in this difficult moment is Tony Willett, a Naval lieutenant, an old friend of the family and former flame of Anne's. Wondering whether the father is a prisoner or dead, the family goes on making its contribution to the community and the war effort as best it can. During a Christmas Eve party, a cable is received that says that Tim Hilton is safe and is returning home.

REVIEWS: "It is a magnificent picture, warm, tender, moving, often glorious, often rich in humor, often poignant with heartbreak, and drenched in that outstanding product of war, women's tears, yet never losing its note of high faith." *The Hollywood Reporter,* July 19, 1944

"It's a box-office mop-up, an audience heart-tug and, in no small measure, a human document of World War II as it affects all of us." *Variety,* July 19, 1944

"[The picture] does come off altogether as a rather large dose of choking sentiment." The *New York Times,* July 21, 1944

ADDITIONAL REVIEWS AND ARTICLES: *Boxoffice* 29 July 1944; *Film Daily;* 19 July 1944 p. 8; *Commonweal* 4 August 1944 pp. 374–375; *Cosmopolitan* August 1944 p. 133; *Films and Filming* (U.K.) October 1981, pp. 46–47; *Harrison's Report* 22 July 1944 p. 119; *Hollywood Reporter* 26 May 1943; *Hollywood Reporter* 2 June 1943 p. 6; *Hollywood Reporter* 2 August 1943 p. 7; *Hollywood Reporter* 10 August 1943 p. 1; *Hollywood Reporter* 17 September 1943 p. 9; *Hollywood Reporter* 1 November 1943 p. 7; *Hollywood Reporter* 3 November 1943 p. 8; *Hollywood Reporter* 4 November 1943 p. 6; *Hollywood Reporter* 5 November 1943 p. 11; *Hollywood Reporter* 12 November 1943 p. 10; *Hollywood Reporter* 15 November 1943; *Hollywood Reporter* 22 November 1943 p. 10; *Hollywood Reporter* 24 November 1943 p. 6; *Hollywood Reporter* 29 November 1943 p. 9; *Hollywood Reporter* p. 30 November 1943 pp. 5, 7, 1; *Hollywood Reporter* 3 December 1943 p. 2; *Hollywood Reporter* 15 December 1943 p. 33; *Hollywood Reporter* 20 December 1943 pp. 3, 4; *Hollywood Reporter* 24 December 1943 p. 3; *Hollywood Reporter* 27 December 1943 p. 4; *Hollywood Reporter* 1 January 1944 p. 4; *Hollywood Reporter* 28 January 1944 p. 15; *Hollywood Reporter* 11 February 1944 p. 9; *Hollywood Reporter* 8 March 1944 p. 3; *Hollywood Reporter* 21 March 1944 p. 5; *Hollywood Reporter* 17 July 1944 p. 2; *Hollywood Reporter* 24 July 1944 p. 6; *Hollywood Reporter* 28 July 1944 p. 3; *Hollywood Reporter* 4 August 1944 pp. 5–44, 48; *Hollywood Reporter* 14 March 1949; *Kinematograph Weekly* (U.K.) 18 December 1952 p. 120; *Kinematograph Weekly* (U.K.) 28 December 1944; *L.A. Times* 9 April 1944; *L.A. Times* 29 October 1944; *Life* 24 July 1944 pp. 53–55; *The London Times* (U.K.) 11 January 1944, p. 6; *Monthly Film Bulletin* (U.K.) January 1945, pp. 6; *Motion Picture Herald* 22 July 1944 p. 2095; *Photoplay* October 1944 p. 21; *Motion Picture Herald Product Digest* 20 November 1943 p. 1635; *Motion Picture Herald Product Digest* 22 July 1944; *New York Herald Tribune* 20 February, 1944; *New York Herald Tribune* 21 July 1944; *New York Motion Picture Critics Reviews* 24 July 1944 pp. 296–298; *The New Yorker* July 29 1944 p. 42. *Newsweek* 10 July 1944 pp. 85–86; *Radio Times* 10 December 1988 p. 29; *Saturday Review* 29 July 1944 p. 16, *Show-*

men's Trade Review 22 July 1944 p. 10; *Theatre Arts* September 1944 p. 543; *Time* June 17 1944 p. 94; *Today's Cinema* (U.K.) 11 December 1952 p. 11; *Today's Cinema* (U.K.) 22 December 1944

AWARDS AND HONORS: Academy Awards: *Won*: Best Music, Scoring of a Dramatic or Comedy Picture: Max Steiner. *Nominated*: Best Picture; Best Actress in a Leading Role: Claudette Colbert; Best Actor in a Supporting Role: Monty Woolley; Best Actress in a Supporting Role: Jennifer Jones; Best Cinematography, Black-and-White: Stanley Cortez, Lee Garmes; Best Art Direction-Interior Decoration, Black-and-White: Mark-Lee Kirk, Victor A. Gangelin; Best Film Editing: Hal C. Kern, James E. Newcom; Best Effects, Special Effects: Jack Cosgrove, Arthur Johns

NOTES: Future stars Guy Madison, Dorothy Dandridge, Ruth Roman and Rhonda Fleming appear in microscopic roles.

I'll Be Seeing You

Selznick International Pictures, Vanguard Films
B&W, 85 minutes
Released January 5, 1945

CREDITS: *Producer:* Dore Schary; *Director:* William Dieterle, George Cukor (uncredited); *Screenplay:* Marion Parsonett, based on the radio play *Double Furlough* by Charles Martin; *Photography:* Tony Gaudio; *Music Score*: Daniele Amfitheatrof; *Settings:* Mark-Lee Kirk; *Supervising Editor:* Hal C. Kern; *Editor*: William H. Ziegler; *Interior Decorators*: Earl B. Wooden, Emile Kuri; *Costumes:* Edith Head; *Makeup*: William Riddle; *Assistant Director:* Lowell J. Farrell; *Sound:* Richard DeWeese; *Special Effects:* John R. Cosgrove; *Song:* "I'll Be Seeing You," words and music by Sammy Fain and Irving Kahal

CAST: Joseph Cotten (Zachary Morgan), Ginger Rogers (Mary Marshall), Shirley Temple (Barbara Marshall), Spring Byington (Sarah Marshall), Tom Tully (Henry Marshall), Dare Harris [John Derek] (Lt. Bruce), Chill Wills (Swanson), Kenny Bowers (Sailor on train), Dorothy Stone: (Saleslady), Fred Aldrich (Sidewalk Cowboy), Margaret Bert (Mother of Boys), Jack Carr (Counterman at Train Station), Robert Dudley (Pine Hills YMCA Hotel Attendant), Gary Gray (Franklin Boy with Toy Machine Gun), Eddie Hall (Charlie Hartman), Joe Haworth (Sailor in Coffee Shop), Olin Howland (Train Vendor), John James (Paratrooper on Train), Earl Johnson (Dog Owner), Mickey Laughlin, Hank Tobias (Boys Outside Theater), Thomas Martin (New Year's Eve Partygoer), Bob Meredith (Soldier-Father on Train), Edmund Mortimer (Floorwalker in Women's Shop), Hal Taggart (New Year's Eve Partygoer)

PLOT: Mary Marshall, on Christmas furlough from the prison in which she is serving a manslaughter sentence, and Sgt. Zachary Morgan, on furlough from the Army hospital where he is under treatment as a neuropsychiatric, meet en route to Pinehill, where Mary is to spend the holidays with her aunt, her uncle and their daughter Barbara. Both Mary and Zach lack confidence in the future. She is under the strain of paying her debt to society for the crime of accidentally killing her former employer, while she was attempting to escape his drunken advances. Having had dreams, as most young business girls do, of eventually marrying and having her own home, a devoted husband and children, she feels now that such things are impossible for an ex-convict.

Zach seems unable to free himself of combat-induced neurosis. Having nowhere to go, he gets off at Pinehill with Mary and arranges to stay at the local YMCA. The love that develops out of their adventures together during the ten days' leave, plus the kindly and steadying influence of the Marshall family, gives Mary and Zach hope for the future. Mary withholds her identity as a prisoner from Zach, fearing the effect the disclosure might have on his greatly improved mental conditions. Barbara inadvertently reveals to Zach the truth about Mary. The sudden shock throws him back emotionally, and their newfound life together is threatened when he rushes to his train without a word of encouragement. But Zach recovers quickly, finds himself completely normal, and when Mary arrives at the prison gates he is there to tell her that he will be waiting for her when she is released.

REVIEWS: "[The picture] has the prime essentials of box-office success, a fascinating moving story and a trio of star names..." *The Hollywood Reporter*, December 19, 1944

"A poignant, romantic drama, done with taste and honesty, and acted superbly, it is sure box-office." *Variety,* December 20, 1944

"[A] simple and straightforward film, which handles this most urgent subject in a sane affecting way." The *New York Times,* April 6, 1945

REVIEW FOR JOHN DEREK: "Good in the cast are Spring Byington and Tom Tully who have important duties. Chill Wills, Dare Harris, Kenny Bowers, Olin Howlin [sic] and others appear." *Los Angeles Times,* December 25, 1944

ADDITIONAL REVIEWS AND ARTICLES: *Boxoffice* 23 December 1944; *Commonweal* 23 March 1944 p. 566; *Film Daily* 20 December 1944 p. 9; *Hollywood Reporter* 31 January 1944 p. 5; *Hollywood Reporter* 24 February 1944 p. 6; *Hollywood Reporter* 28 March 1944 p. 4; *Hollywood Reporter* 31 March 1944 p. 15; *Hollywood Reporter* 3 April 1944 p. 8; *Hollywood Reporter* 4 April 1944 pp. 5–6; *Hollywood Reporter* 25 April 1944 p. 13; *Hollywood Reporter* 28 April 1944 p. 6; *Hollywood Reporter* 3 May 1944 p. 8; *Hollywood Reporter* 26 May 1944 p. 19; *Hollywood Reporter* 19 December 1944 p. 3; *Hollywood Reporter* 9 April 1945 p. 12; *Kinematograph Weekly* (U.K.) 21 June 1945; *Monthly Film Bulletin* (U.K.) November 1945 p. 135; *Motion Picture Herald Product Digest* 27 May 1944 p. 1913; *Motion Picture Herald Product Digest* 23 December 1944 pp. 2237–38; *New York Herald Tribune* 6 April 1945; *New York Motion Picture Critics Reviews* 9 April 1945 pp. 412, 413; *New Republic* 23 April 1945 p. 557; *New Yorker* 14 April 1945 p. 49; *Newsweek* 22 January 1945 p. 88; *Photoplay* March 1945, p. 19; *Theatre Arts* April 1945 p. 231; *Time* 22 January 1945 pp. 91–92; *Today's Cinema* (U.K.) 20 June 1945; *Today's Cinema* (U.K.) 3 April 1950

NOTES: *I'll Be Seeing You* was originally titled *With All My Heart* and *Double Furlough. Lux Radio Theater* broadcast a radio version starring Joseph Cotten and Dorothy McGuire.

Knock on Any Door

Columbia, A Santana Production
B&W, 100 minutes
Premiered in Chicago on February 21, 1949

CREDITS: *Associate Producer*: Henry S. Kesler; *Producer*: Robert Lord; *Director*: Nicholas Ray; *Screenplay*: Daniel Taradash, John Monk, Jr.; Based on the novel by Willard Motley; *Photography*: Burnett Guffey; *Art Director*: Robert Peterson; *Editor*: Viola Lawrence; *Set Decorator*: William Kiernan; *Assistant Director*: Arthur S. Black; *Gowns:* Jean Louis; *Makeup:* Clay Campbell; *Hair Stylist*: Helen Hunt; *Sound:* Frank Goodwin; *Music Score:* George Antheil; *Music Director:* M.W. Stoloff; *Technical Advisers*: National Probation and Parole Association

CAST: Humphrey Bogart (Andrew Morton), John Derek ("Pretty Boy" Nick Romano), George Macready (District Attorney Kerman), Allene Roberts (Emma), Susan Perry (Adele Morton), Mickey Knox (Vito), Barry Kelley (Judge Drake), Dooley Wilson (Piano player), Cara Williams (Nelly) Jimmy Conlin (Kid Fingers), Sumner Williams (Jimmy), Sid Melton (Squint), Pepe Hern (Juan Rodriguez), Dewey Martin (Butch), Robert Davis (Sunshine), Houseley Stevenson (Junior), Vince Barnett (Bartender), Thomas Sully (Officer Hawkins), Florence Auer (Aunt Lena), Pierre Watkin (Purcell), Gordon Nelson (Corey), Argentina Brunetti (Ma Romano), Richard Sinatra (Julian Romano), Carol Coombs (Angie Romano), Joan Baxter (Maria Romano), Evelyn Underwood, Mary Emery, Franz Roehn, Betty Hall, Jack Jahries, Rose Plumer, Mabel Smaney, Sidney Dubin, Homer Dickinson, Netta Packer, Joy Hallward, John Mitchum (Jury members), Frank Arnold (Artist), Ann Duncan, Lorraine Comerford (Bobbysoxers), Chuck Hamilton, Frank Marlo, Ralph Volkie (Bailiffs), Joe Palma, Ed Randolph, Eda Reiss Merin, Joan Danton, Dick Bartell (Reporters), Donald Kerr (Court clerk), Myron Healey (Assistant District Attorney), Jane Lee (Lunch woman), Dorothy Vernon (Knitter), Blackie Whiteford (Tattoo artist), Ned Glass (Fiddler), Brick Sullivan (Policeman on street), William Haade (Policeman with Hawkins), Charles Sullivan (Telescope man), Jack Clisby (Black policeman), Glenn Thompson, Paul Baxley, Lee Phelps (Policemen), Dudley Dickerson (Bootblack), Garry Owen (Larry), George Chandler (Cashier), George Hickman (Pool player–Detective), Chester Conklin (Barber), Jeff York (Hawkins' partner), Frank Pharr (Old man), Wesley Hopper (Boss), Paul Kreibich (Headwaiter), Sid Tomack (Duke), Charles Camp (Waiter), Frank Hagney, Peter Virgo (Suspects), Saul Gorss, Al Hill, Philip Morris (Detectives), Sam Flint (Warden), Helen Mowery (Miss Holiday), Jody Gilbert (Gussie), Curt Conway (Elkins), Edwin Parker, Al Ferguson (Guards)

PLOT: Nick Romano is in court, charged with the murder of a policeman. Andrew Morton, his friend and lawyer, believes Nick is innocent and is battling for his life, blaming society for the boy's other crimes. Nick's life story is seen in flashback. His father died when he was young, he was brought up in the slums, mixed with the wrong people and paid several visits to reformatories where bad treatment expelled any idea of reform in him. He later fell in love with Emma, a young girl whom he eventually married. He tried desperately to reform himself for her sake. He took a job, but then, provoked into a rage by his boss' hostility, he got fired, a fact which caused his pregnant wife to commit suicide. This latter point is played upon constantly by District Attorney Kerman, and this which makes him break down and confess to murder. Nick is sentenced to death and led to the electric chair.

REVIEWS: "A pretentious 'social' melodrama." *New York Times,* February 23, 1949

"*Knock on Any Door* is a message picture of extraordinary effectiveness ... well acted." *Motion Picture Herald,* February 26, 1949

"[A] film which has all of the earmarks of becoming one of the most widely discussed and generously patronized of this or any other season." *Boxoffice,* February 26, 1949

REVIEW FOR JOHN DEREK: "Picture introduces a young man who, to all purposes, is the principal character upon whose shoulders the story burden falls. He is John Derek—a new bobbysoxer dream and a personality who will click with the femmes, motherly or otherwise." *Variety,* February 23, 1949

ADDITIONAL REVIEWS AND ARTICLES: *Boxoffice* 7 August, 1948; *Boxoffice* 25 June, 1949 p. 36; *Brooklyn Eagle* 3 April 1948 p. 14; *Cahiers du cinema* (France) April 1963 pp. 31–32; *Chicago Tribune* 19 June 1948; *Christian Science Monitor* 10 September 1948 p. 10; *Commonweal* 11 March 1949 p. 543; *Dirigido por* (Spain) January 2002; *Film Daily* 21 February 1949 p. 7; *Harrison's Reports* 26 February 1949 p. 35; *Hollywood Reporter* 13 August 48 p. 14; *Hollywood Reporter* 10 September 1948 p. 12; *Il corriere della sera* (Italy) 26 May 1950 p. 2; *Look* March 1949 pp. 100–103; *L.A. Examiner* 8 September 1947; *L.A. Times* 9 March 1949 p. 17; *Modern Screen* April 1949 p. 27; *Modern Screen* June 1949 pp. 99–100; *Monthly Film Bulletin* (U.K.) May 1949 p. 84; *New Republic* 7 March 1949 p. 30; *New Yorker* 5 March 1949 p. 56; *New York Times* 27 February 1949 sec 2. p. 1; *Newsweek* 7 March 1949 p. 91; *Nosferatu* (U.K.) October 2006; *Picture Show* (U.K.) 13 August 1949 p. 8; *Picturegoer* (U.K.) 6 August 1949 p. 18; *Revue des deux mondes* (France) 15 April 1950 p. 746; *Saturday Evening Post* 3 March 1953; *Showman Trade Review* 26 February 1949 p. 22; *Sequence* Summer 1949 pp. 86–88; *Showman Trade Review* 2 April 1949 p. 20; *Sight and Sound* January 2010 p. 89; *Silver Screen* March 1949 p. 18; *Spectator* 29 July 1949 p. 141; *Theatre Arts* April 1949 p. 87; *Time* 14 March 1949 p. 102; *Today's Cinema* (U.K.) 6 Apr 1949, p. 10; *Variety* 1 January 1949; *Woman's Home Companion* May 1949 pp. 10–11

NOTES: The character of Nick Romano was reprised in 1960 by James Darren in *Let No Man Write My Epitaph,* directed by Philip Leacock. The piano player is Dooley Wilson, the man to whom Bogart said, "Play it, once, Sam," in *Casablanca* (1942).

All the King's Men

Columbia, Robert Rossen's Production, B&W, 110 minutes
Premiered in New York on November 8, 1949

CREDITS: *Screenplay-Producer-Director:* Robert Rossen; Based on the novel by Robert Penn Warren; *Photography:* Burnett Guffey; *Art Director:* Sturges Carne; *Editor:* Al Clark; *Editorial Adviser:* Robert Parrish; *Set Decorator:* Louis Diage; *Montages:* Donald W. Starling; *Gowns:* Jean Louis; *Assistant Director:* Sam Nelson; *Makeup:* Clay Campbell; *Hair Styles:* Helen Hunt; *Music Score:* Louis Gruenberg; *Music Director:* Morris Stoloff; *Sound:* Frank Goodwin; *Assistant to the Producer:* Shirley Miller

CAST: Broderick Crawford (Willie Stark), John Ireland (Jack Burden), Joanne Dru (Anne Stanton), John Derek (Tom Stark), Mercedes McCambridge (Sadie Burke), Shepperd Strudwick (Adam Stanton), Ralph Dumke (Tiny Duffy), Anne Seymour (Lucy Stark), Katharine Warren (Mrs. Burden), Raymond Greenleaf (Judge Stanton), Walter Burke (Sugar Boy), Will Wright (Dolph Pillsbury), Grandon Rhodes (Floyd McEvoy), H.C. Miller (Pa Stark), Richard Hale (Richard Hale), William Bruce (Commissioner), A.C. Tillman (Sheriff), Houseley Stevenson (Madison), Truett Myers (Minister), Phil Tully (Football coach), Helene Stanley (Helene Hale), Judd Holdren, Pat O'Malley (Politicians), Reba Watterson (Receptionist), Ted French (Dance caller), Paul Maxey (Local chairman), Frank Mclure (Doctor), Irving Smith (Butler), Louis Mason

(Second minister), John Skins Miller (Drunk), King Donovan, William Cottrell (Reporters), Edwin Chandler (Radio announcer), Paul Ford (Member of state legislature), Frank Wilcox (Man), George Farmer (Bus man), John Giles (Young boy), Wheaton Chambers, Marshall Bradford, Avery Graves, Nolan Leary, William E. Green (Senators), Glenn Thompson, Al Wyatt (State troopers), Harold Miller (Speaker of the house), Mary Bear (File clerk), Stephen Chase (Puckett), Richard Gordon, Tom Ferrandini, George Taylor, James Linn (Politicians), Earle S. Dewey, Roy Darmour, Charles Sherlock (Politicians, Harrison headquarters), Robert Filmer (Editor), Bert Hanlon (Editor), William Tannen, Anthony Merrill (Men in city bar), Al Thompson, Charles Haefeli (Men in cheap bar)

PLOT: Willie Stark makes headlines when he boldly condemns corruption in local civic affairs. Influential urbanites nominate him for governor, in order to split the rural vote and put their own men into office. Willie runs a spectacular campaign but narrowly loses the election. Now, however, Willie, who has cunningly learned a lot of tricks, sets out to be a politician in his own right and gathers together a large group of followers. With the help of Jack Burden, a reporter, and Sadie Burke, his worldly-wise secretary, Willie runs for governor again and he wins in a landslide. His magnetic power has become so great that even aristocratic Anne Stanton, Jack's girl, falls under his spell. Once inside the Governor's Mansion; Willie, although popular with the people, inaugurates an administration of reckless corruption. He becomes alienated from his wife Lucy and, out of sheer vanity, forces his adopted son Tom to play football after being hurt in a car accident. As a result, Tom is crippled for life. Willie's failure to clean up the corruption in his administration causes him to lose the support of Judge Stanton, Anne's uncle. Willie orders Burden to get some unsavory facts on the judge's past, which he does; and the judge commits suicide rather than face exposure. Willie fights impeachment proceedings instituted against him, but while acknowledging the cheers of his supporters, he is shot by Adam Stanton, Anne's brother, who has learned about their affair. Adam, in turn, is shot down by Willie's bodyguard. Burden convinces Anne that together they must destroy the Willie Stark legend.

REVIEWS: "*All the King's Men* is Americana with the strength of legend, although contemporary to this generation." *Showmen's Trade Review*, November 5, 1949

"[M]eticulous attention to production details, inspired scripting and sterling direction ... makes it a triumphant credit for Robert Rossen, who scripted and directed." *Boxoffice*, November 5, 1949

"Consistency of dramatic structure—or of character revelation—is not in it. But it has superb pictorialism which perpetually crackles and explodes." The *New York Times*, November 9, 1949

REVIEW FOR JOHN DEREK: "John Derek has an effective but minor role, as Stark's son." *New York Daily News*, November 9, 1949.

ADDITIONAL REVIEWS AND ARTICLES: *Commonweal* November 19 1949 p. 181; *Cue* 12 November 1949; *Daily Variety* 26 November 1952; The *Daily Mail* (U.K.) April 14, 1950; *The Daily Mirror* (U.K.) 14 April 1950; *The Daily Telegraph* (U.K.) 30 September 1950, *The Evening Standard* (U.K.) 15 April 1950; *Film Daily* 7 November 1949 p. 9; *Film Index* n11 1971, p. 112; *Film Index* n12/13 1971, pp. 113–114; *Films in Review* February 1950 pp. 28–29; *Filmland* (NZ) May 1950 p. 5; *Harrison's Reports* 5 November 1949 p. 179; *Hollywood Reporter* 26 November 1948 p. 16; *Hollywood Reporter* 23 December 1948 p. 4; *Hollywood Reporter* 21 January 1949 p. 16; *Hollywood Reporter* 13 May 1949; *Hollywood Reporter* 29 March 1950 pp. 1, 8; *Hollywood Reporter* 30 March 1950 pp. 1, 7; *Life* 28 November 1949 pp. 11–112; *The Listener* 7 July 1988, p. 35; *L. A. Daily News* 3 July 1947; *L. A. Times* 17 November 1949; *L. A. Times* 22 May 1950; *Monthly Film Bulletin* (U.K.) March-April 1950 p. 42; *Monthly Film Bulletin* (U.K.) February 1986, pp. 56–57; *Motion Picture Herald* 5 November 1949; *Motion Picture Herald Product Digest* 5 November 1949 p. 73; *MovieMaker* Summer 2008 pp. 38–41; *New Republic* 21 November 1949 p. 21; *N.Y. Herald Tribune* 9 November 1949; *New York Times* 27 February 1949 II p. 4; *New York Times* 9 November 1949 p. 37; *New York Times* 13 November 1949 II p. 1; *New York Times* 20 November 1949 p. 5; *The New Yorker* 12 November 1949 p. 101; *Newsweek* 21 November 1949 pp. 91–93; *Picturegoer* (U.K.) 20 May 1950 pp. 12–13; *Picturegoer Annual* (U.K) 1950-51 pp. 71–72; *Saturday Review* 8 January 1955 p. 30; *Sequence* Summer 1950 p. 13; *Sight and Sound* June 1950 pp. 163–164; *Sight and*

Sound July 1950 p. 209; *Sight and Sound* August 1950 p. 264; *Sight and Sound* August 1993 p. 60; *Sight and Sound* September 2001 p. 58; *Silver Screen* March 1950; *Sunday Mirror Magazine* 20 November 1949; *Time* 5 December 1949 p. 102; *The Times* (U.K.) 15 April 1950; *Today's Cinema* (U.K.) 31 March 1950; *The Tribune* (U.K.) April 21 1950; *Variety* 14 May 1947; *Variety* 28 December 1949; *Variety* 29 March 1950.

AWARDS AND HONORS: New York Film Critics Circle Awards: *Won*: Best Film; Best Actor: Broderick Crawford; 3rd Place: Best Actress: Mercedes McCambridge

Venice Film Festival Italy: *Nominated*: Golden Lion: Robert Rossen

Directors Guild of America: *Won*: Outstanding Directorial Achievement in Motion Pictures: Robert Rossen, Sam Nelson

Writers Guild of America: *Won*: Best Written American Drama: Robert Rossen; The Robert Meltzer Award (Screenplay Dealing Most Ably with Problems of the American Scene): Robert Rossen

Golden Globes: *Won*: Best Picture; Best Supporting Actress: Mercedes McCambridge, Best Actor: Broderick Crawford; Most Promising Newcomer—Female: Mercedes McCambridge; *Nominated*: Best Original Score: George Duning; Best Cinematography—Black and White: Burnett Guffey.

Academy Awards: *Won*: Best Picture; Best Actor in a Supporting Role: Mercedes McCambridge, Best Actor in a Supporting Role: John Ireland; *Nominated*: Best Director: Robert Rossen; Best Writing, Screenplay: Robert Rossen; Best Film Editing: Robert Parrish, Al Clark

Blue Ribbon Awards: *Boxoffice Magazine*: *Won*: Best Film; Best Actors: Broderick Crawford, Mercedes McCambridge, Joanne Dru, John Ireland, John Derek

NOTES: "And Introducing John Derek" can be read in the picture's opening credits even though John had already appeared a few months earlier in *Knock on Any Door*.

In 2005, Columbia produced another version of Robert Penn Warren's novel under the same title, directed by Steven Zaillian and starring Sean Penn, Jude Law and Kate Winslet

Rogues of Sherwood Forest

Columbia
Technicolor, 80 minutes
Premiered in New York on June 21, 1950

CREDITS: *Producer*: Fred M. Packard; *Director:* Gordon Douglas; *Screenplay:* George Bruce; *Story*: Ralph Bettinson; *Photography*: Charles Lawton, Jr.; *Art Director*: Harold MacArthur; *Technicolor Color Consultant:* Francis Cugat; *Editor:* Gene Havlick; *Set Decorator:* James Crowe; *Assistant Director:* Wilbur McGaugh; *Gowns:* Jean Louis; *Makeup:* Clay Campbell; *Hair Styles:* Helen Hunt: *Sound*: Jack Goodrich; *Music Score*: Heinz Roemheld, Arthur Morton; *Music Director:* Morris Stoloff

CAST: John Derek (Robin, Earl of Huntingdon), Diana Lynn (Lady Marianne), George Macready (King John), Alan Hale (Little John), Paul Cavanagh (Sir Giles), Lowell Gilmore (Count of Flanders), Billy House (Friar Tuck), Billy Bevan (Will Scarlett), Lester Matthews (Alan-A-Dale), Wilton Graff (Baron Fitzwalter), Donald Randolph (Archbishop Stephen Langton), Harry Cording (Officer posting decree), Matthew Bolton (Abbott), Lois Hall (Pretty girl), Christopher Cook (Little boy), Gavin Muir (Baron Alfred), Olaf Hytten (Charcoal burner), Symona Boniface (Charcoal Burner's wife), Paul Collins (Alfred), John Dehner (Sir Baldric), John George (Peasant), Lumsden Hare (Warwick), Colin Keith-Johnston (Muster), Nelson Leigh (Baron Benedict), George Magrill (Sherwood man), George Suzanne (Acrobat); Patrick Whyte (Officer)

PLOT: In the year 1214, John, evil brother of the late King Richard, reigns over England and plots vengeance against Robin, Earl of Huntington, son of his erstwhile enemy Robin Hood. John raises money to hire mercenaries by levying unjust taxes against the people. Robin defends his tenants against the king's soldiery. He is captured and condemned to be hanged, but the king's ward Lady Marianne, whom Robin loves, frees him and his fellow prisoner Little John. In Sherwood Forest, they reunite Robin Hood's old comrades-in-arms (Friar Tuck, Alan-A-Dale, Will Scarlett and other Merry Men) and proceed to harass the king's soldiery. From Marianne, Robin learns that John plans to assassinate England's three greatest barons. The barons fail to heed Robin's warning, and two of them are killed. The third survives and rouses the remaining barons against John. The king, in a desperate effort to raise the money he needs, promises the hand of his wealthy young ward to the count of

Flanders, against her will. Robin and his men ambush the marriage procession and, in a fierce battle, overcome the king's men. John is forced by the barons to sign the famous Magna Carta and Robin and Marianne are free to be married.

REVIEWS: "The story is good, is spread somewhat thin, but it moves unevenly." *Film Daily,* June 21, 1950

"None may deny the pace and vigor of this astounding slice of English history, which is handsomely decked out in Technicolor before impressive backgrounds of castle and moat and forest." *Today's Cinema* (U.K.), August 10, 1950

"Boisterous adventure story." *Monthly Film Bulletin* (U.K.), September 1950

REVIEWS FOR JOHN DEREK: "Robin Hood, Jr., rides again, and if, in the playing of John Derek, the accent of the English adventurer is more Laguna Beach than Sherwood Forest, it doesn't mean that the young actor isn't equal to the swashbuckling requirements of the role. He's a handsome sight in his Sherwood green as he leads his old man's buddies." *The Hollywood Reporter,* June 16, 1950.

"John Derek does well in carrying off the lead role as Hood's son." *Variety,* June 21, 1950

"John Derek cuts a heroic figure, giving the part all the dash it requires." *Harrison's Reports,* June 17, 1950

ADDITIONAL REVIEWS AND ARTICLES: *Boxoffice* 1 July 1950; *Chicago Tribune* 9 June 1949 p. 59; *Christian Century* 12 July 1950, p. 67; *The Evening Standard* (U.K.) 17 August 1950; *Le Film Complet* (France) 7 August 1952; *Harrison's Reports* 17 June 1950 p. 96; *Hollywood Reporter* 22 August 1949 p. 1; *Kinematograph Weekly* (U.K.) 17 August 1950, p. 30; *Kinematograph Weekly* (U.K.) 19 March 1959, p. 27; *L.A. Times* 9 June 1949 p. 45; *L.A. Times* 11 July 1950 p. 7; *L.A. Times* 14 July 1950; *Modern Screen* July 1950 p. 24; *Motion Picture Herald Product Digest* 17 June 1950 p. 347; *New York Times* 2 October 1949 p. 5; *Novelle Film* (Italy) 13 September 1951; *Picture Show* (U.K.) 19 August 1950; *Picture Show* (U.K.) 16 September 1950; *Picturegoer* (U.K.) 12 August 1950; *Picturegoer* (U.K.) 9 September 1950 p. 15; *Picturegoer* (U.K.) 16 September 1950 p. 21; *Preview* (U.K.) yearly 1951 pp. 158–159; *Rotarian* September 1950 p. 77; *Screenland* February 1950 pp. 34–35; *Screenland* July 1950 p. 18; *The Times* (U.K.) 28 August 1950

Mask of the Avenger
Columbia
Technicolor, 83 minutes
Premiered in New York on June 26, 1951

CREDITS: *Producer*: Hunt Stromberg; *Director*: Phil Karlson; *Screenplay*: Jesse Lasky, Jr.; *Story*: George Bruce. *Adaptation*: Ralph Bettinson, Philip MacDonald, from the novel *The Count of Monte Cristo* by Alexandre Dumas; *Music Director*: Morris Stoloff; *Music Score*: Mario Castelnuovo-Tedesco; *Art Director*: Harold MacArthur; *Gowns*: Jean Louis: *Photography*: Charles Lawton, Jr.; *Editor*: Jerome Thoms; *Set Decorator*: James Crowe; *Sound*: Russell Malmgren; *Makeup*: Clay Campbell, *Hair Stylist*: Helen Hunt; *Technicolor Color Consultant*: Francis Cugat

CAST: John Derek (Capt. Renato Dimorna), Anthony Quinn (Viovanni Larocca), Jody Lawrance (Maria D'Orsini), Arnold Moss (Colardi), Eugene Iglesias (Rollo D'Anterras), Dickie Leroy (Jacopo), Harry Cording (Zio), Ian Wolfe (Signor Donner), Carlo Tricoli (Baron Marchese), David Bond (Marco), Wilton Graff (Count Dimorna), Tristram Coffin (Non-commissioned officer), Chuck Hamilton (Officer), Ric Roman (Guard), Henry Sharp (Doctor), Mario Mariani (Farm lad), Philip Van Zandt (Artillery major), Peter Virgo, George Bruggeman (Apprentices), Jack Low (Follower), Mickey Simpson (Rudolpho), Robert W. Filmer (Merchant), Belle Mitchell (Busybody), Michael Mark (Old townsman), Richard La Marr, Charles Wagenheim (Townsmen), Paul Marion (Colardi's sergeant), Ted Jordan (Sergeant), John Halloran, John Merton (Blacksmiths), Rita Conde (Flower girl), Minerva Urecal (Market woman), Victor Paul (Young fisherman), Laura K. Brooks (Baker's wife), Rose Plumer (Superstitious woman), Trevor Bardette (Farmer), Lester Sharpe (Major domo), Steve Roberts (Comandante), Gregory Gay (Col. Von Falker), Peter Mamakos, Roland Varno (Lieutenants), William H. Yetter, John Doucette (Sentries), Robert R. Stephenson (Stranger), Duke York, Charles Horvath (Loafers), Ben Welden (Tavern loafer)

PLOT: Capt. Renato Dimorna returns from the battlefield to visit his father, a count, in the village of Casamore, on the Austrian-Italian border. He is unaware that the military governor of the province, Viovanni Larocca, has killed his parent: The count was falsely accused of being a traitor and executed after he had discovered Larocca's treachery in agreeing to surrender the village to the Austrians. Renato, attacked by the townspeople "as the son of a traitor," is rescued by Larocca, who takes him to his (Renato's) own castle, which Larocca has been using as his headquarters. At first grateful to the governor, Renato soon begins to suspect him of treachery. These suspicions are shared by Maria D'Orsini, his sweetheart, and several friends, including Rollo D'Anterras, who warn him against Larocca; but Renato pretends to have faith in him. Accusing D'Anterras and his family of treason, Larocca kills Rollo's parents and takes Rollo prisoner. Renato, who has been pretending that he was bedridden because of his injuries, steals out of the castle and, masked, effects D'Anterras' rescue. He then instructs Jacopo, one of his closest friends, to take Rollo and Maria to a hideout, and hurries back to the castle before his absence is discovered. When Renato returns to the hideout, Maria pulls down his mask and learns his identity. The group is determined to expose Larocca by presenting to the townspeople proof of his treachery. That night, Larocca double-crosses his own soldiers and delivers the fort to the Austrians. Forcing Maria to accompany him, the governor attempts to escape into a neighboring country. Renato, aided by the townspeople, recaptures the fort, then pursues and overtakes Larocca. He forces him into a duel and kills him.

REVIEWS: "We won't say that *Mask of the Avengers* [sic] is anybody's *Gone with the Wind*, but as a fast, flashy costumed horse opera, it is energetic, funny and without harm." *The New York Times,* June 27 1951

"*Mask of the Avenger* is a bright show that offers considerable fictional diversion and color." *The Film Daily,* June 27, 1951

"[A] handsome Technicolor adventure drama... [T]he dialogue is a bit stilted at times, but *Mask of the Avenger* is an adventure picture and as such the talk and the plot are definitely secondary to the derring-do." *Motion Picture Herald,* June 30, 1951

REVIEWS FOR JOHN DEREK: "John Derek plays the bold youth with appropriate agility." *The Hollywood Reporter,* June 27, 1951

"John Derek has the right romantic looks and agility for the part of Renato." *Today's Cinema* (U.K.), September 19, 1951

ADDITIONAL REVIEWS AND ARTICLES: *Boxoffice* 30 June 1951; *Boxoffice* 4 August 1951; *Christian Century* 5 September 1951 p. 68; *Film Bulletin* 16 July 1951 p. 20 *Harrison's Reports* 30 June 1951 p. 102; *Hollywood Reporter* 18 September 1950 p. 1; *Hollywood Reporter* 13 October 1950 p. 12; *Hollywood Reporter* 26 October 1950 p. 2; *Hollywood Reporter* 31 October 1950 p. 5; *Hollywood Reporter* 3 November 1950 p. 10; *Il corriere della sera* (Italy) 15 January 1953; *L.A. Times* 24 November 1949; *L.A. Times* 19 July 1951; *Monthly Film Bulletin* (U.K.) October 1951 p. 349; *Motion Picture Daily* 3 July 1951 p. 6; *Motion Picture Magazine* November 1951 pp. 25–27, 55–56; *Picture Show* (U.K.) 1 December 1951; *Picturegoer* (U.K.) 24 November 1951 p. 19; *Variety* 27 June 1951 p. 9

Saturday's Hero

Aka *Idols in the Dust* (United Kingdom title)
Columbia, A Sidney Buchman Production
B&W, 111 minutes
Premiered in New York on September 11, 1951

CREDITS: *Producer;* Buddy Adler; *Director:* David Miller; *Screenplay:* Millard Lampell, Sidney Buchman, based on the novel *The Hero* by Millard Lampell; *Photography:* Lee Garmes; *Art Director:* Robert Peterson; *Editor:* William Lyon; *Set Decorator:* James Crowe; *Assistant Director:* Jack Corrick; *Makeup:* Clay Campbell; *Hair Stylist:* Helen Hunt; *Gowns:* Jean Louis; *Sound:* Richard Olson; *Music Director:* Morris Stoloff; *Music Score:* Elmer Bernstein

CAST: John Derek (Steve Novak), Donna Reed (Melissa), Sidney Blackmer (T.C. McCabe), Alexander Knox (Megroth), Elliott Lewis (Eddie Abrams), Otto Hulett (Coach Preacher Tennant), Howard St. John (Belfrage), Aldo DaRe [Aldo Ray] (Gene Hausler), Alvin Baldock (Francis Clayborne), Wilbur Robertson (Bob Whittier), Charles Mercer Barnes (Moose Wagner), Bill Martin (Joe Mestrovic), Mickey Knox (Joey Novak), Sandro Giglio (Jan Novak), Tito Vuolo (Manuel), Don Gibson (Red Evans), Peter Virgo (Vlatko), Don Garner (Jamieson), Robert Foulk (Butler), John W. Baer (Turner Wylie), Mervin Williams (Dr. Comstock), Peter Thompson (John Fitzhugh), Noel Reyburn (Toby Peterson), Steven Clark (Ted Bricker), Mickey McCardle, Glenn Souers, Hal Braly, Breck Stroschein, Darrel Riggs, Volney Peters, Al Cantor, Newell Oestreich, Frederick Maumetz, Robert "Bob" DeLauer, Edward Saenz, Robert Simpson, Tom Colley, John "Jack"

Zilly, Ralph Pucci, Harold Hatfield, William W. Armstrong, Jack Finlay, Floyd Collier, Hubie Kerns, Don R. Clark, Ray Pourchot, Leon C. McLaughlin, Rod Scott Craig, Howard Hansen, Tony Linehan, George Murphy, Boyd Red Morgan, Albert Carmichael, John Nikcevich (Football players), Paul Cleary (Dobbs), Sunny Vickers (Girl), Fred F. Sears, Don Kohler, Barry Brooks, Clark Howat (Reporters), Ann Duncan (High school girl), James Pierce, Oscar "Dutch" Hendrian (Assistant coaches), Glenn Thompson (Deke Roberts), Charles Horvath (Baldy), Tom Fears (Lineman), Ted Stanhope, Sam Flint (Alumni), Thomas Kingston (Equipment manager), Tom Daly, Dick Cogan (Voices), Thomas Brown Henry (Keppler), Candy McDowell (Girl), Frank Eldredge (Alumni chairman), Lewis Ward (Gamma boy), Sammy McKim (Student), Frances Chaney (Nurse), Luther Crockett (Principal)

PLOT: Steve Novak is a high school athlete and the son of Polish immigrants in a New Jersey mill town. He hopes to escape from the environment by playing football for Jackson, a tradition-bound Southern college,and accepts the Jackson scholarship against the advice of his mentor, newspaperman Eddie Abrams. He also ignores the barbs directed at him by his brother Joey, a maladjusted ex–G.I. who accuses him of wanting to become a snob. Only his father, and Manuel, proprietor of the local bar, back him in his decision. Steve believes he will not only play football, but graduate in engineering and prevent his becoming another football bum. Gradually, he becomes aware that he is nothing but a piece of merchandise to be displayed profitably for the school and specifically for T.C. McCabe, a wealthy and overbearing alumnus. McCabe, Steve learns, is his benefactor. T.C. tries to talk Steve into forgetting his educational ambitions and going to work for him when he is through school. Steve progresses through freshman football into the varsity, and finally becomes the greatest player that Jackson has ever had. T.C. takes him around the country and presents him to a now wildly excited alumni. Unable to study because of the demands on his time, Steve is forced to take passing grades given to him gratuitously because he is a football hero. Eddie Abrams is brought in by T.C. as publicity director to make the school team nationally known. In the flush of football victories, Steve barely perceives what is happening to him. He doesn't because two codes of conduct exist, one for his sort of people and one for the sons and daughters of the wealthy people who have come to the school as a natural and economic "right." Hurt in one game, he insists on going back in. When he is hurt even worse, a brace is built to protect his shoulder. This device fails and he is permanently out of football. He feels that he can't stay on at the college as a charity student, although there is an indication that the school would tolerate this. T.C. learns that Steve and Melissa are in love and intend to get married. Steve is afraid, however, that Melissa will not be able to assert her right to leave T.C. and wants her to make her own decision. His dream is shattered; he hears that his beloved father has died. He returns to his home and to Joey, who is now rehabilitated, has a good job and will help him start anew. Steve is determined to finish his education at night school, work for an honest living among his own people, and marry Melissa when she comes to him, as she has promised to do.

REVIEWS: "General excellence of the story supplies good entertainment values to back full scale ballyhoo." *Variety*, August 22, 1951

"[A] fast and angry film, in which football is played with a venom and the chips fall where they may." The *New York Times*, September 12, 1951

"More sensational than revealing.... *Saturday's Hero* becomes the type of film which is timely, with some interesting glimpses behind the scenes, but of only minor impact and shallow significance." *New York Herald Tribune*, September 12, 1951

REVIEWS FOR JOHN DEREK: "John Derek ... fails to express the lively extrovert personality of the gridiron hero; physically he's not the type." *The Hollywood Reporter*, August 22, 1951

"A highly sensitive performance is turned in by John Derek" *Harrison's Reports*, August 25 1951

ADDITIONAL REVIEWS AND ARTICLES: *Boxoffice* 8 September 1951; *Boxoffice* 27 October 1951 p. 43; *Boxoffice* 3 November 1951 p. 42; *Christian Century* 7 November 1951 p. 1294; *Christian Science Monitor* 4 November 1950; *Daily Variety* 20 March 1950; *Commonweal* 12 October 1951 p. 14; *Daily Variety* 2 August 1950; *Daily Variety* 22 August 51 p. 3; *Daily Variety*

19 October 1951; *Daily Variety* 22 October 1951; *Daily Variety* 24 October 1951; *The Exhibitor* 29 August 1951 p. 3133; *Film Daily* 23 August 1951 p. 6; *Harrison's Reports* 25 August 1951 p. 134; *Hollywood* (Italy) 6 January 1951 p. 5; *Hollywood Citizen-News* 19 October 1951; *Hollywood Reporter* 23 November 1948; *Hollywood Reporter* 25 January 1949; *Hollywood Reporter* 9 June 1950 p. 12; *Hollywood Reporter* 1 September 1950 p. 10; *International Photographer* October 1951 pp. 4, 16–17; *L.A. Daily News* 19 October 1951; *L.A. Examiner* 8 February 1949; *L.A Times* 21 December 1948; *L.A Times* 16 October 1951; *L.A. Times* 19 October 1951; *Look* 15 September 1951 pp. 122–125; *Modern Screen* September 1951 p. 23; *Monthly Film Bullet* March 1952, pp. 31; *Motion Picture* October 1951 p. 56; *Motion Picture Daily* 23 August 1951; *Motion Picture Herald Product Digest* 25 August 1951 p. 989; *Motion Picture Magazine* December 1950 pp. 27, 63–64; *Movie Life* November 1950 p. 27; *The Nation* 29 September 1951 pp. 267–268; *Newsweek* 10 September 1951 p. 98; *New York Times* 7 August 1949; *New York Times* 11 June 1950; *New York Times* 26 August 1951; *New York Times* 11 September 1951 p. 33; *New York Times* 9 Feb 1960; *New York Times* 12 May 1960; *Picturegoer Annual* (U.K.) 1951–1952 pp. 153–155; *Picture Show* (U.K.) 22 March 1952, *Screen World* 1952 p. 79; *Screenland* July 1951 p. 35; *Screenland* October 1951 p. 71; *Time* 15 October 1951 p. 122; *Variety* 10 October 1951; *Variety* 17 October 1951

AWARDS AND HONORS: Writers Guild of America: *Nominated:* The Robert Meltzer Award (Screenplay Dealing Most Ably with Problems of the American Scene): Millard Lampell, Sidney Buchman.

NOTES: Columbia changed the original title, *The Hero*, just a few days before the release date, out of fear that audiences would mistake it as a war film.

The Family Secret

Columbia, A Santana Production
B&W, 85 minutes
Released on October 24, 1951

CREDITS: *Producer*: Robert Lord; *Director*: Henry Levin; *Screenplay*: Francis Cockrell, Andrew Solt; *Story*: Marie Baumer, James Cavanagh; *Associate Producer*: Henry S. Kesler; *Assistant Director*: Sam Nelson; *Photography*: Burnett Guffey; *Art Director*: George Brooks; *Editor*: Al Clark; *Set Decorator*: William Kiernan; *Makeup*: Clay Campbell; *Hair Stylist*: Helen Hunt; *Sound*: Russell Malmgren; *Gowns*: Jean Louis; *Music Director:* Morris Stoloff; *Music Score*: George Duning

CAST: John Derek (David Clark), Lee J. Cobb (Howard Clark), Jody Lawrance (Lee Pearson), Erin O'Brien-Moore (Ellen Clark), Santos Ortega (George Redman), Henry O'Neill (Donald Muir), Carl Benton Reid (Dr. Reynolds), Peggy Converse (Sybil Bradley), Jean Alexander (Vera Stone), Dorothy Tree (Marie Elsner), Whit Bissell (Joe Elsner), Raymond Greenleaf (Mr. Sims), Onslow Stevens (Judge), Elizabeth Flournoy (Cora French), Bill Walker (Larry), Frances E. Williams (Bertha), Mary Alan Hokanson (Miss Martin), Al Eben (Waiter), Peter Thompson (Morton), Jean Willes (Cigarette girl), Fred F. Sears (Laboratory analyst), Joy Windsor, Amanda Blake (Telephone girls), George Spaulding (Inspector), Helen Spring (Mrs. Redman), John Baer (Boy), Paul Dubov (Deputy), Irene Martin (Girl at party), Harry Cheshire (Coroner), Joseph Crehan (Bailiff), Lou Merrill, Paul Marion, Mark Bellaire, Emmett Vogan (Reporters), Jack Roberts (Photographer), Percy Helton (Charlie), Marta Metrovich (Miss Wellington), Teddy Infuhr (Marvin), Shirley Mills (File girl), Lou Marcelle (TV announcer), Robert B. Williams (Detective)

PLOT: David Clark accidentally kills his best friend and fails to report the death to the police, who arrest an innocent man for murder. David's father, a prominent attorney, defends the man, who dies of a heart attack during the trial. David, whose secret is known only to himself and his family, proposes to Lee Pearson and is accepted. He tells her all, and her love gives him the courage to go to the district attorney with a full confession. Lee promises to wait for him.

REVIEWS: "Not a good entertainment. To begin with, the story is depressing, for it deals with a weakling hero..." *Harrison's Reports*, October 27, 1951

"It's the kind of picture that put the dish manufacturers on easy street a few years back." *Theatre Arts,* January 1952

"Though this is quite an ingenious and methodically executed story, the script so emphasizes every clue as to forewarn us of the turn of each event, and so destroys suspense." *Monthly Film Bulletin* (U.K.), July 1952

REVIEWS FOR JOHN DEREK: "[G]ems of acting come from John Derek, the youth; Lee J. Cobb, as the attorney father...." *The Hollywood Reporter,* October 17, 1951

"John Derek portrays a sullen youth whose attitude gains him little sympathy. The role would try many older and more experienced actors." *Los Angeles Times,* October 19, 1951

"Derek, despite the ill-defined character he's required to portray, fares better than might be expected as he puts across the individual scenes." *Variety,* October 24, 1951

ADDITIONAL REVIEWS AND ARTICLES: *Boxoffice* 3 November 1951 p. 1315; *Catholic World* December 1951 p. 223; *Christian Century,* 2 April 1952 p. 415; *Commonweal* 1 February 1952 p. 424; *Daily Film Renter* (U.K.) 14 May 1952, pp. 7; *Daily Variety* 17 October 1951 p. 3; *Film Daily* 24 October 1951 p. 6; *Hollywood Reporter* 19 January 1951 p. 12; *Hollywood Reporter* 9 February 1951 p. 14; *Hollywood Reporter* 17 October 1951 p. 4; *Kinematograph Weekly* (U.K.) 15 May 1952 p. 7; *Kinematograph Weekly* (U.K.) 22 May 1952 p. 16; *Motion Picture Herald* 27 October 1951 p. 1074; *Movie Story* April 1951; The *New York Times* 7 April 1951 p. 8; *Picture Show* (U.K.) 7 June 1952 pp. 4, 7, 10; *Picturegoer* (U.K.) 7 June 1952 p. 17; *Today's Cinema* (U.K.) 14 May 1952 p. 9.

Scandal Sheet

Aka *The Dark Page* (United Kingdom title)
Columbia, A Motion Picture Investors Production
B&W, 82 minutes
Premiered in New York on January 16, 1952

CREDITS: *Producer:* Edward Small; *Director:* Phil Karlson; *Screenplay:* Ted Sherdeman, Eugene Ling, James Poe; Based on the novel *The Dark Page* by Samuel Fuller; *Photography:* Burnett Guffey; *Art Director:* Robert Peterson; *Editor:* Jerome Thoms, *Set Decorator:* William Kiernan; *Assistant Director:* Frederick Briskin; *Makeup:* Clay Campbell; *Hair Stylist:* Helen Hunt; *Sound:* Jack Goodrich; *Gowns:* Jean Louis; *Music Director:* George Stoloff; *Music Score:* George Duning

CAST: Broderick Crawford (Mark Chapman), Donna Reed (Julie Allison), John Derek (Steve McCleary), Rosemary De Camp (Charlotte Grant), Henry O'Neill (Charlie Barnes), Harry Morgan (Biddle), James Millican (Lt. Davis), Griff Barnett (Judge Hacker), Jonathan Hale (Frank Madison), Pierre Watkin (Baxter), Ida Moore (Needle Nellie), Ralph Reed (Joey), Luther Crockett (Jordan), Charles Cane (Heeney), Jay Adler (Bailey), Don Beddoe (Pete), Shirlee Allard (Switchboard operator), Pat Williams (Telephone operator), Raymond Largay (Conklin), Edna Holland (Mrs. Penwick), Kathryn Card (Mrs. Rawley), Cliff Clark (O'Hanlon), Victoria Horne (Mary), Matt Willis (Joe), Eugene Baxter (Edwards), Katherine Warren (Mrs. Allison), Harry Hines (Toothless bum), John "Skins" Miller (Drunk bum), Peter Virgo, Ric Roman, Tom Kingston, Charles Colean, Mike Mahoney (Reporters), Garry Owen (Addled bum), Guy Wilkerson (Janitor), Duke Watson (Policeman), Harry Wilson, Ralph Volkie (Bums)

PLOT: Newspaper editor Mark Chapman, who has built his paper's circulation on headlines selling murder, sex and scandal, is confronted with the dark page of his own past when Charlotte Grant, the wife he deserted years before, threatens to expose him. Mark kills her and tries to make her death look accidental. Chapman's protégé, reporter Steve McCleary, proves the death is murder. Helped by feature writer Julie Allison and spurred by Chapman's drive for sensational headlines. Steve gets on the trail of the killer. Unable to call off his newshounds. Mark watches them uncover clue after clue to his identity as a killer. Steve and Julie finally track him down and Steve writes the front page story with Mark's death while resisting arrest.

REVIEWS: "The story is full of twists and generates fair suspense..." *Variety,* January 9, 1952

"A fairy interesting murder melodrama.... The plot itself is too contrived to be convincing, but those who are not too fussy about story material should find it acceptable." *Harrison's Reports,* January 12, 1952

"[A] mighty suspenseful tale of newspaper men and newspaper women with some rather unique twists..." *Motion Picture Daily,* January 18, 1952

REVIEWS FOR JOHN DEREK: "John Derek is excellent..." *The Hollywood Reporter,* January 9, 1952

"John Derek does a polished job as the star reporter working with Crawford..." *Los Angeles Times,* March 29, 1952

ADDITIONAL REVIEWS AND ARTI-

CLES: *Boxoffice* 2 February 1952 p. 1341; *Christian Century* 12 March 1952 p. 327; *Daily Variety* 9 January 1952 p. 3; *Film Bulletin* 14 January 1952; *Film Daily* 15 January 1952 p. 6; *Hollywood Reporter* 30 August 1950 p. 1; *Hollywood Reporter* 18 September 1950 p. 3; *Hollywood Reporter* 6 April 1951 p. 4; *Hollywood Reporter* 27 April 1951 p. 14; *Hollywood Reporter* 11 May 1951 p. 12; *Hollywood Reporter* 9 January 1952 p. 3; *Il corriere della sera* (Italy) 29 August 1952 p. 2; *Library Journal* 1 February 1952 p. 206; *Modern Screen* April 1952 p. 23; *Monthly Film Bulletin* (U.K.) April 1952 p. 50; *Motion Picture Herald* 12 January 1952, pp. 1186; *N.Y. Herald Tribune* 17 January 1952; *Newsweek* 28 January 1952 p. 89; *Picturegoer* (U.K.) 12 April 1952 p. 18; *Silver Screen* December 1951 p. 33; *Silver Screen* April 1952 p. 14; *The Spectator (U.K.)* April 11, 1952; pp. 481–482; *Time* 4 February 1952 p. 72; *Today's Cinema* (U.K.) 25 February 1952, pp. 12; *Variety* 30 August 1950; *Variety* 2 April 1952.

NOTES: Two films both set in the newspaper world titled *Scandal Sheet* were previously released: one in 1931, directed by John Cromwell for Paramount, and a second one in 1939, directed by Nick Grinde for Columbia.

Rainbow 'Round My Shoulder

Aka *Castle in the Air*
Columbia
Technicolor, 78 minutes
Released on August 8, 1952

CREDITS: *Producer*: Jonie Taps; *Director*: Richard Quine; *Screenplay*: Blake Edwards, Richard Quine; *Photography*: Ellis Carter; *Editor*: Richard Fantl; *Art Director*: George Brooks; *Music Director*: George Duning; *Music Supervisor*: Eddie Franzier; *Choreography*: Lee Scott; *Assistant Choreographer*: Helen Silver; *Assistant Director*: Earl Bellamy; *Set Decorator*: James Crowe; *Sound*: Russell Malmgren; *Technicolor Consultant*: Francis Cugat; *Songs*: "Ain't Misbehavin'," words by Andy Razaf, music by Thomas "Fats" Waller and Harry Brooks; "Wrap Your Troubles in Dreams," words by Ted Koehler and Billy Moll, music by Harry Barris; "There's a Rainbow 'Round My Shoulder," words and music by Billy Rose, Al Jolson and Dave Dreyer

CAST: Frankie Laine, Billy Daniels (Themselves), Charlotte Austin (Cathy Blake), Arthur Franz (Phil Young), Ida Moore (Martha Blake), Lloyd Corrigan (Tobias aka Toby), Barbara Whiting (Suzy Mulligan), Ross Ford (Elliot Livermore), Arthur Space (Joe Brady), Frank Wilcox (Sidney Gordon), John Baer (Red), Broderick Crawford, John Derek, Donna Reed, Gene Autry, Barbara Hale (Themselves), Bess Flowers (Embassy Club Patron/Guest at Benefit), Mira McKinney (Mrs. Abernathy), Frank O'Connor (Sound stage doorman), Richard Quine (Opening narrator/Radio announcer's voice), Fred F. Sears (Director)

PLOT: Orphan Cathy Blake lives with her grandmother Martha and the family butler, Toby. Cathy wants to be in show business but Martha is set against it because she feels it ruined Cathy's father's life. When Cathy gets a job at Columbia as a messenger girl, she hides the fact from Miss Blake. Through a lucky mistake, Cathy gets an audition with Frankie Laine for a picture and makes the grade. Miss Blake clamps down and the girl is forced to withdraw from the movie. Laine and Billy Daniels conspire to showcase Cathy's talents at an affair for Miss Blake's favorite charity. Watching the girl perform, the proud grandma realizes that the youngster belongs in show business and gives her blessing.

REVIEWS: "This is an entertaining filmusical on an unpretentious scale." *Variety*, August 6, 1952

"Glamour, fine singing, good direction and acting, backed by Technicolor photography." *Harrison's Reports*, August 9, 1952

"Modest, light and pleasant." *Film Bulletin*, September 22, 1952

ADDITIONAL REVIEWS AND ARTICLES: *Boxoffice* 16 August 1952; *Daily Film Renter* (U.K.) 25 August 1952 p. 10; *Daily Variety* 6 August 1952 p. 3; *Film Daily* 19 August 1952 p. 7; *Hollywood Reporter* 7 December 1951 p. x12; *Hollywood Reporter* 14 December 1951 p. 14; *Hollywood Reporter* 6 August 1952 p. 3; *Kinematograph Weekly* (U.K.) 28 August 1952 p. 20; *Monthly Film Bulletin* (U.K.) October 1952 p. 145; *Motion Picture Daily* 8 August 1952 p. 4; *Motion Picture Herald* 15 December 1951; *Motion Picture Herald* 9 August 1952 p. 1477; *Today's Cinema* 25 August 1952 p. 6

Thunderbirds

Republic
B&W, 98 minutes
Premiered in Washington on November 20, 1952

CREDITS: *Producer*: Herbert J. Yates;

Associate Producer–Director: John H. Auer; *Screenplay*: Mary C. McCall, Jr.; *Story*: Kenneth Gamet; *Music*: Victor Young; *Photography*: Reggie Lanning; *Art Director*: Frank Hotaling; *Editor*: Richard L. Van Enger; *Assistant Director*: Herb Mendelson; *Technical Advisors*: Major Edward R. Kandel, U.S.A.A.F., Major William C. Burns, U.S.A.A.R.; *Costume Supervisor*: Adele Palmer; *Set Decorators*: John McCarthy, Jr., Otto Siegel; *Special Effects*: Howard Lydecker, Theodore Lydecker; *Makeup Supervisor*: Bob Mark; *Hair Stylist*: Peggy Gray

CAST: John Derek (Gil Hackett), John Barrymore, Jr. (Tom McCreery), Mona Freeman (Lt. Ellen Henderson), Gene Evans (Mike Braggart), Eileen Christy (Mary Caldwell), Ward Bond (Sgt. Logan), Wally Cassell (Pfc. Sam Jacobs), Robert Neil [Scott Elliott] (Keith Watson), Slim Pickens (Pvt. Wes Shelby), Armando Silvestre (Corp. Ralph Mogay), Benny Baker (Pvt. Charlie Klassen), Norman Budd (Pvt. Lou Radtke), Mae Clarke (Mrs. Jones), Sam McKim (Corp. Ray Hanford), Allene Roberts (Mrs. Hanford), Richard Simmons (Capt. Norton), Walter Reed (Lt. Hammond), Suzanne Dalbert (Marie Etienne), Barbara Pepper (Mrs. Braggart), Pepe Hern (Pvt. Jim Lastchance), Victor Millan (Pvt. Joe Lastchance), Else Neft (Mama Jacobs), Helene Wallace (Mrs. David Garrett), Fern Hall (Mrs. Byrnes), Charles Evans (Mr. Watson), Gregory Marshall (Billy Jones), Gil Herman (Train commander), Steve Wayne (Soldier), Frank Wilcox (David Garrett), Rayford Barnes (Sgt. Case), Gene Covelli (Dead soldier), Gayle Kellogg (Military policeman), Richard Reeves (Captain, Q.M. Corps), Richard Grayson (Corpsman), Harry Harvey (Doctor), Martha Bamattre (Proprietor's wife), Eugene Borden (Proprietor), Nadene Ashdown (German girl), John Maxwell (Two-star general), Glen Vernon (Driver), John Albright (Medical corpsman), Albert Szabo (Sniper), Carleton Young (Maj. Alberts), Paul Livermore (Pharmacist's mate), Henry Rowland (German gunner), Bill Froelich (Sergeant), Tony Christian (German soldier)

PLOT: The citizens of Green Hill, Oklahoma, are justly proud of their National Guard unit. Known as the Thunderbird Division, its members have fought in every war. World War II seems far away in the summer of 1940 when they hold their annual maneuvers, but in September, an act of Congress calls up all National Guard units and more than 100 men and boys from Green Hill are suddenly soldiers on their way to regular training at Fort Sill, Oklahoma. Among them are young law students Gil Hackett and Tom McCreery, friends since childhood, both amicably in love with Mary Caldwell. There is Sgt. Mike Braggart, a truck driver, three young Osage Indians; youthful market-owner Sam Jacobs, and Ray Hanford, a clerk whose young wife is pregnant. Left behind are Keith Watson, the town banker's spoiled son, and broken-hearted young Calvin Jones, whose doting mother won't let him join. At Fort Sill, Tom McCreery is impressed by Sgt. Logan, a well-disciplined man with a West Point background. Tom tries to be friendly out of pride that his own father was a West Pointer, killed at St. Mihiel in World War I, but Logan remains coldly aloof. In the Sicilian and Italian campaigns, the Thunderbirds receive their baptism by fire. Ray Handford is killed in battle. Calvin Jones dies happy, the victim of his youthful pride. At Cassino, Tom is wounded and Gil hates Sgt. Logan for refusing to let him go after him. Later, after Logan has been killed and Gil learns that Tom has survived, the truth about Logan comes out. He's Tom's father, court-martialed at the end of World War I for having revealed the position of his company and caused the death of ten men by going back for a fallen comrade. He has changed his name, joined the National Guard and redeemed himself in the eyes of the Green Hill townsfolk and his son Tom. By V-Day, the survivors of the Thunderbirds unit are seasoned warriors and when they come home, the whole town celebrates. Mike Braggart had been killed saving a crowd of German women and children from a hand grenade; his wife proudly receives the posthumous medal. Mary has chosen Tom as the man she wants to marry and Gil has found a bride, pretty Army nurse Ellen Henderson. Keith Watson is now a good soldier and officer. While the others dance, Keith acts as enlisted officer and begins the organization of a new National Guard unit to represent Green Hill in the future.

REVIEWS: "[A] hackneyed screenplay that uses every cliché in the book keeps interest in the personalities involved at a low ebb." *The Hollywood Reporter,* November 21, 1952

"There is no lack of action in this war melodrama ... but there is little in it to distinguish it from countless other war films." *Harrison's Report*, November 29, 1952

"While the picture in toto does not differ greatly from any predecessors of similar theme, the 'home town' angle and the possibility of tie-ups with National Guard units endows it with a new twist..." *Boxoffice*, November 29, 1952

REVIEWS FOR JOHN DEREK: "Performances of both John Derek and Barrymore are too theatrical to have much resemblance to the average infantryman at the front." *Variety*, November 26, 1952

"John Derek and John Barrymore, Jr., portray the devoted buddies with suitable emotionalism." *Today's Cinema* (U.K.) 16 January, 1953

"[Barrymore and Derek] give blunt and lifeless performances." The *New York Times*, March 12, 1953

ADDITIONAL REVIEWS AND ARTICLES: *Boxoffice* 13 November 1952 p. 51; *Daily Variety* 21 November 1952 p. 3; Film Bulletin 3 May 1952; Film Bulletin 19 May 1952; *Film Daily* 3 December 1952 p. 7; *Hollywood Reporter* 14 May 1952 p. 7; *Hollywood Reporter* 14 November 1952 p. 11; *Hollywood Reporter* 2 May 1952 p. 4; *Hollywood Reporter* 23 May 1952 p. 12; *Hollywood Reporter* 25 April 1952 p. 8, *Il corriere della sera* (Italy) 18 December 1952 p. 4; *Kinematograph Weekly* (U.K.) 22 Jan 1953 p. 23; *L.A. Times* 10 December 1952 p. 4; *Monthly Film Bulletin* (U.K.) March 1953 p. 38; *Motion Picture Daily* 20 November 1952 p. 2; *Motion Picture Daily* 25 November 1952 p. 3; *Motion Picture Herald* 16 April 1952; *Motion Picture Herald* 3 May 1952 p. 37; *Motion Picture Herald* 22 November 1952 p. 45; *Motion Picture Herald* 26 November 1952 p. 39; *N.Y. Herald Tribune* 12 March 53 p. 24; *National Parent-Teacher* January 1953 p. 38; *The Film Daily* 3 December 1952 pp. 6; *Today's Cinema* (U.K.) 16 January 1953 p. 12; *Today's Cinema* (U.K.) 6 August 1952 p. 5; *Variety*, 13 January 13 1954

NOTES: According to *Motion Picture Herald*, *Citizen Soldiers* was the picture's original working title. *Bayonet Attack* was also an alternative title.

Prince of Pirates

Columbia, Esskay Pictures
Technicolor, 78 minutes
Released on March 7, 1953

CREDITS: *Producer*: Sam Katzman; *Director*: Sidney Salkow; *Screenplay*: John O'Dea, Samuel Newman; *Story*: William Copeland, Herbert Kline; *Photography*: Henry Freulich; *Art Director*: Paul Palmentola; *Technicolor Color Consultant*: Francis Cugat; *Editor*: Jerome Thoms; *Set Decorator*: Sidney Clifford; *Special Effects*: Jack Erickson; *Assistant Director*: Jack Corrick; *Sound*: Josh Westmoreland; *Music Director*: Mischa Bakaleinikoff; *Unit Manager*: Herbert Leonard; *Hair Stylist*: Dotha Hippe

CAST: John Derek (Prince Roland), Barbara Rush (Countess Nita Orde), Carla Balenda (Princess Maria), Whitfield Connor (King Stephan), Edgar Barrier (Count Blanco), Robert Shayne (Prime Minister Treeg), Harry Lauter (Jan), Don Harvey (Koepke), Henry Rowland (Greb), Glase Lohman (Brenner), Gene Roth (Capt. Brock), Bob Peoples (Carl), Sandy Sanders (Meyers), Joseph F. McGuinn (Gen. DuBois), Al Cantor (Lund), Edward Colmans (Spanish admiral), Stanley Blystone (Capt. Brock's first mate), James Dime (Pirate), Eddie Foster (Sailor), John Hart (Captain of the guards), David Sharpe (Stunt double for John Derek)

PLOT: Prince Roland, younger son of the king of Holland, leads a small band of volunteers to help the French fight the Spanish. When the father of Countess Nita Orde is killed, she joins Roland to avenge his death. Roland learns that his father has died and that King Stephan, his brother, has become king, so he returns home for a conference with Stephan—and quickly discovers that Stephan has allied himself with Spain. Refusing to sell out to a foreign country, Roland is imprisoned. Pretending to be Roland's friend, Prime Minister Treeg releases him. Roland returns to his followers, unaware that he is being trailed; all are captured and cast into a prison ship headed for Fort Bleak. During the voyage, Roland and his men gain control of the vessel and, after capturing a Spanish merchant ship, they sail for Fort Bleak, where they compel the personnel to surrender. Learning that a Spanish princess is due at the fort to marry Stephan, whom she had never seen, Roland masquerades as Stephan and marries her himself, his idea being to learn of Spain's future plans. The fort is attacked after the ceremony, but Roland and his men escape to their ship. He then embarks on a campaign of harassment against incoming Spanish ships, and conceives a scheme whereby he destroys the main Spanish fleet where it arrives. A Spanish shell explodes near Princess Maria and King Stephan, killing both of them. Roland wins complete victory when a force of French soldiers joins him, liquidating the enemy. The victory leaves him and Nita free to resume their romance, which had been interrupted by his strategic marriage to the princess.

REVIEWS: "The story is weak but it has the advantage of fast action and excitement, and of Technicolor photography." *Harrison's Reports,* January 24, 1953

"Considered in the light of the formula escape entertainment the picture sets out to provide, it comes off well." *Motion Picture Herald,* February 7, 1953

"Film offers lots of swashbuckling and slap-bang adventure, plus a vivid coat of Technicolor." *Screenland,* April 1953

REVIEWS FOR JOHN DEREK: "Derek performs his heroics in agile, if brooding style…" *The Hollywood Reporter,* January 19, 1953

"John Derek turns in a good job, pleasing both when swashbuckling and also in his more dramatic moments." *Variety,* January 21, 1953

"John Derek plays the part … with conviction." *Monthly Film Bulletin* (U.K.), July 1953

ADDITIONAL REVIEWS AND ARTICLES: *Box Office* 13 January 1953; *Daily Variety* 19 January 1953 p. 3; *Hollywood Reporter* 15 February 1952 p. 12; *Hollywood Reporter* 22 February 1952 p. 10; *Il corriere della sera* (Italy) 6 August 1954 p. 6; *Kinematograph Weekly* (U.K.) 28 May 1953 p. 15; *L.A. Times* 5 March 1953 p. 11; *Motion Picture Herald* 23 February 1952; *Movie Love* February 1953; *New York Times* 1 February 1952 p. 16; *New York Times* 7 February 1952 p. 31; *Today's Cinema* (U.K.) 21 May 1953, p. 6

Ambush at Tomahawk Gap

Columbia
Technicolor, 73 minutes
Premiered on May 1, 1953

CREDITS: *Producer*: Wallace MacDonald; *Director*: Fred F. Sears; *Story* and *Screenplay*: David Lang; *Photography*: Henry Freulich; *Art Director*: Walter Holscher; *Technicolor Color Consultant*: Francis Cugat; *Editor*: Aaron Stell; *Set Decorator*: Louis Diage; *Assistant Director*: James Nicholson; *Sound*: George Cooper; *Music Director:* Ross Di Maggio; *Publicity Director*: George Lait

CAST: John Hodiak (McCord), John Derek (Kid), David Brian (Egan), Maria Elena Marques (Navajo Girl), Ray Teal (Doc), John Qualen (Jonas P. Travis), Otto Hulett (Stranton), Percy Helton (Marlowe), Trevor Bardette (Twin Forks Sheriff), Steve Clark (Prison Wagon Driver), Harry Cording (Stableman), John War Eagle (Apache chief), Gail Robinson (Frank Egan), John Doucette (Burt—Bartender).

PLOT: Right after the Civil War, four men are released from the Arizona State Prison after serving time for a holdup. McCord, Kid, Egan and Doc reach Twin Forks, where the local sheriff gives them one hour to outfit themselves and leave. McCord, innocent of the holdup, had been framed by the other three so as to protect Egan's brother, who had been holding the loot. Egan now fears that McCord will not only demand a share of the loot but also kill his brother. Shortly after Egan, Kid and Doc ride off, McCord learns that McCord's brother is dead. He sets out after his ex-cellmates and catches up with them in time to help them defeat an attack by Apaches. He then informs them of Egan's brother's death and compels them to declare him in on the loot, which was hidden in the ghost town of Tomahawk Gap. En route they capture a Navajo girl and take her with them. They reach Tomahawk Gap in the midst of a violent sandstorm and take refuge in an abandoned saloon. When the men fall asleep and the girl goes to the well for water, Egan follows her and attempts to attack her. She is saved by an eccentric character named Jonas Travis, the town's only inhabitant. The next day when the men dig for the loot, they discover that it is gone.. They suspect that Egan's brother hid the money in another spot and start tearing up the wooden sidewalks and sides of the buildings. In the complicated events that follow, they become involved with another outlaw and marauding Apaches. This result in a furious battle in which all involved are killed, with the exception of Kid and the Navajo girl, who by this time have fallen in love. They ride off to a new life, unaware that the explosion of a powderkeg had uncovered the money.

REVIEWS: "For audiences demanding action and little else, *Ambush at Tomahawk Gap* will prove satisfactory." *The Hollywood Reporter,* April 23, 1953

"[An] indifferent program melodrama…. The color photography is fairly nice." *Harrison's Reports,* April 25, 1953

REVIEWS FOR JOHN DEREK: "John Hodiak, John Derek, David Brian and Maria Elena Marques, Mexican actress, play their roles convincingly." *Los Angeles Times*, April 23, 1953

"Principals acquit themselves nicely, especially John Derek." *Variety*, May 6, 1953

ADDITIONAL REVIEWS AND ARTICLES: *Boxoffice* 31 January 1953 p. 77; *Boxoffice* 2 May 1953 p. 1471; *Daily Film Renter* U.K 21 July 1952 p. 12; *Daily Variety* 21 April 1953 p. 3; *The Exhibitor* 6 May 53 p. 3513; *Il corriere della sera* (Italy) 4 September 1954 p. 4; *Hollywood Reporter* 3 July 1952 p. 10; *Hollywood Reporter* 17 July 1952 p. 8; *Kinematograph Weekly* (U.K.) 27 August 1953, p. 22; *L. A. Times* 24 June 1952 p. 7; *Motion Picture Herald* 19 July 1952 p. 36; *Motion Picture Herald* 9 May 1953 p. 1829; *National Parent-Teacher* May 1953 p. 47; *New York Times* 10 May 1952 p. 17; *New York Times* 28 June 1952 p. 9; *Today's Cinema* (U.K.) 26 August 1953 p. 9

The Last Posse

Columbia
B&W, 73 minutes
Released in July 1953

CREDITS: *Producer*: Harry Joe Brown; *Director*: Alfred Werker; *Screenplay*: Seymour Bennett, Connie Lee Bennett, Kenneth Gamet; *Story*: Seymour Bennett, Connie Lee Bennett; *Photography*: Burnett Guffey; *Art Director*: George Brooks; *Editor*: Gene Havlick; *Assistant Director*: Jack Corrick; *Set Decorator*: Frank Tuttle; *Music Director*: Ross DiMaggio; *Sound*: Lambert Day

CAST: Broderick Crawford (Sheriff John Frazier), John Derek (Jed Clayton), Charles Bickford (Sampson Drune), Wanda Hendrix (Deborah Morley), Warner Anderson (Robert Emerson), Henry Hull (Stokely), Will Wright (Todd Mitchell), Tom Powers (Frank White), Raymond Greenleaf (Albert Hagen), James Kirkwood (Judge Parker), Eddy Waller (Dr. Pryor), Skip Homeier (Art Romer), James Bell (Will Romer), Guy Wilkerson (George Romer), Mira McKinney (Mrs. Mitchell), Helen Wallace (Mrs. White), Harry Hayden (Davis), Monte Blue (Kane), Rita Conde (Mexican girl), Frank Hagney (Cord), Frank Ellis (Harding) Paul Maxey (Farley), Eugene White (Boy)

PLOT: A posse is formed to hunt and arrest Will, Art and George Romer, brothers who had robbed a bank of $100,000, which they felt theirs, because it had been deposited by Sampson Drune, to whom they have been compelled to sell their cattle cheaply during a severe drought. The posse, formed by Drune and Jed Clayton, is sworn in by drunken Sheriff John Frazier, who is brushed aside when he offers to go along. But four local businessmen join the posse to see to it that the robbers are not killed without the benefit of a trial. Accompanied by his friend Stokely, the sheriff catches up with the posse. In due time he begins to sober up and, when Drune and Clayton take all the supplies and try to outdistance the businessmen, he catches up with them and bests Drune in a fight. Frazier knew that Drune had killed Clayton's father, and he wanted to kill the hunted men because they knew too much. The posse catches up with the robbers and, in a running fight, one robber dies in a fall from a cliff while the remaining two surrender to Frazier. Drune shoots and kills them in cold blood. Frazier then informs Clayton that Drune had killed his father. Clayton then kills Drune, but not before Drune wounds Frazier. The businessmen try to make a deal with Clayton: He will inherit Drune's ranch and they will divide the $100,000 recovered from the robbers. Clayton agrees. The mortally wounded Frazier regains consciousness in a hotel, where a hearing is in progress. He leaves his room to attend the hearing and Clayton seeing him, realizes that he cannot be part of the shady deal with the businessmen. He tells the judge the truth and wins a release. As the judge expresses the town's appreciation to Frazier, it is discovered that he had been dead from the moment he had sat down to listen to the testimony.

REVIEWS: "[T]he entertainment is just fair.... The action stuff is good, however, as are the character performances, and the outdoor lensing of rugged scenery and plot types is excellent." *Variety*, June 10, 1953

"A fair program western melodrama, with the usual shootings and killings. It is a routine picture of its kind..." *Harrison's Reports*, June 13, 1953

"Unpretentious, yet rugged and morally sound..." *Picturegoer* (U.K.), October 24, 1953

REVIEWS FOR JOHN DEREK: "John Derek ... and Charles Bickford ... give conventionally competent performances." *Today's Cinema* (U.K.), May 22, 1953

"John Derek is good as Bickford's adopted son..." *The Hollywood Reporter*, June 8, 1953

"The presence of John Derek as one of the top liners should prove a merchandise advantage." *Boxoffice,* June 13, 1953

ADDITIONAL REVIEWS AND ARTICLES: *Cincinnati Enquiring* 2 October 1952; *Daily Variety* 9 June 1953 p. 3; *Film Western Annual* (U.K.)1954 p. 70; *Hollywood Reporter* 17 October 1952 p. 12; *Hollywood Reporter* 31 October 1952 p. 12; *Kinematograph Weekly* (U.K.)28 May 1953 p. 15; *L.A. Times* 9 July 1953 p. 71; *Monthly Film Bulletin* (U.K.) July 1953 p. 114; *Motion Picture Daily* 19 June 1953 p. 5; *Motion Picture Herald* 13 June 1953 p. 1870; *Philadelphia Enquirer* 12 July 1953; *Picture Show* (U.K.) 19 September 1953 p. 10; *Screenland* September 1953 pp. 17, 73

NOTES: The working title of the film was *Posse.*

Mission Over Korea

Aka *Eyes of the Skies* (United Kingdom title)
Columbia
B&W, 86 minutes
Released in August 1953

CREDITS: *Producer:* Robert Cohn; *Director:* Fred F. Sears; *Screenplay:* Jesse L. Lasky, Jr., Eugene Ling, Martin M. Goldsmith; *Story:* Richard Tregaskis; *Photography:* Sam Leavitt; *Cameramen:* Bill Whitley, Emil Oster, Jr.; *Editor:* Henry Batista; *Art Director:* George Brooks; *Set Decorator:* Frank Tuttle; *Music Director:* Mischa Bakaleinikoff; *Sound:* George Cooper; *Assistant Director:* James Nicholson; *Technical Advisor:* Capt. Paul F. Hopkins; *Songs:* "Gomen-Nasai" (Forgive Me), words by Benedict Mayers, music by Raymond Mattori

CAST: John Hodiak (Capt. George P. Slocum), John Derek (Lt. Pete Barker), Audrey Totter (Kate), Maureen O'Sullivan (Nancy Slocum), Harvey Lembeck (Sgt. Maxie Steiner), Richard Erdman (Corp. Swenson), William Chun (Kilamson Lee aka Clancy), Rex Reason (Major Hacker), Richard Bowers (Singing soldier), Todd Karns (Lt. Jerry Barker), Norma Randall (Gorgeous blonde), Al Choi (Major Kung), Daniel Lim (Interpreter), Chris Alcaide (Army officer), John Crawford (Tech sergeant), John Tarangelo (Air Force private), Sumner Williams (Jeep driver sergeant), John Pickard (Major McGuire), Dick Fortune (Air Force sergeant), Ralph Ahn (Korean radio operator), Robert Human (American radio operator), Herbert Lytton (Ambassador), Janet Brumhall (Annie), James Waters (Radio man), Don Gibson (Sergeant), Tyler McVey (Col. Colton), Weaver Levy (Guerrilla), Edward Colmans (Map Coordinates Officer), Robert Forrest (Medic), Joey Ray (Private), Susan Hawkins (Girl), Walter Flannery (Boy)

PLOT: Capt. George Slocum and his assistant, Lt. Jerry Barker, are stationed at Kimpo Field, Seoul, before the outbreak of war in Korea. They fly the tiny Army L-5 cub planes used for artillery observation, command reconnaissance and aerial photography, and teach Korean recruits with the aid of Major Kung of the Korean Army. Returning from a flight, Slocum is handed a TWX, ordering him back to Japan, where he will be able to see his wife Nancy and their children. In the meantime, Lt. Pete Barker, Jerry's brother, arrives in Japan to take on the job of flying one of the cub planes. Slocum and Pete Barker meet in Brady Field, Japan. Slocum is informed that he can spend just one day with his family. The Korean conflict has erupted suddenly. Pete has met Kate, an Army nurse. But before he can woo her, he and Slocum return to Kimpo Field, which is on fire, the base strewn with the bodies of the defenders. Pete's brother Jerry is wounded fatally and the only survivor is Clancy, a Korean boy who is mascot for the group. A small group of American soldiers arrive and the guerrillas are wiped out. With the GIs are the American ambassador and a distinguished-looking Korean. Slocum and Pete are ordered to fly them to safety at Taegu Airfield. When they arrive, Pete is told that he has flown the president of Korea, Syngman Rhee, to a safe retreat.

Once again, the two flyers are given orders. The battalion had been landed at Suwon and is threatened by encirclement. Unbeknownst to Capt. Slocum, Pete has arranged for a bazooka to be fastened on his tiny cub. Sighting a group of camouflaged tanks, Pete makes a dive for them against Slocum's orders. His bazooka misses its mark and a hail of machine-gun fire disables Pete's plane. He is forced to land. Pete is unconscious and does not know that Slocum has tried to save him. He argues with Slocum about his not trying to save him, until Slocum explains the situation. During the night their unit is attacked by a group of North Koreans. Slocum is seriously injured. Pete, without opermission, takes off to Taejon with the wounded Slocum, who needs immediate surgery. Finishing its run, the tiny L-5 lands near a Red Cross ambulance. From the rear door, Kate and a couple of medics climb out. Slocum is rushed off to a waiting hospital ship. Early the next morning Kate informs Pete that Capt. Slocum is dead. In the meantime the three-man ground crew, consisting of S/Sgt Maxie Steiner, Corporal Swenson and Clancy, arrive at Taejon. Pete informs them that they are now to take aerial pictures of their own lines. The men are horrified to learn of Slocum's death. Clancy is bewildered. He considered Slocum his foster father. Maxie and Pete, taking aerial pictures, spot enemy tanks. Pete notifies the jet command by radio and manages to hold the enemy tank positions until the jet arrive. In doing so, Pete is wounded and Maxie pilots the tiny plane back to Taejon where an ambulance is waiting with Kate standing near it—ready to administer first aid and love to Pete.

REVIEWS: "[F]ully supplied with some tense footage of aerial action.... [T]he first third is over talky...." *The Hollywood Reporter*, July 22, 1953

"The principals do their best with a script that has little of the punch or warmth necessary to elicit audience response." *Motion Picture Daily*, July 23 1953

"[An] ordinary war melodrama that does not rise above the level of program fare." *Harrison's Reports,* July 25, 1953

REVIEWS FOR JOHN DEREK: "Both Hodiak and Derek acquit themselves admirably in their roles..." *Los Angeles Times*, August 27, 1953

"John Derek as the headstrong cub [is] the hapless protagonist of a routine script..." *The New York Times*, September 19, 1953

"John Derek as Barker acts like an overgrown schoolboy..." *Kinematograph Weekly* (U.K.), September 24, 1953

ADDITIONAL REVIEWS AND ARTICLES: *Boxoffice* 16 February 1952; *Boxoffice* 25 July 1953 p. 1498; *Daily Times News* 1 January 1953; *Daily Variety* 16 December 1952; *Film Daily* 23 July 1953 p. 11; *Hollywood Reporter* 13 February 1953 p. 10; *Hollywood Reporter* 6 February 1953 p. 12; *Hollywood Reporter* 7 July 1953; *Il corriere della sera* (Italy) 16 April 1958; *L.A Examiner* 12 January 1953; *L.A Times* 10 February 1953; *L.A Times* 19 February 1953 p. 9; *Monthly Film Bulletin* (U.K.) November 1953 p. 162; *Motion Picture Herald Product Digest* 25 July 1953 p. 1926; *N.Y. Herald Tribune* 19 September 1953; *Philadelphia Enquirer* 12 January 1953; *Picturegoer* (U.K.) 22 May 1954 p. 17; *Pittsburgh Press* 8 March 1953; *Today's Cinema* (U.K.) 21 September 1953 p. 6; *Variety* 25 February 1953

NOTES: Parts of the picture was shot on location in Japan and Korea. In the United Kingdom, *Mission Over Korea* was released in a 72-minute version.

Sea of Lost Ships

Republic
B&W, 85 minutes
Premiered in Washington, D.C., on October 21, 1953

CREDITS: *Presenter:* Herbert J. Yates; *Associate Producer–Director* Joseph Kane; *Screenplay:* Steve Fisher; *Story*: Norman Reilly Raine; *Photography*: Reggie Lanning; *Art Director*: Frank Arrigo; *Music*: R. Dale Butts; *Assistant Director*: Robert Shannon; *Sound:* Earl Crain, Sr., Howard Wilson; *Costume Supervisor:* Adele Palmer; *Set Decorators:* John McCarthy, Jr., George Milo; *Special Effects*: Howard Lydecker, Theodore Lydecker; *Editor*: Richard L. Van Enger; *Makeup Supervisor:* Bob Mark; *Hair Stylist*: Peggy Gray; *Technical Advisor:* Lt. Commander Robert C. Cannon, U.S.C.G.

CAST: John Derek (G.R. Grad Matthews), Richard Jaeckel (Hap O'Malley), Wanda Hendrix (Pat Kirby), Walter Brennan (C.P.O. Chief O'Malley), Tom Tully (Capt. Holland), Barton Maclane (Capt. Matthews), Erin O'Brien-Moore (Mrs. O'Malley), Ben Cooper (Third crewman), Darryl Hickman (Pete Bennett), Roy Roberts (Captain of the *Eagle*), Tom Powers (Rear admiral), Richard Hale (Capt. Welch), James Brown (Ice Patrol Executive Officer), Douglas Kennedy (Helicopter Pilot), Steve Brodie (Lt Rogers), John Hudson (Pilot), Todd Karns (Co-pilot), Andrew Brennan (First crewman), James Lilburn (Radio operator), Nicolas Coster (Wilson), Tom Bernard (Sailor), Edward Ryan (Chet Marshall), Charles Evans (Keane—watch officer), Alden Aldrich, Harry McKim (Second classmen), Rolland Morris (John Logan), Wayne Rourke (Junior officer), Gil Harman (Watch officer), Roydon Clark, Dick Dodge (Seamen), Steve Darrell (Second mate), Richard Crane (Radar man), Richard Walsh (Radio operator)

PLOT: Grad Matthews and Hap O'Malley

have grown up together in the Coast Guard tradition. Grad's father, Capt. Jack Matthews, gave his life to save the Coast Guard base at Argentia, Newfoundland. Chief O'Malley, Hap's father, took Grad home after this tragedy and brought the boy up. The two boys enter the Coast Guard together. They remain allies under the discipline of senior cadet Pete Bennett. Hap helps Grad prove his manhood when their training program takes them on a cruise in an old-fashioned sailing ship and Grad develops a fear of going aloft in bad weather. They quarrel for their first time in their lives over a girl. Hap is passionately in love with Pat Kirby, an admiral's daughter. She tries to convince Hap that he has never been anything more to her than just a casual date. Hap won't accept that, accusing Grad of double-crossing him. Rather than hurt Hap, Grad broke with Pat and gets drunk to drown his grief. He ends up in a car crash, is expelled from the Coast Guard Academy, but is persuaded by his foster father, Chief O'Malley, to start anew in the Coast Guard service as an enlisted man. Grad has a tough time as an enlisted man. It's a bitter pill for him to swallow when Hap, an ensign now, comes aboard the same ship, as a result of hopeful Chief O'Malley's behind-the scenes string-pulling. Grad tries to bury the past and be friendly, but Hap won't meet him halfway. He is barely civil and so the feud continues, in spite of the attempt by everyone, including Pat, makes to bring about a reconciliation at a Christmas reunion at the O'Malley home. The feud finally ends when Grad and Hap display conspicuous heroism, along with Chief O'Malley, on one of the "ice patrols" for which the Coast Guard is famous. All three risk their lives to free the passenger ship *Pleiades* from a monstrous iceberg. When Hap is knocked out by an avalanche of falling ice, Grad carries him to safety. Hap gives Pat and Grad his blessing and asks to act as best man at their wedding. Their former loyalty to each other restored, they carry on their Coast Guard careers.

REVIEWS: "Within the confines of the familiar plot ... producer-director Joseph Kane managed to pack sufficient in the way of movement and heroics to provide showmen with an exploitable and at times engrossing action subject." *Boxoffice*, October 24, 1953

"The action fan should like it very much." *Motion Picture Herald*, October 31, 1953

"The story is loosely constructed and tritely developed, but they are some fairly interesting episodes showing the work of the ice patrol, effective views of icebergs and one particular good shot of a polar bear running and diving." *Monthly Film Bulletin* (U.K.), December 1953

REVIEWS FOR JOHN DEREK: "Stars Derek, Miss Hendrix and Brennan ... bring off their roles satisfactorily under Kane's direction." *Variety*, October 21, 1953

"John Derek and Richard Jaeckal [sic] are fully equal to the roles of the bickering buddies, roles which really make little histrionic demands." *Today's Cinema* (U.K.), October 23, 1953

ADDITIONAL REVIEWS AND ARTICLES: *Boxoffice* 18 July 1953; *Chicago Daily Tribune* 22 October 1953 p. 10; *Chicago Daily Tribune* 23 October 1953 p. 6; *Chicago Daily Tribune* 24 October 1953 p. 14; *Daily Variety* 21 October 1953 p. 3; *Film Daily* 22 October 1953 p. 6; *Film Bulletin* 23 March 1953 p. 12; *Film Bulletin* 1 June 1953 p. 21; *Film Bulletin* 14 September 1953 p. 18; *The Film User* February 1958; *Harrison's Reports* 24 October 1953 p. 170; *Hollywood Reporter* 1 April 1953 p. 7; *Hollywood Reporter* 14 August 1952 p. 5; *Hollywood Reporter* 24 April 1953 p. 14; *Hollywood Reporter* 3 April 1953 p. 8; *Kinematograph Weekly* (U.K.) 29 October 1953 p. 30; *L.A Times* 23 October 1953; *Motion Picture Daily* 22 September 1953 p. 7; *Motion Picture Herald* 11 April 1953 p. 35; *National Parent-Teacher* December 1953 p. 48; *Picturegoer* (U.K.) 27 February 1954 p. 19; *Today's Cinema* (U.K.) 6 August 1952 p. 5

NOTES: Background footage from *S.O.S. Eisberg* (1933) and *Whom the Gods Destroy* (1934) was included in the picture. The film's working title was *American Eagle*.

The Outcast

Republic
Aka *The Fortune Hunter* (United Kingdom title)
Trucolor, 90 minutes
Released on August 15, 1954

CREDITS: *Producer:* Herbert J. Yates; *Associate Producer*: William J. O'Sullivan; *Director:* William Witney; *Screenplay:* John K. Butler, Richard Wormser; Based on the *Esquire* magazine story *Red Horizon* by Todhunter Ballard and his novel *Two-Edged Vengeance*; *Photography*: Reggie Lanning; *Art Director:* Frank Arrigo; *Music:* R. Dale Butts; *Assistant*

Director: A.J. Vitarelli; *Assistant Sound:* T.A. Carman, Howard Wilson; *Costume Designer:* Adele Palmer; *Set Decorators:* John McCarthy, Jr., George Milo; *Editor:* Tony Martinelli; *Special Effects:* Howard Lydecker, Theodore Lydecker; *Makeup Supervisor:* Bob Mark; *Hair Stylist:* Peggy Gray

CAST: John Derek (Jet Cosgrave), Joan Evans (Judy Polsen), Jim Davis (Major Linton Cosgrave), Catherine McLeod (Alice Austin), Ben Cooper (The Kid), Taylor Holmes (Andrew Devlin), Nana Bryant (Mrs. Banner), Slim Pickens (Boone Polsen), Frank Ferguson (Chad Polsen), James Millican (Cal Prince), Bob Steele (Dude Rankin), Nacho Galindo (Curly), Harry Carey, Jr. (Bert), Bill Walker (Sam Allen), Robert "Buzz" Henry (Zeke Polsen), Nicolas Coster (Asa Polsen), Hank Worden (Bartender), Post Park (Weller), Marc Hamilton (Toby MacDonald), Chick Hannan (Baggage Man)

PLOT: After an absence of several years, Jet Cosgrave returns to the rough cattle town of Colton, Colorado, determined to regain his heritage, the wealthy Circle C Ranch, stolen from him by Major Cosgrave, his uncle. Among those who are affected by Cosgrave's arrival are Chad Polsen, a local rancher, whose hatred for Cosgrave's family included Jet himself; Judy Polsen, Chad's daughter; and Alice Austin, Cosgrave's innocent fiancée, who has just arrived from Virginia to marry him. Jet's first move is to hire a group of thugs headed by Dude Rankin, who help to seize the Newmark ranch which Cosgrave had appropriated illegally seven years previously, after the mysterious disappearance of its original owner. Rankin's men round up all the Circle C cattle found on the Newmark range and rebrand them with Jet's mark. The situation flares into violence when Steele kills a Circle C lineman. Jet's men outfight the Circle C crew, but they go over to the other side one by one after being bribed by Cosgrave. Jet's cattle, along with Polsen's herd, are stolen. Jet, wounded in a gun battle, is unable to stop the Circle C gang from recapturing the Newmark range. Polsen, though bitter toward Jed because of Judy's interest in him, joins up with him in a fight against Cosgrave. After much blood is shed, and after one of Polsen's sons is killed, the feud between Jet and Cosgrove comes to an end when the latter is shot dead by Andrew Devlin, an unscrupulous lawyer who had been double-crossed by Cosgrave after helping him to forge the will that deeded him the Circle C Ranch. Devlin himself dies from a bullet wound inflicted by Cosgrave. Alice, disillusioned by the brutality of her late fiancé, returns to Virginia, and Jet, sickened by the slaughter, settles down in peace with Judy as his bride.

REVIEWS: "Although following a routine story line, *The Outcast* has enough action footage to sustain general interest." *Variety,* June 23, 1954

"Grim brutality and tender love make odd contrasts in *The Outcast,* but the film's overall effect is that of a well-made and audience-pleasing period Western." *Motion Picture Daily,* June 25, 1954

"In spite of the fact that the plot elements are familiar, *The Outcast* ... is a better-than-average western." *Harrison's Reports,* June 26, 1954

REVIEWS FOR JOHN DEREK: "John Derek [is] extremely handsome as Jet Cosgrave." *Monthly Film Bulletin* (U.K.), June 1954

"First on the scene is a high-schoolish and somber John Derek." The *New York Times,* July 3, 1954

ADDITIONAL REVIEWS AND ARTICLES: *Albuquerque Journal Sun* 13 September 1953; *Boxoffice* 3 July 1954; *Daily Variety* 17 September 1953; *Daily Variety* 18 December 1953; *Daily Variety* 24 June 1954 p. 3; *Film Daily* 23 June 1954 p. 10; *Hollywood Reporter* 11 September 1953 p. 8; *Hollywood Reporter* 15 September 1953 p. 2; *Hollywood Reporter* 9 October 1953 p. 10; *Hollywood Reporter* 2 October 1953; *Kinematograph Weekly* (U.K.) 13 May 1954 p. 28; *L.A. Times* 14 September 1953; *L.A. Times* 24 June 1954 p. 42; *Motion Picture Herald* 26 June 1954 p. 41; *National Parent-Teacher* September 1954 p. 49; *Picturegoer* (U.K.) 12 June 1954 p. 21; *The Western Film Annual* 1954 (U.K.) pp. 122–125.

The Adventures of Hajji Baba

20th Century–Fox; Allied Artists, A Walter Wanger Production
DeLuxe Color, CinemaScope, 94 minutes
Premiered in Los Angeles on October 7, 1954

CREDITS: *Producer:* Walter Wanger; *Director*: Don Weis; *Screenplay:* Richard Collins; Suggested by the novel by James Morier; *Production Designer*: Gene Allen; *Special Color Consultant*: Hoyningen-Huene; *Costumes:* Renie; *Photography*: Harold Lipstein; *Supervising*

Editor: Lester A. Sansom; *Editor:* William Austin; *Music Director:* Dimitri Tiomkin; *Music Editor:* Robert Tracy; *Sound Editors:* Del Harris, Bruce Schoengarth; *Production Manager:* Rex Bailey; *Assistant Director:* Edward Morey, Jr.; *Art Director:* David Milton; *Set Decorator:* Joseph Kish; *Makeup:* Edward Polo; *Hairdresser:* Mary Smith; *Sound:* Ralph Butler; *Set Continuity:* John L. Banse: *Song:* "Hajji Baba" (Persian Lament) sung by Nat King Cole, music by Dimitri Tiomkin, lyrics by Ned Washington, musical arrangement by Nelson Riddle

CAST: John Derek (Hajji Baba), Elaine Stewart (Princess Fawzia), Thomas Gomez (Osman Aga), Amanda Blake (Banah), Paul Picerni (Prince Nur-El-Din), Rosemarie Bowe (Ayesha), Donald Randolph (Caliph), Melinda Markey (Touareg), Peter Mamakos (Chief executioner), Claude Akins (Chief executioner's aide), Kurt Katch (Caoush), Joann Arnold (Susu), Ed Perry, Bert Arnold, Bob Swan, Anthony George (Guards), Howard Gould (Giant guard), Paul Baxley (Warrior), Veronica Pataky (Kulub), Linda Danson (Fabria), Michael Granger (Musa), Carl Milletaire, Joseph Waring (Captains), Charles Heard (Julnah—horseman), Eileen Howe, Beverly Kidd, Dolly Summers, Leon Corwin, Millicent Rodgers, Ann Carroll, Pat Lawlor, Anna Navarro (Slave girls), Percy Helton (Kerbelai), Peter Leeds (Thin merchant), Leo Mostovoy (Barber), Than Wyenn (Auctioneer), Joe Martorano (Courier), Kenneth Alton, Paul Marion (Messengers), Beverly Thompson, Madeline Witlinger, Marilyn Dean, Pat Sheehan (Handmaidens), Laurette Luez (Meriam), Eugenia Paul (Shireen), Barbara James (Zeenad), Booth Colman (Akim)

PLOT: In a barber's shop in Ispahan, Persia, talk veers from speculation on a marriage for Princess Fawzia to the prospects of young Hajji Baba, a handsome and adventurous young man who is leaving the shop to seek his fortune. In the caliph's palace, Fawzia tries to get her father's consent for her marriage to Nur-El-Din, a rival prince. But the caliph believes his daughter's happiness is with an ally and old friend and intends to send her to him. When a courier comes with word from Nur-El-Din that an escort awaits the princess on the outskirts of the city, Fawzia escapes, disguised in boy's clothes. Hajji, too, leaves the city and is the first to come upon the escort. Hajji is attacked by the escort, who is overpowered by the boy. On Fawzia's arrival, she is puzzled that Nur-El-Din's escort is disguised as a barber but when she learns that Hajji thinks the emerald ring, sent to her by her lover, is the treasure to be delivered, she knows him to be an impostor. In her effort to escape, her turban becomes unbound and Hajji recognizes the princess who, herself, is the treasure Nur-El-Din awaits. Hajji promises to escort her and he asks for the emerald in payment. That night the couple find shelter in the caravan of Osman Aga, who invites them to watch the dancing girls, among whom is the lovely Ayesha. When Hajji and the princess are overtaken by the caliph's guards, a battle ensues when their intended capture is spoiled by an army of Turcoman women. The caliph's men are defeated by the women, and Hajji's life is spared as his good looks and skill attract their leader. Fawzia, however, is lashed up on the rocks under the hot sun, facing a slow death. In the middle of the night, Hajji creeps out of his tent and cuts the princess down. Returning for the emerald, he is seen, captured and strung up beside Fawzia. The following day, Nur-El-Din, learning of the princess's fate and realizing that by marrying her he can control all Persia, quickly rides to her rescue. Hajji is set free too, but later returns with Osman Aga and the Turcoman women to save Fawzia from the prince. As Hajji and the princess return to Ispahan, they are attacked by Nur-El-Din himself. In a fight to the finish, the prince is killed by Hajji, who claims Fawzia as his bride.

REVIEWS: "Eye-filling, voluptuous production […] The plot abounds in sexy situations that would have been more palatable if they had been treated with more wit." *The Hollywood Reporter,* October 7, 1954

"[G]audy, unwholesome and dull." *New York Herald Tribune*, October 9, 1954

"Poor C'Scoped costumer of the sex-and-sand school; a programmer in entertainment quality for the non-discriminating." *Variety*, October 13, 1954

REVIEWS FOR JOHN DEREK: "The actors … behave as though they're making up the story and improvising their own performances as they go along." The *New York Times,* October 9 1954

"John Derek, handsome owner of a fine torso, cuts a rare dash as Hajji." *Kinematograph Weekly* (U.K.) January 20, 1955

"In the title part, John Derek is required simply to be athletic and courageous, to sit a horse well and to make love convincingly. These duties he carries out conscientiously, teaming smoothly with Elaine Stewart." *Today's Cinema* (U.K.) January 17, 1954

ADDITIONAL REVIEWS AND ARTICLES: *America* 16 October 1954 p. 83; *Box Office* 16 October 1954; *Cahiers du Cinéma* (France) March 1958, p. 55; *Chicago Tribune* 3 November 1954 p. 36; *Daily Film Renter* (U.K.) 17 Jan 1955 p. 4; *Daily Variety* 7 October 1954 p. 3; *Film Bulletin* 18 October 1954 pp. 34–35; *Film Daily* 8 October 1954 p. 6; *Films of the Golden Age* Summer 2018 pp. 16–27; *Harrison's Reports* 9 October 1954 p. 162; *Hollywood Reporter* 1 April 1954 p. 5; *Hollywood Reporter* 11 May 1954 p. 5; *Hollywood Reporter* 14 April 1954 p. 1; *Hollywood Reporter* 15 April 1954 pp. 1, 5; *Hollywood Reporter* 16 April 1954 p. 3; *Hollywood Reporter* 17 September 1954 p. 2; *Hollywood Reporter* 19 Apr 1954 p. 6; *Hollywood Reporter* 19 November 1953 p. 10; *Hollywood Reporter* 21 April 1954 p. 4; *Hollywood Reporter* 29 April 1954 p. 5; *Hollywood Reporter* 30 April 1954 p. 3; *Hollywood Reporter* 6 April 1954 p. 3; *Hollywood Reporter* 9 April 1954 p. 8; *Il corriere della sera* (Italy) 25 May 1956; *Library Journal* 1 November 1954 p. 2095; *Life* 27 September 1954 p. 51; *L.A. Times* 24 March 1953; *L.A. Times* 2 April 1954; *L.A. Times* 9 May 1954; *L. A. Times* 8 October 1954 p. 62; *L. A. Times* 11 November 1952; *Monthly Film Bulletin* (U.K.) March 1955, p. 31; *Motion Picture Daily* 7 October 1954 p. 3; *Motion Picture Herald* 16 October 1954, p. 177; *Motion Picture Herald* 17 April 1954, p. 26; *National Newsweek* 8 November 1954 p. 101; *Parent-Teacher* December 1954 p. 39; *Picture Show* (U.K.) 30 April 1955; *Pix* 8 January 1955; *Sight and Sound* August 2007, p. 19; *Time* 1 November 1954 p. 98; *Variety* 21 April 1954

Prince of Players

20th Century–Fox
DeLuxe Color, CinemaScope, 105 minutes
Premiered in New York City on January 10, 1955

CREDITS: *Producer-Director*: Philip Dunne; *Screenplay*: Moss Hart; Based on the book by Eleanor Ruggles; *Music*: Bernard Herrmann; *Photography*: Charles G. Clarke; *Art Directors*: Lyle Wheeler, Mark-Lee Kirk; *Set Decorators*: Walter Scott, Paul S. Fox; *Special Photographic Effects*: Ray Kellogg; *Editor*: Dorothy Spencer; *Wardrobe Director*: Charles LeMaire; *Costumes*: Mary Wills; *Makeup*: Ben Nye; *Hair Stylist*: Helen Turpin; *Sound*: Alfred Bruzlin, Harry M. Leonard; *Assistant Director*: Eli Dunn; *Special Consultant on Shakespearean Scenes*: Eva Le Gallienne; *Color Consultant*: Leonard Doss

CAST: Richard Burton (Edwin Booth), Maggie McNamara (Mary Devlin), John Derek (John Wilkes Booth), Raymond Massey (Junius Brutus Booth), Charles Bickford (Dave Prescott), Elizabeth Sellars (Asia), Eva Le Gallienne (The Queen in *Hamlet*), Christopher Cook (Edwin, age 10), Dayton Lummis (English Doctor), Ian Keith (King in *Hamlet*), Paul Stader (Laertes), Stanley Hall (Abraham Lincoln), Sarah Padden (Mrs. Lincoln), Louis Alexander (John Booth, age 12), Eleanor Audley (Mrs. Montchesington), Jack Raine, Richard Deacon, Ken Christy (Theater managers), Charles Cane (Assistant theater manager), Betty Flint (Lady Macbeth), Mae Marsh (Witch in *Macbeth*), Paul Frees (Francisco), Ben Wright (Horatio), Melinda Markey (Young lady), Percival Vivian (Polonius), George Dunn (Doorman), Ruth Warren (Nurse), Richard Cutting (Doctor), Lane Chandler, Richard Travis (Colonels), Steve Darrell (Major Rithbone), George Melford (Stage doorman), Tom Fadden (Trenchard), Henry Kulky (Bartender), Leo Curley (Rich miner), Burt Mustin, Emmett Lynn, Paul Wexler (Miners), Paul Newland (Drunk miner), Ethan Laidlaw (Drunk), Jack Mather (Man at bar), Barbara Morrison (Actress), Paula Morgan, Michael Granger, Jack Kruschen, Emerson Treacy, Joe Devlin, Paul Kruger (Protesters at theater), Sol Gorss, Charles Regan, John Doucette (Men in audience), Mimi Gibson (Little girl), Harry Denny (Southern gentleman), Nolan Leary (Minister), Tom Hennesy (Man in tavern), Dona Stewart (Farmer's daughter), Edmund Cobb (Farmer), Prudence Beers (Farmer's wife), Henry Rowland (Sergeant), Lawrence Ryle (Actor), Booth Colman (Ghost of Buckingham Palace), Ivan Hayes (Bernardo), Olan Soule (Catesby in *Richard III*)

PLOT: *Prince of Players* opens at the time that Julius Brutus Booth was America's top actor. With his ten-year-old son Edwin accompanying him on his tours, the elder Booth presents Shakespeare in theaters across the country, occasionally missing a performance because he's too drunk to speak his lines, and at other times driven from the stage by his madness. At each performance, Edwin is beneath the stage or in the wings, mouthing the great lines along with his father. Edwin's brother John Wilkes Booth and his sister Asia wait at home on the family farm in Maryland. At the age of 19, Edwin goes with his father to California, where Junius Brutus is scheduled to tour the gold-mining camps playing Shakespeare, but finds himself unable to fill the commitment. Edwin takes his place and is a huge success. His father dies on the way back to Maryland. Returning to the East, Edwin discovers that his brother has taken over the father's costumes and is making a name for himself as an actor, particularly in the South. Edwin goes on tour and soon has outranked John, but he has adopted his father's habit of drinking when he feels he is tainted with his father's madness. After marrying Mary Devlin, an actress, Edwin straightens out and goes to London for a successful season in *Hamlet*. While in England, Mary gives birth to a daughter, Edwina, but also learns that she has tuberculosis. In the U.S., the Civil War has broken out and John, infuriated by his brother's success, seeks to play a greater role by acting as a spy for the South and taking part in the affair at Harper's Ferry. Returning to the U.S. after several years in England's damp climate, Edwin learns that Mary is very ill and must go to Massachusetts for a rest. His manager, Dave Prescott, is readying an opening of *Hamlet* in New York, but Edwin, without Mary's help, again begins to drink. By the time he has sobered up, Mary is dead. Edwin, heartbroken, leaves the stage for several months. Shortly after he returns to acting, Edwin is shocked by the news that his brother has assassinated the president. The shooting of Lincoln creates a surge of anti-theater and anti-actor sentiment. Edwin, opening again in *Hamlet* in New York, is threatened by an ugly mob. Determined to face them, he sits quietly in the center of the stage and asks that the curtain be raised. At first he is booed and pelted with vegetables, but his calm determination eventually impresses the audience, and the catcalls turn to applause.

REVIEWS: "*Prince of Players* is superb from the viewpoint of acting and production." *Harrison's Reports*, January 8, 1955

"*Prince of Players* is singularly lacking in drama and excitement, and Bernard Herrmann's music and Charles G. Clarke's photography do not save it." *Films in Review*, February 1955

"The film is *honestly* conventional, and has an oddly old-fashioned dignity reminiscent of big prestige productions in the 30s; many opportunities are missed ... but the lengthy Shakespearean excerpts are quite interesting." *Monthly Film Bulletin* (U.K.) April 1955

REVIEW FOR JOHN DEREK: "John Derek's work as John Wilkes Booth is skillfully contrasted with that of Burton. [...] Both actors get a note of comedy into their work by an occasional touch of ham." *The Hollywood Reporter*, January 5, 1955

ADDITIONAL REVIEWS AND ARTICLES: *America* 22 January 1955 pp. 434–435; *Box Office* 8 January 1955; *Catholic World* February 1955 p. 383; *Chicago Tribune* 19 January 1955; *Christian Science Monitor* 18 January 1955; *Commonweal* 28 January 1955, p. 455; *Daily Variety* 5 January 1955 p. 3; *Film and Filming* (U.K.) March 1955 p. 24; *Film and Filming* (U.K.) September 1955 p. 21; *Film Bulletin* 10 January 1955 pp. 5, 36; *Film Bulletin* 24 January 1955 p. 27; *Film Bulletin* 7 February 1955 pp. 30–31; *Film Daily* 5 January 1955 p. 12; *Film Score Monthly* December 1998 p. 43; *Hollywood Reporter* 12 November 1954 p. 10; *Hollywood Reporter* 12 October 1954 p. 3; *Hollywood Reporter* 13 September 1954 p. 3. *Hollywood Reporter* 15 September 1954 p. 2. *Hollywood Reporter* 17 June 1954 p. 1; *Hollywood Reporter* 20 August 1954 p. 8; *Hollywood Reporter* 23 August 1954 p. 3; *Hollywood Reporter* 24 September 1954 pp. 6, 12: *Hollywood Reporter* 26 August 1954 p. 3; *Hollywood Reporter* 26 July 1954 p. 3; *Hollywood Reporter* 28 January 1953 p. 2; *Hollywood Reporter* 17 September 1954, p. 10; *Hollywood Reporter* 29 September 1954 p. 4, 16; *Hollywood Reporter* 30 September 1955 p. 2; *Hollywood Reporter* 7 January 1955 p. 1; *Hollywood Reporter* 7 September 1954 p. 6; *Hollywood Reporter* 11 January 1955 p. 3; *Hollywood Reporter* 14 April 1955 pp. 5–7; *Hollywood Reporter* 19 January 1955 p. 3; *Kinematograph Weekly* (U.K.) 3 March 1955, pp. 18; *L.A. Examiner* 16 April 1955; *L.A. Times* 18 January 1955; *Life* 24 January 1955 pp. 55–56; *Modern Screen* April 1955 p. 22; *Motion Picture Daily* 6 January 1955 p. 8; *Motion Picture Herald* 8 January 1955, p. 273; *Music from the Movies* Autumn 1998, pp. 16–17; *The Nation* 22 January 1955 p. 84; *N.Y. Herald Tribune* 12 January 1955;

National Parent-Teacher March 1955 p. 39; *The New Yorker* 22 January 1955 p. 87; *The New York Times* 16 January 1955 sec. II p. 1; *The New York Times* 18 July 1954; *Newsweek* 24 January 1955; p. 9; *Saturday Review* January 22 1955 p. 44; *Sight and Sound* Spring 1955 pp. 196–197; *Time* 7 February 1955 p. 65; *Today's Cinema* (U.K.) 25 February 1955 p. 7

An Annapolis Story

Aka *The Blue and the Gold* (United Kingdom title) and *Navy Air Patrol*
Allied Artists, Technicolor, 81 minutes
Released in New York City on April 10, 1955

CREDITS: *Producer*: Walter Mirisch; *Director*: Don Siegel; *Screenplay*: Dan Ullman, Geoffrey Homes; *Story*: Dan Ullman; *Photography*: Sam Leavitt; *Production Manager*: Allen K. Wood; *Music*: Marlin Skiles; *Art Director*: Dave Milton; *Set Decorator*: Joseph Kish; *Supervising Editor*: Lester Sansom; *Editor*: William Austin; *Second Unit Director*: Austen Jewell; *Sound*: Ralph Butler; *Photographic Effects*: Augie Lohman; *Dialogue Supervisor*: Sam Peckinpah; *Makeup*: Edward Polo; *Hairdresser*: Mary Smith; *Set Continuity*: John L. Banse; *Technicolor Color Consultant*: Mitchell G. Kovaleski; *Technical Advisor*: Commander Marcus L. Lowe, Jr., U.S.N.; *Songs*: "Navy, Blue and Gold" by Joseph W. Crosley; "The Engagement Waltz" by Marlin Skiles

CAST: John Derek (Tony Scott), Diana Lynn (Peggy Lord), Kevin McCarthy (Jim Scott), Alvy Moore (Willie Warren), Pat Conway (Dooley), L.Q. Jones (Watson), John Kirby (Macklin), Barbara Brown (Mrs. Scott), Betty Lou Gerson (Mrs. Lord), Fran Bennett (Connie), Robert Osterloh (Air Group Commander Austin), John Doucette (Boxing coach), Don Kennedy (McClaren), Tom Harmon (Announcer), Don Haggerty (Lt. Prentiss), Lt. Robert Boniol (Lt. Preston), Christian Drake (First classman), Richard Travis (Commander Wilson), James Anderson (Instructor), Robert Pike (Professor), Dabbs Greer (Commander Hallock), Don Keefer (Air officer), George Eldredge (Capt. Lord), John Lehmann (Storekeeper), John Ayres (Superintendent), Sam Peckinpah (Pilot), William Schallert (Tony's instructor), Walter Conrad (Jim's instructor), George Garver, Joel Smith (Boatswain's mates), Richard Carlson (Narrator)

PLOT: At Annapolis Naval Academy, midshipman Tony Scott is individualistic and excels as an athlete, but is not a good student. His brother Jim is a leader all the way through, and both are well liked by their classmates. Jim's engagement to Peggy Lord, daughter of a naval captain, seems practically assured. Tony is injured on a training cruise (Jim saved his life) and Peggy visits him in the hospital. They fall for each other. When Jim hears this from Tony, he bitterly assumes that Peggy wants to marry his brother. The two brothers, once close, are now sharply split, but their careers inevitably keep them near one another. They go to Korea as jet fighter pilots. Peggy in the meantime has gone to Tokyo, where her father has been assigned. Tony gets a leave and meets her there. She tells him that she will not marry him as, in spite of their temporary attraction, she will always love Jim. Tony, disconsolate, returns to his carrier. The next day both brothers go out on a mission. Jim's plane is shot down and he is badly wounded. By radio, Tony gets through to his almost unconscious brother, brings him back to full consciousness and fights off an enemy plane while a helicopter pulls Jim from the sea. Both brothers get back to their carrier safely.

REVIEWS: "The production is expensive-looking and handsomely mounted, forcefully narrated and well enacted..." *Variety*, March 23, 1955

"[A]n old-fashioned, innocuous and pointedly utopian gold-brick of a picture." The *New York Times*, April 9, 1955

"[T]he playing on the whole, lacks flavor." *Monthly Film Bulletin* (U.K.), October 1955

REVIEWS FOR JOHN DEREK: "While [*An Annapolis Story*] does not take [Derek] too far away from the egocentric character he has established, it does let him get, in the later sequences, some believable sympathy." *The Hollywood Reporter*, March 21, 1955

"John Derek and Diana Lynn ... are excellent...." *The Film Daily*, April 1, 1955

"John Derek ... convinces as Tony." *Kinematograph Weekly* (U.K.), August 18, 1955

ADDITIONAL REVIEWS AND ARTICLES: *Box Office* 26 March 1955; *Chicago Tribune* 23 May 1955; *Daily Variety* 21 March 1955 p. 3; *Harrison's Report* 26 March 1955 p. 51; *Hollywood Reporter* 9 November 1953 p. 11; *Hollywood Reporter* 19 November 1953 p. 10; *Hollywood Reporter* 3 June 1954 p. 2; *Hollywood*

Reporter 3 August 1954 p. 1; *Hollywood Reporter* 6 August 1954 p. 8; *Hollywood Reporter* 10 August 1954 p. 2; *Hollywood Reporter* 11 August 1954 p. 8; *Hollywood Reporter* 16 August 1954 p. 4; *Hollywood Reporter* 20 August 1954; *Hollywood Reporter* 24 August 1954 p. 3; *Hollywood Reporter* 3 September 1954 p. 5; *Hollywood Reporter* 20 September 1954 p. 3; *Hollywood Reporter* 22 March 1955; *Il corriere della sera* (Italy) 10 June 1961; *The Independent Film Journal* 2 April 1955 p. 18; *L.A Examiner* 14 July 1955; *L. A. Times* 7 July 1954; *L. A. Times* 15 July 1955 p. 20; *Modern Screen* July 1955 p. 22; *Motion Picture Daily* 25 March 1955 p. 12; *Motion Picture Herald* 26 March 1955 p. 378; *Motion Picture Herald* 8 June 1955 p. 17; *N.Y. Herald Tribune* 9 April 1955; *Today's Cinema* (U.K.) 17 August 1955, p. 7

NOTES: Future director Sam Peckinpah worked on the set as a dialogue coach and appeared briefly as a pilot.

Run for Cover

Paramount, Pine-Thomas Productions
Technicolor, VistaVision, 93 minutes
Premiered in Los Angeles on April 20, 1955

CREDITS: *Producers:* William H. Pine, William C. Thomas; *Director:* Nicholas Ray; *Screenplay:* Winston Miller; *Original story:* Harriet Frank, Jr., Irving Ravetch; *Assistant Director:* Francisco Day; *Photography:* Daniel L. Fapp; *Technicolor Color Consultant:* Richard Mueller; *Special Photographic Effects:* John P. Fulton; *Special Effects:* Farciot Edouart; *Editor:* Howard Smith; *Art Directors:* Hal Pereira, Henry Bumstead; *Set Decorators:* Sam Comer, Frank McKelvey; *Costumes:* Edith Head; *Makeup:* Wally Westmore; *Music:* Howard Jackson; *Sound:* Gene Merritt, John Cope; *Dialogue Coach:* Sumner Williams; *Music Director:* Howard Jackson; *Orchestrator:* Lucien Caillet; *Song* "Run for Cover," music by Howard Jackson, lyrics by Jack Brooks.

CAST: James Cagney (Matt Dow), Viveca Lindfors (Helga Swenson), John Derek (Davey Bishop), Jean Hersholt (Mr. Swenson), Grant Withers (Gentry), Jack Lambert (Larsen), Ernest Borgnine (Morgan), Irving Bacon (Scotty), Trevor Bardette (Paulsen), Ray Teal (Sheriff), John Miljan (Mayor Walsh), Denver Pyle (Harvey), Emerson Treacy (Banker), Gus Schilling (Doc Ridgeway), Phil Chambers (Andrews), Harold Kennedy (Devers), Joe Haworth (Miller—train guard), Bob Folkerson (Hughes), Harold J. Kennedy (Devers—expressman on train), Emmett Lynn (Bartender), Henry Wills (Townsman)

PLOT: After six years in prison for a crime he didn't commit, Matt Dow drifts about the West. He is heading for the cow town of Madison when he meets up with 20-year-old Davey Bishop. Because Davey is almost the age his own son would have been had he lived, Matt warms to him. Davey, whose folks are dead, lives in Madison. As the two ride towards town, they happen to take an idle potshot at a hawk— and a nervous railway clerk on a passing train thinks the train is being held up by the Gentry gang, as it was a few days back. He tosses out the money bags and, on reaching town, gets the sheriff out with a posse to hunt down the "bandits." They ambush Matt and Davey coming in with the retrieved money bags, wound Davey seriously, and nearly hang Matt before they realize their mistake. His leg smashed and close to death, Davey is taken to the Swenson farm where, with the help of Mr. Swanson's attractive daughter Helga, Matt succeeds in saving Davey's life. Matt's wife divorced him while he was in prison and he's had little to do with women since—but during the days he and Helga are together, they fall in love. The townspeople feel they owe Davey and Matt something— particularly Davey, who will be crippled for life—but the boy harshly rejects their offers. Matt, however, accepts the job of sheriff and appoints Davey his deputy, anxious to make Davey feel he can still do a man's job in spite of his crippled leg. Though he never admits it, Matt entertains the hope that Davey will replace the son he lost. Matt's mistake is that he doesn't realize how deeply Davey resents his crippled condition and that his bitterness makes him want to strike back at anyone with two sound legs—even Matt. When two members of Gentry's gang come into town and wound the bank manager, Matt arrests one of them and turns him over to Davey to guard while he goes after the second one. When he returns to town with his prisoner, Morgan—who tried unsuccessfully to buy him off—Matt sees that Davey has let a mob hang his prisoner. Though upset, Matt still has faith in Davey and entrusts him with the task of taking Morgan to another town where the jail is stronger. Again Davey fails, letting the prisoner escape. Not long after this, the Gentry gang rides in and robs the bank. During the hold-up, Gentry recognizes Matt as on old cellmate—a fact which Matt curtly acknowledges to the suspicious townspeople. Familiar with all of Gentry's tricks, he leads a posse in pursuit of the bandits. When they reach Comanche country, the men turn back, leaving only Matt and Davey to go on. They find the gang members massacred by Indians. Now Davey turns to Matt, reveals he has sold out to Gentry—and leaves Matt for dead when Indians attack. But Matt escapes death and grimly goes after Davey, finding him with Morgan. In the final showdown Davey redeems himself by killing Morgan to save Matt—just as Matt, mistaking Davey's intentions, shoots and kills him.

REVIEWS: "*Run for Cover* is a heartening success.... Nicholas Ray's direction is extremely competent." *The Hollywood Reporter*, March 18, 1955

"*Run for Cover* ... is an entertaining picture which owes much of its appeal to the know-how of the producing team ... and to its cast of 'names' and the excellent performances they give." *The Film Daily*, March 18, 1955

"*Run for Cover* is handicapped by a sprawling story and by plot inconsistencies, but on the whole it emerges as a better-than average Western melodrama." *Harrison's Reports*, May 7, 1955

REVIEWS FOR JOHN DEREK: "Derek is wonderfully soft behind a handsome boyish smile."

New York Herald Tribune, April 30, 1955

"Derek is very good as the young man...." *Variety*, March 23, 1955

ADDITIONAL REVIEWS AND ARTICLES: *American Magazine* April 1955 p. 16; *Arts-Spectacles* (France) 5 October 1955 p. 5; *Boxoffice* 26 March 1955; *Cahiers du Cinéma* (France) November 1955 p. 47; *Commonweal* 27 May 1955 p. 208; *Daily Telegraph* (U.K.) 30 April 1955; *Daily Variety* 18 March 1955 p. 3; *Études cinématographiques* (France) Winter 1961 pp. 359–361; *F-Filmjournal (Germany)* August/September 1980 pp. 29–30; *Hollywood Reporter* 28 May 1954 p. 12; *Hollywood Reporter* 21 June 1954 p. 4; *Hollywood Reporter* 25 June 1954 p. 6; *Il corriere della sera* (Italy) 6 August 1954; *Kinematograph Weekly* (U.K.) 28 April 1955 pp. 21–22; *L.A. Times* 21 April 1955; *Monthly Film Bulletin* (U.K.) June 1955, p. 92; *Motion Picture Daily* 18 March 1955 p. 3; *Motion Picture Herald Product Digest* 26 March 1955 p. 378; *Modern Screen* April 1951 p. 26; *National Parent-Teacher* April 1955 p. 40; *The New Yorker* 7 May 1955 p. 132; *Newsweek* 21 March 1955 p. 106; *Picture Show* (U.K.) 4 June 1955; *Scholastic* 20 April 1955 p. 27; *Time* 30 May 1955 pp. 84–88; *Today's Cinema* (U.K.) 21 Apr 1955 p. 7; *Variety* 21 April 1954

The Leather Saint

Paramount
B&W, VistaVision, 86 minutes
Premiered in New York City on June 15, 1956

CREDITS: *Producer*: Norman Retchin; *Director*: Alvin Ganzer; *Story and Screenplay*: Norman Retchin, Alvin Ganzer; *Photography*: Haskell Boggs; *Art Directors*: Hal Pereira, Henry Bumstead; *Special Photographic Effects*: John P. Fulton; *Process Photography*: Farciot Edouart; *Set Decorators*: Sam Comer, Frank McKelvy; *Technical Advisors*: Joe Gray, Herman Schraff; *Costumes*: Edith Head; *Music Supervisor*: Irvin Talbot; *Editor*: Floyd Knudtson; *Assistant Director*: William McGarry; *Makeup*: Wally Westmore; *Sound*: Harry Lindgren, Winston Leverett

CAST: Paul Douglas (Gus McAuliffe), John Derek (Father Gil Allen aka Kid Sunday), Jody Lawrance (Pearl Gorman), Cesar Romero (Tony Lorenzo), Richard Shannon (Tom Kelly), Ernest Truex (Father Ritchie), Ricky Vera (Pepito), Babette Bain (Dolores), Baynes Barron (Tony's henchman), Bill Baldwin (Fight announcer), Cheryl Callaway (Cheryl, girl in iron lung), Court Shepard (Fighter), Donald Wittenberg (Boy), Eddie Sarnez (Fighter in Gil's Third Bout), Edith Evanson (Stella), Edward G. Pagett (Young Yankees fan), Estelle Etterre (Nurse with iron lung), Ethan Laidlaw (Fisherman), Frank Mills (Man in Fight Crowd), Jan Bradley (Secretary), Joe Gray (Referee), Lawrence A. Williams (Fat man in gym), Lou Nova (Tiger), Mary Benoit (Nurse), Mushy Callahan (Referee), Ralph Montgomery (Waiter), Raymond Winston (Young Dodgers fan), Richard Bender (Boy), Robert Cornthwaite (Dr. Lomas), Thomas B. Henry (Bishop Hardtke), William Meader (Bartender).

PLOT: Father Gil Allen, a young Episcopalian minister, is working out in the Los Angeles gymnasium run by his close friend Tom Kelly. The muscular minister catches the eye of fight manager Gus McAuliffe. Mistaking him for a boxer, Gus offers to get him bouts. Without disclosing his identity, the young minister declines. Father Allen visits Bishop Hardtke and tells hi he is in desperate need of money to buy an iron lung and to build a swimming pool for several young polio victims. The bishop promises to do what he can but warns him to have patience as those matters take time. Father Allen returns to his parish, St. Andrew Church in Santa Marta, a few hours from L.A., and reports his failure to raise the money to his superior, Father Ritchie. That night, the two priests are summoned to the children's ward of St. Ambrose Hospital, located on the church grounds. They are shocked to learn that a young girl died because the motor in the hospital's ancient iron lung has failed. Returning to L.A., the minister tells Gus he has changed his mind and is ready to accept his offer. Gus calls Tony Lorenzo, fight promoter, and arranges a bout. Father Allen warns Tom that nobody, Gus included, can know his true identity. Father Allen wins his bout in the first round with a single punch to the jaw. McAuliffe's joy lessens somewhat when his fighter tells him the only time he can train is Saturday morning; the only time he can fight is Saturday night. He offers no explanation to the bewildered McAuliffe. Pearl Gorman, Lorenzo's girl, asks Gus to introduce her to his new boxer, but he refuses. Father Allen returns to Santa Marta and gives father Ritchie $200 for their polio fund. When the old priest asks where it came from, Father Allen tells him it is a donation from a friend in the leather business. The following Saturday, Father Allen again wins his bout in the first round with a single punch. Pearl, slightly tipsy, barges into his dressing room and forces an introduction from Gus. After she leaves, Gus warns his fighter to stay away from her. With a smile, Father Allen agrees. But Pearl is persistent and the next Saturday morning shows up at the gym. She asks him to take her to lunch and he agrees, provided Tom goes along. Pearl manages to ditch Tom and drives Father Allen to Malibu. She is strongly attracted to the handsome young man and, for the first time in years, is inspired to give up drinking for a few hours. Sensing what is happening to the girl, Father Allen insists they return to town. Hurt, Pearl is silent on the way back. That night, following another one-punch victory, Father Allen returns to Santa Marta and discovers that Father Ritchie, anticipating future donations from the friend in the leather business, has purchased an iron lung on the installment plan. Deeply disturbed, Father Allen, who has been on the verge of abandoning his plan, realizes he must continue to fight. He tells Gus he wants some important bouts—and fast. The only trouble is that Gus can't line up any really big matches without Tony Lorenzo's cooperation, and Lorenzo wants to buy Father Allen's contract. After the minister wins his next bout, Pearl follow him to the bus station. While Tom buys his ticket, Father Allen enters the washroom and changes his clothes. Pearl stares in shocked disbelief when he walks out and she discovers he is a man of the cloth. She drives to Santa Marta and learns the reason for the masquerade. Anxious to help, she returns to L.A. and tells Gus what she has learned. Also wanting to help, he schemes with Pearl and Tom and sells Father Allen's contract to Lorenzo for $10,000. The money is turned over to the young minister for his fund. When he learns the cause and sees the wonderful change that has come over Pearl, Lorenzo isn't too upset at the trick played on him. Father Allen is happy too, particularly when he receives forgiveness from Bishop Hardtke for taking matters into his own hands.

REVIEWS: "This is excellently drafted and ably executed entertainment to please most tastes, with a solid assembly star cast, close scripting and honest production values." *Today's Cinema* (U.K.), May 24, 1956

"A fairly good melodrama ... well directed and acted..." *Harrison's Reports*, June 2, 1956

"Humorously scripted ... an unusual story..." *The Film Daily*, June 12, 1956

REVIEW FOR JOHN DEREK: "John Derek pleases in the title role...." *Variety*, May 30, 1956

ADDITIONAL REVIEWS AND ARTICLES: *America* 30 June 1956 p. 332; *Boxoffice* 2 June 1956; *Catholic World* June 1956 p. 224; *Chicago Tribune* 11 January 1956; *Chicago Tribune* 16 October 1956; *Commonweal* 13 July 1956 p. 371; *Daily Variety* 29 May 1956 p. 3; *Film & Filming* (U.K) July 1956 p. 24; *The Film Daily* 12 June 1956 p. 11; *Film Review* (U.K) 1956–1957 p. 119; *Hollywood Reporter* 21 February 1956 p. 9; *Hollywood Reporter* 27 January 1954; *Hollywood Reporter* 6 January 1956 p. 8; *Hollywood Reporter* 7 April 1954 p. 2; *Hollywood Reporter* 8 March 1954 p. 2; *Hollywood Reporter* 9 January 1956 p. 3; *Il corriere della sera* (Italy) 24 November 1955; *Il corriere della sera* (Italy) 5 February 1958; *Kinematograph Weekly* (U.K.) 31 May 1956 p. 32; *L.A. Times* 10 December 1955; *L.A. Times* 14 January 1956; *L.A. Times* 16 September 1954; *L.A. Times* 28 September 1955; *Modern Screen* August 1956 p. 14; *Monthly Film Bulletin* (U.K.) July 1956 p. 92; *Motion Picture Daily* 1 Jun 1956; *Motion Picture Herald Product Digest* 2 June 56 p. 923; *National Parent-Teacher* June 1956 p. 37; *N.Y. Herald Tribune* 16 June 1956; *New York Times* 16 June 1956 p. 12; *Philadelphia Inquirer* 2 June 1956; *Picturegoer* (U.K.) 23 June 1956 p. 16; *Picture Show* (U.K) 14 July 1956 p. 10; *Press and Bulletin Sun* 18 March 1956; *Screenland* October 1956 p. 72; *Today's Cinema* 6 January 1956 p. 8

NOTES: The screenwriters claimed that the story was based on real events. The picture was written for Montgomery Clift, who turned down the role.

The Ten Commandments

Paramount, Cecil B. DeMille Productions
Technicolor, VistaVision, 219 minutes
Premiered in New York City on November 8, 1956

CREDITS: *Producer-Director:* Cecil B. DeMille; *Associate Producer:* Henry Wilcoxon; *Screenplay:* Æneas MacKenzie, Jesse L. Lasky, Jr., Jack Gariss, Fredric M. Frank; Story partially based on the books *The Prince of Egypt* by Dorothy Clarke Wilson, *Pillar of Fire* by Rev. J.H. Ingraham, and *On Eagle's Wings* by Rev. A.E. Southon; *Photography*: Loyal Griggs; *Additional Photography*: J. Peverell Marley, John Warren, Wallace Kelley; *Technicolor Consultant*: Richard Mueller; *Music:* Elmer Bernstein; *Art Directors*: Hal Pereira, Walter Tyler, Albert Nozaki; *Set Decorators*: Sam Comer, Ray Moyer; *Set Construction*: Jerry Cook; *Properties*: Gordon Cole, Robert Goodstein; *Choreography:* Leroy Prinz, Ruth Godfrey; *Dialogue Supervisors*: Frances Dawson, Donald Maclean; *Makeup Supervisor*: Wally Westmore; *Makeup:* Frank Westmore, Frank McCoy; *Hair Stylist*: Nellie Manley; *Sound Recording Supervisor*: Louis H. Mesenkop; *Sound:* Harry Lindgren, Gene Garvin; *Special Photographic Effects*: John P. Fulton; *Optical Photography*: Paul Lerpae; *Process Photographer*: Farciot Edouart; *Costumes*: Edith Head, Ralph Jester, John Jensen, Dorothy Jeakins, Arnold Friberg; *Editor:* Anne Bauchens; *Unit Director*: Arthur Rosson; *Research:* Henry Noerdlinger, Gladys Percey; *Assistant Directors*: Francisco Day, Michael Moore, Edward Salven, Daniel McCauley; *Assistant Director* (Egypt): Fouad Aref; *Production Managers:* Frank Caffey, Kenneth de Land, Donald Robb; *Acknowledgment for valuable cooperation:* Dr. William C. Hayes, Metropolitan Museum of Art, New York; Dr. Labib Habachi Egyptian Department of Antiquities, Luxor, Egypt; Dr. Keith C. Seele, Dr. Ralph Marcus, Dr. George R. Hughes, Oriental Institute, University of Chicago; Rabbi Rudolph Lupo, Jewish Community Library, L.A.

CAST: Charlton Heston (Moses), Yul Brynner (Rameses), Anne Baxter (Princess Nefretiri), Edward G. Robinson (Dathan), Yvonne De Carlo (Sephora), John Derek (Joshua), Debra Paget (Lilia), Nina Foch (Bithiah), Judith Anderson (Memnet), John Carradine (Aaron), Douglass Dumbrille (Jannes), Henry Wilcoxon (Oentaur), Donald Curtis (Mered), H.B. Warner (Amminadab), Cedric Hardwicke (Sethi), Martha Scott (Yochabel), Vincent Price (Baka), Olive Deering (Miriam), Frank De Kova (Abiram), Eduard Franz (Jethro), Lawrence Dobkin (Hur Ben Caleb), Julia Faye (Elisheba), Lisa Mitchell, Joanna Merlin, Joyce Vanderveen, Noelle Williams, Pat Richard, Diane Hall (Jethro's daughters), Abbas el Boughdadly (Rameses' charioteer), Fraser Heston (Infant Moses), Tommy Duran (Gershom), Eugene Mazzola (Rameses' son), Ramsay Hill (Korah), John Miljan (Blind man), Francis J. McDonald (Simon), Ian Keith (Rameses I), Paul De Rolf (Eleazar), Joan Woodbury (Korah's wife), Woodrow Strode (King of Ethiopia), Esther Brown (Princess Tharbia), Arthur Tookoian (Fan bearer)

PLOT: Following a decree that all first sons of the children of Israel be put to the sword, Yochabel, a Jewish mother, places her baby in a basket which drifts down the Nile. Found by Bithiah, daughter of Sethi, king of Egypt, the child is christened Moses and brought up as her son, becoming Seth's favorite over his own offspring Rameses. In manhood, Moses loves Nefretiri, bur remembers she is Rameses' betrothed. Later, Moses' true origin is revealed and Rameses, now king, banishes him to the desert. Moses seeks the word of God, finds it at Mount Sinai and begins his struggle to free the people of Israel from Rameses' tyranny. The Israelites are pursued by the soldiers and chariots of the vengeful Rameses, but the Red Sea parts for them and engulfs their enemies.

Now safe, the freed slaves quickly forget God and Moses, indulge in wild revelry and worship false gods. Moses witnesses the writing of the Ten Commandments, and subsequently the unrepentant idolaters are destroyed. God then condemns the Israelites to 40 years in the wilderness as penance. When they finally approach the Promised Land, Moses hands over the leadership to Joshua, his disciple, and goes alone to Mount Nebo to face his God.

REVIEWS: "[A] moving story ... a rather handsome romance in Mr. DeMille's best massive style ... thrilling and perhaps even spiritually profound." The *New York Times,* November 8, 1956

"*The Ten Commandments* proves, once again and at last again, the power of which the screen is capable...." *Los Angeles Times,* October 28, 1956

"This enormous film is less of a brash, pseudo–Biblical charade than one might at first have expected... [T]he most unsatisfactory of all is the film's totally inadequate approach to character..." *Monthly Film Bulletin* (U.K), January 1958

REVIEW FOR JOHN DEREK: "John Derek and Debra Paget have faces on which neither mind nor heart have left a trace." *Films in Review,* November 1956

ADDITIONAL REVIEWS AND ARTICLES: *America* 1 December 1956 p. 284; *American Cinematographer* November 1956 pp. 658–60, 680–83; *American Cinematographer* April 1983, pp. 46–52, 124–130; *Awake* 8 November 1956 pp. 9–12; *Boxoffice* 6 October 1956; *Boxoffice* 13 October 1956; *Cahiers du Cinéma* (France) 8 February 1958 p. 57; *Chicago Tribune* 29 October 1954; *Chicago Tribune* 21 November 1956; *Cinemagic* Fall 1985 pp. 43; 62; *Cinemagic* Winter 1985–86 pp. 32–36.*Classic Images* October 1993, pp. 48–50; *Classic Images* March 1999 pp. 41–42; *Collier's* 14 September 1956 pp. 90–92; *Commonweal* 30 December 1956 pp. 205–209; *Cue* 10 November 1956; *The Daily Cinema* 28 November 1957 p. 6; *Daily Variety* 5 August 1952; *Daily Variety* 8 August 1952 p. 8; *Daily Variety* 10 October 1953; *Daily Variety* 16 October 1953; *Daily Variety* 3 November 1954; *Daily Variety* 27 July 1955; *Daily Variety* 15 August 1955; *Daily Variety* 5 October 1956 p. 3; *Daily Variety* 15 December 1960 p. 10; *Daily Variety* 28 December 1960; *Daily Variety* 10 November 1965; *Daily Variety* 5 December 1975; *Daily Variety* 24 May 1990; *Daily Variety* 14 March 1997; *Empire (U.K.)* May 1990 pp. 82–83; *Empire* (U.K) May 2006 p. 160; *Evening Telegraph* 9 November 1956; *Film Bulletin* 15 October 1956 p. 16; *The Film Daily* 5 October 1956 p. 7; *Film Quarterly* Fall 1966 pp. 59–60; *Films & Filming* (U.K.) January 1958 pp. 23–24; *Films & Filming* (U.K.) September 1972 pp. 53–54; *Good Housekeeping* April 1956; *Harrison's Reports* 6 October 1956 p. 160; *Hollywood Citizen-News* 8 August 1952; *Hollywood Citizen-News* 22 October 1956; *Hollywood Citizen-News* 26 October 1956; *Hollywood Reporter* 24 March 1952 p. 4; *Hollywood Reporter* 20 May 1953; *Hollywood Reporter* 30 July 1954 p. 2; *Hollywood Reporter* 5 August 1954 p. 4; *Hollywood Reporter* 13 September 1954 p. 7; *Hollywood Reporter* 16 September 1954 pp. 1, 6; *Hollywood Reporter* 20 September 1954 p. 2; *Hollywood Reporter* 13 October 1954 p. 3; *Hollywood Reporter* 14 October 1954 p. 4; *Hollywood Reporter* 15 October 1954 p. 19; *Hollywood Reporter* 19 November 1954; *Hollywood Reporter* 22 November 1954 p. 1. *Hollywood Reporter* 26 November 1954 p. 11; *The Hollywood Reporter* 10 December 1954; *Hollywood Reporter* 25 March 1955 p. 18; *Hollywood Reporter* 4 April 1955 p. 3; *Hollywood Reporter* 6 April 1955 pp. 4, 8; *Hollywood Reporter* 7 April 1955 p. 7; *Hollywood Reporter* 8 April 1955 pp. 4, 7; *Hollywood Reporter* 14 April 1955 p. 2; *Hollywood Reporter* 15 April 1955 p. 11; *Hollywood Reporter* 21 April 1955 p. 9; *Hollywood Reporter* 16 May 1955 p. 2; *Hollywood Reporter* 20 May 1955 p. 5; *Hollywood Reporter* 25 May 1955 p. 8; *Hollywood Reporter* 31 May 1955 p. 6; *Hollywood Reporter* 1 June 1955 p. 3; *Hollywood Reporter* 2 June 1955 p. 11; *Hollywood Reporter* 3 June 1955 p. 2; *Hollywood Reporter* 8 June 1955 p. 14; *Hollywood Reporter* 29 June 1955 p. 15; *Hollywood Reporter* 1 July 1955 p. 17; *Hollywood Reporter* 5 July 1955 pp. 2, 5; *Hollywood Reporter* 7 July 1955 p. 11; *Hollywood Reporter* 8 July 1955 p. 7; *Hollywood Reporter* 26 July 1955 p. 7; *Hollywood Reporter* 8 August 1955 p. 6; *Hollywood Reporter* 3 January 1956 p. 9; *Hollywood Reporter* 5 January 1956 pp. 1, 4; *Hollywood Reporter* 27 January 1956 p. 12; *Hollywood Reporter* 7 February 1956 p. 10; *Hollywood Reporter* 20 March 1956 p. 6; *Hollywood Reporter* 6 April 1956 p. 4; *Hollywood Reporter* 13 April 1956 p. 1; *Hollywood Reporter* 18 April 1956 pp. 1, 4; *Hollywood Reporter* 19 April 1956 p. 3; *Hollywood Reporter* 1 November 1956; *Hollywood Reporter* 9 November 1956 p. 4; *Holly-*

wood Reporter 12 November 1956 p. 4; *Hollywood Reporter* 14 November 1956 p. 2; *Hollywood Reporter* 15 November 1956 pp. 3, 14–51; *Hollywood Reporter* 23 November 1956 p. 11; *Hollywood Reporter* 27 November 1956 p. 8; *Hollywood Reporter* 30 November 1956 p. 6; *Hollywood Reporter* 25 January 1957 p. 16; *Hollywood Reporter* 27 January 1957 p. 6; *Hollywood Reporter* 19 March 1957; *Hollywood Reporter* 5 April 1957 p. 1; *Hollywood Reporter* 4 September 1957 p. 1; *Hollywood Reporter* 7 January 1958 p. 2; *Hollywood Reporter* 8 January 1958 p. 1; *Hollywood Reporter* 10 January 1958 p. 11; *Hollywood Reporter* 20 January 1958 p. 2; *Hollywood Reporter* 7 February 1958 p. 2; *Hollywood Reporter* 12 February 1958 p. 9; *Hollywood Reporter* 21 February 1958 p. 1; *Hollywood Reporter* 25 February 1958 p. 7; *Hollywood Reporter* 12 March 1958 p. 1; *Hollywood Reporter* 21 March 1958 p. 4; *Hollywood Reporter* 28 March 1958 pp. 1, 3–4; *Hollywood Reporter* 4 April 1958 p. 1; *Hollywood Reporter* 11 April 1958 p. 17; *Hollywood Reporter* 4 June 1958 p. 2; *Hollywood Reporter* 16 June 1958 p. 3; *Hollywood Reporter* 8 July 1958 p. 2; *Hollywood Reporter* 14 July 1958 p. 3; *Hollywood Reporter* 18 July 1958 p. 2; *Hollywood Reporter* 23 July 1958 p. 2; *Hollywood Reporter* 7 August 1958 p. 5; *Hollywood Reporter* 18 August 1958 pp. 1, 4; *Hollywood Reporter* 3 September 1958 p. 1; *Hollywood Reporter* 9 September 1958 pp. 1, 6; *Hollywood Reporter* 10 September 1958 pp. 1, 9; *Hollywood Reporter* 29 October 1958 pp. 1, 6; *Hollywood Reporter* 12 November 1958 p. 2; *Hollywood Reporter* 19 December 1958 p. 8; *Hollywood Reporter* 2 January 1959 pp. 1, 3; *Hollywood Reporter* 29 January 1959 p. 6; *Hollywood Reporter* 24 April 1959 p. 2; *Hollywood Reporter* 30 April 1959 p. 3; *Hollywood Reporter* 2 June 1959 p. 2; *Hollywood Reporter* 3 June 1959 p. 6; *Hollywood Reporter* 13 April 1960 p. 3; *Hollywood Reporter* 18 April 1960; *Hollywood Reporter* 14 June 1960 p. 2; *Hollywood Reporter* 11 October 1960 p. 1; *Hollywood Reporter* 28 December 1960 p. 1; *Hollywood Reporter* 7 April 1966; *Hollywood Reporter* 20 July 1966; *Hollywood Reporter* 26 February 1980; *Hollywood Reporter* 11 February 1991; *Hollywood Reporter* 18 April 1995; *Hollywood Reporter* 3 March 1997; *Hollywood Reporter* 13 March 1997; *Hollywood Reporter* February 1980 p. 3; *Hollywood Studio Magazine* September 1975; *Kinematograph Weekly* (U.K) 5 December 1957 pp. 13–14; *Life* 24 October 1955; *Life* 12 November 1956; *Look Magazine* 27 November 1956 p. 9; *L.A. Examiner* 15 November 1956; *L.A. Mirror-News* 5 October 1956; *L.A. Mirror-News* 22 October 1956; *L.A. Mirror-News* 14 November 1956; *L.A. Mirror-News* 15 November 1956; *L.A Times* 23 May 1952 Part III, p. 9; *L.A Times* 14 July 1952; *L.A. Times* 8 August 1952 p. 7; *L.A. Times* 29 December 1953; *L.A. Times* 24 September 1954; *L.A. Times* 29 May 1955; *L.A. Times* 12 February 1956; *L.A. Times* 28 October 1956 p. 1, 4; *L.A. Times* 4 October 1960; *L.A. Times* 16 May 1990 pp. F1, F5; *L.A. Times* 5 March 1997; *L.A. Times* 30 June 1999; *L.A. Times* 27 July 2003; *Motion Picture Daily* 11 August 1955 p. 2; *Motion Picture Daily* 5 October 1956 pp. 1, 5; *Motion Picture Herald* 6 October 1956 pp. 18–20; *Motion Picture Herald Product Digest* 13 October 1956 p. 107; *Movie Maker* August 1980; *Nation* 8 December 1956 p. 506; *New York Herald Tribune* 9 November 1956; *New Republic* 10 October 1956 p. 20; *New York Times* 24 August 1952; *New York Times* 26 September 1954; *New York Times* 24 April 1955; *New York Times* 31 July 1955; *New York Times* 12 August 1956; *New York Times* 9 November 1956 p. 35; *New York Times* 11 November 1956 p. 1; *New York Times* 24 December 1956; *New York Times* 24 February 1957; *New York Times* 10 November 1957; *New York Times* 20 December 1959; *New York Times* 31 December 1961; *New York Times* 16 July 1965; *New York Times* 5 November 1972; *New York Times* 29 January 1978; *New York Times* 25 March 1984 p. 19; *New Yorker* 17 November 1956 p. 101; *NewsLife* 29 September 1953; *Newsweek* 5 November 1956 p. 112; *Parade* 23 June 1996 p. 2; *People* 17 July 1995; *The Picture News Magazine* June 1955; *Picture Show* (U.K.) 30 June 1956 p. 3; *Picture Show* (U.K.) 30 November 1957; *Picture Show* (U.K.) 5 April 1958; *Picturegoer Film Annual* (U.K) 1956–57 p. 30; *Picturegoer Film Annual* (U.K) 1958–59 pp. 122–123; *Popular Man* May 1958 pp. 26–27; *Positif* (France) October 1984, pp. 58–60; *Revista Internacional del Cine* (Spain) December 1959 p. 43; *Saturday Review* 10 November 1956 p. 28; *Scholastic* 15 November 1956 p. 33; *Sight and Sound* Winter 1957/58 p. 148; *Time* 12 November 1956 p. 120; *Time* 19 November 1956 p. 82; *Variety* 26 November 1969; *Variety* 5 October 1966; *Wall St. Journal* 8 April 2001 pp. 1, 12; *Weekly World News* 8 September 1982 pp. 5, 22

AWARDS AND HONORS: Blue Ribbon

Award: *Boxoffice Magazine*: *Won:* Best Picture of the Month: Cecil B. DeMille

Golden Globes: *Nominated:* Best Actor-Drama: Charlton Heston

Academy Awards: *Won:* Best Effects, Special Effects: John P. Fulton; *Nominated:* Best Picture: Cecil B. DeMille; Best Cinematography, Color: Loyal Griggs; Best Art Direction-Set Decoration, Color: Hal Pereira, Walter H. Tyler, Albert Nozaki, Sam Comer, Ray Moyer; Best Costume Design, Color: Edith Head, Ralph Jester, John Jensen, Dorothy Jeakins, Arnold Friberg; Best Sound, Recording: Loren L. Ryder (and Paramount Studio Sound); Best Film Editing: Anne Bauchens

Photoplay Awards: *Won:* Special Award: Cecil B. DeMille: For his creation of one of the screen's greatest emotional and religious experiences.

Fotogramas de Plata: Spain, 1960: *Won:* Best Foreign Performer: Charlton Heston

NOTES: The film's working title was *Prince of Egypt*. In 1990, a restored print of *The Ten Commandments* was re-issued in 70mm Super VistaVision with a six-track soundtrack remixed in Dolby Stereo.

Fury at Showdown

United Artists, Bob Goldstein Productions
B&W, 75 minutes
Premiered in Los Angeles on April 3, 1957

CREDITS: *Producer:* John Beck; *Director:* Gerd Oswald; *Executive Producer:* Bob Goldstein; *Screenplay:* Jason James; Based on the novel *Showdown Creek* by Lucas Todd; *Photography:* Joseph LaShelle; *Music:* Harry Sukman; *Production Manger:* Jack Bernie; *Art Director:* Leslie Thomas; *Editorial Supervisor:* Robert Golden; *Set Decorator:* Howard Bristol: *Property Master:* Max Frankel; *Assistant Director:* Arthur Von Kirbach; *Script Supervisor:* M.E.M. Gibsone; *Wardrobe:* Albert Deano; *Makeup:* Bob Schiffer; *Hair Stylist:* Kay Shea

CAST: John Derek (Brock Mitchell), John Smith (Miley Sutton), Carolyn Craig (Ginny Clay), Nick Adams (Tracy Mitchell), Gage Clarke (Chad Deasey), Robert E. Griffin (Sheriff Clay), Malcolm Atterbury (Norris), Rusty Lane (Riley), Sydney Smith (Van Steeden), Frances Morris (Mrs. Williams), Tyler McDuff (Tom Williams), Robert Adler (Alabam), Norman Leavitt (Swamper), Ken Christy (Mr. Phelps), Tom McKee (Sheriff of Buckhorn), Chet Brandenburg (Waiter), Herman Hack (Fight Spectator), George DeNormand, Kermit Maynard (Townsmen), Buddy Roosevelt (Deputy)

PLOT: Brock Mitchell has unwittingly attained the reputation of "gun-killer." The stigma was first attached to him when he killed Sim Deasey in a fight. As a result, his home town of Showdown Creek turned against him, his girlfriend Ginny rebuffed him and friends turned their backs. Brock left Showdown Creek, and everywhere he was challenged. He served a one-year jail sentence for killing a man who had goaded him into a fight. Now he's free and wants to be left alone. His brother Tracy convinces him that his only salvation is to return home and start anew. Otherwise, Tracy warns, whenever Brock goes, a new gunman will seek to challenge him. As the story opens, Brock returns to Showdown Creek and finds that the town's hatred still lingers. Seeking to goad him into another gunfight is attorney Chad Deasey, Sim's brother. Chad has hired a fast-draw bodyguard, Sutton, and seeks by every method to goad Brock into a gunfight with Sutton. Brock and Tracy have a note due at the bank, and the banker, Van Steeden, says it cannot be extended. But Van Steeden, Brock's lone friend, says he will personally guarantee the note if Brock and Tracy can close a deal with the railroad company. The deal involves the boy's ranch and two other ranches belonging to Norris and Riley; three ranches working together can supply all the food needed by railroad workers moving in to build a railroad. The railroad has agreed to send an agent, Phelps, to sign the contracts. If the note isn't met Chad Deasey, with bank approval, has agreed to buy out the note and take over the boy's ranch. Phelps doesn't arrive on schedule, sending word by the stagecoach driver that he has stopped off in Gunstock on business. The deadline for the notes arrives and still no agent to close the deal. Tracy keeps Brock from fleeing the hatred of the town and hitting the lonely trail again. Brock even takes off his guns to avoid being taunted into a gunfight. Tracy finds Phelps and learns that he had received a letter asking him to wait in Gunstock, signed by Chad, who claimed he was lawyer for Brock and Tracy. Tracy rides back with the letters and an agreement from Phelps. He is ambushed by Sutton and left for dead. However, he manages to get on his horse and reaches town. Sutton has come back to get his money from. Tracy, found by Van Steeden, blurts out the truth before he dies. Sutton is cornered in Chad's office by the sheriff and his men, but shoots his way out and takes Ginny hostage. Brock, forced to use a gun again, kills Sutton. Chad's fate is left in the hands of the law and Brock begins a new life in Showdown Creek with Ginny.

REVIEWS: "Better than average action feature." *The Film Daily,* March 28, 1957

"Some fine direction ... interesting camerawork ... and a fresh approach to a familiar Western plotline... [An] offbeat Western." *Motion Picture Herald,* April 6, 1957

REVIEWS FOR JOHN DEREK: "John Derek is impressive as the hero of the piece..." *Harrison's Reports,* March 30, 1957

"Mr. Derek fits his part..." *The New York Times,* April 20, 1957

"John Derek is okay as the gutsy kid..." *Variety,* May 15, 1957

ADDITIONAL REVIEWS AND ARTICLES: *Box Office* 13 April 1957; *The Daily Cinema* 4 February 1958 p. 3; *Daily Variety* 4 April 1957 p. 3; *The Film Bulletin* 18 March 1957 p. 15; *The Gazette's Magazine* (U.K) 1 December 1957; *Hollywood Reporter* 20 July 1956 p. 11; *Kinematograph Weekly* (U.K.) 6 February 1958 pp. 17–18; *L.A. Times* 28 January 1957; *Motion Picture Daily* 17 January 1956 p. 61 *Motion Picture Daily* 14 March 1957 p. 6; *Movie Life* May 1957; *National Parent-Teacher* September 1957 p. 52; *Screen World* 1958 p. 164; *Screenland* November 1956 p. 14

Omar Khayyam

Aka *The Life, Loves and Adventures of Omar Khayyam* and *The Loves of Omar Khayyam*
Paramount
Technicolor, VistaVision, 101 minutes
Premiered in New York City on August 23, 1957

CREDITS: *Director:* William Dieterle; *Producer:* Frank Freeman, Jr.; *Screenplay:* Barré Lyndon; *Photography:* Ernest Laszlo; *Editor:* Everett Douglas; *Art Directors:* Hal Pereira, Joseph MacMillan Johnson; *Special Photographic Effects:* John P. Fulton; *Process Photography:* Farciot Edouart; *Set Decorators:* Sam Comer, Grace Gregory; *Assistant Director:* Francisco Day; *Makeup Supervisor:* Wally Westmore; *Sound:* Gene Merritt, Winston Leverett; *Music:* Victor Young; *Costumes:* Ralph Jester; *Technicolor Color Consultant:* Richard Mueller; *Technical Advisor:* Abdel Salam Moussa; *Songs:* "The Loves of Omar Khayyam" by Jay Livingston and Ray Evans; "Take My Heart" by Mack David and Victor Young; "Lament" by Moises Vivanco

CAST: Cornel Wilde (Omar Khayyam), Michael Rennie (Hasani Sabah), Debra Paget (Sharain), John Derek (Prince Malik), Joan Taylor (Yaffa), Raymond Massey (The Shah), Maggie Hayes (Queen Zarada), Sebastian Cabot (The Nizam), Perry Lopez (Prince Ahmud), Abraham Sofaer (Tutush), Yma Sumac (Karina), Arthur Tookoian (Courier), Morris Ankrum (Iman Nowafek), Edward Platt (Jayhan), James Griffith (Buzorg), Peter Adams (Master Herald), Henry Brandon (Commander), Kem Dibbs (Tutush's Guard), Paul Picerni (Commander), John Abbott (Yusuf), Ed Agresti, William Bagdad (Assassins), Eric Alden (Commander), Richard Alameda, E.J. André, John Merton, Robert Tafur (Noblemen), Joe Bassett (Prior "Rashidi"), Jugat Bhatia (General), Valerie Allen, Florine Carlan, Emilie Stevens (Harem Wives), Anthony Caruso (Shah's Guard), Roger Creed (Executioner), James Davies (Defender Assassin), Don Diamond (Trooper Captain), Allan Douglas (Townsman/Defendant Assassin), Don Dunning (Prior "Dikar"), Dick Elliott (Tavern Owner), Richard Gilden (Novice Assassin), Frank Griffin (Assassin/Assassin Teacher), Edmund Hashim (Turkoman), Len Hendry (Officer/Courier), Charles La Torre (Army Physician), Frank Leyva (Defender Assassin), Jack Mather (Prior "Sayida"), Lee Belser, Audrey Lowell, Joyce Meadows, Sandra Warner, Sonia Warner (Harem Girls), Abdel Salam Moussa (Shah's Soldier), Mary Ellen Popel (Court Woman), Max Power (Prior "Dastur"); Franz Roehn (Kisrak), Ric Roman (Slavemaster), Paul Salata (Guard), Carl Saxe, Robert St. Angel, Dale Van Sickel (Officers), Mahin S. Shahrivar (Slave Girl), Douglas Spencer (Pigeon Keeper), Marie Tsien (Chinese Girl), Joyce Vanderveen (Hindu Girl), Romo Vincent (Physician), Paul Weber (Q'Adi), Alan Wells (Trooper Scout), Henry Wills (Defender Assassin)

PLOT: In Nishapur, capital of the 11th century Persian Empire, lives Omar Khayyam, poet mathematician and astronomer. Omar loves and is loved by Sharain Mowafek. The Shah is holding audience, and princess and courtiers from every province are arriving in the city to pay homage and to seek appointment for some office. Sharain urges Omar to ask for a court appointment, but he has no desire for advancement. Unlike Omar, the handsome, ambitious Hasani Sabah does seek a high office and arrives in the city with gifts for the Shah. Omar and Hasani gain the Shah's favor—Omar by daring to speak the truth, and Hasani by bringing to the Shah the heads of his two worst enemies. Omar is appointed court counsellor, given an observatory, and ordered to create a new calendar. Hasani is appointed Keeper of the Seal, a position next in power to that of the Nizam. Omar finds no joy in his appointment, for he loses Sherain, who has been chosen by the Shah as his fourth wife. Hoping to divert Omar's thoughts from his loss, the Nizam makes him a gift: Yaffa, a lovely slave girl. The Assassins—a fanatical sect whose headquarters are at Alamut, an impregnable mountain fortress—have threatened the life of Tutush, the Shah's brother. In spite of Omar's precautions, they murder Tutush. At court, Sharain pleases the Shah, earning the anger of Zarada, the queen, his first wife. Zarada is determined that Price Ahmud, her and the Shah's eldest son, shall inherit the throne—though the Shah favors a younger son, Prince Malik. The Shah departs with his army to fight the Byzantines. He is accompanied by Prince Malik, whom he his royal heir after Malik defeated his half-brother in a fight to win the honor. Hassani plots with Queen Zarada and Ahmud. In the meantime, Omar has come to suspect that Hasani (with his lust for power) is the secret leader of the Assassins. Hasani arrives and is revealed as the all-powerful leader. He tells Omar that the Shah and Prince Malik have been wounded in routing the Byzantines, that half of their army is dead, and that Prince Ahmud has risen against his father. Omar spurns Hasani's offer to have him join the Assassins. Hasani lets him depart, and Omar rides to warn the Shah. Omar tells the Shah and Malik that he has a secret plan for destroying the stronghold of Alamut. The Shah dies, and Malik becomes his successor. Yaffa, who went with Asani to Alamut (in order to help Omar), prevents Hasani from sending a message by pigeon to Ahmud—she releases the whole flock of pigeons. The assassins push her from the tower and she falls to her death. Omar's plan for undermining Alamut is successful: The fortress crumbles and collapses and Hasani and Queen Zarada are killed. Malik slays Ahmud in a fierce battle. Malik releases Sharain from her queenly status and restores her to Omar.

REVIEWS: "Opulent sets and costumes set splendid scene for accomplishments of the immortal poet, astronomer. Big names cast will help its sale potential." *The Film Daily*, August 5, 1957

"Sometimes cumbersome and draggy, but lavish and colorful romance." *Variety*, August 7, 1957

REVIEWS FOR JOHN DEREK: "John Derek as the Shah's son ... makes contributions." *The Hollywood Reporter*, August 1, 1957

"A prominent group of players are in support. They include John Derek as the loyal son of the Shah." *New York Mirror*, August 25, 1957

"[Corner Wilde] is well backed by ... John Derek as an honest prince." *News of the World* (U.K), 23 September, 1957

ADDITIONAL REVIEWS AND ARTICLES: *American Cinematographer* 1 April 1956 p. 198; *Boxoffice* 3 August 1957; *Chicago Tribune* 16 September 1957 p. 48; *Daily Film Renter* (U.K) 14 August 1957 p. 3; *Daily Variety* 1 August 1957 p. 3; *Daily Variety* 17 December 1955; *Daily Variety* 26 June 1957; *Film Bulletin* 5 August 1957 p. 7; *Film Daily* 5 January 1956 p. 2; *Daily Telegraph* (U.K.) 23 September 1957; *Films & Filming* (U.K.) November 1957 pp. 25–27; *Historical Journal of Film, Radio and Television* August 2006 pp. 295–309; *Hollywood Reporter* 10 March 1954; *Hollywood Reporter* 2 February 1955 p. 1; *Hollywood Reporter* 6 April 1956 p. 12; *Hollywood Reporter* 19 March 1956 pp. 1, 4; *Il corriere della sera* (Italy) 7 September 1957; *Kinematograph Weekly* (U.K.)15 August 1957 p. 17; *L. A. Examiner* 5 March 1954; *L. A. Times* 22 August 1957; *Monthly Film Bulletin* (U.K.) October 1957 p. 129; *Motion Picture Daily* 6 August 1957 p. 7; *Motion Picture Herald Product Digest* 10 August 1957 p. 481; *National Parent-Teacher* October 1957 p. 34; *Newsweek* 26 August 1957 p. 98; *Picture Show* (U.K.) 16 November 1957 p. 8; *New York Times* 24 August 1957 p. 12; *N.Y. Herald Tribune* 24 August 1957; *The Times* (U.K.) 23 September 1957; *Today's Cinema* (U.K.) 14 August 1957 p. 6.

The Flesh Is Weak

Eros Film Ltd., A Raymond Stross Production
U.K., B&W; 90 minutes

Premiered in London on August 4, 1957
Premiered in New York City on November 8, 1957

CREDITS: *Producer*: Raymond Stross; *Director*: Don Chaffey; *Associate Producer*: Victor Lyndon; *Screenplay*: Leigh Vance; *Original Story*: Deborah Bedford; *Photography*: Stephen Dade; *Art Director*: John Stoll; *Editor*: Charles Hasse; *Production Manager*: Clifton Brandon; *Music*: Tristram Cary; *Night Club Music*: Gerry Levy; *Continuity*: Jane Buck; *Camera Operator*: G. Massy-Collier; *Sound*: Cliff Sandell; *Assistant Director*: René Dupont; *Makeup*: Gerry Fairbank; *Hairdresser*: Anne Box; *Wardrobe*: Betty Adamson

CAST: John Derek (Tony Giani), Milly Vitale (Marissa Cooper), Freda Jackson (Trixie), William Franklyn (Lloyd Buxton), Martin Benson (Angelo Giani), Norman Wooland (Chief Inspector Kingcombe), Patricia Jessel (Millie), Vera Day (Edna), Patricia Plunkett (Doris Newman), Joe Robinson (Lofty), Harold Lang (Henry), Denis Shaw (Saradine), Miriam Karlin (Betty), Charles Lloyd Pack (Salvi), Jack May (Prospective client), Shirley Ann Field (Susan), Roger Snowdon (Benny), Jim O'Brady (Thug), John Paul (Police Sgt. Franks), Emile Stemmier (Joe—café proprietor)

PLOT: Young, innocent Marissa Cooper comes from a small town to seek excitement and a career in London. The proprietress of a nightclub offers her a job as a hostess. Beguiled by expensive clothes and an exotic atmosphere, Marissa fails to realize what her "duties" at the club are until a drunken customer attempts to assault her. A handsome young man named Tony intervenes and persuades Marissa to leave the club. Marissa becomes infatuated by the young man's charm and generosity, unaware that he is one of the n Giani brothers, heads of a London vice racket. As times passes, Marissa falls completely under Tony's domination, so that when he tells her he has lost all he possesses in a gamble for their future happiness and marriage, she eagerly promises to do "anything" to help. She takes to the street to "help us to get out of this mess," as Tony puts it. It is a long, embittering process before Marissa realizes how she has been duped and that Tony is no more in love with her than he is with any of the other Giani girls whose ranks she has now joined. Hardened, disillusioned, yet still in love with Tony, she determines to take to the streets on her own behalf. She is approached by a man named Buxton who wants her to assist in exposing the Giani racket by giving evidence in court. Not until she is framed by Tony does she decide to get out of the pit in which she has fallen. She unhappily testifies in court against Tony and the Giani organization.

REVIEWS: "As entertainment [*The Flesh is Weak*] is rather mediocre stuff which likely will bore the discerning patron and sadly disappoint those in search of cheap thrills." *Variety*, August 14, 1957

"A crudely melodramatic film... [T]he direction is brisk." *Monthly Film Bulletin* (U.K.), September 1957

"A very bad film." *Films & Filming* (U.K.), September 1957

REVIEWS FOR JOHN DEREK: "Mr. Derek, as despicable as he is handsome, is completely convincing..." The *New York Times*, November 9, 1957

"A peculiarity of this film is that Mr. Derek ... is more often undressed than Miss Vitale.... Exposing Mr. Derek seems to have pre-occupied the director more than revealing Miss Vitale." *New York Herald Tribune*, November 9, 1957

"Derek ... again shows himself as a dull, flat and expressionless actor." *Los Angeles Times*, November 21, 1958

ADDITIONAL REVIEWS AND ARTICLES: *ABC Film Review* (U.K.) January 1958 pp. 12–13; *Il corriere della sera* (Italy) 16 April 1957 p. 4; *Confidential* November 1957; *Daily Film Renter* (U.K.) 25 July 1957 p. 6; *Daily Herald* (U.K) 2 August 1957; *Daily Mail* (U.K.) 2 August 1957; *Daily Worker* (U.K.) 27 July 1957; *Evening Standard* (U.K.) 1 August 1957; *Films & Filming* (U.K.) May 1957 p. 29; *Films & Filming* (U.K.) March 1971 pp. 18–22; *Journal of British Cinema and Television* n.2 2006 pp. 266–283; *Kinematograph Weekly* (U.K.) 25 July 1957 p. 21; *Motion Picture Daily* 5 September 1957 p. 5; *Motion Picture Daily* 31 December 1957 p. 2; *New Statesman* (U.K.) 3 August 1957; *Photoplay* July 1957 pp. 12–13; *Picture Show* (U.K.) 17 August 1957 p. 3; *Picture Show* (U.K.) 25 January 1958 p. 9; *Reynolds News* (U.K.) 4 August 1957; *The Star* (U.K.) 2 August 1957; *The Sun Baltimore* 18 January 1958; *The Times* (U.K.) 29 July 1957; *Today's Cinema* 25 July 1957 p. 10

NOTES: *Women of the Night* was the picture's original title. *The Flesh Is Weak* was

High Hell

Paramount, A Princess Production, A Rich and Rich Production
B&W, 87 minutes
Released on February 19, 1958

CREDITS: *Producers:* Burt Balaban, Arthur L. Mayer; *Director:* Burt Balaban; *Screenplay:* Irve Tunick, based on the novel *High Cage* by Steve Frazee; *Photography:* Jimmy Wilson; *Editor:* Eric Boyd Perkins; *Music Composer and Director:* Phil Cardew; *Art Director:* Frank White; *Production Manager:* Eddie Pike; *First Assistant Director:* Jimmy Shingfield; *Camera Operator:* Desmond Davis; *Continuity:* June Randall; *Makeup:* George Claff; *Hair Stylist:* Eileen Warwick; *Casting Supervisor:* Sally Nicholl; *Production Secretary:* Trix Wilkin; *Assistant Art Director:* David Catley; *Dubbing Editor:* Janet Davidson; *Production Supervisor:* William N. Boyle; *Song:* "A Man's Man," music by Phil Cardew, lyrics by Sonny Miller, sung by Dick James.

CAST: John Derek (Craig Rhodes), Elaine Stewart (Lenore Davidson), Rodney Burke (Danny Rhodes), Patrick Allen (Luke Fulgham), Jerold Wells (Charlie Spence), Al Mulock (Frank Davidson), Colin Croft (Dell Malverne), Nicholas Stuart (Jed Thomas)

PLOT: In a valley at the foot of a peak in the Canadian Rockies, Craig Rhodes and Dell Malverne have met in unfriendly circumstances. Rhodes is determined to take his miners, Luke Fulgram, Danny Rhodes and Charlie Spencer, up the mountain to Malverne's gold mine, but Malverne fears that blasting might bring avalanches down on the village. Rhodes promises to use his dynamite cautiously. Through unexpected snowstorms, they fight their way to the mine site's cabin, but to their surprise they find their partner Frank Davidson and his wife Lenore waiting for them. Furious, Rhodes tries to get Lenore down the mountain, but the weather is too bad. As winter drags by, tensions grow. Lenore and Frank don't get along, and each man wishes Lenore were his wife. Rhodes finally banishes her to a small storehouse to sleep and live alone. A rich vein of gold is discovered, but Rhodes stubbornly allows only one blast of dynamite one night, intending to use every stick in one big blast. Rhodes catches them at it, a gunfight breaks out and Luke fall to his death. Frank has been frantically preparing the dynamite while Lenore pleads with him. They struggle and Lenore is hurried toward the main entrance. But Frank falls against a prop and brings the roof down on himself, an instant after Rhodes pulls Lenore out. The mine is now sealed beyond hope of being reopened. Rhodes has lost his gold but kept his promise to the town.

REVIEWS: "[A] modest programmer that fails to wring out the full potential of basic plot ideas and physical backgrounds." *Variety*, April 2, 1958

"A routine adult adventure melodrama that does not rise above the level of a supporting feature for lower-half billing. Moreover, the writing, direction, acting and photography leave much to be desired." *Harrison's Reports*, April 5, 1958

REVIEWS FOR JOHN DEREK: "John Derek is tough and masterful as the leader of the mining operation." *The Daily Cinema* (U.K.) May 7, 1958

"The acting ranges from grim (John Derek), to grotesque (Al Mulock, Patrick Allen) to ghastly (Elaine Stewart)." *Picturegoer* (U.K.) June 28, 1958

ADDITIONAL REVIEWS AND ARTICLES: *Boxoffice* 7 April 1958; *Daily Variety* 2 April 1958 p. 3; *Film Daily* 31 March 1958 p. 18; *Film Facts* vol. 1 1958 p. 45; *Harrison's Reports*, 29 March 1958 p. 51; *Il corriere della sera* (Italy) 11 June 1959 p. 6; *Kinematograph Weekly* (U.K.) 8 May 1958 p. 16; *L.A. Times* 22 September 1957; *Miami News* 29 July 1958; *Monthly Film Bulletin* (U.K.) June 1958 p. 76; *Motion Picture Daily* 14 March 1958; *Motion Picture Herald Product Digest* 29 March 1958 p. 772; *The Palm Beach Post* 10 November 1957; *Picturegoer* (U.K.) 3 May 1958 p. 9; *The Times* (U.K.) 22 November 1957; *The Times* (U.K.) 2 February 1957; *Variety* 7 August 1957; *Variety* 4 June 1958

Il Corsaro della Mezza Luna

Aka *La belle et le corsaire* (*The Pirate of the Half Moon*)
Glomer Film Produzione (Rome)
Ferraniacolor, CinepanScope, 95 minutes
Released in Italy on March 7, 1958

CREDITS: *Producer:* Enzo Merolle;

Director: Giuseppe Maria Scotese; *Story:* Alma Neille, Riccardo Pazzaglia, Giuseppe Maria Scotese; *Screenplay* and *Additional Dialogue:* Alma Neille, Kay Ously, Riccardo Pazzaglia, Mario Amendola, Giuseppe Maria Scotese; *Photography:* Adalberto Albertini; *Production Manager:* Ignazio Luceri; *Production Supervisors:* Sergio Merolle, Renato De Pasqualis; *Assistant Directors:* Hugo Velona, Daniele Luisi; *Camera Operator:* Carlo Fiore; *Music:* Renzo Rossellini; *Music Director:* Alberto Paoletti; *Script Supervisor:* Mario Caiano; *Editor:* Nino Borogli; *Production Designer:* Saverio D'Eugenio; *Set Decorator:* Franco Fontana; *Matte Artist:* Joseph Nathanson; *Makeup:* Giuseppe Annunziata; *Costumes:* Ugo Pericoli; *Choreography:* Wilbert Bradley; *Song:* "Magica Notte" (Magic Night), music by G.F. Lavagnino, lyrics by S. Simoni

CAST: John Derek (Nadir El Krim/Paolo di Valverde), Ingeborg Schöner (Angela), Gianna Maria Canale (Infanta Caterina), Alberto Farnese (Capt. Alonzo de Carmona-Ugo van Berg), Raf Mattioli (Vasco), Camillo Piliotto (Baron Alfonso di Camerlata), Gianni Rizzo (Visconte di Grand), Paul Muller (Carlo V), Yvette Masson (Rosa), Raf Baldassari (Pirate), Carol Corter (Dancer), Fausto Guerzoni (Master Anselmo), Ignazio Leone (Nicola), Amina Pirani Maggi (Nurse Gertrude), Carlo Hintermann (Il ticinese), Fanny Landini (Marchesa di Gredon), Alberto Varelli (Tatun), Piero Giagnoni (Antonio), Mimmo Poli (Fat Pirate), Silvio Lillo (Vazquez), Andrea Fantasia (Carlo V's helper)

PLOT: In 16th century Italy, nobleman Paolo di Valverde is driven to piracy by Capt. Alonzo de Carmona, a traitor whose real name is Ugo van Berg. Carmona has seized power in Carlo V's kingdom by controlling the elite palace guard of the Baron Alfonso di Camerlata. Disguised as a pirate, Valverde sneaks into the castle of the baron to kidnap the Infanta Caterina, who is visiting the nobleman. Meanwhile, Angela, the baron's niece, has been promised, against her will, as the bride to Carmona. Nadir erroneously kidnaps Angela in place of the Infanta. On his boat, Nadir discloses his true identity to the woman he thinks is the Infanta, revealing his desire of revenge on Carmona who has ruined his family. Angela and Nadir quickly fall for each other. Nadir's brother Vasco is killed shortly before the pirates succeed in taking the castle. Finally, the troops of Charles V are called to rescue the besieged. Nadir and Carmona fight on the beach by the castle and Nadir prevails.

REVIEWS: "An unpretentious adventure picture with some efficacious set reconstructions and appropriate period costumes." *Segnalazioni Cinematografiche* (Italy), vol. XLII, 1957

"This naïve and colorful story is characterized by a breakneck speed and very distinguished players" *Cinémonde* (France), January 8, 1959

REVIEW FOR JOHN DEREK: "John Derek doesn't lack allure." *Télérama* (France), March 22, 1995

ADDITIONAL REVIEWS AND ARTICLES: *Cinefoto (Italy)* September 1958; *Il corriere della sera* (Italy); 24 March 1959; *Films & Filming* (U.K.) October 1957 p. 28; *Die Filmwoche* (Germany) 16 September 1961 p. 7; *La Stampa* (Italy) 8 March 1958 p. 8.

NOTES: In the U.S., the picture did not have any theatrical distribution. It was first shown on U.S. television in March 1965.

Prisoner of the Volga

Aka *I Battellieri del Volga* and *The Boatmen*
Transmonde-Film (Rome), Rialto Films (Paris), Fidés Film (Paris)
Eastman Color, TotalScope, 102 minutes
Released in Italy on January 13, 1959
Released in New York on June 1, 1960

CREDITS: *Producer:* Arnaldo Genoino; *Directors:* Victor Tourjansky, Arnaldo Genoino; *Screenplay:* Damiano Damiani, Arnaldo Genoino, from an original screenplay by Salka Viertel, Al Lyx; *Adaptation:* Viktor Tourjansky, Annalena Limentani; *English-language dialogue:* Duncan Elliot, Barbara Sohmers; *Photography:* Mario Montuori; *Production Manager:* Gianpaolo Bigazzi; *Assistant Director:* Robert Martin; *Camera Operator:* Alfio Contini; *Editor:* Roberto Cinquini; *Assistant Editor:* Daniele Alabiso; *Art Director:* Vlastimir Gavrik; *Costumes:* Enzo Bulgarelli; *Music:* Norbert Glanzberg; *Sound:* Mario Amari

CAST: John Derek (Alexei Orlof), Elsa Martinelli (Mascha), Dawn Addams (Princess Irina), Rik Battaglia (Lisenko), Charles Vanel (Gen. Gorew), Gert Fröbe (Professor), Nerio Bernardi (Elagin), Ingmar Zeisberg (Olga), Jacques Castelot (Jakowlew), Nitza Constantin (Grisha), Feodor Chaliapin, Jr. (Fomitsch),

Nino Marchetti (Michailow), Arturo Bragaglia (Principe), Wolfgang Preiss (Ossip)

PLOT: In 19th-century Czarist Russia, a young cavalry officer, Alexei, marries Princess Irina, the beautiful ward of General Gorew, the governor of the province. After the ceremony, Alexei learns the general consented to the wedding only because Irina was bearing his child and he wished to avoid scandal. Infuriated, Alexei publicly attacks the general and, as a consequence, is stripped of his rank and sent to a far-off disciplinary camp. The remorseful Irina arranges his escape but she is shot and killed before she and Alexei can reach safety. After arranging for her burial, Alexei befriends some Volga boatmen as well as a peasant girl named Mascha who hides him in her room. As Alexei continues to evade pursuing Cossacks, Gorew is exposed by his superiors and deprived of his rank. He sets out to find and kill Alexei. But in a final battle, he and his men are killed by Alexei and the Volga boatmen. After being reunited with his regiment and restored to his former rank, Alexis asks Mascha to be his wife.

REVIEWS: "Colorful production of a bulky, contrived period adventure yarn.... Unsuitable for healthy U.S. booking." *Variety*, May 18, 1960

"A stolid, frankly old-fashioned swashbuckler in color with heavy, ornate sets depicting nineteenth century Russia." *The New York Times*, June 2, 1960

"Implausible adventure tale.... Dubbing ... is a major flaw, dulling whatever grace notes this romantic rigmarole might have had." *New York Herald Tribune*, June 2, 1960

REVIEWS FOR JOHN DEREK: "Derek is satisfactory as the oppressed officer..." *The Hollywood Reporter*, May 2, 1960

"Derek's Alexis Orloff [sic] is patently charming and precise, attractively bashful and when he does swagger the act is softly sold." *Motion Picture Herald*, May 7, 1960

"John Derek is an agreeable Alexis." *The Daily Cinema*, October 16, 1960

ADDITIONAL REVIEWS AND ARTICLES: Die Filmwoche (Germany) 7 November 1959 p. 8; *The Film Daily* 2 May 1960 p. 8; *Filmblätter* (Netherland) 9 May 1959 p. 435; *FilmFacts* v. III 1960 p. 113; *Harrison's Reports* 7 November 1959 p. 180; *Harrison's Reports* 7 May 1960 p. 75; *Il corriere della sera* (Italy) 12 June 1959; *Intermezzo* (Italy) 31 March 1959 p. 6; *Kine Weekly* 20 October 1960 p. 23; *La Cinématographie Française (France)* 19 September 1959 p. 2: *La Stampa* (Italy) 17 January 1959 p. 8; *Le Film Français* (France) 4 September 1959 p. 14; *Monthly Film Bulletin* (U.K.) December 1960 p. 168; *Screen World* 1961 p. 194

Exodus

United Artists, Otto Preminger Productions
Technicolor, Panavision 70, 212 minutes
Premiered in New York City on December 15, 1960

CREDITS: *Producer-Director:* Otto Preminger; *Screenplay*: Dalton Trumbo; Based on the novel by Leon Uris; *Art Director:* Richard Day; *Associate Art Director:* Bill Hutchinson; *Set Dresser:* Dario Simoni; *Music:* Ernest Gold; *Photography:* Sam Leavitt; *Editor:* Louis R. Loeffler; *Camera Operator*: Ernest Day; *Electrical Supervisor:* James Almond; *Construction Manager:* Peter Dukelow; *Key Grip:* Morris Rosen; *Special Effects*: Cliff Richardson; *Music Editor:* Leon Birnbaum; *Sound:* Paddy Cunningham, John Cox, Red Law; *Sound Effects Editor*: Win Ryder; *Costume Coordinator*: Hope Bryce; *Miss Saint's Clothes Designer:* Rudi Gernreich; *Wardrobe:* Joe King, May Walding, Margo Slater; *Makeup:* George Lane; *Hairdresser:* A.G. Scott; *Property Master*: Robert Goodstein; *Script Supervisor:* Angela Martelli; *General Manager*: Martin C. Schute; *Production Manager:* Eva Monley; *Assistant Production Managers:* Mati Raz, Ivan Lengyel, Lionel Lober; *Assistant to Producer*: Max Slater; *Speech Consultant:* Simon R. Mitchneck; *Technical Advisors*: Ilan Hartuv, Anan Safadi; *Production Secretary*: Noreen Hipwell; *First Assistant Director:* Gerry O'Hara; *Assistant Directors*: Otto Plaschkes, Yoel Silberg, Larry Frisch, Christopher Trumbo; *Assistant Art Director*: Arnon Adar; *Production Secretary*: Noreen Hipwell; *Titles:* Saul Bass

CAST: Paul Newman (Ari Ben Canaan), Eva Marie Saint (Katherine "Kitty" Fremont), Ralph Richardson (Brigadier Gen Sutherland), Peter Lawford (Major Fred Caldwell), Lee J. Cobb (Barak Ben Canaan), Sal Mineo (Dov Landau), John Derek (Taha), Hugh Griffith (Mandria), Gregory Ratoff (Lakavitch), Felix Aylmer (Dr. Lieberman), David Opatoshu (Akiva Ben Caan), Jill Haworth (Karen Clement Hansen), Marius Goring (Von Storch), Alexandra Stewart (Jordana), Michael Wager (David Ben Ami), Martin Benson (Mordekai),

Paul Stevens (Reuben), Betty Walker (Sarah), Martin Miller (Dr. Samuel Odenheim), Victor Maddern (Sergeant), George Maharis (Yaov), John Crawford (Capt. Hank Schlosberg), Samuel Segal (Proprietor), Dahn Ben Amotz (Uzi), Ralph Truman (Colonel), Peter Madden (Dr. Johann Clement), Joseph Furst (Avidan), Paul Stassino (Driver-Guide), Michael Wynne (Man), Marc Burns (Lt. O'Hara), Esther Reichstadt (Mrs. Hirshberg), Zeporah Peled (Mrs. Frankel), Philo Hauser (Novak), Yossi Graber (Jake), Anna Maria Millo (Woman Onlooker), Amos Mokadi (Expert for explosions), Hannah Norbert (Yetta), Paul L. Smith (Peretz Geffner—Jewish prisoner), John Van Eyssen (Detective)

PLOT: It's 1947, and Kitty Fremont, an American nurse, arrives in Cyprus to see the British commander, General Sutherland. She wants to know details about the death of her husband, a newspaper photographer who saw action with the general in Palestine and was killed there. Cyprus has been turned into a vast prison camp. The docks are packed with Jewish refugees from ships headed for Palestine, but intercepted by the British navy and brought into Famagusta harbor. Some 30,000 Jews are interned on the island. At their meeting, Sutherland suggests that she help out the refugee camp where facilities and medical personnel are desperately limited. Elsewhere on Cyprus, Ari Ben Canaan, a top agent of Hagannah, the Jewish underground organization in Palestine, has landed under cover of night on a daring mission: to defy the British blockade of the Palestine coast and to take and to take all the refugees into Israel. In this operation he is sided by Cypriots patriot, Mandria. In the detention camp, Kitty meets some of the people with whom she is to become deeply involved in the months to come. They include young Karen; David Ben Ami; and old Dr. Odenheim. Ari obtains a leaky old Greek ship, the Olympia, and fits her for the trip to Palestine. Disguised as a British officer, he commandeers arms, trucks and supplies from a British depot and, with the help of forged papers, he convoys the Star of David group on board the vessel which he now calls "The *Exodus*." The ship's path is promptly blocked by British destroyers. The Jews vow to blow themselves up if boarded by British troops, and starve to death rather than return to their barbed-wire confinement. Among the leaders of the hunger strike is Lakavitch. Kitty, fearing for Karen's health and safety, boards the *Exodus* and pleads with Ari for the child's release. But Karen refuses to leave, and the hunger strike continues for more than 100 hours before world opinion and Sutherland's intervention in London force British authorities to permit the *Exodus* to sail. Kitty stays on board to help look after the children. The sharp difference between factions working and fighting within Israel are brought into focus almost immediately after the refugees land at Haifa. The *Exodus* youngsters are taken from the port to Gan Dafna, a youth village in Galilee, where they were welcomed by Bark, a Palestinian pioneer and father of Ari. He also introduces Taha, the Mukhtar of a nearby Arab village and a life-long friend of Ari. Barak, chairman of the executive committee of the Jewish Palestine Agency, represents the Hagannah position, which calls for the use of force only to defend the interests of the country or to maintain advantage already gained. By contrast, the Irgun is convinced that only through terrorism can the British be induced to leave Palestine. Dov escapes from the Haifa docks, but is arrested by British police. After his release, Dov joins the group and soon becomes one of the most daring and effective members. In Jerusalem, Kitty again meets Ari and, despite their strong and obvious differences, they are attracted to each other. Ari seeks out Akiva, his uncle, to try and dissuade him from carrying further terrorist acts on the eve of the U.N. vote. Hagannah feel that these acts hurt the Israeli causes, but Akiva turns him down. On the way to Ari's home, Kitty and Ari confess their love for each othet. Kitty goes to Gan Dafna where she is reunited with Karen, whom she wants to adopt and bring to America. The Irgun blows up a wing of the King David Hotel. Akiva and other Irgun leaders are caught by the British and condemned to die, but Dov escapes. Ari joins forces with the Irgun to free the men from prison. Dov gives himself up in order to help engineer the break. Akiva is fatally wounded in the escape and Ari is badly hurt. Kitty helps smuggle Ari past British guards to Taha's home, where she nurses him back to health. The U.N. votes for partition on November 29, 1947, and Arabs attacks on Israeli settlements immediately mount. Syrian commandos led by a German officer demand that Taha join an operation to wipe out Gan Dafna. Taha warns Ari and Kitty of the impending attack and Gan Dafna is evacuated at night. The German, suspecting Taha, calls off the Gan Dafna raid. But when Israeli forces enter Taha's village, they find it empty and many of his inhabitants brutally murdered. Taha is found hanged, a huge swastika smeared in red on the side of his house. Karen, whose affection for Dov has grown into real love, is senselessly killed by a refugee Arab. With Taha, she is laid to rest in a moving ceremony, even as the trucks go roaring into the night, heading for another fight.

REVIEWS: "An unemotional blaze that remains unkindled.... *Exodus* lacks emotional impact." *The Hollywood Reporter*, December 14, 1960

"The very bigness of Preminger's theme makes his film an important one and well worth seeing—its defects by no means offset the excellences." *New York Herald Tribune*, December 16, 1960

"Otto Preminger's extremeely long film ... has enough action, romance, suspense and humor to please most patrons." *Harrison's Reports*, December 17, 1960

REVIEW FOR JOHN DEREK: "John Derek's mukhtar lacks credibility." *Los Angeles Times*, December 22, 1960

ADDITIONAL REVIEWS AND ARTICLES: *America* 7 January 1961 p. 451; *American Cinematographer* February 1961 pp. 90–91, 110-11, 113–15; *American Cinematographer* April 1961 p. 231; *Boxoffice* 19 December 1960 p. 9; *Boxoffice* 26 December 1960; *Cahiers du Cinéma* (France) July 1961 p. 45; *Cinéaste* (France) n.2 1996 pp. 24–29; *Cinéma* (France) January 1961 p. 52; *Cinéma* (France) July 1961 p. 108; *Cinémonde* (France) 2 May 1961; *Commonweal* 16 December 1960 p. 316; *Cosmopolitan* November 1960; *Cue* 19 November 1960 p. 13; *Daily Variety* 26 May 1958; *Daily Variety* 3 April 1962; *Film Daily* 10 May 1960 p. 6; *Film Daily* 15 December 1960 p. 5; *Film Quarterly* Spring 1961 pp. 56–59; *Filmfacts* 30 December 1960 pp. 301–304; *Films and Filming* (U.K.) June 1961 pp. 22–23; *Films and Filming* (U.K.) September 1960 pp. 28–30; *Films in Review* December 1960 pp. 611–613; *Hollywood Reporter* 21 September 1959 p. 1; *Hollywood Reporter* 9 December 1959 p. 4; *Hollywood Reporter* 14 December 1959 p. 2; *Hollywood Reporter* 18 December 1959 p. 2; *Hollywood Reporter* 20 January 1960 p. 1; *Hollywood Reporter* 21 January 1960 p. 1; *Hollywood Reporter* 4 February 1960 p. 1; *Hollywood Reporter* 8 February 1960 p. 3; *Hollywood Reporter* 10 February 1960 p. 2; *Hollywood Reporter* 12 February 1960 p. 3; *Hollywood Reporter* 15 February 1960 p. 2; *Hollywood Reporter* 23 February 1960 p. 2; *Hollywood Reporter* 25 February 1960 p. 2; *Hollywood Reporter* 25 March 1960 p. 12; *Hollywood Reporter* 29 March 1960 p. 1; *Hollywood Reporter* 9 August 1960 p. 1; *Hollywood Reporter* 6 November 1995; *Kinematograph Weekly* (U.K.) 11 May 1961 p. 131; *L.A. Mirror* 28 January 1961; *L.A. Mirror-News* 20 May 1960 p. 6; *L.A. Times* (Sunday Magazine) 11 December 1960 p. 3; *L.A. Times* 8 May 1960; *Life* 12 December 1960 pp. 70–77; *McCalls's* February 1961 p. 168; *Monthly Film Bulletin* (U.K.) June 1961 p. 74; *Motion Picture Daily* 15 December 1960 pp. 1, 3; *Motion Picture Herald* 17 December 1960 p. 10; *Motion Picture Herald* 31 December 1960 p. 973; *Movie* September 1962 pp. 24–25; *National Review* 17 December 1960 p. 30; *New Republic* 19 December 1960 pp. 21–22; *N.Y. Post* 6 December 1960 p. 72; *N.Y. Times* 1 January 1961 sec.2 p. 1; *N.Y. Times* 15 May 1960; *N.Y. Times* 17 April 1960; *N.Y. Times* 18 January 1970; *N.Y. Times* 20 January 1960; *N.Y. Times* 24 August 1960; *N.Y. World Telegram and Sun* 16 December 1961 p. 24; *New Yorker* 17 December 1960 pp. 136–137; *Newsweek* 19 December 1960 pp. 87–88; *Positif* (France) November 1993 pp. 74–77; *Radio Times* 15 November 1986 p. 26; *Saturday Review* 17 December 1960 p. 30; *Seventeen* February 1961 p. 20; *Sight and Sound* Summer 1961 pp. 146–147; *Time* 19 December 1960 p. 69; *Variety* 18 May 1960 pp. 3, 22; *Variety* 28 October 1959; *Variety* 8 July 1959; *Variety* 20 July 1960; *Variety* 22 February 1961; *Variety* 5 July 1961; *Variety* 4 October 1961; *Variety* 3 April 1962

AWARDS AND HONORS: Golden Globes: *Won:* Best Supporting Actor: Sal Mineo. *Nominated:* Best Original Score: Ernest Gold; Most Promising Newcomer—Female: Jill Haworth

Academy Awards: *Won:* Best Music, Scoring of a Dramatic or Comedy Picture: Ernest Gold. *Nominated:* Best Actor in a Supporting Role: Sal Mineo; Best Cinematography, Color: Sam Leavitt.

Grammy Awards *Won:* Best Soundtrack Album or Recording of Music Score from Motion Picture or Television: Ernest Gold.

Laurel Awards: *Won:* Golden Laurel: Top Male Supporting Performance: Sal Mineo. *Nominated:* Top Male Dramatic Performance: Paul Newman; Top Male Supporting Performance: Lee J. Cobb

Nightmare in the Sun

Afilmco Inc., A Ricky DuPont Presentation
DeLuxe Color, 80 minutes
Released in October 1964

CREDITS: *Producer-Director:* Marc Lawrence; *Associate Producer:* Douglas Stewart; *Screenplay:* Ted Thomas, Fanya Lawrence; *Story:* Marc Lawrence, George Fass; *Production Manager:* Jerry A. Baerwitz; *Assistant Director:* Frank Parmenter; *Script Supervisor:* John Dutton; *Photography:* Stanley Cortez; *Key Grip:* Fred Russell; *Editors:* Douglas Stewart, William Shenberg; *Art Director:* Paul Sylos; *Set Decorator:* Ray Boltz; *Property Master:* George MacKinnon; *Wardrobe Supervisor:* Pat Cummings; *Makeup:* Harry Thomas; *Hairdresser:* Carmen Dirigo; *Music Composer and Conductor:* Paul Glass; *Music Editor:* Lee Osborne; *Sound Effects:* William Shenberg; *Sound Mixer:* Max Hutchinson

CAST: John Derek (The Hitch-hiker), Aldo Ray (The Sheriff), Arthur O'Connell (Sam Wilson), Ursula Andress (Marsha), Sammy Davis, Jr. (Truck driver); Allyn Joslyn (Scout-master), Keenan Wynn (Junk dealer); John Marley (Hogan, gas station owner), George Tobias (Gideon), Lurene Tuttle (Gideon's wife), Robert Duvall (Motorcyclist), Richard Jaeckel (Motorcyclist), Chick Chandler (Bartender), Bill Challee (Old coot in bar), Michael Petit (Philip), John Sebastian (Sheriff's deputy), Darby Hinton (Kid)

PLOT: Sam Wilson is the older husband of Marsha, a Swiss-born sex kitten. In a late morning call at their ranch house, an unscrupulous and amoral sheriff is tossing Marsha out of her bed. The sheriff is there while Wilson is drowning his sorrows in town. Marsha endeavors to ward off the sheriff's crude advances. Returning to the ranch, Wilson, with growing suspicion, confronts his wife. She decides to leave, and the highway, picks up a hitch-hiker thumbing his way back home to patch up his broken marriage. Marsha offers to drive him to the city, first returning to the ranch on the pretext of packing an overnight bag. They are alone in the house. She teases him. At first, he is amused but soon falls for her. She lures him into the pool; Marsha begs the man to take her away from her unhappy life with Wilson. But the hitch-hiker resists further temptation, intent on returning home. He repulses the amorous girl and leaves. As he walks down the road, he is spied by a drunk and sulking Wilson, whose suspicions grow. As he comes into the house, he accuses his wife and in a blind rage shoots her. Her body is discovered by the ranch hands, who summon the sheriff. He wrings a confession from Wilson. He sees a scheming maneuver to cover up for Wilson and shouts: "Remember you didn't kill her!" Aware of the hitch-hiker's rendezvous at the ranch and Marsha's two-timing ways, the sheriff seeks a scapegoat in the man, who is soon apprehended. The hitch-hiker is subdued and is handcuffed, but in the struggle escapes from the sheriff. A manhunt ensues, and finally he is overtaken. Back at the ranch, Wilson, drunk and torn by conscience, battles with the sheriff. In the fight, the latter is killed. Wilson confesses to both slayings. The hitch-hiker is cleared of the charge and continues on his way.

REVIEW: "It is not so much the story as the way it is put over that makes this picture into an above average example of its kind." *Kine Weekly* (U.K.), December 31, 1964

REVIEWS FOR JOHN DEREK: "John Derek imparts a fine amount of audience sympathy." *Boxoffice*, December 7, 1964

"John Derek is as handsome as ever and sweats convincingly as the hero." *The Daily Cinema* (U.K.), December 30, 1964

"Derek's aging boyishness serves the film well with his non-heroic connotation." *Films and Filming* (U.K), March 1965

ADDITIONAL REVIEWS AND ARTICLES: *Boxoffice* 16 September 1963 p. 11; *Boxoffice* 21 October 1963 p. 17; *Cahiers du Cinéma* (France) May 1967 p. 73; *Il corriere della sera* (Italy) 28 August 1964; *Screen World* 1966 p. 113; *Variety* 10 February 1965.

NOTE: John Derek co-directed the film without credit.

Once Before I Die

Aka *No Toys for Christmas*
F.8 Productions, Seven Arts Pictures, Vitri Film International, A Goldstone Film Enterprises Release
Eastmancolor, 97 minutes
Released on December 2, 1966

CREDITS: *Producer-Director:* John Derek; *Screenplay:* Vance Skarstedt, based on the novel *Quit for the Next* by Anthony March; *Photography:* Arthur E. Arling; *Associate Producers:* Allen Pinson, Vance Skarstedt; *Executive Producer:* Wray Davis; *Art Directors:* Francisco Balanquit,

Sergio Manaluang; *Unit Production Manager:* Vincente Nayve; *Sound:* Joseph Keener, Blandino Acuin; *Assistant Cameraman:* Romigio Young; *Camera Operator:* Primitivo Magpayo; *Supervising Editor:* Maurice Wright; *Editor:* John Davisson; *Sound Effects Editor:* Del Harris; *Wardrobe:* Carson Shade; *Makeup:* Baby Buencamino, Juliet Buencamino; *Assistant Director:* Fred Galang; *Music Composer-Conductor:* Emanuel Vardi; *Song:* "Once Before I Die," words and music by Norman Gimble and Ralph London, sung by Lenny Welch

CAST: Ursula Andress (Alex), John Derek (Major Bailey), Richard Jaeckel (Lt. Custer), Rod Lauren (Young Captain), Ron Ely (Soldier), Jock Mahoney (Major), Allen Pinson, Greg Martin, Renato Robles, Fred Galang, Nello Nayo, Mario Taquibulos, Rod Francisco, Eva Vivar, Lola Boy, Armando Lucero, Vance Skarstedt, Fred Galang, Andress Centera, Mario Taquibulos, Poch Apostol, Lucien Pan, Bessie Barredo, Max Roio, Renato Langit, Jimmy Cruz, Fred Castro, Estanislao Fernandez, Raymundo Galvez

PLOT: Shortly after the Japanese attack on Pearl Harbor, a U.S. cavalry troop, stationed in the Philippines and commanded by Major Bailey, is attacked. Bailey's first concern is for his fiancée Alex, and he hurriedly persuades her to drive to Manila where he hopes she will find safe conduct to the U.S. with her father. After discussing plans with his captain and the war-loving Lt. Custer, the major begins to march his company through the jungles to Manila. Once on the narrow roads, he spots Alex in her car, stalled and surrounded by evacuating natives. Afraid that she will never make it on her own, Bailey lets her join him. Later, the isolated troop is attacked by an enemy plane which they shoot down. The captured pilot is executed and Lt. Custer is thrilled with his first taste of killing. Major Bailey and Alex ride into a deserted village to search for food and they locate supplies in a barn. The major is forced to shoot the farmer and is himself accidentally killed by a hand grenade. The captain, aware that the Japanese are not far behind, orders the men to march on. Alex, torn by grief at her lover's death, has no choice but to continue the journey with them. Lt. Custer, machine gun in hand, demands to be left behind to face the enemy alone. That night, at a small outpost, he rejoins the company, reporting he has gunned down over a dozen enemy soldiers. While the rest of the men are preparing to trap a Japanese tank, a young soldier goes to Alex. He tells her he has never made love to a woman and does not want to die without becoming a man. Alex, deeply moved, later goes to him and offers herself. After destroying the tank, the soldiers move on until Custer's bloodthirstiness leads the men into an encounter with a Japanese-held village. Ultimately there are no survivors on either side. Alex wanders down to a beach to await her inevitable fate.

REVIEWS: "This is a pointless, dull and stupid story, beautifully photographed." *Kinematograph Weekly* (U.K.), September 16, 1967

"*Once Before I Die* is an out-of-the-ordinary 'small' film that has some of the qualities and, unfortunately, all the shortcomings of Marc Lawrence's *Nightmare in the Sun,* an offbeat picture which starred the same husband-and-wife team." *Films and Filming* (U.K.), March 1968

REVIEWS FOR JOHN DEREK: "Derek, quite aside from the excessiveness of his cinematic effects and over-indulgence in artsy-crafty pyrotechnics, is a young filmmaker worthy of major assignment." *Boxoffice,* March 13, 1967

"An expert still photographer, Derek ... has a marvelous eye for the vivid effect, but not much idea of how to use it in the context of a gripping movie." *The Daily Cinema* (U.K.), September 8, 1967

"John Derek's overheated direction is more than the material can stand." *Monthly Film Bulletin* (U.K.), November 1967

ADDITIONAL REVIEWS AND ARTICLES: *The Daily Cinema* 19 January 1968 p. 8; *Detroit Free Press* 16 September 1966 p. 8 C; *Evening News* (U.K.) 18 January 1968; *Film Daily* 18 June 1964; *Films in Review* December 1973 pp. 636–637; *FilmFacts* vol. IX 1966 p. 385; *The Guardian* (U.K.) 19 January 1968; *La Stampa* (Italy) 21 June 1968 p. 20; *Newsweek* July 20 1964 pp. 79–80; *Screen World* 1968 p. 107; *Sunday Express* (U.K.) 21 January 1968; *Sunday Telegraph* (U.K.) 21 January 1968; *The Times* (U.K.) 18 January 1968; *Variety* 19 May 1964 p. 19; *Variety* 10 June 1964 p. 5

NOTES: *Once Before I Die* was released internationally as *No Toys for Christmas* and *The 26th Cavalry.*

Film Shorts

The Nest
(USA) 16mm, B&W, 20 minutes, silent (with records as a soundtrack)
1943
  CREDITS: *Screenplay-Producer-Director*: Kenneth Anger.
  CAST: Dare Harris [John Derek] (Boy friend), Bob Jones (Brother), Jo Whittaker (Sister)
  PLOT: A brother and a sister relate to mirrors and each other until a third party breaks the balance, seducing both into violence. Ablutions and the act of dressing and making upare observed as a magic rite. The binding spell of the sister-sorceress is broken by the brother, who walks out.
  NOTES: *The Nest* was never released. It is considered Derek's screen debut.

As Director

Once Before I Die (1966)
See the entry in the Actor filmography.

A Boy ... a Girl
Aka *The Sun's Up* (1970 re-release title)
A Cinema J. Production, Jack Hanson Productions
Color, 69 minutes
Premiered in Los Angeles on April 25, 1969
  CREDITS: *Producer*: Jack Hanson; *Screenplay-Director-Photography-Costumer*: John Derek; *Editors*: John H. Post, Bob Raff, Sonic Editorial Services; *Composer*: Joe Greene; *Musical Performers*: The Jamme; *Lyrics*: John Derek
  CAST: Dino Martin, Jr. (The Boy), Airion Fromer (The Girl), Karen Steele (Elizabeth), Kerwin Mathews (Mr. Christian), Peggy Lipton, Trace Vernell, Gene Walker, Michael-Maxim Nader
  PLOT: Two 15-year-olds fall in love, have an affair and part when the girl falls for a neighbor more than twice her age, who owns a stable of horses.
  REVIEW: "There are understandable moments of incoherence ... but at a benevolently brief 69-minute running time, the film can hope for limited success in a few first-run arties." *The Hollywood Reporter*, April 28, 1969
  ADDITIONAL REVIEWS AND ARTICLES: *Associated Press Newspapers* 26 April 1969; *Billboard* 17 May 1969 p. 80; *L.A. Times Sunday Magazine* 26 November 1967 p. 46; *L.A. Times* 10 April 1969; *L.A. Times* 11 April 1969; *L.A. Times* 14 April 1969 sec. IV p. 12; *L.A. Times* 25 April 1969; *L.A. Times* 4 May 1969; *Screen World* 1970 p. 118
  NOTES: *A Boy ... a Girl* was shot in 16mm and later blown up to 35mm. Apparently the picture had three different cuts, 69, 76 and 85 minutes.

Childish Things
Aka *Confessions of Tom Harris* and *Tale of the Cock*
A Braintree Productions Release, Film-World Productions, Gateway Films
Technicolor, 93 minutes
Premiered in Beverly Hills, California, on July 2, 1969
Re-released as *Confessions of Tom Harris* on November 8, 1972
  CREDITS: *Associate Producers*: Tom Harris, Maurice Wright; *Producers*: Don Murray, Jeffrey M. Sneller; *Directors*: John Derek, David Nelson: *Screenplay*: Don Murray, suggested by the life of Tom Harris; *Photography–Camera Operator*: John Derek; *Editors*: Maurice Wright, Martin Dreffke; *Composer:* Joe Greene; *Music Producer*: Don Perry; *Sound Mixer*: Rod Sutton; *Hair Stylist*: Judih Scott; *Makeup*: Mark Snegoff; *Production Manager*: Jonathan Haze; *Construction Manager*: Fernando Valento
  CAST: Don Murray (Tom Harris), Linda Evans (Pat Jennings), David Brian (Jennings), Angelique Pettyjohn (Angelique), Don Joslyn (Kelly), Gypsy Boots (Gypsy), Rod Lauren (Rod), Leroy Jenkins (Preacher), Logan Ramsey (Mr. Simmons), Erik Holland (First Fighter), Jack Griffin (Jack), William Kerwin (Mr. Sullivan), Brooke Valerie (Girl), Gene LeBell (Peanut Man), Ed Bennett (Carousel Man), Seamon Glass (Ex-Fighter), George Atkinson (Last Fighter), Peter Tenen (Gene), Claire Kelly (Sharon), Gary Clarke (Dr. Brown)
  PLOT: Amateur boxer Tom Harris is violent in and out of the ring. After being dishonorably discharged by the Navy, he steals a Corvette, which breaks down. He gets picked up by a fight promoter who gives him a job as a

fighter in Las Vegas. Tom also works as a collector for a racketeer, spending his free time getting drunk and getting in fights. One day on a California beach, he rapes Pat Jennings, a pretty young blonde, under a pier. A few months later, Tom runs into Pat, who doesn't recognize her abuser. He's drawn to her purity and naïve character. He begins stalking her, and ends up at a farm-commune for recovering alcoholics run by her father. The old man sees great potential in Tom, who suddenly experiences a cathartic religious conversion. His spiritual awakening convinces him to help other alcoholics.

REVIEWS: "[*Childish Things*] has its interesting moments but lacks the full ingredients for a dramatically sustained picture." *Variety*, July 2, 1969

"The religious theme ... is worked in naturally." *Boxoffice*, January 8, 1973

"Obviously aimed at the Bible audiences.... The movie has more recognizable faces behind the camera than in front with John Derek and David (Ozzie and Harriet) Nelson having co-directed." *The Independent Film Journal*, January 8, 1973

ADDITIONAL REVIEWS AND ARTICLES: *Cinema* July 1966 pp. 18–19; *L.A. Times* 2 July 1969; *The Tennessean* 25 January 1970 p. 110; *The Town Talk* 7 November 1972, *Screen World* 1970 p. 123; *South African Film and Entertainment Industry* November 1982 p. 30

NOTES: The movie was shot and copyrighted in 1966. *Cock a Doodle Doo* and *Night on the Street* were working titles. It was shelved for three years and finally promoted as *Childish Things* in hopes of attracting a distributor. In Australia, the film was released in November 1970 as *The Tale of the Cock*. In 1972, it received nationwide North American re-release with several cuts, under the title *Confessions of Tom Harris*. The real Tom Harris, whose life events inspired the film, worked as technical advisor and was credited as an associate producer.

Love You!

A Take Seven Productions Release, Essex Films
Technicolor; 85 minutes
Premiered at the SeaVue Theatre in Blaine, Washington, in April 1979

CREDITS: *Producer*: Bo Derek; *Director-Screenplay-Photography-Editor*: John Derek; *Music*: Nieman-Tiller

CAST: Annette Haven (Charlie), Wade Nichols (Steve), Lesllie Boveé (Lynn), Rob Everett (Mark), Blair Harris (Third Fantasy Guy), Paul Thomas (First Fantasy Guy)

PLOT: Steve and Mark agree on wife-swapping. Their spouses are not too excited about the idea, but Lynn, Mark's spouse, is willing to go along with it to please her husband. Charlie, Steve's wife, would rather not, but she is outnumbered. On a secluded Hawaiian island, they bare themselves not only in the literal sense, but also opening up to each other and discussing their most intimate feelings.

ADDITIONAL REVIEWS AND ARTICLES: *Gin Film* (Italy) December 1988; *Parade* 16 December 1979 p. 14; *Chicago Tribune* 26 February 1980; *New York Daily News* 26 February 1980; *Reelingback.com* Blog 1 December 2015

NOTES: Rated X, *I Love You!* is essentially a porn film.

Actor Eric Edwards was billed as Rob Everett.

"Directed by John Derek," along with the four main actors' names, are the only credits presented in the film. On the original 1979 Italian film poster and on the official DVD cover, different credits appear. However, none of the following names could be confirmed as authentic: *Screenplay*: Gail Sterling, John Derek; *Story*: Robert B. Corr; *Photography*: Arthur King; *Music*: Bob Vosse; *Editor*: Thomas Brown.

Fantasies

Aka *And Once Upon a Time*; *Once Upon a Love*; *Bo Derek's Fantasies*
Kevin Casselman Productions; P.G. Professional Group Services, A Klempner-Arnow Productions Presentation, A Joseph Brenner Associates Release
Color, 86 minutes
Premiered in New York City on November 6, 1981

CREDITS: *Producer*: Kevin Casselman; *Director-Screenplay-Photography*: John Derek; *Associate Producers*: Murray Jordan, Dick Stewart, Burt Weinstein; *Editors*: Bret Weston, Marsha Murphy; *Executive Producers*: R. Edmund McMullan; *Cameramen*: George Antonakis, Nicos Paizanos; *Key Grip*: George Alexopoulos; *Gaffer*: Nicos Lagos; *Best Boy*: Socrates Sadas; *Art Director*: Peter Kapouralis; *Wardrobe*: Diane Ionas; *Makeup*: Mary Collins; *Location Manager*: Yuri Kowalenko; *Script Supervisor*:

Carol Davidson; *Production Secretary:* Teresa Lydi; *Music:* Jeffrey Silverman; *Music Editor:* Michael R. Sloan; *Songs:* "We Have Loved Forever" and "Once Upon a Love Song," music by Jeffrey Silverman, lyrics by Walter Willison, sung by Walter Willison

CAST: Cathy Collins [Bo Derek] (Anastasia), Peter Hooten (Damir), Anna Alexiadis (Cleopatra, the mayor), Phasdon Gheorghitsis (Photographer), Nicos Paschalidis (Priest), Constantine Beladames (Godfather), Therese Bohlin (Model), Boucci Simma (Beautifuloni), Vienneula Koussefhane (Sales lady)

PLOT: Damir and his younger sister Anastasia return to their birthplace, a tiny Greek island, to establish a business to develop tourism. The boy starts flirting with Beautifuloni, the wealthy daughter of a cruise ship owner. She agrees to have her father's tourist-filled ships stop at Damir's island, after he promises to get the local population to refurbish their places to make the island more attractive. In the meantime, brother and sister seem to experience mutual strong sexual feelings. Eventually they learn, through the help of Cleopatra the local mayor, they aren't really related, so they can freely fall in love for each other.

REVIEWS: "The movie is very solemn. It is also very badly done. It celebrates its star's adolescence... [I]t's not pornography, and it barely earns even its R rating." The *New York Times*, November 7, 1981

"Other than some fleeting nudity there's not much to exploit here ... a curio somewhere between a home made movie and professional filmmaking." *Variety*, November 11, 1981

REVIEWS FOR JOHN DEREK: "As a director, John Derek also seems to lack the slightest intuition as how two shots should connect with each other or how a dramatic script should proceed." *The Hollywood Reporter*, November 17, 1981

"With this clinker, John Derek proves he was just as vapid a director years ago as he is today." *Soho Weekly News*, December 8, 1981

ADDITIONAL REVIEWS AND ARTICLES: *Boxoffice* 21 October 1974 p. 8; *Daily Variety* 5 November 1980; *Fort Lauderdale News* 9 September 1981; *Hollywood Reporter* 12 January 1981; *Hollywood Reporter* 8 February 1981; *Hollywood Reporter* 3 October 1986; *Honolulu Star Bulletin* 4 August 191 pp. C1, C4; *Los Angeles Times* 20 January 1982 p. 6; *Los Angeles Times* 31 August 1986 p. 13; *Parade* 16 December 1979 p. 14; *People Magazine* February 11, 1980; *The Philadelphia Inquirer* August 25, 1981; *Prevue* November-December 1981 pp. 22–29, 47; *Screen International* 31 October 1981; *Variety* 28 November 1973; *Variety* 7 January 1981 p. 4, 19; *Variety* 4 November 1981

NOTES: *Fantasies* was filmed in 1973 and released eight years later, after the box office success of 1981's *Tarzan, the Ape Man*.

Tarzan, the Ape Man

MGM, Svengali Productions
Metrocolor, 111 minutes
Premiered in New York City on July 24, 1981

CREDITS: *Producer:* Bo Derek; *Director-Photography:* John Derek; *Screenplay:* Tom Rowe, Gary Goddard; Based on the novel by Edgar Rice Burroughs; *Production Executive:* Eva Chun; *Unit Production Managers:* Jack Oliver, Tom Shaw; *Production Coordinator (Sri Lanka):* Chandran Rutnam; *Production Assistant:* Kerry Collins; *Production Assistants (Sri Lanka):* Rohan Jayantilika, Jayantha Jayantilika; *Assistant Directors:* Jack Oliver, Michael Lally; *Assistant Director (Sri Lanka):* Warner Warnasiri; *Camera Operator (Sri Lanka):* Somapala Dharmapriya; *Camera Sssociate:* Wolfgang Dickmann, *Editor:* James B. Ling; *Art Director:* Alan Roderick-Jones; *Assistant Art Director (Sri Lanka):* J.A. Vincent; *Costumes:* Patricia Edwards; *Title Designer:* Burke Mattsson; *Hairdresser:* Norma Collins; *Music:* Perry Botkin; *Orchestrators:* James Harbert, Bill Stafford; *Music Supervisor:* Harry V. Lojewski; *Music Editor:* Curt Sobel; *Music Consultant:* Dan Carlin, Jr.; *Sound:* William Randall; *Sound Re-recordists:* Robert Knudson, Robert Glass, Don MacDougall; *Supervising Sound Editor:* Don Warner; *Sound Editors:* Pamela Bentkowski, Allan Bromberg, Jack Cheap, David B. Cohn, Gini Cook, Robert Waxman; *Stunt Coordinator:* Jock Mahoney; *Technical Adviser (mountain climbing):* Allan Placko; *Head Animal Trainer:* Paul Reynolds; *Animal Trainers:* Fess Reynolds, Bill Gage, David Mcmillan, Joe Campassi

CAST: Bo Derek (Jane Parker), Richard Harris (James Parker), John Phillip Law (Harry Holt), Miles O'Keeffe (Tarzan), Akushula Selayah (Nambia, "Africa"), Steve Strong (Ivory King), Maxime Philoe (Riano), Leonard Bailey (Feathers), Wilfrid Hyde-White, Laurie Mains,

Harold Ayer (Club Members), C.J. (The Orangutan)

PLOT: Jane Parker, daughter of famous explorer James Parker, arrives in the African jungle from England to join her father's latest expedition: a search for the fabled Elephant Graveyard. Jane has never seen her father, who deserted her mother when she was born. She catches a ride on a boat carrying equipment for the Parker Expedition. Her unexpected arrival surprises her father and his companions, including Holt, a photographer; Riano, a guide; and Africa, Parker's native wife. In the morning, the safari begins, with Parker leading a large group of bearers en route to the Escarpment, a towering cliff face that is the gateway to the Elephant Graveyard. After nightfall, the cry of Tarzan is heard in the distance—a sound that panics the natives, most of whom desert the expedition. Parker explains to his daughter that this is Tarzan, an ape man who is rumored to be 100 or even 1000 feet tall. In the morning, the party begins the climb up the Escarpment; Riano dies in a fall. Reaching the summit, the safari proceeds, with a group of Christian native girls as bearers. Once again hacking their way through the jungle, Parker's abbreviated expedition comes upon the fabled Inland Sea. Jane bathes in the surf, only to find a lion on the beach stalking her. Before the animal can strike, Tarzan arrives to save her. He flees when Parker and the rest of the expedition come running, thinking that Tarzan has endangered Jane. Resuming the march, Parker's group is stalked by treacherous ivory hunters who capture the woman Africa and harass the expedition members. Thinking that Tarzan is responsible for the kidnapping, Parker threatens to kill the ape man and stuff him. The next day, Tarzan kidnaps Jane and takes her away from the camp. When Jane orders Tarzan to leave her alone, he does so in the middle of the jungle, where a giant python drags her into a lagoon. Her screams once again bring Tarzan to her rescue. During his battle with the snake, he is badly bitten and later collapses, but he is nursed back to health. Jane begins to fall in love with him. Tarzan retreats into the jungle rather than face the rifles of Parker and Holt. Jane explains to her father that the ape man is harmless, that he is a man, not an animal. The expedition members are captured by the ivory hunters. Transported to their camp, Parker, Jane, Holt and Africa are bound and gagged. Jane is about to be raped by the sumo wrestler–like king when her father breaks his bonds and hurls himself toward the king. Parker dies but Jane is saved when Tarzan smashes his way into the camp and in a brutal fight kills the king. Jane asks Holt to return to civilization to inform her father's explorers' club of his great discoveries. Jane decides to remain behind and start a new life with Tarzan.

REVIEWS: "The most messed-up movie of the season." *Christian Science Monitor,* September 3, 1981

"[The moviemakers] have done what one would not have thought possible—turned a vibrant, powerful, richly allusive story into pure and undiluted tedium." *Films and Filming* (U.K.), December 1981

"All the display of Bo's body cannot divert attention from the ludicrous ineptness of the enterprise. Nothing breaks a tumid erotic spell, faster than giggling." *Time,* August 3, 1981

REVIEWS FOR JOHN DEREK: "Although John Derek's direction remain loose and uninspired, he does know how to shoot pretty pictures of Sri Lanka and more particularly, Bo." *Variety,* July 29, 1981

"Mr. Derek is a great still photographer, favoring scenes shot against backgrounds so brilliantly lighted you can't see what's going on in the foreground." *The New York Times,* August 7, 1981

"John Derek, who has directed this inept and hilarious film, seems to be trying for a mood of primal eroticism.... As a promoter, an exploiter of his wife's golden tan, John Derek is a success. It's only as a pornographer that he's a failure. He's hopeless as a filmmaker too, but probably nobody cares." *New York Magazine,* August 17, 1981

ADDITIONAL REVIEWS AND ARTICLES: Actuà Ciné (France) September 1981 p. 7; *Boxoffice* 1 September 1981 pp. 43–44; *Ciné-Revue* 23 July 1987 p. 31; *Cinefantastique* December 1981 p. 11; *Daily Variety* 14 February 1980; *Daily Variety* 15 February 1980; *Daily Variety* 25 February 1980; *Daily Variety* 23 May 1980; *Daily Variety* 25 June 1980; *Daily Variety* 10 July 1980; *Daily Variety* 9 January 1981; *Daily Variety* 3 July 1981 pp. 1–2; *Daily Variety* 14 July 1981 pp. 1, 18; *Daily Variety* 28 July 1981 pp. 3, 12; *Daily Variety* 1 June 1982; *Hollywood Reporter* 26 August 1980; *Hollywood Reporter*

13 January 1981; *Hollywood Reporter* 17 June 1981; *Hollywood Reporter* 21 December 1981 p. 11; *Hollywood Reporter* 1 June 1982; *Hollywood Reporter* 16 July 1982 p. 14; *Il corriere della sera* (Italy) 19 September 1981 p. 19; *Il corriere della sera* (Italy) 20 September 1981 p. 19; *L.A. Herald Examiner* 27 July 1980 p. A2; *L.A. Herald Examiner* 6 March 1981 p. A2; *L.A. Herald Examiner* 8 April 1981 p. A2; *L.A. Herald Examiner* 14 July 1981 p. A2; *L.A. Herald Examiner* 13 August 1981; *L.A. Herald Examiner* 21 August 1981; *L.A. Times* 11 July 1981 pp. 3, 5. *L.A. Times* 15 July 1981; *L.A. Times* 25 July 1981 p. 3; *L.A. Times* 9 July 1981 pp. 1, 5; *L.A. Times* 9 September 1981; *The Listener* 1 Oct 1981 p. 385; *Monthly Film Bulletin* (U.K.) November 1981 pp. 225–226; *Motion Picture Product Digest* 19 August 1981 pp. 21–22; *N.Y. Daily News* 24 May 1980 p. 9; *N.Y. Daily News* 29 July 1981 p. 39; *N.Y. Daily News* 7 August 1981 p. 39; *N.Y. Post* 2 October 1980 p. 7; *N.Y. Post* 23 July 1981 p. 33; *N.Y. Post* 7 August 1981 p. 39; *N.Y. Times* 19 July 1981 pp. B2, 24; *N.Y. Times* 9 August 1981 pp. B1, 25; *N.Y. Times* 19 August 1981 p. C23; *N.Y. Times* 10 June 1982 p. C19; *On Cable* August 1982 pp. 10–12; *People Magazine* 27 July 1981 pp. 70–74; *People Magazine* 10 August 1981 p. 43; *Prevue* November-December 1981 pp. 22–29, 47; *San Francisco Chronicle* 27 July 1981;*Screen International* 26 September 1981 p. 27; *The Soho News* 11 August 1981 p. 35; *StarBurst* November 1982 pp. 7–8; *Variety* 11 June 1980; *Variety* 10 July 1980; *Variety* 2 July 1980; *Variety* 21 May 1980; *Variety* 29 June 1981; *Variety* 27 July 1981; *The Village Voice* 5 August 1981 p. 36; *Wall Street Journal* 16 May 1980; *Wall Street Journal* 7 August 1981

NOTES: *Tarzan, the Ape Man—Me Jane* was the film's working title. The picture got six nominations in the 1981 Razzie Awards, including John as Worst Director.

Bolero

Golan-Globus Productions, City Films, Cannon Films
Color; 105 minutes
Released on August 31, 1984

CREDITS: *Producer:* Bo Derek; *Director-Screenplay-Photography*: John Derek; *Executive Producers*: Menahem Golan, Yoram Globus; *Associate Producer*: Rony Yacov; *Location Manager*: Francisco Ruiz; *Post-Production Supervisor*: John Amicarella; *Assistant Directors*: Yousaf Bokhari, Alfredo Berlinchon;: *Assistant Photographers*: Nicholas Starkmeth, Michael Bartlett, Klaus-Peter Venn; *Production Designer*: Alan Roderick-Jones; *Assistant Art Director*: Miguel Chang; *Set Dresser*: Juan Jesus Escudero; *Wardrobe*: Tony Pueo, Sally Turner; *Makeup*: Cristóbal Criado; *Hairdresser:* Norma Bass; *Composer-Conductor:* Peter Bernstein; *Music (Love Scene)*: Elmer Bernstein; *Orchestrator:* Christopher Palmer; *Sound:* William Randall; *Sound Re-recordist*: Chris Jenkins, Gary Alexander, Larry Stensvold; *Post-Production Dialogue Recording*: Norman B. Schwartz; *Supervising Sound Editors*: Bob Henderson, Alan Murray; *Sound Editor:* Gordon Davidson, Song "As Time Goes By" written by Gus Kahn and Herman Hupfeld

CAST: Bo Derek (Ayre McGillivary), George Kennedy (Cotton Gray), Andrea Occhipinti (Angel Contreras), Ana Obregón (Catalina Terry), Greg Bensen (Sheik), Olivia d'Abo (Paloma), Ian Cochrane (Robert Stewart), Mirta Miller (Evita), Mickey Knox (Moroccan Guide), Paul Stacey (First Young Valentino), James Stacey (Second Young Valentino)

PLOT: The year is 1926; Ayre McGillivary and her companion Catalina are beautiful and have no shortage of male admirers, but none match up to the sheik of Ayre's dreams. After graduation, Ayre throws both garments and discretion to the wind on the college grounds, much to the embarrassment of her chauffeur Cotton. She receives her inheritance and vows to find a sheik to relieve her of her virginity. Destiny smiles at Ayre as she is introduced to her first sheik in the depths of the Casbah and offers him her most precious gift ... her virginity. Rather taken aback, the sheik vows to fly her to his desert paradise and deflower her in a night of unbridled passion than she will never forget. After an imaginative first course with milk and honey of the desert, the sheik passes out from the effect of too much opium. Intact but undaunted, Ayre and Catalina travel to Spain in search of greater conquests. While attending a bullfight, Ayre is summoned by the most celebrated Rejoneador in Spain, Angel Contreras. Angel, however, is tied to both his family and his wild gypsy lover, taken by Angel on her 14th birthday. Ayre's ruse of asking to buy one of Angel's stallions does not work: He explains that he deals only in bulls and wine. Finally, at Catalina's suggestion, she buys his whole vineyard. Angel gives her a horse and promises to meet Ayre in her bedchamber at dawn. After an evening of exhaustive preparations, he enters her room to fulfill her desires. In a scene of erotic passion, they achieve the ecstasy she has so longed for. The next day, disaster strikes in the bullring and Angel, horribly gored, faces a future of impotency. But Ayre is devoted to him and despite his shame and anger she promises to restore his manhood and desire by learning the skill of a Rejoneador which he holds so dear. Disaster threatens to strike again when the lusty sheik returns for a second attempt at seduction. He kidnaps Ayre, only to be thwarted when she escapes. Angel's recovery is slow, but Ayre restores his flagging potency by riding naked on a charger in the bullring and by showing amazing skill in handling a bull. She enables him to give his most stunning performance.

REVIEWS: "*Bolero* sounded at least mildly arousing, but the sex is 'tasteful' and soft-focus, as someone screwed up and smeared the KY jelly on the camera lens instead of the performers." *The Village Voice*, September 18, 1984

"The shapeless characterizations and fragmentary background render the quest for passion both implausible and remarkably uninteresting despite Bo Derek's proportions, offered to us from all angles until tedium yawns." *Monthly Film Bulletin* (U.K.), December 1984

REVIEWS FOR JOHN DEREK: "The plot sounds like that of a straight porn film, which is what *Bolero* would have become with anyone other than John Derek directing." *New York Times*, September 1, 1984

"When not lingering over his wife's private parts, photographer Derek has an obsession with extreme closeups of her face, presumably because as a writer he repeatedly pens lines about her being the 'most beautiful girl in the world.'" *Variety*, September 4, 1984

"Mr. Derek has done a good job of keeping everything, especially the male everything, camouflaged and out of sight." *Boxoffice*, November 1, 1984

ADDITIONAL REVIEWS AND ARTICLES: *Actua Ciné* (France) January 1985 p. 2; *Chicago Tribune* 26 August 1984 pp. L5–7; *City Limits* 26 October 1984 p. 23; *Daily Express* (U.K.) 28 June 1983 p. 3; *Daily Express* (U.K.) 28 January 1984; *Daily Express* (U.K.) 26 October 1984 p. 21; *Daily Mail* (U.K.) 23 June 1983 p. 9; *Daily Mirror* (U.K.) 13 October 1982 p. 3; *Daily Telegraph* (U.K.) 26 October 1984 p. 17; *France Soir* (France) 1 January 1985; *France Soir Magazine* (France) 5 January 1985 pp. 25–27; *Film-Echo/Filmwoche* (Germany) 12 Aug 1983, p. 6; *Filmfaust* (Germany) Feb/Mar 1985 pp. 14–15; *Films and Filming* (U.K.) December 1984 p. 32; Financial Times *(U.K.)* 26 October 1984 p. 21; *Hollywood Reporter* 27 January 1984 pp. 1, 4; *Hollywood Reporter* 4 September 1984 pp. 3, 54; *Il corriere della sera* (Italy) 8 January 1985 p. 19; *Mail on Sunday* (U.K.) 28 October 1984 p. 39; *Le Parisien* (FRANCE) 2 January 1985 p. 26; *N.Y. Post* 1 September 1984; *Screen International* 16 October 1982 p. 6; *Screen International* 18 February 1984 p. 6; *Screen International* 27 October 1984 p. 278; *The Sun* (U.K.) 27 September 1984 pp. 16–17; *Sunday People* (U.K.) 26 June 1983 pp. 20–21; *Sunday Express* (U.K.) 8 April 1984 p. 23; *Sunday Express* (U.K.) 28 October 1984 p. 22; *Sunday Times* (U.K.) 28 October 1984; *Time* 10 September 1984 p. 44; *Times* (U.K.) 26 October 1984 p. 22; *Variety* 8 February 1984 p. 6; *Time Out* 25 October 1984 p. 45.

NOTES: *Bolero*'s alternate titles were *Exstasy*, *Bo-bolero*, *Bolero: An Adventure in Ecstasy* and *Bolero Extasy*. Bo's mother Norma Bass and Bo's sister Kerry Collins were on the crew. *Bolero* received Razzie Awards for Worst Director and Worst Screenplay.

Ghosts Can't Do It

Epic Production, Sarlui/Diamant, Triumph Releasing
USA, Color, 90 minutes
Released in the U.S. on June 1, 1990

CREDITS: *Producer*: Bo Derek; *Director-Screenplay-Photography-Camera Operator*: John Derek; *Associate Producer*: Chandran Rutnam; *Music*: Junior Homrich, Randall Tico; *Editor*: John Derek: *Casting*: Ellen Lang; *Hair and Makeup:* Norma Bass; *Production Manager:* Anthony M. Ray; *Special Assistant*: Claude G. Albuquerque; *Assistant Cameraman*: Nikolaus Starkmeth; *Dialogue Supervisor*: Mickey Knox; *Script Supervisor*: Eva Banhidi; *Sound Mixer:* Tony Smyles; *Production Accountant*: Tink Ten Eyck; *Still Assistant*: Frank Brouille; *Production Controller*: Avram "Butch" Kaolan; *Production Coordinators:* Gail Schacht, Suzanne Unvert; *Production Accountants*: Catherine Roehl, Bettina Paladini

CAST: Bo Derek (Katie O'Darey), Anthony Quinn (Scott), Don Murray (Winston), Julie Newmar (Angel), Victoria Burgoyne (Sabine), Henry Jayasena (Mayor), Mickey Knox (The Pill Man), Wade Collings (Reverend), Leo Damian (Fausto Garibaldi), Gerry Spence (Wyoming Preacher), Richard Sherman (Dr. Frank), Cotton Gray (Cotton), Jane Damian (Lizabeth), Sy Tanney (Marriage Priest), Carole J. Fleck (Nurse), Imaging Spence (Funeral Woman), Polo (The Dog), Donald Trump (Himself), Jon T. Benn (Banker)

PLOT: Katie is madly in love with her wealthy and much older husband, Scott, who is terminally ill. Unwilling to be a burden for his wife, he commits suicide at their Wyoming mansion. Katie is pleasantly surprised when Scott appears to her as a ghost. Later she travels to South Sea Island, their favorite vacation spot, where he reappears. Together they plan to find a healthy young man whose body Scott can inhabit, so they can continue their sexual passion. In the meantime, Katie is forced to go to Hong Kong to fight magnate Donald Trump, who's looking to acquire the corporate empire Scott left her. With invisible Scott advising her in her ear and the help of Winston, a loyal corporate financial advisor, Katie outsmarts Trump. Back on the resort island, she considers hunky Fausto as the perfect body for Scott. Since Scott can only take over a body at the moment of death, Kate must kill Fausto. Fate steps in when Fausto, diving in the ocean, gets caught in nets. Katie saves him and brings him back to life, just in time so he can die again. Scott's spirit and Fausto's body are united for Katie's satisfaction.

REVIEWS: "Film styles of the rich and famous, Part One.... Mr. Trump's role is likely to be the main attraction of *Ghost Don't Do It*." *The Independent* (U.K.), January 19, 1989

"Derek seemed have to spent the entire special effects budget for this movie about the supernatural indulging his lady's passion for bizarre headgear. This movie should have been called 'Women Can't Do Anything'" *The Boston Globe,* June 2, 1990

"In concept and execution, there's enough Ernest Hemingway here for an Old Man and the CPR, a Farewell to Garments and lifetime of entries in the dialog contest at Harry's Bar." *Variety,* June 13, 1990

ADDITIONAL REVIEWS AND ARTICLES: *Entertainment Weekly* 26 October 1990; *The Film Journal* 1 September 1988 p. 77; *The Hollywood Reporter* 24 August 1988 p. 14; *Jackson Hole News* 8 February 1989 p. 6; *L.A. Times* 19 May 1989; *L.A. Times* 17 June 1990 p. 28; *N.Y. Daily News* 13 February 1991 p. 21; *Screen International* 27 August 1988 p. 1; *Palm Beach Post* 9 February 1989; *Screen International* 12 November 1988 p. 13; *Variety* 1 February 1989 p. 2

NOTES: John Derek won a Razzie Award as Worst Director in 1991.

Commercials, Music Videos and Videos

Evel Knievel at Caesar Palace

USA, 2 minutes, color; Las Vegas, December 31, 1967.

Motorcycle stunt performer Evel Knievel asked Derek to film his Caesars Palace motorcycle jump over the fountains.

Spanish Jeanswear Company

TV Commercial, Spain, color, 1982. John directed this commercial showing a day in Bo Derek's life at their Santa Ynez ranch.

"Whose Bed Have Your Boots Been Under?"

Music Video, USA, 4 minutes, color; released on January 2, 1995, performed by Shania Twain. Directed by John Derek

"Any Man of Mine"

Music Video, USA, 4 minutes, color; released on April 26, 1995, performed by Shania Twain. Directed by John Derek and Charlie Randazzo

The video won the Canadian Country Music Award for Video of the Year (1995), AOL's Online Music Award for Hottest Country Video (1995) and CMT Europe's Video of the Year (1995)

Television Appearances

"Tomorrow's Men"

The Ford Television Theatre
NBC, 30 minutes, B&W, Drama
Aired October 29, 1953

CREDITS: *Producer*: Fred Briskin; *Director*: James Neilson;

Screenplay: Karen DeWolf; *Original Story:* William R. Scott

CAST: Pat O'Brien (Spud Malone), John Derek (Allan Malone), Ann Doran (Mrs. Malone), Frances Helm (Judy Essex), John Eldredge (Dr. Essex), William E. Green (Dr. Miller), Chester Marshall (Bob Marshall), Bob Kelley (Announcer)

PLOT: When college senior Allan Malone hears a freshman criticizing the football coach for not letting him play, he tells him his own story. In flashbacks, sophomore Allan is convinced that he is the school's best football player and feels that the coach, who happens to be his father, refuses to let him play for fear of being accused of favoritism. On the day of the big game, the coach finally allows his son in the game. After a couple of hard tackles and mistakes, Allan realizes that he isn't as great as he thought. The coach is fired because this loss tops off a two-year losing streak.

REVIEW: "[A] compact, thoroughly entertaining football story … pointedly avoiding the clichés which usually seem to beset such grid entries." *Variety*, November 2, 1953

"A Place in the Sun"
Lux Video Theatre
CBS, 60 minutes, B&W, Drama
Aired January 28, 1954

CREDITS: *Producer:* Cal Kuhl; *Director:* Buzz Kulik; *Screenplay:* Sandy H. Barnett; Based on the novel *An American Tragedy* by Theodore Dreiser

CAST: John Derek (George Eastman), Ann Blyth (Angela Vickers), Marilyn Erskine (Alice Tripp), Raymond Burr (District Attorney R. Frank Marlowe), Paul Frees (Rev. Morrison), Herbert Heyes (Charles Eastman), Paul Maxey, Regis Toomey, Louis Jean Heydt

PLOT: Young George Eastman falls in love with Alice Tripp, a factory co-worker. But later he switches his affections to Angela Vickers, a wealthy young lady. When Alice tells George she's pregnant, things take a bad turn.

REVIEWS FOR JOHN DEREK: "John Derek was moodily photogenic but little more as the boy whose shabby romance with a factory girl ends in disaster." *Variety*, January 29, 1954

"Derek was fairly convincing." *Variety*, February 3, 1954

ADDITIONAL ARTICLE AND REVIEWS: *Detroit Free Press* 17 January 1954; *The Evening Sun* 1 February 1954; *The Hollywood Reporter* 28 January 1954 p. 11; *The Hollywood Reporter* 1 February 1954 p. 8; *Lincoln Sunday Journal and Star* 7 February 1954 p. 10 D; *L.A. Times* 21 January 1954; *The Observer* 4 February 1954; *Photoplay* March 1955 p. 22; *Variety* 13 January 1954 p. 31; *Variety* 29 January 1954

The Big Moment
NBC, 25 minutes, B&W, Drama
Aired May 2, 1954

CREDITS: *Producer:* Mel Epstein; *Director:* Jerry Juran [Nathan Juran]; *Writer:* Don Mankiewicz; *Music:* Irving Talbot; *Casting:* Bill Meiklejohn; *Editor:* Frank Bracht; *Photography:* Lionel Lindon; *Assistant Director:* Mickey Moore; *Art Director:* Henry Bumstead

Presented by the United Jewish on behalf of the United Israel Appeal and United Service for New Americans

CAST: Donna Reed (Deborah), John Derek (Avram), Robert Young (Narrator), Eduard Franz (Dr. Berg), Forrest Tucker (Uri), Thomas Mitchell (Blumenau), Stevie Roberts (Joseph), Don Bender (Ricky), Ray Galli (Ruffian), Henry Corden (Policeman), Gil Warren (Registrar), Booth Colman (Dr. Bauman), Grace Hayle (Agnes), Josephine Whittell (Marie), Harry Harvey (Ben), Laurence Dobkin (Worker)

PLOT: Divided in three different segments, this 25-minute film tells the story of people located in different parts of the world who don't always make the headlines or the history books, whose prospects are changed from despair to hope through the aid of the Allied Jewish Appeal. Derek and Donna Reed portray Avram and Deborah, a settler and a Holocaust survivor in love with each other, living in an Israel border settlement.

ARTICLES: *Jewish Exponent* 30 April 1954; *L.A. Times* 29 March 1954 p. 59; *Motion Picture Daily* 28 September 1954 p. 2; *The Wisconsin Jewish Chronicle* 25 September 1954

AWARDS AND HONORS: United Jewish Appeal Award: Awards for outstanding service and devotion to the work of saving lives, building Israel and strengthening the free way of life: Donna Reed, John Derek, Robert Young, Eduard Franz, Forrest Tucker, Thomas Mitchell, Don Bender, Ray Galli, Harry Harvey, cast; Mel Epstein, producer; Irvin Talbot, music director; Bill Meiklejohn, casting director; Frank Bracht, film editor; Lionel Lindon, photographer; Mickey Moore, assistant director; Henry Bumstead, art director.

Entertainment 1955

NBC Network; 90 minutes, Color; Music, Variety,
Aired March 27, 1955

CREDITS: *Producer-Director*: Jack Rayel; *Associate Producers*: Bob Henry, Roy Montgomery; *Other Directors*: Dick McDonough; Bob Banner (Hollywood), Max Lieberman, Kirk Browning (New York); *Writer*: Charles Isaacs; *Music Director*: Ross Miller; *Costumes*: Grady Hunt; *Art Director*: Jay Krause; *Lighting*: Al Scarlett; *Choreography*: Nick Castle, Miriam Nelso

CAST: Fred Allen (Host), Dinah Shore, Sylvester "Pat" Weaver, B.A. Graham, Robert Sarnoff, Helen Hayes, John Derek, Jimmy Durante, Ralph Edwards, Judy Holliday, Bob Hope, Cesar Romero, Adolph Zukor, Karl Malden, The Double-Daters, Leontyne Price, Elizabeth Montgomery, Josh Wheeler (Guests)

PLOT: A TV special that highlights the year in entertainment. Helen Hayes introduces a scene from the play *The Desperate Hours* and presents the Tony Awards for Best Broadway Play and Direction of the Best Play to author Joseph Hayes, producer Howard Erskene (not present) and director Robert Montgomery (his daughter Elizabeth Montgomery accepts on his behalf) for *The Desperate Hours*. Also included are appearances by NBC President Sylvester L. "Pat" Weaver, Robert Sarnoff of NBC, and Sunbeam Corp. president B.A. Graham; excerpts from Puccini's "Tosca," performed by Leontyne Price and Josh Wheeler; and additional sketches and segments featuring Derek, Fred Allen, Jimmy Durante, Ralph Edwards, Judy Holliday, Bob Hope, Cesar Romero and Adolph Zukor.

REVIEW: "Accustomed to the network's usual high excellence in previous spectaculars, this particular effort was disappointing." *Broadcasting*, April 4, 1955

The Birthday Present Matinee Theatre NBC, June 27, 1956, episode 170: Some sources erroneously credit John with an appearance. No evidence of his participation has been found.

"Black Jim Hawk"

The Ford Television Theatre
ABC, 30 minutes, B&W, Drama
Episode aired October 31, 1956

CREDITS: *Producer*: Lou Breslow; *Director*: Arthur Hiller; *Teleplay*: Russell S. Hughes; *Story*: Harold Shumate

CAST: John Derek (Jim Hawk), Marcia Henderson (Maude Collins), George Keymas (Cherokee Hollister), Donald Randolph (Sam Houston), Chris Alcaide (Luke), Sydney Mason (Wayne), Paul Petersen (Jim Hawk as a Boy)

PLOT: Texas outlaw "Black" Jim Hawk became one of the South's most feared lawbreakers after his own outlaw father was hanged for murder. The child Hawk pleads with Tennessee governor Sam Houston to pardon his condemned father. When Houston allows the sentence to be carried out, the boy vows to become an outlaw himself and one day murder Houston. Hawk leads a life of crime once he grows up, commanding a group of bandits, including Cherokee Hollister, who is responsible for reading everything for the illiterate Hawk. Throughout their crime spree, Hawk never kills anyone, promising to save all his murderous urges for one man—Sam Houston. When the outlaw settles for a while in Texas, though, a reluctant schoolteacher named Maude Collins agrees to help him learn to read and write. Hawk's newfound knowledge proves a burden when he attempts to murder Houston, now the governor of Texas

REVIEW FOR JOHN DEREK: "John Derek, seen too infrequently in teledramas, contributes a forceful performance which dominates *Black Jim Hawk*, an interesting well-written story." *Variety*, November 5, 1956

ADDITIONAL ARTICLE: *The Daily Reporter* 31 October 1956

"Massacre at Sand Creek"

Playhouse 90
CBS, 90 minutes, B&W, Western
Aired December 27, 1956

CREDITS: *Screenplay-Producer*: William Sackheim; *Director*: Arthur Hiller; *Photography*: Ray Cory; *Editor*: Henry Batista; *Art Director*: Cary Odell

CAST: John Derek (Lt. Norman Tucker), Everett Sloane (Col. John Templeton), Gene Evans (Sgt. Maddox), H.M. Wynant (Free

Horse), Ken Mayer (Maj. Downing), William Schallert (Capt. Kingsley), Roy Roberts (Collery), Michael Granger (Little River), Rick Vallin (Henshaw), William Bryant (Calhoun), Anthony Lawrence (Reed)

PLOT: Col. John Templeton is in command of troops stationed in Kansas territory. The colonel hates all Indians bitterly; his methods tend to prolong war rather than work toward peace. He even goes as far as to move the Cheyennes out of their fertile homeland to the barren area of Sand Creek. Norman Tucker, a young lieutenant assigned to Templeton's command, tries in vain to make him realize that his tactics are high-handed. When Templeton orders the regiment to fire on sleeping, unarmed Cheyennes, Tucker refuses to obey the command.

REVIEW: "[A] lot of drama, even for the 90-min. length, but yet well-knit in the teleplay by producer Sackheim, and moves with continuous excitement and emotions." *Variety*, December 31, 1956

ADDITIONAL ARTICLES: *The Bristol Daily Courier* 27 December 1956; *L.A. Times* 24 October 1956; *TV Guide* 27 December 1956 p. A-17; *Variety* 10 October 1956 p. 30; *Variety* 2 January 1957 p. 34.

"There Were Four"

Zane Grey Theater
CBS Network, 30 minutes, Western
Episode aired March 15, 1957

CREDITS: *Director*: Christian Nyby; *Producer*: Hal Hudson; *Writers*: Berne Giler; *Story*: Steve Frazee; *Editorial Supervisor*: Bernard Burton; *Art Director*: Duncan Cramer; *Photography*: George E. Diskant; *Production Supervisor*: Frank Baur; *Editor*: Desmond Marquette; *Story Editor*: Coles Trapnell; *Unit Manager*: William Dario Faralla; *Music Supervisor*: Hollywood Music Service; *Assistant Director*: Jack Sonntag; *Set Decorator*: Budd S. Friend; *Makeup*: Karl Herlinghaus

CAST: John Derek (Andy Todd), Dean Jagger (Bert Ensign), David Janssen (Danny Ensign), James Gavin (Dutch), Dick Rich (Campion), Grant Withers (Sheriff Carl Metz), Jimmie Komack (Deputy Whitey), Kenneth MacDonald (Jury Foreman), Dick Powell (Himself—Host)

PLOT: Young Andy Todd and pal Bert Ensign turn to cattle rustling to get revenge on a wealthy rancher.

Climb Aboard the Six-Five Special

Aka *The Six-Five Special*
BBC Television (U.K.), 18 minutes, Variety, Musical
April 20, 1957

CREDITS: *Producer*: Josephine Douglas; *Writer*: Trevor Peacock; *Additional Research*: Kenneth Midwood

CAST: Josephine Douglas (Presenter), Pete Murray (Presenter), Tony Crombie and His Rockets (Musicians); Dickie Bennett, Ronnie Hilton, Jackie Collins (Singers), Leonora Mila (Pianist), Graham Stuart and His Jazz Band (Musicians), Freddie Mills (Sports presenter), John Derek (Special Guest)

PLOT: The "Star Spotlight" segment is on John Derek, who appears in a light-hearted interview.

"Storm Over Eden"

Zane Grey Theater
CBS Network, 30 minutes, Western
Episode aired May 4, 1961

CREDITS: *Director*: Dick Moder; *Writer*: Stephen Lord

CAST: John Derek (Chet Loring), Nancy Gates (Ellen Gaynor), Robert Middleton (Whitney "Whit" Gaynor), Harry Dean Stanton (Fletcher), Roberto Contreras (Estrada), Dick Powell (Himself—Host)

PLOT: Chet Loring kills Bill Gaynor in self defense, but Bill's father Whitney Gaynor is determined to track down Loring. In his quest for vengeance, Gaynor ignores the pleas of his daughter Ellen, who plans to wed Chet. When Ellen helps Loring escape to a ghost town where they once played as children, her father and his two henchmen, Fletcher and Estrada, follow and discover the hideout.

Frontier Circus

CBS Network, 60 minutes, B&W, Western
26 Episodes (October 5, 1961–May 24, 1962):

CREDITS: *Production Company*: Calliope Productions; *Executive Producer*: Richard Irving; *Series Writing Creator*: Samuel A. Peeples; *Set Decorator*: John McCarthy, Jr.; *Makeup*: Florence Bush; *Costumes*: Vincent Dee; *Music Supervisor*: Stanley Wilson; *Animal Supervisor*: Ralph Helfer

MAIN CAST: Chill Wills (Col. Casey Thompson), John Derek (Ben Travis), Richard Jaeckel (Tony Gentry)

PLOT: Two friends run a small traveling circus right after the Civil War.

REVIEWS: "It isn't any worse than a lot of cow-hand drama; it isn't a bit better, either." *New York Daily News*, October 6, 1961

"[The show] unfolded as a cross between an adult Western and a horse-drawn study of mental cases." *New York Times*, October 6, 1961

"*Frontier Circus* at least has the advantage of novelty, which in itself makes it a standout show of the current TV season.... If it can sustain the pace of its opener, could be a real winner." *The Hollywood Reporter*, October 9, 1961

OTHER ARTICLES AND REVIEWS: *The Courier Journal* 6 October 1961; *Daily Mail* (U.K.) 12 October 1961; *New York Times* 16 October 1961 p. 59; *The Orlando Sentinel* 19 November 1961 p. 23 F; *Sunday Times* (U.K.) 8 October 1961; *TV Guide* 16 December 1961 pp. 10–11; *Television Mail* (U.K.) 24 November 1961 p. 21; *TV Guide* 3 February 1962 pp. 21–24; *TV Mirror* December 1961 p. 64; *Variety* 11 October 1961; *Weekly Television Digest* 27 February 1961 p. 6

NOTES: Although John Derek's name appears in the credits, he did not appear in the last episode, "Incident at Pawnee."

Frontier Circus Episode Guide

"The Depths of Fear"

Air Date: October 5, 1961; *Director:* William Witney; *Writer:* Samuel A. Peeples; *Guest Stars*: Aldo Ray (Toby Mills), James Gregory (Jacob Carno), Bethel Leslie (Millie Carno), Vito Scotti (Jaybo the Clown), Frank Ferguson (Fred)

"The Smallest Target"

Air Date: October 12, 1961; *Director:* William Witney; *Writer:* Samuel A. Peeples; *Guest Stars*: Barbara Rush (Bonnie Stevens), Brian Keith (Dan Osborne), Roy Barcroft (Pete Andrews), Mike Ragan (First Bill Poster)

"Lippizan"

Air Date: October 19, 1961; *Director:* William Witney; *Writer:* Lawrence Kimble; *Story:* Dorothy C. Fontana

Guest Stars: Vera Miles (Maureen McBride), H.M. Wynant (Talby), Gordon Jones (Rousty), Dick Wessel (Smith), Kay Kuter (Will Cutler), Howard Wright (Dolliver), Joan Staley (Anna-Marie), Otto Kruger (Gen. Frederic Jellich)

"Dr. Sam"

Air Date: October 26, 1961; *Director*: John English; *Writer:* Jean Holloway; *Guest Stars*: Irene Dunne (Dr. Sam Applewhite), Ellen Corby (Abby), J. Pat O'Malley (Duffy), Sue England (Mary), Jon Locke (Jerry Jones), Jean Howell (Janet Jones), Norman Leavitt (Willoughby), Robert Gunner (Harry), Jay Silverheels (Chief Red Cloud), Iron Eyes Cody (The Indian)

"The Hunter and the Hunted"

Air Date: November 2, 1961; *Director*: Alan Crosland, Jr.; *Writer:* Frank Price; *Guest Stars*: Eddie Albert (Dr. Payton Jordan), Rip Torn (Jess Evans), Cloris Leachman (Anna), Jocelyn Brando (Mrs. Phyllis Jordan), Warren Kemmerling (John Bowman), Michael Vandever (Grant), John Anderson (Carl)

"Karina"

Air Date: November 9, 1961; *Director*: Sydney Pollack; *Writer:* Jean Holloway; *Guest Stars*: Elizabeth Montgomery (Karina Andrews), Barbara Stuart (Melda), Tod Andrews (Jeff Andrews), Brian Hutton (Greg Andrews), J. Pat O'Malley (Duffy), Nora Marlowe (Madame Sonya), Albert Paulsen (Rodales)

"Journey from Hannibal"

Air Date: November 16, 1961; *Director*: Don Weis; *Writer:* Frank Price; *Guest Stars*: Thelma Ritter (Bertha Marie Beecher), Arte Johnson (Charles Gippner), Clem Bevans (McPhee), James Flavin (Boyle), Bill Zuckert (Sheriff Barnett), John War Eagle (First Indian)

"Winter Quarters"

Air Date: November 23, 1961; *Director*: John English; *Writer:* Ken Pettus; *Guest Stars*: Robert Wilke (Jack Gance), Alex Viespi (Nino Sanchez), Walter Sande (Jake), Roy Barcroft (Gore), Lane Bradford (Borden)

"The Patriarch of Purgatory"

Air Date: November 30, 1961; *Director*: William Witney; *Writer:* Les Crutchfield; *Guest Stars*: Royal Dano (Jethro Hedges), Carolyn Kearney (Susannah Hedges), Robert Sampson (Mark Hedges), Jane Chang (Shan Lu), Warren

Kemmerling (Boss), Abbagail Shelton (Mitzi), George Barrows (Clint), Pete Kellett (Sled), Harold Fong (Li Po)

"The Shaggy King"

Air Date: December 7, 1961; *Director:* Richard Irving; *Writer:* Samuel A. Peeples; *Guest Stars:* Dan Duryea (Terrence Tyber), Dick York (Jeb Randall), Frank de Kova (Karl Maynard), Michael Pate (Michael Smith), Paul Newlan (Dr. Turner), Jack Lambert (Hark Baker), Lorrie Richards (Molly), Alan Carney (Circus Cook)

"Coals of Fire"

Air Date: January 4, 1962; *Director:* William Witney; *Writer:* Shimon Wincelberg; *Guest Stars:* Sammy Davis, Jr. (Cato Richards), R.G. Armstrong (Uriah Foster), Larry Blake (Interlocuter), Marx Hartman (Roustabout), Chief Yowlachie (Indian Leader)

"The Balloon Girl"

Air Date: January 11, 1962; *Director:* Gilbert L. Kay; *Writer:* Vance Skarstedt; *Guest Stars:* Stella Stevens (Katy Cogswell), Claude Akins (Powcheek), Chick Chandler (Luke Turlock), Stacy Morgan (Clarence Wexler), Hal Needham (Ralph Wexler)

"Mr. O'Grady Regrets"

Air Date: January 25, 1962; *Director:* Don Weis; *Writer:* Lawrence Kimble; *Guest Stars:* Charles Ruggles (Will Grady), Anne Helm (Rosa Blanchard), Crahan Denton (Marshal Beckett), Michael Forest (Roy Clatter), Richard Le Pore (Jake Gard), Lillian Bronson (Dorothy Barker), Dorothy Neumann (Mrs. Hoskins), Anthony Jochim (Dr. Benson), S. John Launer (Warden Martine), Tim Graham (Williams)

"Quick Shuffle"

Air Date: February 1, 1962; *Director:* Robert Gist; *Writer:* Robert E. Thompson; *Guest Stars:* Gilbert Roland (Luke Santos), Patricia Barry (Amy), Carl Benton Reid (Judge Salem), George Mitchell (Sheriff), William Challee (Arnold), Richard Reeves (Gruber), Myron Healey (Card Player), Robert Ball (Nappy)

"The Courtship"

Air Date: February 15, 1962; *Director:* Hollingsworth Morse; *Writer:* Frank Price; *Guest Stars:* Jo Van Fleet (Amelia Curtis), Henry Jones (Marshal Harry Longstreet), Jeanette Nolan (Amanda Curtis), Lloyd Corrigan (Willis), Willard Waterman (Parker), Sheila Bromley (Mrs. Parker)

"Stop Over in Paradise"

Air Date: February 22, 1962; *Director:* Earl Bellamy; *Writer:* Bob Barbash; *Guest Stars:* Carolyn Jones (Amy Tyson), Adam Kennedy (Sam Hagen), Robert F. Simon (Jess Bailey), Robert Hinkle (Dave), Jackie Russell (Janet), James Anderson (Hobie), Don Hix (Perkins), John Cliff, Bob Williamson (Roustabouts)

"Calamity Circus"

Air Date: March 8, 1962; *Director:* Lesley Selander; *Writer:* Samuel A. Peeples; *Guest Stars:* Mickey Rooney (Arnold), Nico Minardos (The Great Roberto), Ina Victor (Lana), Parley Baer (Sheriff), Howard McNear (Judge Stuart), Dennis Rush (First Boy)

"The Inheritance"

Air Date: March 15, 1962; *Director:* Sydney Pollack; *Writer:* Steven Ritch; *Guest Stars:* Marc Marno (Yuki Yamoto), Tsuruko Kobayashi (Hideko Yamoto), Alan Hale, Jr. (Lait), J. Pat O'Malley (Duffy), Donald Barry (Martin), Tracey Roberts (Rowena), Peter Leeds (Rolando), Wally Brown (Sheriff Tom Bender), Sidney Tomack (Toby), Ken Hudgins (Mr. Jeffers), Delores Wells (Marie)

"Naomi Champagne"

Air Date: March 29, 1962; *Director:* Don Weis; Writer: Steven Ritch; *Guest Stars:* Richard Conte (Dan Diego Montoya), Constance Ford (Naomi Champagne), Marguerite Chapman (Theresa Haskill), Neil Hamilton (Jason Glass), George Keymas (Rafael), David Faulkner (Prater), Alex Montoya (Juan), Roberto Contreras (Pablo), Robert H. Harris (John Haskill)

"Mighty Like Rogues"

Air Date: April 5, 1962; *Director:* Alan Crosland, Jr.; *Writer:* Frank Price; *Story:* Lawrence Kimble; *Guest Stars:* Glenda Farrell (Ma Jukes), Jena Engstrom (Betsy Ross Jukes), J. Pat O'Malley (Duffy), Renee Godfrey (Stella), Roger Mobley (Andy Jukes), Ruth Carlsson, Carl Carlsson (Jugglers), Joby Baker (George Washington Jukes)

"Never Won Fair Lady"

Air Date: April 12, 1962; *Director:* Hollingsworth Morse; *Writer:* Shimon Wincelberg; *Guest Stars:* Red Buttons (Earl Youngblood), Gloria Talbott (Pamela), Christopher Dark (Manfredi), Paul Newlan (Gen. Youngblood), Richard Reeves (The Custom)

"The Good Fight"

Air Date: April 19, 1962; *Director:* John English; *Writer:* Steven Thornley; *Guest Stars:* George Macready (John Duncan), Lisabeth Hush (Hannah Cabot), Stephanie Hill (Evvy Sanders), Jason Evers (Judd Halleck), Kenneth MacDonald (Canfield), Kenneth Tobey (Sheriff Walden), Ray Daley (Luke Sanders), Gordon Jones (Jase), William Fawcett (Postmaster)

"The Clan MacDuff"

Air Date: April 26, 1962; *Director:* Charles Haas; *Writer:* Thomas Thompson; *Story:* Steven Ritch; *Guest Stars:* James Barton (Angus MacDuff), Chris Alcaide (Paul), Don Wilbanks (Carl), John Considine (Robin MacNeil), Robert Ivers (Sandy MacNeil), Jackie Russell (Patricia MacDuff), Nan Peterson (Mary MacDuff), Jess Kirkpatrick (The Sheriff)

"The Race"

Air Date: May 3, 1962; *Director:* Ty Garnett; *Writer:* Ric Hardman; *Guest Stars:* Edward Andrews (Duke Felix Otway), Skip Homeier (Col. Rastatt), Jim McMullan (Charlie), Harry Carey, Jr. (Anderson), Don Haggerty (Marshal Walworth), Jeff Bell (Dave), Ronnie R. Rondell, Jr. (Italy), Allen Pinson (France), Leroy Johnson (Swede)

"The Daring Durangos"

Air Date: May 17, 1962; *Director:* Robert Gist; *Writer:* Lee Erwin, Donn Mullally; *Guest Stars:* Nehemiah Persoff (Paco Durando), Margarita Cordova (Maria Durando), David White (F.X. Farnum), Jack Searl (Cal Soper), Anita Sands (Tina Durando)

"Incident at Pawnee Gun"

Air Date: May 24, 1962; *Director:* Sydney Pollack; *Writer:* N.B. Stone, Jr.; *Guest Stars:* Paul Carr (Young Gun), Robert Foulk (Logan), Kathie Browne (Mauvereen), Robert Lowery (Marshal Taggert), John Pickard (Deputy Murdoch), Walter Sande (Shanghai), Kenneth Tobey (Frank Mitchell), Joe Maross (Al Buchanan), John Hart (Deputy Fred), William Phipps (Cowboy), Dick Haynes (Deputy Phillips), Bob Woodward (Deputy)

Archival Footage and Personal Appearances

Stars in Rio de Janeiro

(March 9, 1951) Hearst Newsreel, 5 minutes

John Derek, Ricardo and Georgiana Montalban, Lizabeth Scott, Wendell Corey, Joan Fontaine, June Havoc, June Haver, Patricia Neal, Florence Marly.

Screen Snapshots: Hollywood Awards

(May 17, 1951) 10 minutes

At the annual *Photoplay* award dinner, Ralph Staub interviews Derek, Farley Granger, Loretta Young and Mercedes McCambridge. Master of ceremony Ronald Reagan presents awards to Broderick Crawford, John Wayne, Gregory Peck and *All the King's Men* writer-director Robert Rossen.

The Ken Murray Show

CBS-TV (September 8, 1951) 60 minutes

Derek appears with Johnny Johnston, ogling actress-singer Anita Gordon.

Author Meets the Critic

NBC-TV (September 9, 1951) 30 minutes

Moderated by John McCaffery, panel members (including Derek) debate "Is college football over-commercialized and tough business?" Subject stemmed from the upcoming release of *Saturday's Hero*. Six key scenes from the film are also played during the program.

Screen Snapshots: Meet Mr. Rhythm, Frankie Laine

(March 20, 1952) 10 minutes

Frankie Laine and his wife Nan Grey open up an antique store in Hollywood. Stars drop by to wish them success: John Derek, Joanne Dru, Smiley Burnette, Jock Mahoney, John Ireland and Ruth Warrick.

Screen Snapshots: Hollywood's Mr. Movies

(April 17, 1952) 10 minutes

Adolphe Menjou is presented a trophy and proclaimed Mr. Movies at a meeting of the Saint and Sinners Club in Los Angeles. Derek appears among many guest stars.

Art Linkletter's House Party

CBS-TV (February 24, 1953) 30 minutes

Dean Miller interviews Derek and Dr. Paul Popenoe.

Screen Snapshots: Hollywood Stars to Remember

(February 25, 1954) 10 minutes

A compilation of archival footage and photographs and stories about early stars Lon Chaney, Douglas Fairbanks, Carole Lombard, Wallace Reid and Will Rogers. Derek reminisces over the Hollywood greats.

Paramount Presents VistaVision

Technicolor (February 1955) 20 minutes

Derek appears in clips from *Run for Cover* in this short featurette heralding upcoming Paramount's productions.

Thailand Premier Visits Hollywood

(April 25, 1955) 01:28
Paramount, Pathé Newsreels

The premier of Thailand visits Paramount with his wife and daughter. They watch the production of *The Ten Commandments*. The Thai prime minister shakes hands with studio vice-president Frank Freeman, director Cecil B. DeMille and stars Derek, Yul Brynner and Charlton Heston.

Two pre-teen girls from Toronto, Canada, winners of safety contest, tour Paramount Studios in 1956

(April 3, 1956) 00:32, Paramount, Pathé Newsreels

Ten-year-old Elizabeth Allport and 11-year-old Carolyn Mullen on the set of *Omar Khayyam* with Derek, Michael Rennie, Cornel Wilde and Peter Adams.

Screen Snapshots: Mr. Rhythm's Holiday

(June 22, 1956) 10 minutes

Ralph Staub talks to Peter Lawford and Las Vegas hotel owner Wilbur Clark. Footage from 1952's *Screen Snapshots: Meet Mr. Rhythm, Frankie Laine* is shown, remembering the day when Laine and his wife opened their antique store in Hollywood. Derek is one of the stars visiting the shop.

La Settimana Incom

(July 24, 1958) 02:28, Italian Newsreel

Derek is shown along with Dawn Addams, Elsa Martinelli and Rik Battaglia on the Belgrade, Yugoslavia, set of *I Battellieri del Volga*.

Playboy Video Magazine

Documentary TV series (1980) 12 min.

An intimate conversation with John and Bo Derek at their secluded California ranch. The couple discusses their thoughts and feelings about charges that John is a Svengali, their friendship with John's former wives and more. There is also a photomontage of naked Bo photos taken by John.

The Barbara Walters Summer Special

(April 1, 1980) ABC-TV

Barbara Walters interviews John and Bo Derek.

The Today Show

(July 24, 1981) NBC-TV

John and Bo Derek discuss with Gene Shalit their controversial new film *Tarzan, the Ape Man*.

The Mike Douglas Show

(1981) Syndicated

John and Bo Derek discuss *Tarzan, the Ape Man* with host Douglas.

60 Minutes

(1981) CBS-TV

Bo and John Derek, interviewed on their 46-acre ranch in Santa Ynez, California, discuss friendships, lifestyles, Bo's career, family plans, fantasies, and what it's like being lovers 24 hours a day.

People Now

(August 3, 1981) CNN
"John & Bo Derek"

An interview with Bo and John Derek. A clip from *Tarzan, the Ape Man* is shown.

Entertainment Tonight

(September 14, 1981) CBS-TV

Host Marjorie Wallace reports on the legal

entanglements about royalties from the film *Tarzan, the Ape Man*.

Entertainment Tonight
(March 1, 1982) CBS-TV
  John and Bo Derek discuss the release of her old exploitation film.

Bo Derek at the Academy Awards
(March 24, 1986) Getty Images
  Bo and John Derek are interviewed at the Dorothy Chandler Pavilion in Los Angeles.

The Today Show
(June 27, 1988) NBC-TV
  John and Bo are interviewed at the Carlyle Hotel in New York City. John recalls his first meeting with Bo, stating that he needed a young actress for a movie he was making. He adds that his second wife actress Linda Evans recommended Bo. A movie clip features 16-year-old Bo. John describes his living arrangements in Mexico while Bo lived in Los Angeles. He expresses anger over constant criticism from the media.

The 50th Barbara Walters Special
(November 29, 1988) ABC Network
  Footage from Walters' 1980 interview with the Dereks is shown on this retrospective of the past 50 shows.

The Today Show
(January 21, 1994) NBC-TV
  Bo talks about her life, marriage and a new TV movie.
  Clips from some of her films (including *Tarzan, the Ape Man* and *Bolero*) are shown. She reminisces about her relationship with John and the 30-year difference between them. She also discusses her friendship with Linda Evans.

Entertainment Tonight
(July 1998) CBS-TV
  Two months after John's death, Bo talked about her grieving. Footage of John Derek is shown.

E! True Hollywood Story
(October 7, 1999) E! Television
"Bo Derek"
  Bo Derek's biography including a segment dedicated to John's life and career.

Larry King Live
(March 10, 2000) CNN
  King interviews Bo Derek for the full hour. Several of John's photographs are seen in the background while Bo discusses being his wife and muse.

Intimate Portrait
(October 23, 2000) Lifetime TV
"Linda Evans"
  Evans talks about her life and career. Images of John are shown.

Great Romances of the 20th Century
(March 6, 2001) BBC (U.K.)
"John and Bo Derek"
  A 26-minute documentary about John and Bo. Footage from some of John's films is shown. A French-dubbed version of this documentary was released in DVD by Gala in 2004 under the title *Les couples legendaries du 20e siècle*.

Intimate Portrait
(October 17, 2003) Lifetime TV
"Bo Derek"
  Bo talks about her life and career. Images and clips of John are seen throughout the program.

Biography
(September 1, 2007) A&E
"Bo Derek: The Perfect 10"
  Bo Derek's *Biography* includes several clips and photography with John.

Radio Programs

The Lux Radio Theater—Movie Time U.S.A.
  CBS Network; Air Date: September 24, 1951. Sponsored by: Lux. William Keighley (host), John Milton Kennedy (Announcer), Rudy Schrager (Music Director), Earl Eby (Director), Charlie Forsyth (Sound Effects).
  A program celebrating the "Fiftieth Anniversary of 'The Movies.'" The program features scenes from *Saturday's Hero* with Derek, Donna Reed and Mickey Knox.

Awards and Honors

Man of the Year Award, USA, October 1949: *Photoplay* magazine

Blue Ribbon Award, USA, February 1950: *Boxoffice Magazine*

Golden Apple Award, USA, Most Cooperative Picture Star, 1951

Silver Medal from the Uruguayan Government as active participant to the Punta del Este Film Festival, Uruguay, 1951

International Stardom Award, given by the Foreign Press Association of Hollywood, 1952

United Jewish Appeal Award, USA, a plaque given for outstanding service and devotion to the work of saving lives, building Israel and strengthening the free way of life, as an actor in *The Big Moment*, 1954.

Star on the Walk of Fame, Hollywood, California, February 8, 1960

Sour Apple Award, USA, Least Cooperative Director, 1984

Projects with Derek's Name Attached as Actor or Director

Valentino
(Columbia) 1948

While Derek was playing in *Knock on Any Door*, producer Edward Small was interested in having him play the lead in a Rudolph Valentino biopic. *Valentino* was made in 1951 with Anthony Dexter in the main role.

The Gainesville Circus
(Columbia) 1949

While Derek was making *Rogues of Sherwood Forest*, it was announced that he would be cast in a semi-documentary film built around the history and activities of the Gainesville Community Circus. The project was never realized.

The Patent Leather Kid
1949

According to the *Los Angeles Times*, producer Jerry Wald hoped to persuade Columbia to lend him Derek, to star in a remake of the 1922 First National silent film. It was never produced.

Golden Boy
(Columbia) 1950

According to the *Los Angeles Times*, Columbia planned a remake of their 1939 hit *Golden Boy*. Derek trained for two months as a boxer with champion Mushy Callahan. The remake never materialized.

Strong Arm
(Columbia) 1950

After Columbia denied the *Golden Boy* remake, a studio spokesman claimed that they had an original prizefight story by Roy Huggins which could have reunited Derek and Broderick Crawford after *All the King's Men*. The picture was never made.

Strangers on a Train
(Warner Bros) 1951

According to Sean Derek, Alfred Hitchcock was interested in casting her father as Guy Haines in this thriller. Columbia refused to lend him and the part was assigned to Farley Granger.

The Wheel Man
(Columbia) 1951

Columbia purchased the rights of this unpublished magazine story by James Benson Nablo and planned to make it into a film with Derek and either Terry Moore or Jody Lawrance. The picture was made in 1954 under the title *Drive a Crooked Road* starring Mickey Rooney and Dianne Foster.

Murrieta
(Paramount) 1952

Derek intended to play the real-life Mexican character of Joaquin Murrieta, one of history's most famous Robin Hood–like personages. Derek pitched the project first in 1952 with Columbia and in 1955 with Paramount; neither studio showed an interest. A 1965 film entitled *Joaquín Murieta,* produced by a Spanish company, starred Jeffrey Hunter.

Renegade Canyon
(Columbia) 1953

It was announced that Derek would play a young cavalry officer of the 1880s in this film adaptation of a *Saturday Evening Post* serial by Peter Dawson, produced by Kenneth Gamet from John K. Butler's screenplay. It was never produced.

From Here to Eternity
(Columbia) 1953

Columbia Pictures head Harry Cohn wanted Derek in the role of Private Robert E. Lee Prewitt, but the role was assigned to Montgomery Clift, who got an Academy Award nomination.

Angels Cooking
(Paramount) 1954

It was announced that Derek would play one of the three leads in the picture that was later renamed *We're No Angels* (1955). He was replaced by Aldo Ray.

The Vagabond King
(Paramount) 1954

The United Press indicated that Derek was assigned to play a trusted young officer in the court of Louis XI in this film, under the direction of Michael Curtiz. The picture was released in 1956 without Derek.

Chief Red Sleeves
(United Artists) 1956

There were press reports that Derek signed with producer Aubrey Schenck for two pictures a year for the next five years. The first film he was scheduled to make was *Chief Red Sleeves*. Derek never signed such a contract. The picture was made in 1957 as *War Drums* with Lex Barker.

Love Is My Shame
1957

The press announced that newlyweds Derek and Ursula Andress would make this film in Italy. It was not made.

Bronco
1957

John Derek wanted to shoot his own Western series entirely in Mexico. The show was later produced by ABC-TV (1958–1962) with Ty Hardin. Except for some exteriors shot in Arizona, it was entirely filmed at Warner Brothers in Burbank.

A Gaucho Project
1959

In a February 25, 1959, letter to a friend in Israel, John said he was in Uruguay with Ursula Andress trying "to put together a Gaucho picture." The project was never made.

Butterfield 8
(MGM) 1960

According to an Elizabeth Taylor's biographer, Derek asked Taylor to use her influence to get him cast as the second male lead in the picture. The role was given to Eddie Fisher.

The Colossus of Rhodes
(MGM) 1961

John Derek was fired after falling out with director Sergio Leone. Rory Calhoun replaced him.

May the Sea Take This Island
1962

The press announced in March 1962 that Derek, after completing the TV show *Frontier Circus*, would direct his wife Ursula Andress in a movie he wrote, set to be filmed in Yugoslavia. The project was never realized.

Butch Cassidy and the Sundance Kid
(20th Century–Fox) 1969

According to a Paul Newman biographer, John asked the blue-eyed actor to campaign for him to play the Sundance Kid. Robert Redford got the role.

Wildflowers
1969
Aka **Wild Flowers**

Derek wrote, produced and directed his third wife Linda Evans in this film about incestuous sibling relationships. Partially shot on the Swiss Alps in 1969, it was never released. A few photographs appeared in *Playboy* magazine in July 1971.

Harold Robbins' 79 Park Avenue
1977

According to Bo Derek, John declined a $1 million offer to star in this TV series based on Harold Robbins' bestseller.

Candy's Man and The Ice Box
1978

According to an interview in the *Los Angeles Times,* John had scripted two major features, *Candy's Man*, in which John Wayne was apparently interested, and *The Ice Box*. No other information was found about those two unrealized projects.

The Girl with the Golden Hair
(20th Century–Fox) 1979

New York Daily News columnist Marilyn Beck announced that John was expected to co-produce (with Marty Ransohoff) this film starring Bo Derek. It was later made as *A Change of Season* (1980) without John's participation.

Monte Carlo
1980

Derek was supposed to direct a film produced by Harry Saltzman starring Bo Derek and Ursula Andress. A story centered on the reconciliation of a mother and a daughter after a separation of 20 years. It was never realized.

The Dazzler
1981

Screenwriter Gary Goddard was commissioned to write a script for a Bo Derek film based on Marvel's comic heroine Dazzler. The project was abandoned because of several creative differences between John Derek, the prospective director and the leading investors, who eventually backed out.

Never-Never Land
1981

A never-made sword-and-sorcery film involving the Dereks and *Tarzan* co-writer Gary Goddard.

Pirate Annie
1981
Aka *Sea Mistress* and *The Flag*
CBS Films

An $8 million movie inspired by the life of pirate Anne Bonny. John planned to direct with Bo to star. The picture was never due to creative differences and budget problems with CBS Theatrical Films.

Adam and Eve
1982
Aka *Eve and That Damned Apple*
Universal

A comedy based on Mark's Twain's *The Diary of Adam and Eve* that John had in mind for several years. It never came to pass due to an argument between the Dereks and Universal. It was rumored that Richard Harris would play God and George Hamilton the Devil.

A Knight of Love
1986

The press reported that John would direct Bo in a film based on the German fairy tale *Ondine*, the story of a nymph who is tired of being immortal. After falling in love with a human, she ends her endless and boring existence. The project was never realized.

O
1990

In an interview with a French newspaper, Bo revealed that John was planning *O*, a romantic comedy about an extra-terrestrial, stranded on Earth, who wants to go back to his planet. Unrealized.

Driven
(Undated)

A script Derek wrote for Bo about cattle ranchers. Apparently he was unable to find financing.

Published Photographic Work

Magazines

Note: Much of the photographic work of John Derek for *Playboy* has been reprinted in several international versions of the magazine or sold to other foreign publications. The references below indicates the original photographic spread as it first appeared in the U.S. publications.

Look Magazine, "Ursula Andress Success Story of a Lazy Beauty," November 5, 1963

Playboy, "She ... is ... Ursula Andress," June 1965

Playboy, "Ursula," July 1966

Playboy, "Blooming Beauty," July 1971

Playboy, "The Return of Ursula Andress," November 1973

Playboy, "Bold.... Beautiful.... Breathtaking," March 1980

Playboy, "Bo Encore!," August 1980.

Playboy, "Tarzan & Bo," September 1981

Playboy, "John Derek Perfect '30' Ursula Linda & Bo," January 1982

Playboy, "Bo Derek X Rated," July 1984

Playboy, "The Prime Time of Linda Evans," June 1986

Playboy, "A Perfect '40,'" December 1994

Playboy, "An Eye for Beauty," October 1998

Books

John Derek, *Bo*, New York: Walleby Books—Simon & Schuster, 1980

A color photo essay book celebrating Bo Derek, with photographs by John.

Robert Vavra, *An Eye for Beauty. John Derek Photographer, Bo Derek: Model and Muse*, Chula Vista, CA: International Institute of Photographic Arts, 2008.

A book celebrating Bo Derek's life and career through John's photographs, with quotes from friends and colleagues.

Chapter Notes

Chapter 1

1. *Everyone's*, May 17, 1922, 10.
2. John Derek, "The Truth About Me," *Hello*, May 21, 1988, 59.
3. Bo Derek, *Riding Lessons* (New York: ReganBooks, 2002), 72.
4. Phyllis Pope, "Brave or Foolish," *Motion Picture and TV Magazine*, July 1955, 70.
5. Russell Harlan, "He Might Have Been My Son," *Modern Screen*, January 1951, 26, 71.
6. John Derek, "On the Level," *Movieland*, June 1950, 41.
7. John Derek, "The Road I Traveled," *Motion Picture and TV Magazine*, February 1952, 67.
8. Derek, "The Truth About Me," 60.
9. Harlan, "He Might Have Been My Son," 71.
10. Jerry Asher, "Robert Wagner: I'm Still Not a Star," *Motion Picture and TV Magazine*, May 1954, 60.
11. Pope, "Brave or Foolish," 70.
12. Brac Stevens, "Handsomest Guy in Hollywood," *Silver Screen*, June 1949, 67.
13. "Hollywood Digest," *Film Daily*, December 6, 1943, 10.
14. "Studio Contracts," *Variety*, December 29, 1943, 4.
15. Stevens, "Handsomest Guy in Hollywood," 67.
16. *Film Culture*, N°32- Spring 1964, 8.
17. Elizabeth Taylor, *Elizabeth Taylor. An Informal Memoir* (New York: Harper & Row, 1965), 6.
18. Darwin Porter Danforth Prince, *Elizabeth Taylor: There Is Nothing Like a Dame* (New York: Blood Moon Productions, 2012), 43–44.
19. Dick Richards, *Ginger—Salute to a Star* (Brighton, UK: Clifton Books, 1969), 106–107.
20. Sean Catherine Derek, *Cast of Characters* (New York: Dorchester Publishing, 1982), 29.
21. Shirley Temple Black, *Child Star* (London: Headline, 1989), 359–360.
22. *Ibid.*, 360.
23. Robert Wagner, *I Loved Her in the Movies: Memories of Legendary Actresses* (New York: Viking, 2016), 16.
24. Black, *Child Star*, 360–361.
25. J. Derek, "The Truth About Me," 61.
26. J. Derek, "On the Level," 84.
27. J. Derek, "The Truth About Me," 61.
28. S.C. Derek, *Cast of Characters*, 29–30.
29. Pope, "Brave or Foolish," 32.
30. "Star's Mother Takes Lethal Pills," *The Long Beach Independent*, July 16, 1948, 43.

Chapter 2

1. Hedda Hopper, "Make a Way for Youth!" *Modern Screen*, June 1949, 100.
2. John Derek, "The Role I Liked Best…," *Saturday Evening Post*, March 28, 1953.
3. Steranko, "The Uncensored Bo," *Prevue*, November-December 1981, 28.
4. Patrick McGilligan, *Nicholas Ray. The Glorious Failure of an American Director* (New York: It Books, 2011), 166.
5. *Ibid.*, 160.
6. *Ibid.*, 161.
7. *Ibid.*, 166.
8. Pauline Swanson, "Too Big for My Britches," *Motion Picture and TV Magazine*, October 1953, 36.
9. Stevens, "Handsomest Guy in Hollywood," 67.
10. Humphrey Bogart, "Listen to Me, Kid," *Photoplay*, September 1949, 34.
11. *The Hollywood Reporter*, February 21, 1949, 4.
12. Howard Barnes, *N.Y. Herald Tribune*, February 23, 1949.
13. *Boxoffice*, February 26, 1949.
14. J. Derek, "The Role I Liked Best."
15. A.H. Wieler, "By Way of Report," *New York Times*, February 20, 1949, X 5.
16. "Screen Beauty Arrives for Role," *L.A. Times*, January 9, 1946.
17. Patti (Sic) Behrs, "My Kind of Man," *Modern Screen*, February 1950, 44.
18. *Ibid.* 88.
19. *The Wilke Barre Record*, October 23, 1949, 18.
20. John Derek, "The Amazing Story of John Derek in His Own Words," *Hello*, May 28, 1988, 115.
21. Robert Rossen, "Fact and Fiction Behind 'All the King's Men,'" *New York Times*, November 20, 1949.
22. Robert Penn Warren, *Selected Letters Volume 3, Triumph and Transition, 1943-1952* (Baton Rouge: Louisiana State University Press, 2015) April 18, 1949.
23. Broderick Crawford, "He Tries Too Hard," *Motion Picture and TV Magazine*, November 1951, 73.

24. "Malaya Bans 'King's Men,'" *New York Times*, May 15, 1950.
25. Jack Gaver, "Female Shrieks and Whistles Startle John," *The Des Moines Register*, November 13, 1949, 62.
26. Florence Pritchett, "Speaking of Love and Kisses," *Silver Screen*, April 1950, 41.
27. Steranko, "The Uncensored Bo," 28.

Chapter 3

1. Pritchett, "Speaking of Love and Kisses," 63.
2. Favius Friedman, "Don't Be a Hero!" *Motion Picture Magazine*, December 1950, 63.
3. Ronald L. Davis, *Just Making Movies: Company Directors on the Studio System* (Jackson: University Press of Mississippi, 2005), 196.
4. Thomas F. Brady, "Columbia to Film 'Big Top' Feature," *New York Times*, August 23, 1949, L 29.
5. Louella O. Parsons, "John Dereks' Expect Baby Next July," *International News Services*, November 22, 1949.
6. J. Derek, "The Amazing Story of John Derek in His Own Words," 115.
7. S.C. Derek, *Cast of Characters*, 111.
8. Patrick McGilligan and Paul Buhle, *Tender Comrades* (Minneapolis: University of Minnesota Press, 2012), 397–398.
9. Jay Fultz, *In Search of Donna Reed* (Iowa City: University Press of Iowa, 1984), 83.
10. *Cue*, September 15, 1951.
11. Tim Cohane, "Saturday's Hero," *Look Magazine*, September 15, 1951, 123.
12. "Cristo Legend Put to Actionful Use," *The Hollywood Reporter*, June 27, 1951, 3.
13. James S. Barstow, Jr., "On the Screen," *N.Y. Herald Tribune*, June 27, 1951, 17.

Chapter 4

1. *The Hollywood Reporter*, October 17, 1951, 4.
2. Fultz, *In Search of Donna Reed*, 85.
3. Crawford, "He Tries Too Hard," 73.
4. *Ibid*.
5. Earl Wilson, *L.A. Daily News*, September 20, 1951.
6. *L.A. Times*, March 3, 1953, Part III, 11.
7. S.C. Derek, *Cast of Characters*, 30.
8. *Monthly Film Bulletin*, October 1953.
9. *Picturegoer*, October 24, 1953.
10. *The Hollywood Reporter*, June 8, 1953, 3.

Chapter 5

1. George Armstrong, "Is Hollywood Destroying John Derek," *Photoplay*, April 1953, 48.
2. Michelangelo Capua, *Montgomery Clift. A Biography* (Jefferson, NC: McFarland, 2002), 84.
3. Louella Parsons, *Albuquerque Journal*, October 1, 1952, 23.
4. Ben Cook, "Hollywood Food Shop," *Panama City News Herald*, February 10, 1952.
5. Wheeler Winston Dixon, *Lost in the Fifties* (Carbondale: Southern Illinois University Press, 2005), 83.
6. Untitled newspaper clipping, February 19, 1953.
7. Ben Cook, "Actors Are Suffering of Inferiority Complex," *The Pittsburg Press*, March, 1953.
8. Gene Freese, *Richard Jaeckel, Hollywood's Man of Character* (Jefferson, NC: McFarland, 2016), 39.
9. J. Derek, "The Amazing Story of John Derek in His Own Words," 116.
10. Helen Weller, "From Grim to Grin," *Silver Screen*, December 1953, 9.
11. Roderick Mann, "Come Back for John Derek?," *Los Angeles Times*, November 5, 1978, 40.
12. Jack Moffitt, *The Hollywood Reporter*, June 24, 1954, 3.
13. Maxine Arnold, "The Big Gamble," *Photoplay*, April 1955, 95.
14. Ruth Rowland, "The Last of Mr. Pretty Boy," *Silver Screen*, June 1954, 25.
15. *Ibid*.
16. John Derek, "Turn of a Career," *Photoplay*, March 1955, 23.
17. Edward A. Harris, "A 'Pretty Boy,' but There's More to Him Than That," *St. Louis Post-Dispatch*, November 20, 1955, 96.

Chapter 6

1. Hyatt Downing, "Miracle at Crossroad," *Photoplay*, October 1954, 117.
2. *Ibid*.
3. *Ibid*.
4. "His Face Was (Not) His Fortune," *Picturegoer*, July 10, 1954, 17.
5. Matthew Bernstein, *Walter Wanger. Hollywood Independent* (Berkley: University of California Press, 1994), 191.
6. Stuart M. Kaminsky, *A Biographical Study of the Career of Donald Siegel* (Evanston, IL: Northwestern University, 1972), 91.
7. Paul Picerni, *Step to Stardom—My Story* (Albany, GA: BearManor Media, 2007).
8. Jean Pierre Coursodon, *American Directors. Volume II* (New York: McGraw-Hill, 1983), 360.
9. Dee Phillips, "You Need Love in Your Life," *Photoplay*, August 1955, 95.
10. Arnold, "The Big Gamble," 94.
11. Ernest Borgnine, *Ernie. The Autobiography* (New York, Citadel Press, 2008) 115.
12. McGilligan, *Nicholas Ray*, 258.
13. James Cagney, *Cagney by Cagney* (New York: Doubleday, 1976), 132.
14. Bosley Crowther, *The New York Times*, April 30, 1955, 10.
15. Phillips, "You Need Love in Your Life," 95.
16. Don Siegel, *A Siegel Film* (London: Faber & Faber, 1996), 174.
17. *Ibid*.
18. Lawrence Suid, *Sailing on the Silver Screen: Hollywood and the U.S. Army* (Annapolis, MD: U.S. Naval Institute Press, 1996) 112.

19. Jack Moffitt, "An Annapolis Story Good Popular Entertainment," *The Hollywood Reporter*, March 21, 1955, 3.
20. Philip Dunne, *Take Two. A Life in Movies and Politics* (New York: McGraw-Hill, 1980), 269.
21. Richard Burton, *The Richard Burton Diaries* (New Haven: Yale University Press, 2014), 634.
22. Bob Thomas, "Lincoln Being Shot Again in New Film," *The Paris News*, September 29, 1954, 4.
23. Arnold, "The Big Gamble, 94.

Chapter 7

1. Scott Eyman, *Empire of Dreams. The Epic Life of Cecil B. DeMille* (New York: Simon & Schuster, 2010), 441.
2. "John Derek Gets Tough!" *Popular Man*, May 1958, 27.
3. Phillips, "You Need Love in Your Life," 49.
4. Henry Wilcoxon, *Lionheart in Hollywood: The Autobiography of Henry Wilcoxon* (Metuchen, NJ: The Scarecrow Press, 1991), 256.
5. Phillips, "You Need Love in Your Life," 49.
6. Ibid.
7. "Taking a Big Plunge," *Movie Life*, November 1955, 29.
8. Tony Crawley, *Film Illustrated*, March 1980, 275.
9. Louella Parson, "John Derek, Wife Part; 'Nothing in Common,'" *L.A. Examiner*, September 10, 1955.
10. Harrison Carroll, "Derek Says Wife Cruel, Asks Divorce," *Herald Express*, September 16, 1955.
11. "False Suicide Report," *L.A. Evening Herald Express*, October 20, 1955.
12. Diane Scott, "The Truth Behind John Derek's Bust Up," *Photoplay*, December 1955, 88.

Chapter 8

1. Gordon White, "Love Without Marriage," *Motion Picture*, March 1956, 56.
2. J. Derek, "The Amazing Story of John Derek in His Own Words," 116.
3. White, "Love Without Marriage," 56.
4. "I Was a Playgirl of Sort: Ursula," *Sunday News*, April 30, 1967, 28.
5. J. Derek, "The Amazing Story of John Derek in His Own Words," 116.
6. Robert Vavra, *An Eye for Beauty. John Derek Photographer, Bo Derek: Model and Muse* (Chula Vista, CA: International Institute of Photographic Arts, 2008), 151.
7. *Cincinnati Enquirer*, February 19, 1956, 29.
8. Aline Mosby, "Derek Raps Arty Actors in TV, Films," *Courier-Post* (Camden, NJ), January 14, 1956, 4.
9. *The Hollywood Reporter*, May 29, 1956, 3.
10. Ken Ferguson, "At Last—A British Film with Guts," *Photoplay U.K.*, July 1957, 13.
11. James L. Boyd, "Did You Hear What Happened to John Derek in London?" *Confidential*, November 1957.
12. "Memphis Bans Flesh," *Motion Picture Daily*, December 31, 1957, 2.
13. *Harrison's Reports*, August 3, 1957, 122.
14. *Fury at Showdown*, Press Release, 1957.
15. *The New York Times*, April 20, 1957, 21.
16. *Variety*, November 5, 1956.

Chapter 9

1. "John Derek and Friend Saved After Sea Spill," *L.A. Times*, January 6, 1957 B1.
2. Elsa Martinelli, *Sono come sono* (Milano: Rusconi, 1995), 188.
3. Darwin Porter, *Paul Newman: The Man Behind the Baby Blues: His Secret Life Exposed* (Blood Moon Productions, 2009), 335.
4. Fred Hift, "Exodus Harrassed by Reds, Arabs," *Variety*, May 25 1960.
5. Bosley Crowther, *The New York Times*, December 16, 1960, 44.
6. *Variety*, December 14, 1960, 6.
7. Christopher Frayling, *Sergio Leone. Something to Do with Death* (London: Faber & Faber, 2000), 101.
8. Ibid., 102.

Chapter 10

1. Joe Hyams, "John Derek, a Disillusioned Guy," *N.Y. Herald Tribune*, September 28, 1961, 19.
2. Isobel Ashe, "Frontier Circus Has Something for Everyone," *Ithaca Journal*, November 18, 1961, A 5.
3. "Actor Sues Over Slide," *Citizen-News*, August 14, 1962.
4. Anthony Slide, *Actors on Red Alert* (Lanham, MD: Scarecrow Press, 1999), 84.
5. *Variety*, March 17, 1965.
6. *Monthly Film Bulletin* (U.K.), February 1965, 26.
7. *Newsweek*, July 20, 1964, 80.
8. Ibid.
9. Ben G. Pinga, "Filipino Missing Boat, Derek Claims," *Film Daily*, June 18, 1964.
10. Freese, *Richard Jaeckel*, 83.

Chapter 11

1. Vavra, An Eye for Beauty, 166.
2. Roderick Mann, "Ursula Andress Discusses Money, Men," *EL Paso Herald-Post*, August 6, 1966, 4.
3. Linda Evans, *Recipes for Life. My Memories* (New York: Vanguard Press, 2011), 34.
4. John Derek, "Linda and Bo," *Hello*, June 4, 1988, 89–90.
5. Curtis Lee Hanson, "Cock a Doodle Doo," *Cinema*, no. 3, July 1966, 19.
6. Donald Zec, "One Bizarre Encounter: Note Sturdy Rib Cage," *The Brandon Sun*, September 9, 1966, 12.
7. Reva Berger, "Director Out of Uniform," *L.A. Times Sunday Magazine*, November 26, 1967, 46.

8. *The Chanute Tribune*, April 26, 1969.
9. Eugenia Sheppard, "Hanson Drives to Film Field," *L.A. Times*, April 14, 1969, sec. IV, 12.
10. J. Derek, "Linda and Bo," 90.
11. Michael Freedland, *Linda Evans* (New York: St. Martin's Press, 1986), 36.
12. "Blooming Beauty," *Playboy*, July 1971, 138.
13. *Hello*, June 4, 1988, 91.

Chapter 12

1. J. Derek, "Linda and Bo," 91.
2. Evans, *Recipes for Life*, 70.
3. *Ibid*.
4. B. Derek, *Riding Lessons*, 111.
5. S.C. Derek, *Cast of Characters*, 287–288.
6. Michael Walsh, "I Made It for Women," unpublished *Variety* news report originally submitted in 1979; available at http://reeligback.com/articles/_i_made_it_for_women_i_.
7. *Ibid*.
8. "Film Revival of Bo Derek, At 16, Broadly Pacted," *Variety*, January 7, 1981.
9. B. Derek, *Riding Lessons*, 120.
10. *The Barbara Walters Summer Special*, ABC Network, April 1, 1980.
11. "Derek-ed," *N.Y. Daily News*, March 24, 1980, 9.

Chapter 13

1. Steranko, "The Uncensored Bo," 22.
2. *Variety*, April 5, 1981.
3. Cathleen McGuigan, "The Making of a Goddess," *Newsweek*, December 10, 1979, 139.
4. "John Derek Plays 'Tarzan' for Real and Decks a Sailor," *N.Y. Post*, October 29, 1980, 7.
5. Steranko, "The Uncensored Bo," 23.
6. *Ibid*. 22.
7. David Lewin, "Bo Derek Brings 'Tarzan' Back Alive," *N.Y. Times*, July 19, 1981, 24 D.
8. *Ibid*.
9. *Ibid*.
10. Sue Reilly and David Wallace, "A Torrid Tarzan," *People*, July 27, 1981, 74.
11. J. Derek, "Linda and Bo," 93.
12. B. Derek, *Riding Lessons*, 156.
13. Joy Gould Boyum, *Wall Street Journal*, August 7, 1981, 19.
14. Vincent Canby, *N.Y. Times*, August 7, 1981, 10 C.
15. Jennifer Selway,"Live Fast, Grow Old, Get Rich," *Time Out London*, October 2, 1981, 17.
16. *Today Show*, NBC Network, July 24, 1981.
17. Scott Tracy Griffin, *Tarzan on Film* (London: Titan Books, 2016), 170.
18. Reilly and Wallace, "A Torrid Tarzan," 74.
19. Steranko, "The Uncensored Bo," 64.
20. B. Derek, *Riding Lessons*, 171.

Chapter 14

1. David Lewin, "She Leaves Latin Lovers in the Cold," *Sunday People* (UK), June 26, 1983 20.
2. George Kennedy, *Trust Me. A Memoir* (New York: Applause, 2011), 118–119.
3. Edward Owen, "Bo's Film Lover Sacked in Row with Husband," *Daily Express* (UK), June 23, 1983, 3.
4. Kennedy, *Trust Me. A Memoir*, 128.
5. Lewin, "She Leaves Latin Lovers in the Cold," 21.
6. Jeff Silverman, "X Ratings and Egos: The Fury Behind Bo's Bolero," *Chicago Tribune*, August 26, 1984, L5.
7. *Ibid*.
8. Clipping from *GQ* (USA), March 2008.
9. John Derek "Why I'm Happy with Bo," *Hello*, June11, 1988, 113.
10. Liz Smith, *NY Daily News*, October 3 1980, 8.
11. Betty Goodwin, "Sean Derek Is No 'Daddy's Girl,'" *L.A. Herald-Examiner*, November 29, 1982, D1.
12. Marilyn Beck, "Dereks in Snit Over Bio," *N.Y. Daily News*, October 20, 1980, 49.
13. Robin Adams Sloane, *Daily News*, clipping undated approx. 1980.
14. Peter H. King, "Disabled Criticized Olympic Organizer," *L.A. Times*, March 1, 1984, 36.
15. Leonard Klady, "Bo's Got Spirits," *L.A. Times*, June 29, 1989.
16. Pat H. Broeske, "Outtakes," *L.A. Times*, June 17, 1990, 28.
17. Vavra, *An Eye for Beauty*, 226.
18. *Variety*, September 14, 1994.
19. Shania Twain, *From This Moment On* (New York: Atria, 2011) 264.
20. *Ibid*. 264–265.
21. Vavra, *An Eye for Beauty*, 232.
22. Twain, *From This Moment On*, 265.
23. Douglas Thompson, *Hollywood People* (London: Pan Books, 1995) 123.
24. Cork Millner, *Portraits* (Santa Barbara, CA: Fithian Press, 1994), 99.
25. Thompson, *Hollywood People*, 123–124.
26. Liz Smith, *L.A. Times*, June 4, 1998.
27. Steve Kurutz, "Ranch Dressing," *N.Y. Times Magazine—Men's Fashion of the Times*, September 22 2002, 77.
28. Millner, *Portraits*, 106.

Bibliography

Books

Allan, Blaine. *Nicholas Ray. A Guide to Reference and Resources.* Boston: G.K. Hall, 1984.

Ann-Margret. *Ann-Margret. My Story.* London: Orion, 1994.

Bernstein, Matthew, and Walter Wanger. *Hollywood Independent.* Berkley: University of California Press, 1994.

Blottner, Gene. *Columbia Picture Movies Series 1926–1955.* Jefferson, NC: McFarland, 2012.

Borgnine, Ernest. *Ernie. The Autobiography.* New York: Citadel Press, 2008.

Buhle, Paul, and David Wagner. *Radical Hollywood. The Untold Story Behind America's Favorite Movies.* New York: New Press, 2002.

Burton, Richard. *The Richard Burton Diaries.* New Haven: Yale University Press, 2014.

Cagney, James. *Cagney by Cagney.* New York: Doubleday, 1976.

Capua, Michelangelo. *Montgomery Clift. A Biography.* Jefferson, NC: McFarland, 2002.

Carey, Harry Jr. *Company of Heroes.* Lanham, MD: Taylor Trade Publishing, 2013.

Casty, Alan. *The Films of Robert Rossen.* New York: The Museum of Modern Art, 1969.

Ciaccia, Maria. *Dreamboats: Hollywood Hunks of the '50s.* New York: Excalibur, 1992.

Coursodon, Jean-Pierre, and Pierre Sauvage. *American Directors. Volume II.* New York: McGraw-Hill, 1983.

Davis, Ronald L. *Just Making Movies: Company Directors on the Studio System.* Jackson: University Press of Mississippi, 2005.

DeMille, Cecil Blunt. *The Autobiography of Cecil B. DeMille.* New York: Garland Publishing, 1985.

Derek, Bo. *Riding Lessons: Everything That Matters in Life I Learned from Horses.* New York: Regan Books-HarperCollins, 2002.

Derek, John. *Bo.* New York: Walleby Books-Simon & Schuster, 1980.

Derek, Sean Catherine. *Cast of Characters.* New York: Dorchester, 1982.

Dewy, Donald. *Lee J. Cobb: Characters of an Actor.* Lanham, MD: Rowman & Littlefield, 2014.

Dickens, Homer C. *The Complete Films of James Cagney.* Secaucus, NJ: Citadel Press, 1989.

Dixon, Wheeler Winston. *Lost in the Fifties. Recovering Phantom Hollywood.* Carbondale: Southern Illinois University Press, 2005.

Douglas, Mike. *I'll Be Right Back.* New York: Simon & Schuster, 2000.

Dunne, Philip. *Take Two. A Life in Movies and Politics.* New York: McGraw-Hill, 1980.

Edwards, Paul M. *A Guide to Films on the Korean War.* Westport, CT: Greenwood Press, 1997.

Evans, Linda. *Recipes for Life. My Memories.* New York: Vanguard Press, 2011.

Eyman, Scott. *Empire of Dreams. The Epic Life of Cecil B. DeMille.* New York: Simon & Schuster, 2010.

Fitzgerald, Michael G., and Boyd Magers. *Ladies of the Western.* Jefferson, NC: McFarland, 2002.

Frayling, Christopher. *Sergio Leone. Something to Do with Death.* London: Faber & Faber, 2000.

Freedland, Michael. *Linda Evans.* New York: St. Martin's, 1986.

Freese, Gene. *Richard Jaeckel. Hollywood's Man of Character.* Jefferson, NC: McFarland, 2016.

Frischauer, Willi. *Behind the Scenes of Otto Preminger.* London: Michael Joseph, 1973.

Fujiwara, Chris. *The World and Its Double: The Life and Work of Otto Preminger.* New York: Faber & Faber, 2008.

Fultz, Jay. *In Search of Donna Reed.* Iowa City: University Press of Iowa Press, 1984.

Fury, David. *Kings of the Jungle.* Jefferson, NC: McFarland, 1994.

_____. *Maureen O'Sullivan. No Average Jane.* Minneapolis: Artist's Press, 2007.

Geoff, Andrew. *The Films of Nicholas Ray.* London: Letts, 1991.

Godfrey, Lionel. *Paul Newman Superstar: A Critical Biography.* New York: St. Martin's Press, 1979.

Groffin, Scott Tracy. *Tarzan on Film.* London: Titan Books, 2016.

Groom, Arthur. *Frontier Circus.* London: Purnell, 1961.

Hammontree, Patsy G. *Shirley Temple Black: A Bio-Bibliography.* Westport, CT: Greenwood Press, 1998.

Hare, William. *L.A. Noir. Nine Dark Visions of the City of Angels*. Jefferson, NC: McFarland, 2004.
Hutchinson, Alice L. *Kenneth Anger*. London: Black Dog Publishing, 2004.
Hyams, Joe. *Bogie: The Definitive Biography of Humphrey Bogart*. New York: New American Library, 1966.
Jeffers, Paul H. *Sal Mineo. His Life, Murder, and Mystery*. New York: Carroll & Graff, 2000.
Joyner, C. Courtney. *The Westerners. Interviews with Actors, Directors, Writers and Producers*. Jefferson, NC: McFarland, 2009.
Kaminsky, Stuart M. *A Biographical Study of the Career of Donald Siegel*. Evanston, IL: Northwestern University, 1972.
Keaney, Michael F. *British Film Noir Guide*. Jefferson, NC: McFarland, 2011.
Kennedy, George. *Trust Me. a Memoir*. New York: Applause, 2011.
Kreidl, John Francis. *Nicholas Ray*. Boston: Twayne Publisher, 1977.
Lamparski, Richard. *Whatever Became of…? Fourth Series*. New York: Crown Publishers, 1973.
Landis, Bill. *Anger: The Unauthorized Biography of Kenneth Anger*. New York: HarperCollins, 1995.
Marrill, Alvin H. *The Films of Anthony Quinn*. Secaucus, NJ: Citadel Press, 1975.
Martinelli, Elsa. *Sono Come Sono*. Milano: Rusconi, 1995.
McCarty, Clifford. *The Complete Films of Humphrey Bogart*. Secaucus, NJ: Citadel Press, 1995.
McGilligan, Patrick. *Cagney. The Actor as Auteur*. London: A.S. Barnes, 1982.
_____. *Nicholas Ray. The Glorious Failure of an American Director*. New York: It Books, 2011.
_____, and Paul Buhle. *Tender Comrades*. Minneapolis: University of Minnesota Press, 2012.
Meier, Patrick, and Philippe Durant. *Ursula Andress*. Lausanne: Favre, 2009.
Michael, Paul. *Humphrey Bogart: The Man and His Films*. Indianapolis: Bobbs-Merrill, 1965.
Millner, Cork. *Portraits*. Santa Barbara, CA: Fithian Press, 1994.
Munn, Michael. *Charlton Heston*. London: Robson Books, 1998.
_____. *Richard Burton. Prince of Players*. London: J.R. Books, 2008.
Nini, Britt. *Ursula Andress*. Paris: Éditions PAC, 1980.
Orrison, Katherine. *Written in the Stone. Making Cecil B. DeMille's Epic the 10 Commandments*. Lanham, MD: Vestal Press, 1999.
Parish, James Robert. *The Swashbucklers*. New Rochelle, NY: Arlington House, 1976.
Penn Warren, Robert. *Selected Letters Volume 3, Triumph and Transition, 1943–1952*. Baton Rouge: Louisiana State University Press, 2015.
Pettigrew, Terence. *Bogart. A Definite Study of His Film Career*. London: Proteus, 1981.
Picerni, Paul. *Step to Stardom-My Story*. Albany, GA: BearManor Media, 2007.
Pike, Andrew, and Ross Cooper. *Australian Films 1900–1977*. Melbourne: Oxford University Press, 1981.
Pilato, Herbie J. *The Essential Elizabeth Montgomery*. Lahman, MD: Taylor Trade Publishing, 2013.
Pilling, Jayne, and Michael O' Pray. *Into the Pleasure Dome: The Films of Kenneth Anger*. London: BFI, 1989.
Porter, Darwin. *Paul Newman: The Man Behind the Baby Blues: His Secret Life Exposed*. New York: Blood Moon, 2009.
_____, and Danforth Prince. *Elizabeth Taylor: There Is Nothing Like a Dame*. New York: Blood Moon, 2012.
Preminger, Otto. *Otto Preminger: An Autobiography*. New York: Doubleday, 1997.
Prince, Danforth, and Darwin Porter. *James Dean. Tomorrow Never Comes*. New York: Blood Moon, 2016.
Quirk, Lawrence J. *Paul Newman*. Dallas: Taylor Publishing, 1996.
Reade, Eric. *The Australian Screen*. Melbourne: Lansdowne Press, 1975.
_____. *Australian Silent Films*. Melbourne: Lansdowne Press, 1970.
_____. *History and Literature. The Saga of Australian Film 1896–1978*. Sydney: Harper & Row, 1979.
Richards, Dick. *Ginger. Salute to a Star*. Brighton, U.K.: Clifton Books, 1969.
Ringgold, Gene, and DeWitt Bodeen. *The Films of Cecil B. DeMille*. Secaucus, NJ: Citadel Press, 1974.
Rovin, Jeff. *The Films of Charlton Heston*. Secaucus, NJ: Citadel Press, 1980.
Rubython, Tom. *And God Created Burton*. Myrtle Press, 2011.
Ryan, Tom. *Otto Preminger Films Exodus: A Report*. New York: Random House, 1960.
Scott Royce, Brenda. *Donna Reed: A Bio-Bibliog"raphy*. Westport, CT: Greenwood Press, 1990.
Shiller, Ralph. *The Complete Films of Broderick Crawford*. Lulu.com, 2016.
Siegel, Don. *A Siegel Film*. London, Faber & Faber, 1996.
Slide, Anthony. *Actors on Red Alert*. Lanham, MD: Scarecrow Press, 1999.
Suid, Lawrence. *Sailing on the Silver Screen. Hollywood and the U.S. Army*. Annapolis, MD: U.S. Naval Institute Press, 1996.
Taylor, Elizabeth. *Elizabeth Taylor. An Informal Memoir*. New York: Harper & Row, 1965.
Temple Black, Shirley. *Child Star*. London: Headline, 1989.
Thompson, Douglas. *Hollywood People*. London: Pan Books, 1995.

Twain, Shania. *From This Moment On*. New York: Atria, 2011.
Vavra, Robert. *An Eye for Beauty. John Derek Photographer, Bo Derek: Model and Muse*. Chula Vista, CA: International Institute of Photographic Arts, 2008.
Wagner, Robert. *I Loved Her in the Movies: Memories of Legendary Actresses*. New York: Viking, 2016.
Wilcoxon, Henry. *Lionheart in Hollywood: The Autobiography of Henry Wilcoxon*. Metuchen, NJ: Scarecrow Press, 1991.
Wilkerson, Tichi, and Marcia Bore. *The Hollywood Reporter: The Golden Years*. New York: Arlington House, 1984.
Williams, Chris. *The Richard Burton Diaries*. New Haven, CT: Yale University Press, 2012.

Newspaper and Periodicals

Albert, Katherine. "Hold That Man!" *Photoplay*, May 1951.
_____. "Hollywood's Young Marriages." *Photoplay*, February 1951.
"All the King's Men Gala Premier." *Silver Screen*, March 1950.
Armstrong, George. "Is Hollywood Destroying John Derek." *Photoplay*, April 1953.
Arnold, Maxine. "The Big Gamble." *Photoplay*, April 1955.
_____. "Have a Heart." *Photoplay*, February 1950.
Asher, Jerry. "Robert Wagner: I'm Still Not a Star." *Motion Picture and TV Magazine*, May 1954.
"Baby-Faced Killer." *Silver Screen*, March 1949.
Baskette, Kirtley. "Pretty Tough." *Modern Screen*, April 1952.
Behrs, Patti [sic]. "My Kind of Man." *Modern Screen*, February 1950.
Berger, Reva. "Director Out of Uniform." *L.A. Times Sunday Magazine*, November 26, 1967.
"Blooming Beauty." *Playboy*, July 1971.
Bogart, Humphrey. "Listen to Me, Kid." *Photoplay*, September 1949.
"Bogart's Bet." *Picturegoer*, August 6, 1949.
Boyd, James L. "Did You Hear What Happened to John Derek in London?" *Confidential*, November 1957.
Brasselle, Keefe. "The Lightning Kid." *Movieland*, May 1953.
Brooks, Caroline. "John Speaks for Himself." *Photoplay*, June 1952.
Bulnes, José. Les immortels du cinema: John Derek." *Ciné Revue* (France), October 4, 1984.
"The Case of the 'Desert-ing' Husbands." *Movie-World*, March 1952.
Cohane, Tim. "Saturday's Hero." *Look Magazine*, September 15, 1951.
Coons, Robbin. "Meet John Derek." *Movie Stars Parade*, July 1949.
"Country Squire." *Movie-World*, July 1953.
Crawford, Broderick. "He Tries Too Hard." *Motion Picture and TV Magazine*, November 1951.
"Day of Rest." *Movie Secrets*, August 1955.
Derek, Bo. "Bo Derek Her Life Story in 4 Parts." *Hello* (U.K.), November 12, 1994.
Derek, John. "The Amazing Story of John Derek in His Own Words in 4 Parts." *Hello*, May 21, 1988.
_____. "I Have a Terrible Time." *Photoplay*, August 1953.
_____. "I Won't Be Pushed Around." *Motion Picture Magazine*, March 1953.
_____. "Is Divorce Justified?" *Photoplay*, January 1957.
_____. "My First Screen Kiss." *Movie*, August 1950.
_____. "The Road I Traveled." *Motion Picture Magazine*, February 1952.
_____. "The Role I Liked Best..." *Saturday Evening Post*, March 28, 1953.
_____. "The Truth About Me." *Hello*, May 21, 1988.
_____. "Turn of a Career." *Photoplay*, March 1955.
_____. "What Does a Guy Have to Do?" *Movieland*, March 1951.
_____. "What Hollywood Divorce Has Taught Us." *Movieland*, November 1951.
_____. "Why I Hate Publicity." *Picturegoer* (U.K.), May 3, 1958.
_____. "Why I'm Happy with Bo." *Hello*, June 11, 1988.
_____, as told to Alice L. Tildesley. "On the Level." *Movieland*, June 1950.
_____, as told to Jane Morris. "What I Want for My Son." *Movieland*, June 1951.
Derek, Pati. "He's Funny That Way." *Motion Picture Magazine*, May 1954.
_____. "I'm in Love with a Wonderful Guy." *Movieland*, July 1949.
_____. "My Man, John." *Motion Picture Magazine*, February 1952.
_____. "Our Third Year of Marriage." *Silver Screen*, March 1951.
_____. "The Quiet One." *Photoplay*, August 1952.
"The Dereks Visit Disneyland," *Clipping*, December 1955.
"Don't Envy Derek." *Movieland*, May 1952.
Douglas, Nan. "Go Ahead and Swoon." *Motion Picture Magazine*, February 1950.
Downing, Hyatt. "Miracle at Crossroad." *Photoplay*, October 1954.
_____. "When Does a Husband Think Divorce Is Justified." *Photoplay*, October 1956.
"Father's Day." *Photoplay*, June 1953.
Ferguson, Ken. "At Last—a British Film with Guts." *Photoplay* (U.K.), July 1957.
Friedman, Favius. "Don't Be a Hero!" *Motion Picture Magazine*, December 1950.
_____. "On Location with John Derek." *Motion Picture Magazine*, November 1951.
"Future Unlimited." *Movieland*, October 1955.

Garavan, Frank. "Beautiful Bo Derek Fears About Her Husband." *Weekend Magazine* (U.K.), September 8, 1982.

"The Gentleman Prefers Blondes." *Playboy*, January 1982.

Gittelson, Natalie. "Bo Derek: The Even "10" Takes an Odd Turn." *McCall's*, January 1981.

Harlan, Russell. "He Might Have Been My Son." *Modern Screen*, January 1951.

"His Face Was (Not) His Fortune." *Picturegoer* (U.K.), July 10, 1954.

Hopper, Hedda. "Make a Way for Youth!" *Modern Screen*, June 1949.

"JJ Is for John." *Movie Life*, May 1950.

"John Derek." *Movie Spotlight*, April 1951.

"John Derek Dies Age 71." *Hello* (U.K.), 1998.

"John Derek Gets Tough." *Popular Man*, May 1958.

"John Derek—It's Part of My Time." *Film Show Annual* (U.K.), 1956.

"John Derek, Pop." *Movie Life*, November 1950.

Kurutz, Steve. "Ranch Dressing." *N.Y. Times Magazine-Men's Fashion of the Times*, September 22, 2002.

"Letter from Liza." *Silver Screen*, December 1949.

"The Life Story of John Derek." *Picture Show* (U.K.), September 23, 1950.

"The Life Story of John Derek." *Picture Show* (U.K.), July 14, 1956.

"The Life Story of John Derek." *Picture Show* (U.K.), December 21, 1957.

"Luau." *Motion Picture Magazine*, December 1951.

Marshack, Laddie. "Just Don't Call Me Jane." *TV Guide*, February 3, 1962.

McGuigan, Cathleen. "The Making of a Goddess." *Newsweek*, December 10, 1979.

Moore, Viola. "Good Skates." *Modern Screen*, March 1949.

More, Marie. "One Man's Three Beautiful Women." *Modern Screen*, July 1980.

"Movie Life of John Derek." *Movie Life*, July 1950.

O'Leary, Dorothy. "Giorni Duri Per John Derek." *Hollywood* (Italy), September 2, 1950.

"The Other Love." *Movie Star Parade*, November 1950.

Parsons, Louella. "In Hollywood with Louella: John Derek." *L.A. Examiner*, July 17, 1949.

Perkins, Lynn. "Photolife of John Derek." *Photoplay*, July 1951.

Phillips, Dee. "You Need Love in Your Life." *Photoplay*, August 1955.

Pope, Phyllis. "Brave or Foolish." *Motion Picture and TV Magazine*, July 1955.

"Present Perfect." *Movie Life*, June 1954.

Pritchett, Florence. "Speaking of Love and Kisses." *Silver Screen*, April 1950.

"Private Life of John Derek." *Movie Stars Parade*, July 1951.

"Private Life of John Derek." *Movie Stars Parade*, July 1955.

Reeves, Michael. "Me Jane." *On Cable*, August 1982.

Reilly, Sue, and David Wallace. "A Torrid Tarzan." *People*, July 27, 1981.

Rhodes, Charles. "Catalina Holiday." *Motion Picture and TV Magazine*, July 1952.

_____. "John Derek." *Motion Picture and TV Magazine*, December 1954.

Ross, Lincoln. "Danger Ahead." *Motion Picture and TV Magazine*, November 1953.

"Round-up, Weekend." *Photoplay*, June 1950.

Rowland, Ruth. "The Last of Mr. Pretty Boy." *Silver Screen*, June 1954.

Scott, Diane. "The Truth Behind John Derek's Bust Up." *Photoplay*, December 1955.

Selway, Jennifer. "Live Fast, Grow Old, Get Rich." *Time Out London*, October 2, 1981.

Sheff, David. "John and Bo Derek: The Bitter Battle Over Hollywood's Hottest Couple." *People*, February 11, 1980.

"Speaking Frankly." *Movies*, October 1952.

Steranko. "The Uncensored Bo." *Prevue*, November-December 1981.

Stevens, Brace. "Handsomest Guy in Hollywood." *Silver Screen*, June 1949.

Swanson, Pauline. "Too Big for My Britches." *Motion Picture and TV Magazine*, October 1953.

"Taking a Big Plunge." *Movie Life*, November 1955.

"This Is the Life." *Filmland*, November 1949.

"Together Again." *Silver Screen*, December 1951.

"Too Handsome to Fight." *Filmland*, July 1951.

Trent, Susan. "New Baby-New Happiness." *Modern Screen*, March 1954.

_____. "Our Son." *Modern Screen*, August 1950.

Tusher, Bill. "Everything's Jake for John Derek." *Photoplay*, December 1953.

"Ursula Major." *Newsweek*, July 20, 1964.

Valentine, Duane. "Bluebird on Their Window Sill." *Modern Screen*, April 1950.

Waterbury, Ruth. "The Kid Who Never Cried." *Photoplay*, December 1949.

_____. "The Triumphant Years." *Photoplay*, May 1954.

Weller, Helen. "From Grim to Grin." *Silver Screen*, December 1953.

_____. "How to Find the Right Guy." *Silver Screen*, July 1954.

Weller Hover, Helen. "The John Dereks' Near Tragedy." *Movieland*, November 1950.

Werner, Laurie. "The Man Behind Those Beautiful Women." *Cosmopolitan*, June 1981.

White, Arnold. "Amour Fools." *Film Comment*, February 1987.

White, Gordon. "Love Without Marriage." *Motion Picture*, March 1956.

York, Call. "Inside Stuff: His and Hers." *Photoplay*, September 1955.

Zeitlin, Ida. "Now It Can Be Told." *Photoplay*, October 1950.

Index

Adam and Eve see *Eve and That Damned Apple*
Adams, Nick 77
Addams, Dawn 81, 180
The Adventures of Hajji Baba 55–57, 61, 65, 89, 95, 96, 145–147
The Adventures of Ozzie and Harriett 96
The Adventures of Robin Hood 25
The Alamo 89
Albuquerque, Claude 117
All the King's Men 1, 18, 21–24, 38, 39, 45, 129–131, 179, 182
Allégret, Marc 19
Ambush at Tomahawk Gap 42–43, 44, 46, 140–141
American Eagle see *Sea of Lost Ships*
An American Tragedy 51, 174
And Once Upon a Time see *Fantasies*
Andress, Ursula 1, 68, 69–71, 75, 79, 80, 81, 83–84, 85, 89–94, 95, 96, 97, 100, 102, 105, 107, 108, 115, 120, 122, 183, 184, 185
Angel's Cooking see *We're No Angels*
Anger, Kenneth 9, 167
Anglemyer, Kenneth see Anger, Kenneth
Ann-Margret 101
An Annapolis Story 59–61, 149–150
Any Man of Mine 121, 173
Arnow, Max 14
The Asphalt Jungle 90
Austin, Charlotte 39
Author Meets the Critic 31, 179
Autry, Gene 39, 41
Avedon, Richard 94

Bacall, Lauren 15, 16
Bachelor, Barbara 69
Bachelor Father 96
The Bad and the Beautiful 56
Bailey, Mary 120
Baker, Snowy 8
Balaban, Barney 80
Balaban, Burt 80, 81
Ballard, Todhunter 49
Banacek 102
Bandits of the Sherwood Forest see *Rogues of the Sherwood Forest*
The Barbara Walters Summer Special 106, 180

Barrymore, John Drew 41, 42
Bass, Norma 101, 102, 110, 172
Battaglia, Arturo "Rick" 180
Baum, Martin 107
Baumer, Marie 35
Baxter, Anne 39, 47
Bayonet Attack see *Thunderbirds*
The Beautiful Blond from Bashful Bend 20
Behrs, Andre 18–19
Behrs Eristoff, Pati 14, 18–21, 23, 24, 27–28, 32, 40, 41, 49, 51, 67–68, 70–71, 77, 87, 94, 122
The Bells of St. Mary 74
Belmondo, Jean Paul 94–95, 102
Bernstein, Elmer 115
Bernstein, Peter 115
Bickford, Charles 43, 44
The Big Moment 53, 174–175, 182
The Big Valley 95, 96, 98
Black, Noel 106
Black Jim Hawk 78, 175
The Blue and the Gold see *An Annapolis Story*
Blyth, Anne 51, 52
Bo-bolero see *Bolero*
Bo Derek's Fantasies see *Fantasies*
Bogart, Humphrey 1, 14, 15, 16, 17, 21, 22, 37, 129
Bolero 113, 114–117, 171–172
Bolero: An Adventure in Ecstasy see *Bolero*
Bolero Extasy see *Bolero*
Bonny, Anne 112, 184
Booth, Edwin 61
Booth, John Wilkies 61, 62
Borgnine, Ernest 58
A Boy ... a Girl 98–99, 167
Boys Town 73
Brand, Bob 20
Brand, Candy 20
Brando, Marlon 14, 18, 70
Braun, Zev 112
Brazzi, Rossano 75
Breathless 94
Brennar, Walter 48
Brian, David 42
The Bridge on the River Kwai 110
Brynner, Yul 66, 180
Buchman, Sidney 29, 31
Burnette, Smiley 179
Burr, Raymond 51
Burroughs, Edgar Rice 108, 111, 112

Burton, Richard 61
Bus Stop 96
Bush, Pres. George H.W. 120
Buttons, Red 89
Bye, Bye Birdie 101
Byington, Spring 10

Cagney, James 54, 57–59
Calhoun, Rory 13, 85, 183
Callahan, Mushy 72, 182
Callan, Karen 105
Caltabiano, Alfio 85
Canby, Vincent 111
Camp, Roy 66
Canalito, Lee 109
Carey, Harry, Jr. 50
Carmen Jones 84
Casablanca 129
Casino Royale 96
Casselman, Kevin 101, 102, 105
Cavanagh, James 35
Chaffey, Don 74
Chandler, Jeff 64
Chaney, Lon, Sr. 3, 180
A Change of Season 105
Childish Things 96–97, 167
Christian, Linda 56
Chun, Eva 110
Circumstance 4
Citizen Soldiers see *Thunderbirds*
Clearly, Paul 30
Cleopatra 67
Clift, Montgomery 18, 45, 47, 60, 51, 71, 153, 183
Climb Aboard the Six-Five Special 176
Cloak and Dagger 90
Cobb, Lee J. 35, 83
Cock a Doodle Doo see *Childish Things*
Cocteau, Jean 9
Cohane, Tim 31, 188
Cohn, Harry 15, 21–22, 27, 29, 32–33, 37–38, 42, 45, 183
Cohn, Robert 42, 46
Colbert, Claudette 10
Collins, Colin 101
Collins, Kelly 101
Collins, Kerry 101
Collins, Mary Cathleen see Derek, Bo
Collins, Paul 101
Collins, Richard 55

195

Colorado see *Run for Cover*
The Colossus of Rhodes 85–86, 183
Confessions of Tom Harris see *Childish Things*
Cook, Ben 47
Cooke, Bob 31
Cooper, Gary 5
Il Corsaro della Mezza Luna 81–82, 160–161
Cotten, Joseph 10
The Count of Monte Cristo 33
Craig, Carolyn 77
Crain, Jeanne 51
Crawford, Broderick 21, 22, 24, 38–39, 43, 182
Crawford, Christina 118
Crawford, Joan 118
Crawford, Mary Alice 24
Crosby, Bing 39, 73
Crowther, Bosley 59, 84
Cukor, George 11, 13
Curtis, Tony 40, 64
Curtiz, Michael 55, 64, 183

Dandridge, Dorothy 10
Da Re, Aldo see Ray, Aldo
Da Re, Mario 30
The Dark Page see *Scandal Sheet*
A Daughter of Australia 4
Dawson, Peter 47–48
Dean, James 18, 70, 71
Dean, Loomis 40
De Laurentiis, Dino 79
DeMille, Cecil Blunt 1, 5, 54, 64–66, 67, 71, 82, 180
Derek, Bo 1, 3, 100, 1001–106, 107–109, 110, 111, 112, 113, 114, 115, 116, 117, 118, 119, 120–122, 123, 173, 180, 181, 183, 184, 185
Derek, Pati see Behrs Eristoff, Pati
Derek, Russell Andre 28–29, 32, 37, 40, 67, 68, 77, 87, 94, 122
Derek, Sean 3, 12, 27, 50, 67, 68, 71, 77, 87, 99, 100, 104, 117–118, 122
Dexter, Anthony 25, 182
Dieterle, William 11, 75
Dr. No 89, 90, 105, 107
Double Furlough see *I'll Be Seeing You*
A Double Life 13
Douglas, Gordon 25, 27
Douglas, Kirk 89
Douglas, Mike 180
Douglas, Paul 75
Duggan, Pat 55
Dunne, Irene 89
Dunne, Philip 61, 62
DuPont, Ricky 90, 91
Duvall, Robert 91
Dynasty 96

Edwards, Blake 104–105, 106
Edwards, Eric 168
Edwards, Vince 64
Ely, Ron 91–92, 94
Les Enfants Terribles 9
Entertainment 1955 175
Epstein, Mel 53
Erskine, Albert 22

Erskine, Marilyn 51, 52
Evans, Jack 23
Evans, Linda 1, 94, 95–98, 100–102, 103, 104, 118, 120, 122, 181 183, 185
Eve and That Damned Apple 172, 185
Everett, Rob 104
Exodus 1, 82–84, 162–164
Extasy see *Bolero*
Eyes in the Skies see *Mission Over Korea*

Faber, Dr. Luke 122
Fairbanks, Douglas 25, 34, 112, 180
The Family Secret 30, 35–36, 73, 135–136
Fantasies 105–106, 168–169
Faulkner, Edith 25
Faulkner, Ralph 25, 34, 112
Fighting Caravans 5
Fishbein, Sanford 90–91
Fleming, Eric 64
Fleming, Ian 89
Fleming, Raymond B. 42
Fleming, Rhonda 10
The Flesh Is Weak 74–75, 158–160
Flynn, Errol 15, 25, 26, 112
Fontaine, Joan 179
Ford, John 50
Forsythe, John 75, 96
Foss, Fanya 90, 91
Franzetta, Frank 107
Frazee, Steve 80
Freeman, Frank, Jr. 75, 180
Freeman, Mona 41
From Here to Eternity 45, 183
Fromer, Airion 99
Frontier Circus 87–89, 90, 91, 177–179, 183
Fuller, Samuel 37
Fury at Showdown 77–78, 156–157

Gaffey, Burnett 43
The Gainesville Circus 27, 182
Ganzer, Alvin 71, 72–73
Gaver, Jack 23
Gaynor, Mitzi 40
Genoino, Arnaldo 82
Ghent, Derek 8
Ghosts Can't Do It 119–129, 172–173
Giant 78
Gibson, Virginia 40
Globus, Yoram 113
Goddard, Gary 108, 112, 184
Going My Way 73
Golan, Menahem 113, 115, 116
Golden Boy 72, 182
Goldstein, Bob 77
Goldstein, Leonard 71
Gone with the Wind 10
Grable, Betty 20
Grahame, Gloria 51
Granger, Farley 33, 51, 179
Grant, Marshall 27
Grayson, Kathryn 64
The Greatest Show on Earth 64
Greystoke 108
Grinde, Nick 137
Grizzard, George 120

Hale, Alan 25
Hale, Barbara 39
Hamilton, George 112, 184
Hanson, Jack 98, 99
Harlan, Russell "Russ" B. 5–6, 7, 8, 9, 28
Harris, Elizabeth Hawley 3
Harris, Frank 120
Harris, Richard 103, 108, 110, 112, 184
Harris, Tom 98, 168
Harris, William James 3
Harris, William Lawson 3–4, 5, 6, 8, 13
Hart, Moss 61
Haven, Annette 104
Hawks, Howard 37
Hedegaard, Caspar 119
Hefner, Hugh 94, 103
Hellinger, Mark 14
Hendrix, Wanda 43
Hepburn, Audrey 70
The Hero see *Saturday's Hero*
Herod the Great 82
Heston, Charlton 66, 180
Higgins, Ernest 4
High Hell 79–81, 160
Hiller, Arthur 78
Hinds, Anthony 91
Hitchcock, Alfred 32, 33, 37, 71
Hodiak, John 42, 43, 46–47
Holden, William 38, 39
Hollywood Stars to Remember 39, 180
Hollywood's Mr. Movies 39, 179–180
Hooten, Peter 101
Hopalong Cassidy 5
Hopkins, Anthony 105
Huggins, Roy 182
Hunter, Jeffrey 182
Hyams, Joe 87

I'll Be Seeing You 10–11, 75, 127–128
Ireland, John 21, 179

Joan of Arc 40
Joaquín Murrieta 35–37, 77, 182
Johnny Guitar 57
Johnson, Delevan D. 3
Johnson, Dolores 3, 4, 5, 6, 8, 12, 13, 40–41, 71
Jones, Bob 9, 10
Jones, James 45
Jones, Jennifer 8
Jourdan, Louis 47

Karlson, Phil 34, 38
Keith, Brian 64
Kennedy, George 114–115
Key Largo 90
Keys of the Kingdom 73
Kirkop, Oreste 64
Kissinger, Henry 79
Knievel, Evel 98, 173
Knock on Any Door 1, 13, 14–18, 20, 23, 35, 45, 57, 59, 79, 115, 128–129, 131, 182

Index

Knox, Alexander 31
Knox, Mickey 74, 115, 181
Knute Rockne All American 50
Krim, Arthur 82
Kulik, Buzz 51, 52
Kurutz, Steve 123

Ladd, Alan 37
The Lady's Not for Burning 61
La Gallienne, Eva 62
Lampell, Millard 18, 29, 31
Lang, Richard 105
Lasky, Jesse 33
The Last Knight 119, 184
The Last Posse 42, 43–44, 141–142
Laura 84
Law, Jude 131
Law or Loyalty 4
Lawford, Peter 83, 180
Lawrance, Jody 34, 35, 36, 73
Lawrence of Arabia 87
Lawrence, Mark 90–91
Lazarus, Paul, Jr. 31
Leacock, Philip 129
The Leather Saint 71–74, 151–153
Leavitt, Sam 60
Leone, Sergio 79, 85, 183
Let No Man Write My Epitaph 129
Levin, Henry 35
Long, Huey P. 21
The Long Gray Line 50
Lord, Bob 14, 15, 35
Love Is My Shame 79, 183
Love Story 78
Love You! 103–104, 168–169
Lynn, Diana 25, 26, 27, 60

MacArthur, Harold 26
Macready, George 25, 179
Madison, Guy 10, 12, 127
Mahoney, Jock 39, 92, 109
Malden, Karl 74
Maltz, Albert 82
Mangano, Silvana 79
Mann, Roderick 95
The Many Loves of Casanova 70
March, Anthony 91
Marley, Florence 179
Martin, Dean 98
Martin, Dino Paul 98–99
Martinelli, Elsa 81, 82, 180
The Mask of Monte Cristo see *Mask of the Avenger*
Mask of the Avenger 30, 32–34, 36, 73, 132–133
Massacre at Sand Creek 78, 175–176
Massey, Raymond 61, 75
Mathews, Kerwin 99
Matinee Theatre 175
May the Sea Take This Island 90, 183
McCaffery, John 31, 179
McCallum, Lorice C. 4
McCambridge, Mercedes 22
McCardle, Mickey 30
McCarthy, Kevin 61
McDowall, Roddy 9–10
McLaine, Shirley 105

McLean, Donald 65
McMullen, Edmund 102
McNamara, Maggie 61, 63
McQueen, Steve 99
Men of Boys Town 73
Meet Mr. Rhythm, Frankie Laine 39, 179
Meiklejohn, William 54
Meyer, Arthur 80
Miles, Vera 89
Miller, David 29, 30
Miller, Winston 57
Mineo, Sal 82
Minnelli, Vincent 56
Mirisch, Walter 59
Mission Over Korea 45–47, 142–143
Mr. Rhythm's Holiday 39, 180
Mitchell, Thomas 53
Monks, John, Jr. 14
Monroe, Marilyn 19, 40, 96
Montalban, Ricardo 37
Monte Carlo 107, 184
Montgomery, Elizabeth 89, 175
Moore, Terry 10, 24, 182
Moore, Tom 8
Motley, Willard 14, 15
Murray, Don 96, 120
Murray, Ken 20, 179
Murrieta, Joaquin 35, 36–37
My Four Wives 117

Nader, George 64
Neal, Patricia 37
The Nest 9, 167
Neville, John 75
Newman, Paul 83, 84, 183, 77, 182
Newmar, Julie 120
Nichols, Wade 104
Night on the Street see *Childish Things*
Nightmare in the Sun 90–91, 165–166
No Toys for Christmas see *Once Before I Die*

Obregon, Ana 114
O'Brien, Hugh 64
O'Brien, Pat 50
O'Brien Moore, Erin 35
Occhipinti, Andrea 116
O'Cotter, Pat 3
O'Keeffe, Miles 109, 111
O'Mahoney, Jock 39, 92, 109
Omar Khayyam 75–77, 157–158, 180
On the Waterfront 74
Once Before I Die 92, 93, 94, 98, 165–166, 167
Once Upon a Love see *Fantasies*
Ondine see *The Last Knight*
Orca—The Killer Whale 103
Oster, Emil, Jr. 46
O'Sullivan, Maureen 46, 47, 108
The Outcast 49–50, 144–145
Owen, Tony 29

Pace, Frank, Jr. 42
Paget, Debra 60, 65, 75

Palance, Jack 29
Parks, Larry 32
Parsons, Louella 27, 45, 67
Pate, Michael 64
The Patent Leather Kid 27
Pavis, Marie see Pavis, Yvonne
Pavis, Yvonne 4
Peck, Gregory 73, 179
Peckinpah, Sam 61, 150
Peeples, Samuel A. 87
Pembroke, Percy "Scott" 4
Penn, Sean 131
Peppard, George 102
Peters, Jean 19
Picerni, Paul 56
Pichel, Irving 33
Pine, William 57
Pirate Annie 112, 184
The Pirate of the Half Moon see *Il Corsaro della Mezza Luna*
A Place in the Sun 51–52, 174
Playhouse 90 175
Pollack, Sydney 89
Ponti, Carlo 112
The Posse see *The Last Posse*
Power, Tyrone 17, 56
Preminger, Otto 1, 82–83, 84
Prince of Egypt see *The Ten Commandments*
Prince of Pirates 40, 41, 81, 139–140
Prince of Players 59, 61–63, 65, 147–149
Prisoner of the Volga 81–82, 161–162, 180

Quinn, Anthony 34, 120

Rachmill, Lew 108
Railsback, Buddy 79
Rainbow 'Round My Shoulder 39, 137
Rampling, Charlotte 103
Ransohoff, Marty 105, 184
Ratoff, Gregory 83
Ray, Aldo 30, 45, 55, 89, 91, 183
Ray, Nicholas 14, 15, 16, 57, 58, 59
Ray, Tony 120
Reagan, Pres. Ronald 53, 179
Red Horizon see *The Outcast*
Redford, Robert 183
Reed, Donna 29–30, 31, 38, 39, 53, 181
Reed, Oliver 108
Remée, Vera 4
Remy, Ronald 92
Renegade Canyon 47, 182
Retchin, Norman 71
Rewald, Ronald 118
Richardson, Ralph 83
Riefenstahl, Leni 94
Riot in Cell Block 11 55
Ritter, Thelma 89
Robbins, Harold 103, 183
The Robe 61
Robertson, Dale 64
Robinson, Edward G. 37
Robinson, Jay 61
Rogers, Ginger 10, 11
Rogers, Roy 41

Index

Rogers, Will 8, 180
Rogues of the Sherwood Forest 25–28, 112, 131–132
Roman, Ruth 10
Romero, Cesar 20, 73
Rooney, Mickey 89, 178, 182
Roosevelt, Pres. Theodore 114
Rossen, Robert 18, 21, 22, 179
Ruggles, Eleanor 61
Run for Cover 55, 57–59, 150–151, 180
Rush, Barbara 40, 41, 89

Saint, Eva Marie 83
Salkow, Sidney 40
Saltzman, Harry 107, 184
Samuels, Leo 90
Sanforth, Clifford 27
Saturday's Hero 29, 30–32, 34, 79, 115, 133–135
Scandal Sheet 24, 37–39, 136–137
Schenck, Aubrey 183
Schneider, Benno 34
Scott, Lizabeth 37, 179
Sea Mistress see *Pirate Annie*
Sea of Lost Ships 48–49, 88, 143–144
Sears, Fred F. 42, 43, 46, 47
The Secret see *The Family Secret*
Selznick, David O. 8–9, 10, 11, 12, 13
The 7th Voyage of Sinbad 99
Shalit, Gene 111, 180
Sharpe, David 26
Sharpe, Karen 29
She 91, 93
Shirley, Arthur 3, 4
Siegel, Don 55, 60–61
Sinatra, Frank 15, 23
Since You Went Away 10, 125
The Sinner see *Childish Things*
The Six-Five Special see *Climb Aboard the Six-Five Special*
Skarstedt, Vance 91
Slater, Bob 31
Small, Edward 25, 182
Smith, Bob 62
Smith, John 77, 78
Smith, Liz 117, 123
Smith, Roger 101
Sorrell, Helena 13, 14
S.O.S. Eisberg see *Sea of Lost Ships*
Spiegel, Sam 87
Stanwyck, Barbara 95
Staub, Ralph 39, 179, 180
Stevens, George 51

Stevens, Stella 89
Stewart, Elaine 56, 80
Stewart, James 24
Storm Over Eden 87, 176
Strangers on the Train 32, 33, 182
Stross, Raymond 74
Sumac, Yma 75
The Sun's Up see *A Boy ... a Girl*
Sunshine Sally 4
Swords of the Sherwood Forest see *Rogues of the Sherwood Forest*

Tajiri, Vince 94
Tale of the Cock see *Childish Things*
Tanney, Herb 118
Taradash, Daniel 14, 15
Tarzan (TV series) 92
Tarzan, the Ape Man 107–112, 117, 169–171
Taylor, Elizabeth 3, 9–10, 51, 78, 183
Tchltchinadze, Gogi 20
Temple, Shirley 10, 11
10 104–105, 106, 107, 110, 113
The Ten Commandments 1, 54, 64–67, 69, 71, 74, 84, 153–156, 180
Testi, Fabio 115
Thomas, Ted 90
Thomas, William 57
Thorpe, Richard 72
The Three Worlds of Gulliver 92
The Throwback 3, 4
Thunderbirds 41–42, 137–139
Tillman, A.C. 21
Today Show 111, 180, 181
Todd, Lucas 77
Tolstoy, Leon 18
Tomorrow's Man 50, 173–174
Totter, Audrey 47
Tourjansky, Victor 82
Towne, Col. Clair 59
Tracy, Spencer 21, 73
Trumbo, Dalton 82
Trump, Donald 120
Tucker, Forrest 53
Tully, Tom 10
Turzhanskiy, Vyacheslav Kostantinovich see Tourjansky, Victor
Twain, Mark 112, 184
Twain, Shania 120–121, 173
The 26th Cavalry see *Once Before I Die*
Two Women 101

Uris, Leon 82

The Vagabond King 64, 183
Valentino, Rudolph 25, 182
Vance, Leigh 74
The Vanity Fair Girls 5
Vavra, Robert 185
Viertel, Salka 82
Vitale, Milly 74, 75

Wagner, Robert 7, 11, 75
Wagon Train 87
Wald, Jerry 27, 182
A Walk in the Sun 5
Walker, Clint 64, 65
Wallace, Marjorie 180
Walters, Barbara 106, 180, 181
Wanger, Walter 55–56
Warren, Earl 22
Warren Penn, Robert 18, 21, 22, 131
Wayne, John 41
Weis, Don 55, 56, 89
We're No Angels 55, 183
Werker, Alfred 43
Werker, Judge Henry 111, 112
Whitley, Bill 46
Whittaker, Jo 9
Whom the Gods Destroy see *Sea of Lost Ships*
Whose Bed Have Your Boots Been Under 121
Wilcoxon, Henry 65
Wilde, Cornel 25, 64, 75, 76
Wildflowers 100, 101, 183
Williams, Cara 15
Wills, Chills 88, 89
Willson, Henry 8
Wilson, Dooley 129
Wilson, Earl 40
Winslet, Kate 131
Winters, Shelley 51
Witney, William 49, 50, 89
Women of the Night see *The Flesh Is Weak*
Wood, Natalie 77, 78
Worsley, Wally 89
Wyle, Noah 123
Wynn, Keenan 91

Yellow 5
Young, Gig 25
Young, Robert 53

Zaillian, Steven 131
Zane Grey Theatre 87, 176
Zanuck, Darryl 8, 19, 61
Zec, Donald 97
Zinnemann, Fred 45

www.ingramcontent.com/pod-product-compliance
Ingram Content Group UK Ltd.
Pitfield, Milton Keynes, MK11 3LW, UK
UKHW050525150426
5217IPUK00026B/1805